ETERNAL ROME

ETERNAL ROME

THE CITY AND ITS PEOPLE
FROM THE EARLIEST TIMES TO
THE PRESENT DAY

BY

GRANT SHOWERMAN

PROFESSOR OF CLASSICS IN THE UNIVERSITY OF WISCONSIN
DIRECTOR OF THE SUMMER SESSION, THE AMERICAN ACADEMY IN ROME

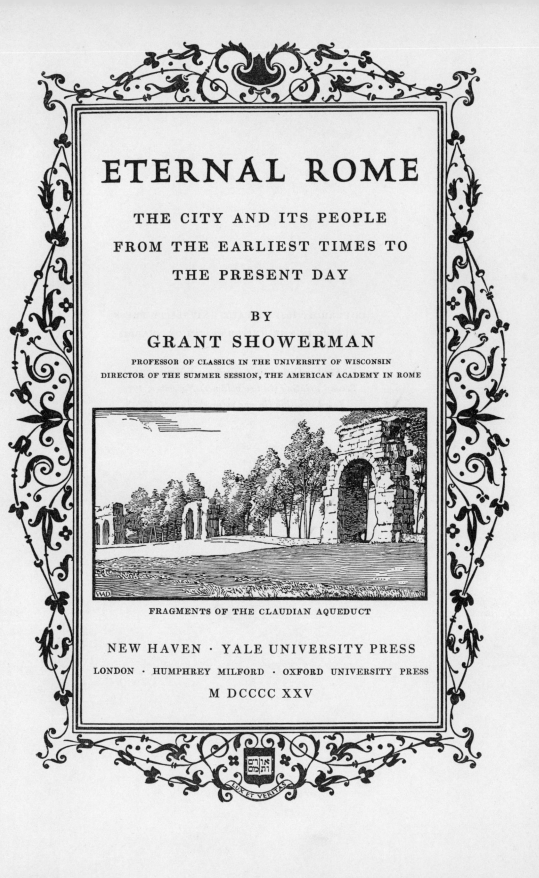

FRAGMENTS OF THE CLAUDIAN AQUEDUCT

NEW HAVEN · YALE UNIVERSITY PRESS
LONDON · HUMPHREY MILFORD · OXFORD UNIVERSITY PRESS
M DCCCC XXV

LUX ET VERITAS

First published (in two volumes) May, 1924
Second printing (in two volumes) November, 1924
Third printing (in one volume) August, 1925

FRANZ CUMONT
GEORGE LINCOLN HENDRICKSON
ET MIHI ET INTER SE
AMICIS

TABLE OF CONTENTS

LIST OF ILLUSTRATIONS

I.

EARLIEST LATIUM

Romulus æternæ nondum firmaverat urbis
Moenia consorti non habitanda Remo,—

No Romulus had yet appeared,
    No strong-built walls yet rose in air;
No Rome Eternal stood, in which
    Remus was fated not to share.

Tibullus II: 5: 23-24

ROME FROM THE VILLA AURELIA

BEYOND THE TIBER, FROM LEFT TO RIGHT,
ARE THE MONUMENTO VITTORIO EMANUELE, THE CAPITOLINE,
THE BASILICA OF MAXENTIUS, AND THE PALATINE

1.

THE LAND OF LATIUM

T HE drama of Eternal Rome begins with an empty
stage.

No great City with towers and domes and many-
windowed palaces and green trees and monumental
ruins flung like a great garment over valley and height.
No River winding an eddying way at the foot of sacred
Hills. No wide reaches of purple-brown fields tumbling
away to Albans, Apennines, and sea. No white villages
and green vineyards and gardens girdling the far slopes
of a solitary Mountain. No Rome, no Tiber, no Seven
Hills, no Campagna, no Alban Mount, no Land of the
Latin People.

Everywhere instead the swinging blue waves of the
Tyrrhenian sea, a far-extended bay one hundred and
fifty miles long and thirty broad, whose shore-line sweeps
along under grey masses of the Apennines. Nothing
above the waters but a huge island of rock confused with
the mainland at the south; the Mount of Circe standing
apart from it, like a sentinel; and the serrate crest of
Soracte, another mountain-island, at the north. The
waves wash the bases of the steep limestone barriers and
reach far inland in many a cove and inlet to meet
streams that come dashing out of rocky fastnesses or
careering over the cliffs. The Anio plunges headlong
into the sea from its mountain cleft at Tivoli. The Tiber
mouth is beyond Soracte, forty miles from the sea of
today. There are no men upon the earth.

Beneath the great bay runs the northern extremity

of the long line of weakness in the earth's crust whose southern limit is the region of Ætna. In the course of time the energies confined in the caverns of the earth begin to stir. Now gradually, now with violence, the floor of the bay begins to heave. It is just appearing here and there above the waters, and in other places still lies deep beneath, when the energies explode. The earth opens, beneath or at the surface of the sea, and vomits forth its depths.

Again time passes; a second and mightier explosion occurs, and still a third. An infinite quantity of cinders and ash is furiously blown from giant craters in the north, and from others in the south when the northern are spent. It descends from the air upon islet, coast, lagoon, and open sea, or it surges away from craters still submerged and mingles with the waves. It spreads itself three hundred feet deep over all the plain beneath the waters, over all the plain already appeared above the waters. It pushes its way into the inlets and clefts of the mountain wall. According as it finds its place below the surface of sea or lagoon, or falls on dry land above them, according as it is denser or less compact, it settles at length into ruddy or greyish rock, or lies in violet-brown beds of heavy ash, the building-stone and cement of the City that is to come.

But another great force is at work in the forming of the plain. While the slow lifting of the sea-floor and the blowing forth of scoriæ and ash beneath and above are extending the surface of the land, mighty streams of fresh water descend from the Apennines. It is the age of a great glacial retreat. From the melting snows and ice of the north, impetuous torrents come roaring through the mountain valleys and pour themselves

THE TIBER VALLEY NORTH OF ROME

FROM VILLA GLORI, THREE MILES FROM THE CITY
AND NOT FAR FROM ANTEMNÆ

forth to mingle in surging rivalry with the waves and currents of the sea. One of the great eruptions has left an irregular line of fracture, a crevice from north to south across the bottom of the bay. The mightiest of all the mountain streams follows this line and makes the crevice its channel. Lesser streams have followed other natural paths and formed their channels in similar manner. By the time the center of the plain has risen above the waters, the Tiber is flowing in definite course.

The great explosion to the south that rears the Alban Mount occurs. It fills the bottom of the Tiber bed and throws rocky obstructions across its channel. For long time the river is a mighty flowing lake with banks half submerged and bosom dotted with dark islets, the summits of the future Hills. It wears the obstructions away or washes a course around them. It sweeps along through a winding and ever-deepening bed until its great highway to open sea is established.

The great eruptions whose ashy débris covers the land or sinks to the bottom of the sea are at an end; but the plain is not yet at rest. The great cone-craters in the north and south are broken and scarred at the rims by lesser explosions that send forth streams of basalt or blow high in air more scoriæ to settle into banks of rock or powdery ash. The rim of the Alban crater crumbles and loses shape, and about its outer slopes appear the smaller bowls that later become the Alban lake and Nemi and the vale of Aricia. The lofty central cone of Monte Cavo is reared within the great crumbled rim, and its rim also falls away on the north. Torrential rains and overflowing waters fissure the slopes of all the craters with radial valleys that cut the ash and rock till they reach the larger channels in the lower land.

When at length the violence and thundering uproar of the greatest upheavals have given place to the gentler action and lesser rumor of tumbling cascades and rapidly gliding streams and washing waves, and the glacial freshets have begun to subside and to leave the slowly rising land a real plain, the aspect of the region has changed indeed. Instead of blue sea are everywhere the somber reaches of ruddy and yellowish-grey volcanic rock and purple-brown ash. The dark mass of the Alban Mount rises with sweeping lines three thousand feet in air. It looks down to the south and west upon an uncertain coast of marsh and lagoon, and of sand cast up by the sea, and to the north on a rolling, tumbling, furrowed landscape that grows higher and wilder until it reaches the distant crater-cone of Bracciano and the height of Rocca Romana and mingles with the lines of the horizon. The Tiber is a mighty, lake-like current winding a resistless way between worn hills and plateaus of rock and clay, a hundred feet deep and in places a mile from bank to bank. Compared with its mammoth flow, the Tiber of historic times, three hundred feet wide but lost and wandering in the vast expanse of its prehistoric bed, is the merest rivulet. Its ever-flooded affluents are twenty-seven; the Anio, rushing from its cascades at the edge of the Apennines, itself a great river swollen by fourteen tributaries, is chief of them. Twelve streams besides the Tiber pour their waters directly into the marshy borders of the sea. The lesser tributaries and independent streams are numberless. Their swiftly coursing floods have worn and seamed and furrowed and fissured the soft rock and looser ash until all the area through which they rush is wrought into gully, ravine, and valley, and into little hills and hummocks and rolling slopes and rounded table-lands. Four parts of the plain are hills; one part is valley bottom.

The glacier recedes still farther on its northward retreat; the waters continue slowly to subside. While they are still high, the warmth has changed to humid heat. The Tiber about the hills is still a broad, flowing lake, when its banks and the higher places of the plain become clothed with vegetation. Gigantic elephant and ox appear, and others of their kind. They roam the leafy glades on the shores of the stream and leave their bones in the ooze. After long time the glaciers and the cold approach once more. Again the streams are swollen and again in the course of the years subside, this time to flow within the limits of historic times, or to disappear except in the season of rains. They have not only furrowed and fissured the plain, but filled the valleys and clothed the slopes with soil eroded from the rocks and ash of the hills, and embroidered the line of the coast with a wide and watery jungle. The Tiber's mouth, once at Soracte, again at Monte Mario north of the Seven Hills, has advanced to Ponte Galera, ten miles to the south of them. In Roman times it will be at Ostia, five miles farther into the sea.

The Land of Latium, a broad expanse of hill and valley that seems to the distant eye a level plain with a single mountain mass in its midst, is ready for human habitation. What men will enter into the land to possess it?

THE EARLIEST MEN OF LATIUM

THE first men to set foot on the soil of Latium were
the nomad cave-men of the old stone age. When
they began their straggling existence in the Tiber region, their brethren had long been wandering in England, Belgium, France, and Spain, inhabiting caverns
and mountain clefts and frequenting valley and stream.
They were scattered thickly over Italy, but were few in
Latium, and left scarcely a trace behind. They lived the
life of the cave ten thousand years before Rome came
into being. They saw the majestic Tiber before it was
altogether shrunk within its shores, the Alban Mount
while its fires were still alight.

A new race appeared in Italy after them. The men
of the late stone age descended from the western Alps
and France, and came up from the south and Sicily.
They conquered, but did not destroy, the race of
strangers they found. They populated all the peninsula,
and at last advanced to the Tiber region, where they
stopped on the lower ridges and foothills of the Apennines and the Albans, and on the high places of the volcanic plain. The Alban Mount especially invited them.
Its genial wooded slopes and rich pastures, its lakes and
springs and running streams, were lifted above the
vapors of the plain, whose network of valley and ravine
sequestered many a stagnant pool, and whose lower
lands were so little raised above the sea that the water
never left their marshy thickets. They sheltered themselves in cave and cleft or in rounded cabins of brush or

reeds and clay half sunk in the rock or earth, with a
single door for themselves and light and air and smoke.
In Latium they were less advanced than their brethren;
a hunting and a shepherd race, clothed in the skins of
their game and herds and flocks. When they engaged in
the chase or went forth to war, their weapons were of
horn and wood and stone. Their ornaments were of like
material. Their pots were earthen and rude. They could
spin and weave, they polished their weapons and implements, and in the course of time their pottery came to
merit the name of art. They laid their dead to rest in
caves or tombs resembling the homes of the living; sometimes in a crouching or sitting posture, more often lying
on the side with knees drawn up and head reclining on
the open hand. Sometimes they divested the dead of
their flesh, whether at burial or after natural dissolution, and reddened their bones with vermilion.

Like their predecessors of the old stone age, the men
of the late stone age represent long reaches of time.
They were the primordial wanderers of the Mediterranean race that issued from Africa and peopled the
shores of the great inland sea. Their later generations
at the dawn of bronze were to leave the dolmen along
the African coast and over the west of Europe, and
sometime rear the massive city defences that dot the
Mediterranean lands of east and west from Troy to
Spain. Before their descendants in the Latin region
were lost to sight in the inundation of an invading race,
their eyes and ears were astonished by many an outburst from the near-by hills, and their hearts quaked in
alarm at many a rocking of the ground beneath their
feet.

The wave of rude invaders which was to descend upon

the Mediterranean stock had long been on the way.
Moving slowly from east to west across the face of
nearer Asia and Europe to the neighborhood of the
Balkan range, they were driven by a last stirring of the
nomadic instinct, or by the pressure of their kinsmen
farther north, to cross the great barriers that stood between them and the sunnier south. They surged through
the passes of Hæmus and descended into the precincts
of Greece. They overwhelmed the Mediterranean men
of Mycenæ, Tiryns, and Crete, and became the Achæans
of Homeric song. A second time they surged across the
mountain barrier, repeated the process of conquest and
amalgamation, and became the Dorian Greeks of history.

It was not much later when the migrant race arrived
at the bulwarks of the Alps. Impelled by the same
forces, it burst open the gates of Italy. It thronged the
passes of the Alps as the Achæans thronged the Balkan
passes, and descended by ever pleasanter paths to the
leafy and grassy plains of the Po. In blankets of rough
wool or linen or in skins, unkempt and fierce, haggard
and sinewy from long wandering and deprivation,
carrying lance, arrow, or battle-axe tipped and headed
with stone, the warriors of the nation led the way. Along
the rugged cliffs, over the snowy passes, and down the
now greener inclines, followed the long trains of jolting
and creaking wagons, loaded with women, children, and
the aged, and with the tents and implements of a migrant
people.

The richness and warmth of the wooded valleys and
plain were pleasant to the strangers. They treated with
or beat back and dispossessed the ancient dwellers in
the land, and made homes for themselves on the con-

quered soil. The first arrivals were lake-dwelling men, and fixed their abodes about the shallows of Como, Varese, and Garda. The later, descending from the eastern Alps, were of different habit, and made for firmer ground. In clearings along the streams and by the lakes and on the hills, in the heavy forests of chestnut, ilex, and elm, they prepared the ground and laid out their cities; little, compact hamlets of straw, reeds, brush, and clay, on rough platforms carried by piles, the whole surrounded and sharply defined by the embankment palisaded with the trunks and branches of trees, and fronted by the moat of running water. Whether at edge of lake or stream or on higher ground, the plan was the same; long practice had fixed it, the practice of their fathers and their fathers' fathers in central and eastern Europe. A principal street from north to south was crossed by a shorter street from east to west, in the manner of the later city-camps of Rome. The larger street might be a half mile in length, or even a mile. The village might cover from two to more than twenty acres. The house might be from ten to twenty feet in diameter.

Village succeeded village on the same spot. Untutored, careless, and hardy, the tenants of the round huts let fall through the platform their waste of every description, until generations had passed and the space between the piles below was full. The whole area was levelled then, and a second village reared above the first. Or fire broke out, and the whole assemblage of reedy cabins, platform, piles, and all, was reduced in an hour to ashes and débris, and the building of the new abode thus hastened.

The life of the northern men on their entrance into

the valley was rude in the extreme. They used the skins
of animals, and knew how to spin and weave their clothing of wool or linen. Their utensils were of wood or
stone, their arms nearly all of stone. They were acquainted with bronze, but casting, and not forging, was
their method of shaping it; it was still so rare that the
owner of weapon or ornament was looked upon with
envy. Their arms in war were the stone axe, the flint-
headed lance and arrow, and perhaps the sling. The
sword was either unknown or of wood that has left no
trace behind. The usual implements of peace were of
bone or horn, of wood, leather, and clay. They worked
their pottery by hand and dried it in the sun or at the
open fire. Their women wore the comb, the pin, and
other ornament, and these, with their pottery, were
often of gracious form; but the sense of art in general
was hardly more developed in the race than the ideal of
cleanliness or hygiene. They worshipped no images, and
burned their dead. Their bones were placed in earthen
containers and buried in cities of the dead laid out like
cities of the living.

Their occupations, when they were not at war, were
quiet and domestic. They drove their herds and flocks
to woodland pasture and stream. They had the cow, the
hog, the goat, the sheep, the horse, the dog, and perhaps the ass. They pursued the stag, the wild boar, and
the bear.

Their agriculture was hardly worthy of the name.
They sowed and reaped the principal grains, but the
fruits they enjoyed, with few exceptions, were probably
wild. Their food was the product of the herd and flock,
the chase, and the yield of forest and field. Women
ground at the mill of roughly shaped stones, and made

the coarse meal into dough, or merely softened it with
water, and baked it at fires from the abundant fuel of
the woodland. The vine was already known to them,
or soon became known, but they made no wine. The
olive had not yet appeared.

But the day was coming, after many generations in
the northern valley of the Po, and after many more in
the wide plains to its south, when the little villages, with
their fosses, palisades, piles, and round cabins, were to
be left behind. Their people were at the dawn of the
iron age, when perhaps another migratory wave came
rolling down from the unknown regions beyond the
Alps; or perhaps the homes about the Po were full and
overflowing. The villagers in their turn were crowded
from the fertile plain. The march begins again. Fighting, sojourning, dispossessed and dispossessing, they
move to the south on the eastern slope of the Apennines
and along the coast. They begin at length to cross the
mountain range. The sunlit valleys of Umbria afford
them homes for another period, until other impulses,
from the north and from within, once more drive them
on. They separate. Some continue in Umbria. Some follow the Apennines toward Samnium. A few arrive as
far even as Tarentum. Others complete the passage of
the mountains of central Italy. They people the hills and
valleys of the Sabine and the Volscian Apennines, and
finally one day look down into the Latin plain itself and
across to the Alban Mount. It is a thousand years before
the Christian era, and long before the founding of
Rome.

The sojourn in the valley of the Po and the southward movement across the Apennines had extended over
many centuries, and the long procession of years had

brought its changes. It had seen the advance from stone
to bronze, and from bronze to iron. It had seen the
gradual modification of custom as knowledge and means
had increased and environment had varied. The pile-
village of lake and marsh had changed on firmer ground
to the hamlet of moat and palisade, and the moat and
palisade of the northern lowlands had given place to
the wall of the hill-town farther south. The cabin upon
the platform in the valley of the Po had become the hut
built on or partially into the rock or soil of central Italy.
The single opening of the door had been supplemented
by an orifice in the roof, and the window was known.
The rough clay jars for the ashes of the dead were now
often replaced by tasteful urns that imitated the houses
of the living. A currency in cattle had evolved from the
crude transactions of the migrants. The manner and the
blood of the stone-age men had entered into theirs.
They had met with men and products from the east, had
learned to forge their bronze, and knew the more precious metals. They had slowly made advances in art.
While they were wandering in the uncertain ways of
semi-savagery and blindly seeking the established state
of civilized men, Assyria, Phœnicia, Egypt, and Crete
were old and stable cultures. While they were slowly
building a new culture from the wreckage of the Mediterranean race their arms had crushed, their brethren
invaders from the Balkans had destroyed the Mycenæan
and Cretan power and begun their swifter climb on the
rich débris toward the heights of Hellenism.

The newcomers conquered and mingled with the
earlier hill-men on the ridges and slopes of the Apennines that overlooked the plain of Latium, and in the
event gave their towns new life and growth. They de-

scended into the plain and climbed the foothills of the
Alban Mount to continue the process. From among the
towns they conquered and re-created or themselves
brought into being, there were certain ones that emerged
as the heads of their little territories. In addition to
Tibur, on the brow of the Sabines where the Anio took
its leap into the plain, and Præneste, looking down on
the gap between the Sabines and Volscians and the
Alban Mount, there arose on the ridge and slopes of
the Alban crater-lake the cities of Alba Longa and
Lanuvium, and many lesser towns.

The Alban volcano was not even yet extinct. Some
of the homes of the new race were buried by an outburst from the mountain. It was at most no more than
an interruption; the growth went on. The thriving populations of the higher towns overflowed now to the lesser
heights at the base of the mountains. They pushed out
into the plain. The harder conditions of life in the lowlands were met and overcome, and the lonely, rolling
waste was dotted with the rude hamlets of shepherd and
farmer. Gabii, Antemnæ, Lavinium, and Ardea, on the
little heights in the plain, became leaders among the
lowland towns, and ranked with the cities on the mountain-sides.

The lowlands and the high places to the east and
south of the Tiber had thus become the seat of a new
civilization. Rude and shapeless as it was, however, it
was already composite. Its basis was the culture of the
original Mediterranean men. Their settlements at the
time of the hostile inundation were sparse, their means
scant, and their character unaggressive, but they had
long been on the ground, and their culture had the persistence of native things. The energetic invader had

contributed vigor and action to the tribal life, and had
altered dimensions and outward forms, but nature had
not yielded her own. Neither the long-heads themselves
had disappeared, nor the intimate, inbred ways of a life
long since grown out of physical circumstance. As in
the flooding of the Mycenæan areas by the broad-headed
northern Greek, so in Latium the native culture had
been overwhelmed, but had silently emerged again
until blended with the northern into one. Nor were these
two the only components of the Latin culture, though
they were the chief. The Phœnician from his merchant-
ships, and the Mycenæan with distant approaches from
east and south, had touched it, though ever so lightly,
during its southward march. A deeper impression was
made by another and a nearer civilization. The descending race had hardly finished settling the hills and valleys
of the Apennines and extending its homes throughout
the Tiber region before an enterprising race of strange
and mysterious men from unknown lands beyond the
sea had occupied the coasts and mountain valleys to the
north of Latium. The superior means and culture of
the Etruscans were already a leaven, however slight, in
the crude and unformed mass of the Latin civilization.

The newly established population of Latium was
neither a single racial strain nor possessed of an unmixed culture. Much less was it a nation. The great
family of wanderers to which it belonged was itself
hardly at the goal of its progress to the heart of Italy
before it had fallen apart into three, and Umbrian to
the north, Oscan to the south, and Latin about the
Tiber, had begun to diverge in language, manners, and
interest. The men of Latium were hardly settled on
their mountain-ridges and hill-towns in the plain when

THE CAMPAGNA AT PRATTICA DI MARE

THIS IS THE SITE OF ANCIENT LAVINIUM

they too fell apart. The centuries of their fighting pere-
grination had taught them too well the spirit of aggressive self-dependence and the use of arms. Scarcely
had they overcome the common foe when they turned
their weapons each against his neighbor. The shepherd
hamlets perched on the lonely hills glowered one at
another across disputed pasture lands, and met in the
shock of battle over stolen oxen and sheep. The men of
the mountains raided the fields of the men of the plain.
Treaties were made and broken. Misunderstandings and
jealousies arose. There were tiny groups of towns that
clustered about their miniature capitals, but even these
groups were loosely knit. The walk of an hour might
leave the tribesman on foreign soil. The word for stranger and guest and host and enemy was one and the same.
The Mediterranean tongue had not yet died, nor was
the tongue of the newcomers fixed. Diversity of interest
and position began to be followed, even within these
narrow limits, by divergence in speech. There was no
commanding common purpose, there was no commanding dialect, there was no leader whose judgments were
respected and whose word was law. There was no Rome
upon the Seven Hills.

II.

EARLIEST ROME

Quam ob rem, ut ille solebat, ita nunc mea repetet oratio populi originem; libenter enim etiam verbo utor Catonis,—

Well, then, just as he of whom we speak was wont to do, I too will now go back and tell of the Origin of our people; for I am glad to make use also of this term of Cato's.

CICERO, De Republica, II: 1

1.

THE TIBER AND THE SEVEN HILLS

AMONG the innumerable elevations of soft volcanic rock which, with their intersecting valleys and ravines, made up the surface of the Latin plain, was the group of hills later covered by the city of Rome. They differed neither in origin nor in nature from the other hills of the neighborhood. Before the streams of the Campagna had yet lost the volume of geologic times, the mighty current of the Tiber, swollen still more by the waters of the Anio, came sweeping down between the broad plateau on its left and the long ridge which formed its right bank from Monte Mario to the Janiculum, until, three miles below the confluence, it reached the site of Rome. At that point its waters, rushing with augmented violence because of the narrowed and impeded channel, cut out of the plateau on the eastern bank the little islands of tufa rock which, after the subsidence of the river and the coming of men, were to receive the names of the Capitoline, the Palatine, and the Aventine hills. At the same time, to the east and north of these island elevations, the powerful though smaller tributaries of the main stream, hurrying to lose themselves in its bosom, cut deep gorges through the plateau and formed the broad Cælian, the expansive Esquiline with its abrupt spurs of Cispian and Oppian, the tongue-like Quirinal and Viminal, and the rugged Hill of Gardens today called the Pincian.

When the waters had gradually sunk and the Tiber bed was reduced to its present narrow proportions, the

broad area which had been covered by the river-lake at
the site of Rome was transformed into a low expanse of
rich alluvial soil traversed by a little stream descending
from the hills, and dotted by marshy pools. This was the
Campus Martius, the plain of Mars, the soldiers' field
of the later Romans. Looking down into it at the eastern
edge like outposts of the plateau of which they formed
the fringe, stood the northern hills of Rome. At its
southern limit, continuing the line of the Quirinal across
a narrow channel, rose the twin peaks of the Capitoline
and the former islands of the Palatine and the Aventine,
the last at the Tiber's edge, the other two but slightly
removed. Between the Capitoline and the Palatine, and
between the Palatine and the Aventine, were low and
easily flooded valleys through which flowed rivulets
from various springs, and little tributaries from the
adjacent hillsides and ravines. Opposite all these, on the
right and western bank, lay the long and irregular
clayey ridge of the Janiculum, the Tiber almost washing
its base.

The Hills of Rome were thus only the jutting, ragged
edge of the plain where the Tiber cut a winding way
deep through its surface. Their elevation above the sea,
compared with that of the towns on the Alban foothills
or the ridges of the Sabines, was insignificant. The highest ground in the neighborhood, the summit of Monte
Mario, was only five hundred feet, and the highest of
all the hills of Rome was less than three hundred. Of
the hills on the eastern bank, the Aventine and the
Capitoline were one hundred and fifty feet, and the
Palatine one hundred and sixty. The various spurs
which overlooked the Campus Martius, running back
like the fingers of a hand to unite in the plateau, ranged

MONTE MARIO

AT THE EDGE OF THE TIBER VALLEY,
TWO MILES NORTH OF ROME

from the two hundred and five feet of the Quirinal to the one hundred and fifty-five of the Cælian. The Tiber itself was only twenty-two feet above the sea, and the lower places in the valleys between the hills but a trifle above the level of the stream.

On to these spur-plateaus and little hills came the men of Earliest Rome. Who were they, and what were the circumstances of their coming? What advantages of position, or what traits of character, or what accidents of fortune brought them at first to be the leading community in the neighborhood, and finally made their city mistress of the plain?

2.

EARLIEST ROME AND THE POETS

THE vision of the ancient Roman had less difficulty than that of the modern scholar in penetrating the mists of the prehistoric past. By the time of Cicero and Cæsar and Virgil and Augustus, the scant and faded web of fact preserved through the centuries when men's mouths were the only record of days gone by had been woven upon and embroidered by story-teller in verse and prose, and by the less disinterested glorifier of the family past, until it presented a pattern beautifully traceable and clear.

Let us borrow the vision of the ancient of Augustan times as we follow the fortunes of the earliest men of Rome. Let us look on the early Seven Hills through the willing eye of those who listened to or read the pages of a Virgil, a Cicero, a Livy, a Tibullus, an Ovid. It will be the poet's eye through which we look; for, whether in epic, oration, essay, history, or lyric, the ancient tale of Rome is always the shaping of the poet. What do we see?

A rugged and leafy Palatine and Capitoline rise from the marshy borders of the Tiber, their summits and the neighboring heights the abode of scattered shepherds roaming the hills and plain and offering simple sacrifice of milk and fruits to the rustic deity. Among them we see arrive a band of rovers from Greek Arcadia, and Evander their leader. The new chieftain teaches the little realm he wrests from them, or forms in peace, the ways to please the shepherd gods. We see Æneas the goddess-born and his sea-bronzed men, after weary years of wandering in blind obedience to the will of Heaven, sail into the Tiber between the great forest banks where it pours its eddying yellow volume into the sea, and set foot in the land of their destiny. We see his high ships as they sail inland and emerge from the shady woods of the winding river, an amazing apparition to the now venerable Evander and his people at their feasting on the Palatine, and we follow in their steps as with the royal guide they traverse the village streets and the paths of the grassy Forum to the woodland thickets of the Capitoline. We see Æneas in his wars with Latinus, king of the Aborigines, and their end in his union with Lavinia, daughter of the king. We see the outraged Turnus rouse the land to arms and summon the Etruscan princes from beyond the Tiber, we witness the defeat and death at Æneas' hand of his ill-starred rival.

The walls of Lavinium rise, and Æneas leaves the mortal scene to be united with the gods. The young prince Ascanius leads from the overflowing capital a band of colonists to found Alba Longa on a foothill or ridge of the Alban Mount. Ascanius dies, and Silvius reigns in his stead. And Silvius begets a second Æneas, and Æneas begets Latinus Silvius, who leads forth colonists called the Prisci Latini, and Latinus Silvius begets Alba, and Alba Atys, and Atys Capys, and Capys Capetus, and Capetus Tiberinus, whose drowning as he crosses the Albula gives the river its name among later generations; and Tiberinus begets Agrippa, and Agrippa Romulus Silvius, and Romulus Silvius Aventinus, who is buried on the hill in after times a part of Rome, and gives it a name; and Aventinus begets Proca, and Proca begets Numitor and Amulius.

Numitor is unjustly deprived of the Alban throne, his son is slain, and his daughter made a Vestal Virgin. But the Vestal becomes divinely the mother of twin boys. The usurper takes her life, and sends the babes to be drowned in the Tiber. The stream is beyond its banks, and difficult of approach; the assassins leave the twins in shallow water at the corner of the Palatine nearest the channel, and report the deed as done. The providential wolf is attracted by their crying and offers her breasts, until a woman of the near-by shepherds comes and takes them up. Under the rude discipline of shepherd tasks and shepherd company they grow to vigorous manhood, the leaders of devoted comrades. An accident reveals their identity, they slay the tyrant and reinstate the injured king, their grandsire, on the Alban throne, and themselves are off to found a city of their own at the place of their rescue and rearing by the Tiber-side. They begin the building of walls about the Palatine, Remus pays with his life the price of offending his high-spirited brother, and Romulus reigns alone.

The king completes the wall, annexes the Capitoline and other contiguous parts, and fills the vacant spaces of the unsettled town by opening the Asylum and inviting the discontented and ambitious from neighboring towns to unite their fortunes with those of the growing state. He seizes the Sabine women to gratify his men and to prolong the city's existence. He defeats the Sabine army, treats with Tatius the Sabine king, and rules conjointly with him until the death of Tatius restores him the undivided sway. He makes the Campus Martius a military ground, conquers Cænina, Crustumerium, and Antemnæ, not many miles to the north of Rome, and defeats the Etruscans at their nearest towns

of Fidenæ and Veii. To add to his kingly dignity, he
adopts the dress and state of the Etruscan princes, and
provides himself with lictors. He creates the Roman
senate of a hundred Fathers, whose sons are the first
patricians. He is better loved by the common people and
soldiery than by the upper class. He reigns with great
success for forty years, and finally, while holding a great
review in the Campus Martius, divinely disappears, in
the presence of all the state, in a crashing thunderstorm.
There are murmurs that jealous patricians know more
of his death than they care to tell.

The reverend figure of the Sabine Numa Pompilius
next appears. He becomes religious guide and law-giver
to the rude soldiers and shepherd-farmers of Romulus.
We see him build the temple of Janus at the edge of the
Forum, and close it for the first of the three times before Livy that Rome is at peace with all peoples. We
see him meet for nocturnal counsel with Egeria, to learn
what rites and what priests are acceptable to the gods.
He creates the flamen of Jupiter and the pontifex
maximus, and establishes the ancient Alban worship of
Vesta and her virgins. He divides the year into twelve
months of lunar length, and provides for the interposi-
tion of a corrective month. His reign is for three-and-
forty years.

Tullus Hostilius, the impetuous warrior-king, succeeds to the peaceful reign of the priest-king of early
Rome. He wars on Alba Longa because its men have
raided the fields of Roman farmers and cattle-men, and
the issue is decided by the spectacular combat of the
Roman triplets Horatii and the Alban triplets Curiatii.
He takes Fidenæ, the dangerous outpost of the Etruscans on the near side of the Tiber seven miles to the

north of Rome. To punish the Albans for defection in
the fight with the men of Fidenæ, he condemns their
general to death and their city to destruction; Alba
Longa, four centuries old, is razed to the ground, and
its people transported to Rome. He annexes the Cælian
and assigns it as their quarter. He erects the senate
house at the northwest corner of the Forum. He is
scornful of religion until the people are seized by a
devastating plague and he himself is smitten, when he
becomes the superstitious observer of every real or fancied rite, and is at last reduced to ashes, together with
his palace, by the lightning-stroke of a Jupiter profaned
and outraged by the inexpert performance of a rite. The
reign of Tullus is for two-and-thirty years.

In the four-and-twenty years of Ancus Martius'
reign, the Aventine is added to the city and made the
residence of the men of conquered Ficana, Politorium,
and Tellenæ. The city grows in strength as well as in
area; the Janiculum is fortified against the encroachments of the ever-expanding Etruscan power. The first
bridge, of wood, is built. The increase of the lawless element necessitates the building of the Tullianum at the
head of the Forum. The Prisci Latini revolt and are
overcome by the taking of Medullia, and their men
transported and assigned to the valley between the
Aventine and Palatine. Ostia is founded at the mouth of
the Tiber, and the salt-marshes are established. Rome
has reached the sea.

One day in the reign of the well-poised Ancus, a
carriage appears on the brow of the Janiculum, to
descend and cross the wooden bridge to Rome. In it are
Lucumo, grandson of Demaratus, refugee from Corinth

to Tarquinii, and Tanaquil, his Etruscan wife. He takes
the name of Lucius Tarquinius Priscus, cultivates king
and courtiers, and at length, through native talent for
intrigue and the aid of Tanaquil, is elected successor
of Ancus and reigns for eight-and-thirty years as Tarquin the First. He wars with the Latins and the Sabines, levels and drains the easily flooded Forum, plans
the Circus Maximus between the Palatine and Aventine, lays the foundations of the great temple of Jupiter
on the Capitoline, enlarges the senate and the city, and
at his murder by the revengeful sons of Ancus is making
ready to erect a great ring-wall about the capital.

Tarquin has no heir of age, and the sons of Ancus
are in exile, but the resourceful Tanaquil is ready with
a successor in the person of a young man reared in the
palace, the son of a captive Sabine lady of noble blood
become gossip to the queen, and married to the princess
her daughter. Servius Tullius reforms the constitution
by providing for the distribution anew of obligation and
privilege. His count of the city shows a total of eighty
thousand, though Fabius Pictor in after times will have
the number mean only those who bore arms. He adds to
the urban area the Quirinal and the Viminal, honors and
increases the Esquiline by making it his seat, and girdles
the now large city with a strong and stately wall of
stone more than five miles long. He wars against Veii,
after Fidenæ the nearest and most dangerous of the
Etruscan strongholds. He builds the temple of Diana
on the Aventine to be a common sanctuary for all the
Latins in like manner as the shrine of Ephesus is common to all the Greeks, hoping thus to win the tacit confession of Rome's leadership among the Latin cities. He

is murdered after four-and-forty years of reign by the ambitious son of Tarquin the First.

Tarquin the Arrogant reigns five-and-twenty years. He completes the temple of Jupiter on the Capitoline, and builds the great sewer Cloaca Maxima by walling over the natural stream that descends from the hills and through the Forum. He wars with the Volscians, plants on their ground the Roman colonies of Signia and Suessa Pometia, by patient treachery captures Gabii, on the road from Rome to Præneste, and makes the city of Rome the acknowledged capital of the Latin tribes. But he and his court are arrogant and domineering toward both their equals and the common people. The murmurs of discontent swell to cries of rage at the final act of crime and cruelty in the rape of Lucretia by a son of the king. The royal house is driven out, and the Roman character receives the impress of hatred for kingly rule which will remain its most visible mark until five centuries later, when weariness of popular mistakes and the conflicts of selfish demagogues have reconciled it to autocratic power in the person of Augustus.

Such is the story of the earliest men of Rome as told by historian and poet of Augustan times, as taught the Roman boy in school, as recited by the guide to those who came to see the Eternal City, as recorded by successive writers of Roman history from Livy to modern times. It was known by the judicious to be mingled of the stuff of poetry, but accepted by the common run of men as truth, and by even the more exacting critic as representing essentially the truth. "The poetic tales of tradition," says Livy in his preface, "it is not my intention either to present as truth or to refute. We allow

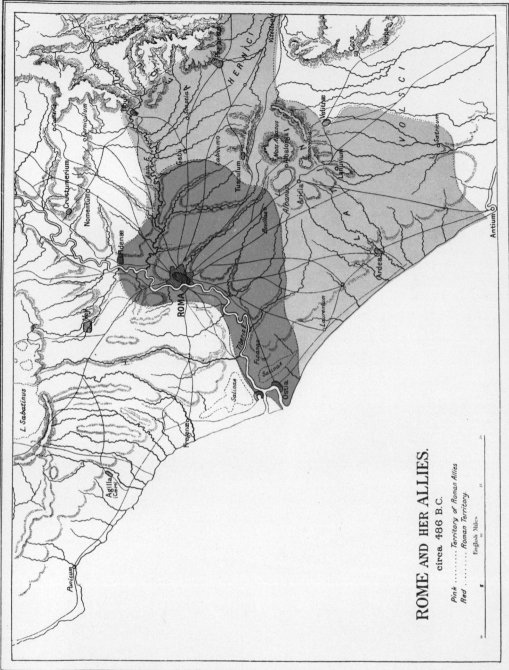

ROME AND HER ALLIES.

circa 486 B.C.

Pink .... Territory of Roman Allies.

Red .... Roman Territory.

English Miles.

THE ROMAN SWAY

IN 486 B.C.

SUGGESTING THE ROME

OF THE

ETRUSCAN PERIOD

antiquity to have its way in mingling the work of the gods with the work of men to make the beginnings of its cities more august . . . but these matters and others like them, in whatever manner they shall be noted or judged, I for my part shall make of no great account."

EARLIEST ROME AND THE CRITIC

THE rise of a more exacting method has altered our vision. The critical historian and the archæologist have sponged out in part, and then retouched and restored, the picture of early Roman times. The critic has removed from it the figures of individual men with names and dates, and we see no longer actual persons on the hills of Rome. He has removed the individual scene with its dramatic circumstance, and we no longer thrill at the sight of heroic figures in action. He has directed our attention to the politics and economics and general movement of a growing society rather than to the fortunes of warriors and kings, to the progress of man rather than to the achievements of men. The archæologist has gone hand in hand with the critic. He has enlisted the aid of geology, and taught us to read the origin of the actual ground the earliest Romans trod. He has led us to their local habitations, and taught us of the houses in which they lived, the roads on which they travelled, the goods they gave and received in trade, the peoples with whom they exchanged, the routes over which their commerce moved. He has shown us the ornament they wore, the pottery from which they ate and drank, the tools with which they wrought, the arms with which they went forth to war, the graves in which their bones or ashes were laid. He has helped us to conceive of the mind in which they sought God, if haply they might feel after him, and find him.

Historian and archæologist may seem at first sight to

have ruined the picture by their obscuration of the well-known lines and their reduction of the brilliant lights; but, if they have taken from its sharp distinctness, they have given it richer and warmer color, a greater unity, and a deeper reality. If we look again, with amended vision, upon the hills of Rome and their earliest men, it will be with no less pleasure.

Again the Palatine and its neighbors rise from the reedy surroundings, their masses of rugged reddish rock half hidden in the verdure of oaks and pines and dark shrubbery that crown their summits and hang upon their sides. Their only inhabitants are the birds and the beasts, until one day a hunter or shepherd gone farther afield than his wont appears in the thickets and glades of the upland silences to the north and east, and picks an exploring way along the low ridge that leads to the solitary Palatine. The invading race from the valley of the Po has at last completed the occupation of the old sites on the mountain-sides and the multiplication of new sites on the high places in the plain, and the wave of its expansion has advanced to the hills by the Tiber.

Other shepherds come in the days that follow. One of them throws up a rude shelter of poles and branches and returns from time to time. Another follows example. A group of cabins becomes lodged on the Esquiline, another on the Palatine, another on the Quirinal. The lightly trodden paths of random flocks of sheep become well-worn ways that wind about the hills and descend to the drinking-places in the valleys. The cabins become huts, the huts become permanent dwellings, the groups become villages, the paths become roads and streets that are clouds of dust in summer and channels of mud and water in the winter months of rain.

The villages are swelled by shepherd, drover, and farmer. Their number multiplies. The neighborhood in time is dotted by miniature cities in grey thatch that look across the valleys to other miniature cities in grey. Their general form and content are those of the palisaded towns of the Po. Their round and oblong huts of reeds and straw supported by poles and clay resemble in shape the American Indian wigwam or tepee; their principal garment is not unlike the Indian blanket. They learn to scarp the rocky side of the cliff and dress it with stone from the bed of the hill, and to moat and dike the level approaches. Fold and pen are within the walls or close at hand. The chieftain's hut, larger than the rest and perhaps of wood or stone, is at the village center. From the apex of a rounded hut near by rise the light heat waves and wisps of smoke from the common village fire. The chieftain's daughter keeps it alight, the Vestal Virgin that is to be.

The villagers have no temples. Though every object of earth and air for them is immanent with deity, they know no gods in human form. Beyond the gates they bury their dead. Some they cremate and deposit in urns of clay or stone; some they lay to rest in coffins of hollowed logs or of earthenware. The eastern border of the Forum valley is one of their burial-places, the broad plateau of the Esquiline another; cities of the dead that will lie unknown for twenty-seven centuries under the ever-mounting strata of life above them.

Their contacts with each other and with the world are simple. They meet in central places for the exchange of oxen and sheep and such simple produce as the times and place afford, and for mutual agreement on matters of interest between the tribes. They know little of the world beyond the hills and mountains that limit their vision. They are all kinsmen, yet the village across the valley may belong to a different branch of the common race, and speak a tongue already divergent from that of its neighbors. Perhaps the settlers on the Esquiline are of Sabine stock, and those on the Palatine are their Alban cousins. The stranger from Etruria sometimes appears among them with his dazzling wares, but does not remain in the rude surroundings. The trading-vessel from the Tyrrhenian sometimes ascends the Tiber, or the wagon-pack comes up the roads from the south or over the mountains from the east, bringing the rich and highly colored stuffs of Greece and the Orient. They barter and go their ways. The awakening of the little group of towns is slow. The civilization of the Latin plain in general is barren and backward.

But the awakening comes. The Palatine begins to emerge at the head of the group. Perhaps it is an older and better-knit community; perhaps its position is better for defence or aggression; perhaps its chiefs are men of dynamic character. The hill receives the name Palatium from the shepherd-goddess Pales; the city itself is known as Roma, the River-city. The strong man who first gives the city greatness may really bear the name of Romulus, chief of the River-city. The gate to the Tiber is Porta Romanula, the River-gate. The gate to the north that leads to the ridge of the Velia and across to the Esquiline, is Mugonia, the Lowing-gate. This is the earliest form of the city Rome. The earliest Romans are cattle-owners.

The River-city compels or persuades its neighbors to submission; or it admits them to its protection against a common foe. To its own two parts, the Palatium and the Germalus, it unites the Velia, immediately at hand, the Oppian, the Fagutal, and the Cispian, which reach out toward it from the Esquiline, and the Sucusa, adjacent on the edge of the Cælian. It encloses the seven precincts, each with its village, within a single defence. The second form of the city of Rome receives the name of Septimontium. The tribal chieftain has become a king, his strong men a council.

The momentum of growth increases. The overflowing villages meet in the valleys, and grow into a whole. Their fields and pastures are extended farther and farther into the plain. The limits of the city are pushed beyond the wall. They include the Palatine, the Capitoline, the Quirinal, the Viminal, the Esquiline, the Cælian. In the course of time the boundary is again defined and fixed, and the third form of the city of Rome comes into being. It is a city of four regions, or wards: the Palatina, the Esquilina, the Collina, the Suburana. This is the city of the middle kings. It is no longer the simple shepherd village. Its principal streets are paved; their large squared stones are seamed, and the unpaved ways and alleys are deeply rutted, by the passage of laboring two-wheeled carts from the country drawn by long-horned cattle. It is a city of markets and public places, with temples and public buildings beginning to cluster about the Forum valley, and larger houses rising from favored spots on the hills. There are shops of a simple sort, but most of the city's barter is done in the open. Men and women in homespun blanket and body-garment mingle in the market and jostle in the street. The king on horseback or in his car with guard about him goes by on his way to the senate. Squads of soldiers with shield and lance come tramping up the street. The

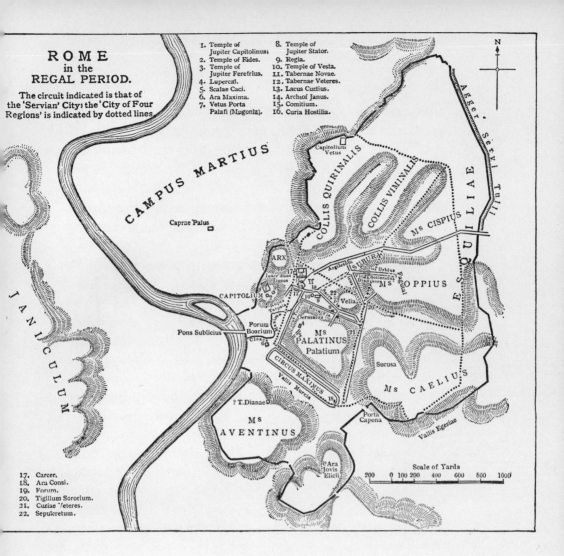

ROME
in the
REGAL PERIOD.

The circuit indicated is that of
the 'Servian' City; the 'City of Four
Regions' is indicated by dotted lines.

1. Temple of Jupiter Capitolinus.
2. Temple of Fides.
3. Temple of Jupiter Feretrius.
4. Lupercal.
5. Scalae Caci.
6. Ara Maxima.
7. Vetus Porta Palati (Mugonia).
8. Temple of Jupiter Stator.
9. Regia.
10. Temple of Vesta.
11. Tabernae Novae.
12. Tabernae Veteres.
13. Lacus Curtius.
14. Arch of Janus.
15. Comitium.
16. Curia Hostilia.

17. Carcer.
18. Ara Consi.
19. Forum.
20. Tigillum Sororium.
21. Curiae Veteres.
22. Sepulcretum.

EARLIEST ROME

SHOWING THE FIRST FOUR FORMS OF THE CITY

REPRODUCED BY PERMISSION OF THE CAMBRIDGE UNIVERSITY PRESS
FROM LIVY, BOOK I, EDITED BY H. J. EDWARDS

world beyond the hills and mountains that limit their vision. They are all kinsmen, yet the village across the valley may belong to a different branch of the common race, and speak a tongue already divergent from that of its neighbors. Perhaps the settlers on the Esquiline are of Sabine stock, and those on the Palatine are their Alban cousins. The stranger from Etruria sometimes appears among them with his dazzling wares, but does not remain in the rude surroundings. The trading-vessel from the Tyrrhenian sometimes ascends the Tiber, or the wagon-pack comes up the roads from the south or over the mountains from the east, bringing the rich and highly colored stuffs of Greece and the Orient. They barter and go their ways. The awakening of the little group of towns is slow. The civilization of the Latin plain in general is barren and backward.

But the awakening comes. The Palatine begins to emerge at the head of the group. Perhaps it is an older and better-knit community; perhaps its position is better for defence or aggression; perhaps its chiefs are men of dynamic character. The hill receives the name Palatium from the shepherd-goddess Pales; the city itself is known as Roma, the River-city. The strong man who first gives the city greatness may really bear the name of Romulus, chief of the River-city. The gate to the Tiber is Porta Romanula, the River-gate. The gate to the north that leads to the ridge of the Velia and across to the Esquiline, is Mugonia, the Lowing-gate. This is the earliest form of the city Rome. The earliest Romans are cattle-owners.

The River-city compels or persuades its neighbors to submission; or it admits them to its protection against a common foe. To its own two parts, the Palatium and the Germalus, it unites the Velia, immediately at hand, the Oppian, the Fagutal, and the Cispian, which reach out toward it from the Esquiline, and the Sucusa, adjacent on the edge of the Cælian. It encloses the seven precincts, each with its village, within a single defence. The second form of the city of Rome receives the name of Septimontium. The tribal chieftain has become a king, his strong men a council.

The momentum of growth increases. The overflowing villages meet in the valleys, and grow into a whole. Their fields and pastures are extended farther and farther into the plain. The limits of the city are pushed beyond the wall. They include the Palatine, the Capitoline, the Quirinal, the Viminal, the Esquiline, the Cælian. In the course of time the boundary is again defined and fixed, and the third form of the city of Rome comes into being. It is a city of four regions, or wards: the Palatina, the Esquilina, the Collina, the Suburana. This is the city of the middle kings. It is no longer the simple shepherd village. Its principal streets are paved; their large squared stones are seamed, and the unpaved ways and alleys are deeply rutted, by the passage of laboring two-wheeled carts from the country drawn by long-horned cattle. It is a city of markets and public places, with temples and public buildings beginning to cluster about the Forum valley, and larger houses rising from favored spots on the hills. There are shops of a simple sort, but most of the city's barter is done in the open. Men and women in homespun blanket and body-garment mingle in the market and jostle in the street. The king on horseback or in his car with guard about him goes by on his way to the senate. Squads of soldiers with shield and lance come tramping up the street. The wars of Rome have carried its lands and dominion, on the east and south, far toward the mountains and the sea. On the west and north it looks with growing uneasiness upon an ever-expanding enemy of alien blood and manners. It has developed a commanding character. It has made of Latin and Sabine within its walls a strong amalgam, and impressed upon it the Latin traits. It is envied, feared, or loved by its neighbors and subject-allies according to circumstance. It is different from the older cities. It has become Roman. It is filled with the vigor of youthful things, and soon will be the Latin capital.

It was not mere chance that set Rome apart from other cities of the Latin land. Nor was her rise due directly to an advantageous site. It was men that made her great, men as the instrument of necessity. The character of the early men of Rome was forged on the anvil of hardship. It was a rough life in the open that the shepherd-farmers of the first kings led, the worthy tradition of the life of their migrant northern fathers. The advantages of situation praised by their patriotic descendants of the days when Rome had become part of the outside world, to them were hardly present.

"Not without reason," Camillus is made to say in Livy, when, after the taking of Rome by the Gauls, he argues against the removal of the Romans from their devastated city to Veii, "not without reason did gods and men choose out this spot for the beginnings of our city: these healthful hills, the convenient river on which to bring down the produce of inland regions and over which we are reached by the commerce of the seas, a position near enough the coast for convenience, yet not so near as to be imperilled by stranger ships, a location central to Italy, a site uniquely adapted to the expansion of a city."

Neither these advantages, nor the abundant springs, the breezy hills, and the shady valleys praised by Cicero in similar strain of loyalty were the causes of Rome's beginnings and rise. Necessity determined its founding. Necessity fixed its site. Necessity dictated its expansion. Necessity moulded the character of its men. The city was not well watered until centuries after its foundation. The Tiber above Rome could have had little to do with commerce at any time, and became of service below only after the city had long existed. The Ciceronian "healthful hills among pestilential surroundings" is praise for the orator's home high-raised on the Palatine, "in full view of all the city," but hardly praise for the ground within and without the city into which the earliest Romans were compelled to expand. The phrase is suggestive of undrained valleys and water-soaked fields and marshy thickets, and of the sole-surviving and immortal deity of the Latin lowlands, the goddess Fever.

There was not only the struggle with unwilling nature to harden the Roman character. There was the discipline of struggle with men, to temper as well as to harden. From the day the Sabines reached the hills from the north and east and the Latins reached them from the south, the men of Rome were never wholly at peace. As the city increased, broils with Sabine neighbors and nearer kinsmen were succeeded by wars both with them and with remoter kinsmen of the Apennines where they touched the plain. Distrust and envy of Rome as an equal were followed by combination and league against her as she emerged superior. There was the constant strain of anxiety, the constant exercise of arms and

diplomacy. The rude men by the Tiber were men of the
world, though their world was small.

But a greater danger was at hand, and a greater
discipline. The powers with whom Rome fought to the
east and south of the Tiber were never of great dimensions, and never of totally alien blood. It was not so
with the enemy that threatened from the north.

The sons of the Alpine race had not been many centuries in the Latin land, and the shepherd-farmers had
hardly settled their homes on the hills by the Tiber,
when their kinsmen who stopped in the western Apennines and the coastal plain to the north of Latium were
the victims of sudden invasion. About eight hundred
years before the Christian era, a race of men from unknown lands in Asia Minor whose speech and appearance were altogether alien to the men of Italy, and
whose language still remains cryptic after upwards of
three thousand years, appeared in the Tyrrhenian and
descended upon the simple civilization they found on
its shores. They captured and settled first the line of
hill-towns from Cære to Vulci, and in the course of no
long time, as their numbers were swelled by successive
waves of armed invaders and colonists, possessed the
whole of the land between the Arno and the Tiber.

Already of superior culture, the growth of the Etruscans in wealth and accomplishment was rapid. The
mounded rock-hewn tombs of their great cemeteries
are still rich with sculpture and luminous with beautifully painted walls. Their funeral couches were strewn
with bronze and silver and gold in rare design and exquisite craftsmanship. They expanded to the east into
Umbria. They established themselves in the fertile gardens of Campania. They connected their north and

south by a line of roads and fortresses of which the already ancient Præneste, commanding the valley between the Sabines and the Albans and Volscians, was the principal one. They shared the sea with the Carthaginian, and with him kept the Greek from the western Mediterranean until their joint defeat at the Himera on the day of Salamis.

The Etruscan encroachments upon Latin soil began early and were persistent. They conquered or founded Fidenæ, north from Rome on the Latin bank of the Tiber, and made it their outpost. A few miles farther away, on the Cremera, a northern tributary of the Tiber, lay one of their twelve great capitals, the strong city of Veii. From the west, they advanced to the Tiber's edge, where at Rome they found a fortress on the Janiculum guarding the bridge to the city. They threatened constantly the whole of the Latin land, which lay between them and their rich Campanian holdings and divided their empire.

Meanwhile they treated and traded with Rome, and mingled with the Romans. Their hucksters and merchants, their fortune-tellers, the migrant spirits among them, were attracted to the rising Latin capital. They lodged in numbers to the south of the Forum, between the Palatine and the Tiber, and formed the Etruscan quarter. Some of their more ambitious men of means and consequence sought greater fortune and fame in the higher circles of the city's life. Among them there may have been the sons, less alien to the Romans, of exiled or enterprising Greeks who had married Etruscan women. It may even be that their presence at Rome was not without ulterior design. Etruscan wealth and Etruscan merchandise, Etruscan skill of hand, Etrus-

ETRUSCAN TOMBS AT CERVETERI

THE SITE OF ANCIENT CÆRE,
THIRTY MILES NORTH OF ROME,
NEAR THE COAST

can fortune-telling and bird-lore among the common
people, Etruscan culture and Etruscan suavity among
the upper classes, were not without their effect. However it may have been, whether by dint of quiet penetra-
tion, whether by astute diplomatics, whether by sudden
coup and peaceful seizure or by siege and long campaign, Etruria gained her end, and one day the Romans
found themselves with a king of Etruscan blood. This
was the fourth form of Rome.

For a hundred years the stranger sat in the seat of
the Roman kings. He seized and subdued the cities already in league with Rome, and warred upon those
who had not yielded to arms or persuasion. He strengthened the route to the Capuan plain by the conquest of
Gabii, on the road between Præneste and Rome. The
fortress-town of Præneste itself became the seat of
wealthy and powerful princes. The sober grey of life
at Rome was enlivened by the bright hues of Etruscan
luxury. The noble families and kingly connection
brought with them not only new modes of administration, but with them came also Etruscan manners and
dress, Etruscan painting, sculpture, and building,
Etruscan augural lore, Etruscan regal and religious
custom, Etruscan pomp. The prestige of Etruscan
wealth and culture, of Etruscan commerce on sea and
land, of Etruscan connection with Carthage, Greece,
and the Orient, was communicated to Rome and the
Latin people. By the sixth century, the already thriving
population of the Roman territories was not only enriched by Etruscan patronage, but through it enjoyed a
contact with distant parts of the Mediterranean world.
Roman and Latin markets were bright with eastern
merchandise, the homes of richer men were warm with

eastern color and graced by delicate vases of clay and metal, and women were good to look upon in eastern stuffs and jewels.

But the Etruscan domination could not endure. The culture of the wealthy hill-towns was too strange to blend with Latin culture, and Latin character had grown too strong and too distinct to be absorbed by a culture already past its climax. Whether because their sway in Etruria had been only in the nature of exploitation and had exhausted the resources of the lands they seized; or because the use of luxury had undermined physique and character; or because their ancient and high-bred blood was of a strain too alien to fertilize or be fertilized by the vigorous current that pulsed through native Italian veins, Etruscan discipline had begun to weaken, Etruscan power to wane. The arrogance of Etruscan nobles and men of wealth at Rome, the high-handedness of kings who assumed that Romans would crook the knee in Etruscan fashion, provoked at last in a people waxing in strength as well as restiveness the outburst of fury that expelled the stranger from their gates and started him on the descent whose end was to be his overthrow in turn by Roman arms.

THE ROMANS AND ROME IN
TARQUIN'S TIME

THE Rome that had driven out the kings and now defeated the united efforts of Etruscan army and Latin ally to reinstate them, emerged from the trial no longer a city in the dread and fear of kings from any source. It emerged not only free from the Etruscan, but, thanks to the increase in strength and size conferred by his vigorous rule, as an equal and rival. It emerged also as potential leader and mistress of all the Latin land. Its character as a city, and the character of its men, were established. As Rome itself was different from Etruscan cities and from her sisters on Latin soil, so the name of Roman was now possessed of distinctive content.

The Roman of just before the Republic was a blend of the Latin and the Sabine, and each of these in turn was a blend of the Alpine invader with his neolithic predecessor. The main ingredient of the blend was Latin; the Mediterraneans with whom the northerners had mingled were sparser in the plain than in the mountains where the fathers of the Sabines came among them, and communication between the city and the Latins had always been immediate and open. The result was essentially a Latin city and Latin men.

The Roman blood and the Roman character were thus firm and consistent, if not entirely homogeneous. The Hellenic strain as yet had really entered into

neither. By even Etruscan blood and character, they
had been but lightly touched. The century of Etruscan
occupation had been only an episode in the Roman experience. Of the changes it had wrought, but few concerned the essential. It had affected the form far more
than the essence of both Rome the city and the life of
Rome. It had left its mark on officialdom; the lictors,
the curule chair, the purple-bordered gown, were part
of its legacy. It had left its impress on the manner of
religious observance, and added somewhat to religious
content. It had taught to priest and populace the lore
of birds and of lightning and thunderbolt, and how to
read the future in the shape and movement of the fresh-
slain victim's vital parts. It had loaned them the Etruscan gods, and helped their rustic imaginations to see
deity in the image of man. It had helped them to plan
the house with atrium for central room, to employ the
arch in the building of their drains and sewers, to rear
and ornament their temples and public buildings. It had
ministered for the time to their material good, and
hastened their discovery of the outside world. It had
not changed, however, or even greatly modified, the language of the Roman. It had not altered perceptibly his
manner of living; he might on occasion eat and drink
from Etruscan plate, and adorn his women with Etruscan jewels, but this was not his settled mode of life. The
Etruscan kings themselves had modified their ways in
the presence of the Roman, and become less foreign on
Roman soil. They had left at Rome no princely tombs
such as those their cousins left on the mountain-side of
Præneste. Their presence, with all their following,
except as it had educated the Roman to patience and
self-reliance, and stamped deep into his soul the hatred

of kings, had left him in race and temperament the same
as it found him.

The Roman remained essentially the shepherd-farmer
of his fathers' times. The city had grown in population,
and the rise of urban needs had created the usual urban
occupations, but the center of interest for men of consequence and for the mass of the less important was beyond the gates. Their possessions were in the fields that
lay within sight of the city; their occupations and their
incomes dependent first of all upon the fields. Even
during the times of expansion under Etruscan kings
their main concern had never been commerce, and in
the period that ensues their trading was largely confined to Latium and the nearer parts of Italy. Their
gains were the produce of pasture, farm, and garden.
Daily they rode afield from city or farmhouse to over-
see the tasks of shepherd and husbandman. There were
larger estates of pasture land whose hills were dotted
with countless sheep and goats and kine. There were
the larger tracts of farm land that were made by intensive cultivation to blossom like the rose; they were
tilled by dependent and slave supervised by heads responsible to the master in the city. There were smaller
farms and garden tracts whose tillers were the owners
themselves. The men who possessed the land and the
flocks and herds, as well as the men who guarded and
worked, were dressed in homespun from the wool and
flax of pasture and farm; the rustic in simple body-
garment, with the rudest of wraps in the colder season,
the shepherd in fleece, the master in tunic and oblong
cloak. The men of the fields were barefoot, bareheaded,
and bronzed, with shaggy beards and hair. The men of
the city on occasion wore a simple sandal, but rarely a

hat. The food of both was from the fields and of the season: the milk and cheese of sheep and goats and cows, the flesh of sheep and goats and swine, unleavened cakes and porridge, the fruits of orchard and garden. The flesh of their oxen they did not eat; the ox was sacred to the gods. Of wine and olives they hardly knew the use. Their sugar was honey, their salt was brought from the marshes by the sea.

Their religion was still essentially the rustic faith of primitive cultures. The more advanced who formed the influential class had learned, from near Etruria and more remote Marseilles or Cumæ, something of deity clothed in human form and possessed of human sentiment; in the city they had even erected temples and lesser shrines, and peopled them with images; yet all but the few, impressed though they were by the mystic splendor of the new and strange, still practiced the faith of the fields and the open air. For them every object they saw or touched was quick with an inner and unseen spirit. Sky, forest, fountain, and beast, and man himself, were indwelt by a vague and shadowy second self. Not only every object, but every act, was thus the abode of deity; there was a god for the birth of the babe or the lamb, a god for his feeding, a god for his growth, a god for his walking, eating, and drinking. There were gods for sowing and reaping, for marriage, for all the processes that make up the life-experience of men and things, to the separation of soul from body. The number of gods was limited only by the number of objects in the contacts of life and the number of acts that make the day. They did not roam the earth at will in the manner of Homer's gods; they could not exist apart from the acts or objects proper to them. They were jealous gods. They must be approached through perfectly definite formulæ; mistake, or even variation, would bring failure, misfortune, or even wrathful destruction.

Generation after generation since the arrival of men in the land had added to knowledge and improved upon rite and formula, until the body of divine lore could no longer be contained by the mind of the ordinary man. The affairs of men and of the state had been often endangered by inexpert observance. The priest had long since risen, the special agent between man and god. But the Roman god was just, as well as jealous. He required no paraphernalia, and did not delight in the death of man. The simple and homely act, the time-honored invocation and prayer, the sacrifice of milk, or cheese, or fruits, or flowers, or of roasted flesh or sacred meal,—let them be clear and unequivocal, in exact accord with prescription, and the result was assured; the deity had no choice.

Some few of these multitudinous gods had slowly emerged from the populous limbo of the spirit-world. There were Faunus and Fauna, of the wilder life of field and forest; Janus and Vesta, of beginnings and the hearth; Consus and Ops, of horses and harvests; Liber and Libera, of the forces of nature in grains and fruits; Jovis, of the sky, the sunshine, and the rain; and a score of others. Yet, paired as they were, they sustained no marriage relation, no genealogies accounted for them, they were subjects of no rich body of legend. They were but dimly bodied forth in the worshipper's imagination as having human form and attributes. They had no statues, and none but Vesta, whose everlasting fires required a shelter, dwelt in a temple made with hands. The groves were the Roman god's first temples.

A still smaller number rose in time to greater distinction. They were lodged in the sparse temples about the Forum valley. Etruscan and Greek had quickened the Roman imagination. Saturn, the ancient god of seed-time and harvest, long worshipped at the base of the Capitoline, was among the first to see the rude altar converted into a sheltered abode. Mars was conceived of as something more than a mystic lance. The round hut of Vesta and her maidens was transformed from wood and clay into stone. The formless Jovis, whose token was the flint, was transformed to Jupiter, wielder of the thunderbolt. The trinity of Jupiter, Juno, and Minerva took form on the Capitoline. The cult statue appeared, to fix the type of the god in the worshipper's mind. Yet these were but the apex of the pyramid whose base was firmly set in the nature of primitive man.

It is a rude and stern society that has its seat by the Tiber five hundred years before the Christian era, yet it is not untouched by enlightenment. The early men of Rome excel in war. Its constant practice has made them strong and enduring in body and spirit. They surpass in the management of men. The centuries of continual toil and constant danger have taught them the need and the method of unity. The family is a unit, the clan a larger unit, the state a unit that includes them all. Their heads are supreme, even to the power of life and death; the householder over son and daughter, dependent, and slave, the chief of the clan over the heads of the aggregated families that constitute his larger family, the king over the chiefs of clans who with him form the visible state. It is a society whose basis is the austere practice of authority, yet not a society where irresponsibility reigns and freedom is crushed. The son finds his safe-

guard against paternal tyranny in the family council
and public opinion, the clansman in the council of family
heads, the citizen in the council of the chiefs of clans,
the senate. So well on one side has the lesson of discipline been learned, so well on the other the lesson of
self-restraint and justice, that flagrant abuses are rare,
and wrongs of lesser degree are likely to find their
remedy.

But, even with these virtues, the early men of Rome
are not yet highly civilized. Their rustic simplicity and
ruggedness are also narrowness and roughness. They
are still a provincial race. The horizon of life for them
is the line that circumscribes their own immediate interests. They are not yet conscious of the ultimate uses of
art, or of education for other purpose than the fitting
of their sons for the plain duties of family and state, and
of their daughters for the duties of motherhood. Women
they hold in esteem as the breeders of men. Continued
warring has made of their city an armed camp; it has
bred them to be hard and aggressive, and on occasion
cruel and unjust.

The city that sits at the center of this society is
equally distinct in character, and equally mingled of
the crude and the civilized, the rustic and the urban. Its
five miles of massive stone defence are built against the
beetling rocks of the ruggeder parts of the circuit, and
continued across the level reaches as moat and high-
walled dike. Its people have already filled it and grown
beyond the barriers. In poorer quarters and on the
skirts of the city, the old-time huts of clay and reeds
may still be seen. Elsewhere their places are filled by
a motley assemblage of squared and oblong dwellings
of wood and sun-dried brick with sloping roofs of wood.

The more pretentious houses are of the rectangular type, with rooms about a court which is open to the sky, and with garden at the rear. There are temples here and there in the city's heart, some square, some round, of roughly dressed blocks of stone and with painted upper members in wood. The rectangular type prevails, with columned portico in front and gabled roof of tile whose ends and sides are gay with brightly colored earthen figurines or sculptured plaques. One peak of the Capitol frowns as a fortress; on the other reposes the temple of Jupiter Best and Greatest. The valley of the Forum is free of water, and teeming with the business of senate, tribunal, temple, and market. The woman from the Palatine is there with water-pot on head, the country-woman with vegetable-basket comes and goes. The field of Mars, between the walls and the Tiber, is vociferous and dusty with the drilling of men. The streets that traverse the hills and valleys are crooked and narrow, the paths of long ago. Many are still unpaved and thick with dust or mud. It is a city of dun and grey, but little relieved by color, yet picturesque in the expansive rise and fall of irregular streets, and beautiful from afar in the rhythmic roll of the masses of roofs that rest like a garment upon the hills. Sometimes at dead of night the thoroughfares are choked by the infinite living stream of sheep and bleating lambs on the way across the city to fresher pastures.

III.

THE REPUBLIC

Is dicere solebat ob hanc causam præstare nostræ civitatis statum ceteris civitatibus, quod in illis singuli fuissent fere qui suam quisque rempublicam constituissent legibus atque institutis suis . . . nostra autem respublica non unius esset ingenio sed multorum, nec una hominis vita sed aliquot constituta sæculis et ætatibus,—

He used to say that for this reason our state stood out before all others, because in them it was generally true that individual men had brought the commonwealth into being by dint of laws and institutions of their own devising . . . whereas our commonwealth was grounded in the genius not of one man but of many, in the life not of one man but of a succession of ages and generations.

Cicero, De Republica, II: 1

Moribus antiquis res stat Romana virisque,—

Rome's roots are deep in the morals and men of the olden times.

Ennius, Annales, 500

1.

SOVEREIGNTY AND CITIZENSHIP

TO follow the fortunes of Rome from the time of the kings to their culmination in the best days of the Republic is gradually to advance from the dim uncertainties of dawn and the half-lights of early morning toward the perfect light of day. The spade and the literary legend find reinforcement in the pen of the ancient historian. The shadowy Rome whose power has been increased and whose character deepened by the episode of Etruscan rule is seen at the time of Cato's death and the uprooting of Carthage with her features distinct. By the middle of the second century before the Christian era, three hundred and fifty years from the last of the kings, the authority of the city-state has touched the farthest shores of the Mediterranean sea, and Roman character has assumed the form under which it is to be the inspiration of time to come.

It may indeed be that, with the expulsion of the Etruscan and the upheaval of the revolution, the sphere of Rome's authority was for a time contracted, and her contact with the world diminished. The royal house made desperate efforts to regain the throne, and the Latin cities hastened to seize on the opportunity that seemed to offer of asserting total independence and setting a limit to the power of the rising capital. The halt occasioned by the opposing forces, however, was only momentary. The vitality of the city and her men was too robust to permit a long quiescence. Rome not only met the onslaughts of the enemy and faced these dangers

down, but initiated advances of her own, and was soon
once more on the road which led to ultimate domination.
To the south, to the east, to the north, to the farther
south and across the straits and the seas, she extended
her arms and her civilization until the natural term of
growth was reached.

The hostility of the Latin cities was manifest in the
league of the year 500, in which Rome had no part, and
in 495 the Æquians in the mountain borders to the east
and the Volscians to the southeast first appear as her
enemies. But Rome asserted her leadership. The new
Latin league of 493 not only included her, but demonstrated her importance; the understanding being that
Rome was to be protected against Etruria on the north
and west, and the Latin cities to the south against the
Æquians and the Volscians. In 487, with the breaking
by Rome of the Hernican power in the hill-towns of the
gap between the Æquians and Volscians, the way was
prepared for another alliance, that of 486, by which
Romans, Latins, and Hernicans made common cause
against Æquian and Volscian, thus driving a wedge between them. By 431, the power of these enemies was
broken, and Rome was the acknowledged leader, if not
the mistress, of the mountain peoples to the immediate
east and southeast, and of the plain from Fidenæ and
Veii on the north to the Tiber mouth and Anxur at the
foot of the Mount of Circe on the south. In 385 she was
strong enough to declare the closing of the Latin
league to those outside its thirty full members and
seventeen participants, and reserved for herself the admission of new allies.

Meanwhile, on the north, the Etruscan enemy was
being managed. The defeat of Carthaginian by Sicilian

Greek at the Himera in 480, and the crushing of Carthaginian and Etruscan naval power at Cumæ in 474, hastened the decline of the one-time dangerous foe of Rome. The ever-smouldering hostility of Etruria was fanned to a blaze in the border wars of 438 to 425, and again in the famous ten-year siege of Veii at the end of the century. The taking of Veii in 396, and the downfall of Falerii and Volsinii in the following year, were the end of serious danger from the Etruscans as a power. The sway of Rome was extended beyond the Tiber between the Apennines and the sea toward the Arno in the distant north.

The roving, lawless, fluid Italian Gaul was another peril from the north. The great raid of about 390, with the capture and burning of Rome, was more a calamity for the capital city than for the Roman power at large. The year following saw Rome again in the paths of victory. In 386-370 she dealt with troublesome Volscian and Latin about Signia, Cora, and Velitræ, and in 358 and 350 demonstrated her power to beat back the Gauls in other attempted raids. She met a formidable revolt of the Latin towns, whose demand for one Latin consul had been refused, in 338 overwhelmed them at Antium, and brought all the Latins under Roman control. Her sway was now secure from the Arno to Anxur-Tarracina.

But another power had arisen to stand in the onward path of Rome. The hardy Samnite mountaineers, in the heart of the Apennines to the east and south, already in 400 a strong power, collided with Rome in three wars in the course of fifty years, until in 295 their final effort, together with that of Umbrian, Etruscan, and Gaul, convinced them that resistance was futile.

The fortress-colony of Venusia, twenty thousand strong, was planted, and the Roman standards had advanced to the borders of Magna Græcia.

The soil of Magna Græcia itself soon resounded with the tread of Roman legions. Roman aid in response to a call from Thurii resulted in collision with Tarentum, for centuries supreme in the region. The efforts of the Greek capital were in vain; not even the help of Pyrrhus, would-be Alexander of the west, with Macedonian phalanx and elephants, enabled her to make head against the Romans. The hard-won victory over Pyrrhus and the fall of Tarentum left the conquerors still stronger, and still more conscious of their strength. By 272, Rome was mistress from the Arno and the Gauls on the north to Tarentum and the Sicilian strait on the south, and from Tyrrhenian to Adriatic. Ptolemy the Second of Alexandria had recognized her importance by sending a friendly embassy.

Three miles of water was all that separated the Sicilian shore from Italy, but to cross it was to set foot in the distant and dangerous land of world ambition. When the Romans accepted the invitation of their brigand kinsmen in Messana to rescue them and the city from the Carthaginian, they entered upon a trial of arms with the greatest power in the western sea. At the end of the first Punic war, in 241, Rome was mistress of Sicily, and soon afterward of Sardinia and Corsica. The end of the war with Hannibal in 201 established her in Spain and strengthened her hold on northern Italy and the valley of the Rhone. From Malta to Gibraltar the Mediterranean sea was swept by Roman oars, and Rome had learned from Sicilian Greek and Carthaginian for

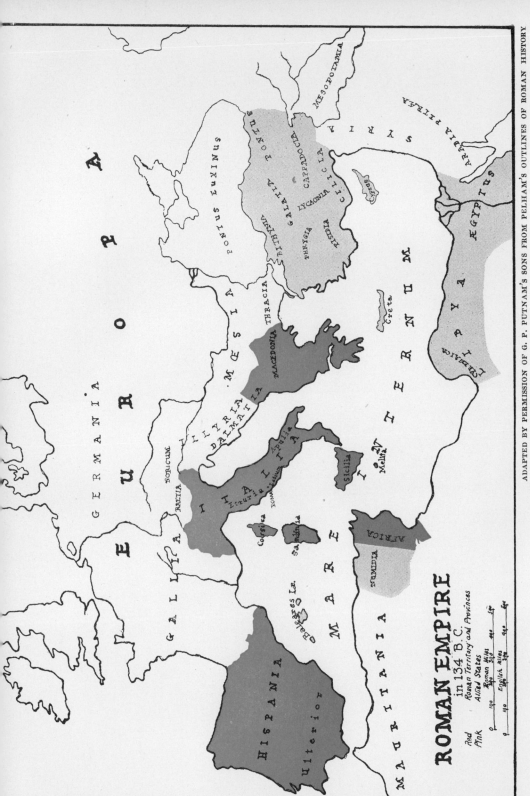

ROMAN EMPIRE
in 134 B.C.

Red   Roman Territory and Provinces
Pink   Allied States

THE ROMAN SWAY IN 134 B.C.

ADAPTED BY PERMISSION OF G. P. PUTNAM'S SONS FROM PELHAM'S OUTLINES OF ROMAN HISTORY

the first time the attractions of the tribute system of government.

There remained the Adriatic and the east. The war with Pyrrhus and the triumph over Carthage had removed all fear from the Roman heart. The war against Philip of Macedon, already declared in the midst of the struggle with Hannibal, was prosecuted with vigor. The Macedonian empire crumbled, and Greece was liberated, to be protected at first by Roman benevolence, and finally to yield to Roman authority. The setting of the Macedonian house in order drew the Roman legions into Asia. In the last days of Cato the censor, when the final crash of Carthage was almost audible, the hand of Rome was felt from Syria to Spain and from Africa to the Rhone, and the Mediterranean was a Roman sea.

What were the motives that impelled the city-state by the Tiber in the course of her long career of expansion?

To seek them wholly, or even largely, in the greed of citizen or state is to forget the consistent moral bent of the Roman character, and to miss the fact that Rome was never a great commercial center, nor the Romans of the Republic a race of tradesmen. If it is true that the acquisition of lands by citizen and state, rather than trade, was the Roman form of economic effort, it is also to be remembered that the immediate gain in land accrued to no single citizen or limited group of citizens, but to the commonwealth, and that its distribution, in holdings almost miniature, was actuated first of all by concern for the establishment of Roman authority among the conquered and the increase of solidarity among the citizenship. At the end of the war with Han-

nibal the state was in control of two million acres of
land. The allotments to citizen-settlers on conquered
soil were more like garden-plots than farms. The abuses
of capitalistic absorption were not the immediate effect
of conquest, but the slower growth of ordinary times.

To look for motives in the personal or patriotic ambitions of individual men of genius for action is equally
to go astray. Rome had no Alexander, no Cyrus the
Great, to energize her people into a unified and personal
whole that swept all things before it. She had not even
a. Solon or a Lycurgus, at least in historic times, to
mould her into the perfect image of his idea.

Nor are we to seek the springs of action wholly in
the growing consciousness of a mission to perform. It is
true that the Roman never forgot the superior worth of
his own race as compared with the half-formed nations
about him, and was proudly patronizing to even Greece
and the east, and that the benevolent improvement of
backward or decadent peoples was both a powerful ar-
gument in the mouth of the expansionist before aggression and a justification after; but to regard him as a
self-denying missionary is to forget the stern, hard-
headed, and unimaginative practicality that dominated
Roman character.

Least of all did the Roman have a settled and far-
sighted plan for the domination of the world. The advances of Rome to the leadership of the world were step
by step, with the vision rarely reaching beyond the step
of the moment. The step was often on uncertain and
dangerous ground, and sometimes taken in the dark.
Aggression pure and simple was rare. The forward
movement was invited, or even compelled, by circumstances involving the safety of the state or its faithful-

ness to friend and ally. The forward movement of today brought unsuspected consequences that necessitated the forward movement of tomorrow. Rome was not a military state in the sense that the soldier was all in all; she was not bred to the lust of conquest for conquest's sake. It has even been said that Rome was less warlike than the races she conquered. Her armies were not the end, but the instrument, of her ambition. There was frequent blundering. There was no civil service worthy of the name. The responsible head of the state was not a single person with the map of future empire spread before him, but a provincially-minded body of hundreds whose concern was the practical need of the moment. The extrication of army and state from dangers begotten by rashness or inexperience was accomplished only by dint of the natural vigor of a growing organism.

This touches the root of the matter. The growth of the Roman power was grounded in nature. The Roman state was not a fortuitous or forced assemblage of heterogeneous parts, but an organism instinct with life. Its expansion was a process of living accretion and assimilation. Its protoplasm was the family. The family was added to the family, the clan to the clan, the community to the community, the people to the people, the nucleus gradually growing larger, more compact, and more vibrant with life, until the term of growth was reached in the latter days of the citizen-soldier, and the organism began to decay and fall apart, in turn to give life to a different form. There is a sense in which all that exists is only the product of nature, and whatever is, is right; but the process of Roman growth was peculiarly free from the mingling of artifice with nature. The arteries of Rome pulsed with the bounding blood of unspoiled youth. Her expansion was the irresistible push of healthy, growing things. The Romans of the later and more conscious age were nearer the truth than they were aware when they talked of the Will of the Gods and the Destiny of Rome.

The assimilative, organic character of Roman expansion is conveniently discerned in the story of Romanization in Italy. The leaven of Rome began to work in her neighbor city-states before she became their mistress. By force of example, by treaty relations providing for mutual privilege and duty, her methods and spirit were communicated abroad. When alliance was changed to possession, the conquered city-state was either merged in the Roman state as a municipium with or without the right of local self-government, or became a citizen-colony. In either case the ultimate status was Roman citizenship for all free men. The colony especially might be the effective instrument of the state. A third of the conquered city's land, taken over by Rome, was allotted to a permanent garrison of citizen-soldiers who derived subsistence from it for themselves and their families while they kept the region safe for the mother city, and, gradually blending with the subject population, transformed it to Roman character and Roman citizenship. The number of citizens sent on these missions might vary from the three hundred that were customary to the twenty-five hundred that were settled at Luceria, the four thousand at Sora, or the twenty thousand at distant Venusia. The so-called Latin colonies were of a special type and special effectiveness.

The enumeration of citizen and Latin colonies will thus not be an arid list of unfamiliar names, but a testimonial to the slow and steady extension of the life of

Rome throughout the members of Italy. Besides the tradition of the refounding of Signia and the settling of Cora, Norba, Suessa Pometia, and Velitræ in the Volscian land in 486, and of Ardea in 442, there is the record of the following colonies in the fourth and third centuries, to the end of the war with Hannibal: in Volscian territory, Antium, Anxur-Tarracina, Fregellæ, Pontiæ, Interamna, Sora; among the Æquians, Alba Fucens and Carseoli; on the coast of Etruria, Alsium, Fregenæ, and perhaps Cosa and Pyrgi; in Umbria, Narnia, Æsium, Spoletium; in Picenum, Hatria, Castrum Novum, Firmum; in Samnite lands, Saticula, Beneventum, Æsernia; in Campania and its vicinity, Cales, Suessa, Minturnæ, Sinuessa; in Lucania, Pæstum; in Apulia, Luceria and Venusia; in Calabria, Brundisium; in Gallic territory, Sena Gallica, Ariminum, Cremona, Placentia. Within the forty years that followed, a score of others were planted, among them Parma, Mutina, Luna, Luca, Bononia, and Aquileia.

With the extension of Roman sway, or following it in the course of time, went Roman citizenship. On the final overthrow of the allied Latin cities in 338, the Latins were admitted to the privileges of alliance as well as burdened with the penalties of defeat. The Sabines and Picentes later received like privileges. By the beginning of the second century, the Latins were probably all in possession of full civic rights, and their neighbors to the east well on the way to the same position. A broad band of Roman citizenship covered the center of Italy from Tyrrhenian to Adriatic. And with the spread of Roman rule and the dissemination of Roman privilege went the Latin language, supplanting or rising above the primitive local dialects, and already being forged and tempered by constant trial into the most effective instrument that civilization has ever employed.

But to talk of expansion is to deal only with the members of the body. The heart of the Roman organism was the city by the Tiber. It is there we must go to appreciate the strength of the vital impulses compelling the growth of the state.

The foundations of Roman greatness were laid in authority: in the obedience of son to father, of clansman to chief, of subject to king. They were not laid, however, in authority undisputed, or in obedience that was blind. The will of a despot may carry his people forward for the time, but the state he governs is an unresisting, unorganic, lifeless mass, incapable of character. The life of Rome was constant struggle, the struggle that makes for strongly tempered character. The blood that ran in her veins was rapid and hot. There never was question of the principle of authority; the struggle lay in the discipline of authority. There never was question of the principle of liberty; the struggle lay in the discipline of liberty. The story of Rome from the kings to the fall of the republic is the story of the clash of wills: of the will of the few on the will of the many, of the will of the arrogant on the will of the unsubmissive, of the will of those who plan the advance and issue the order on the will of those who march and fight. The monarchy abuses its power, and the king is driven out, but not authority. Authority remains, but authority under surveillance and discipline. The consuls still are kings, but kings for the term of a year and each a check upon the other, with the people as court of appeal when the citizen's life is at issue.

But the unforeseen result of the new régime was the growing power of the ruling few; the old-time jealousies of king and senators were no longer present as mutual checks to protect the people against excess on the part of their masters. By 494, only fifteen years from the fall of the monarchy, the wrong had become intolerable, and the tribunes of the people were created to check the consular group. By 457, the tribunes had increased from two to ten, and were checks upon each other as well as upon the patricians.

Another source of abuse must be removed. The laws must be made more definite, and be set before the public. The knowledge of their intricacies by the patrician few was placing the weak at the mercy of the strong. A dozen years of struggle and turbulence preceded the drafting and confirmation of the famed Twelve Tables.

The assaults of the nameless many on the noble few continued. The quæstorship was opened to the people in 447, two years after the Twelve Tables had triumphed. In 445, the people demanded the right to elect one consul from their own ranks, and were put off with the creation of the military tribunate with consular power. In the same year, they won at last the right to marriage with the patricians. In 443, or within a few years of it, the censorship was established, a sign of the growing power of the senate, and destined to become its strong ally. In 393, the colonial distributions of land began, with the double purpose of confirming the rule of the state in doubtful territory and of providing the citizens with homes. In 367, the Licinian laws, securing the people the right to one consul, and providing for easement of debt and the limitation of holdings in public lands to three hundred acres, marked another stage in the struggle between the many and the few. The first plebeian election to the censorship occurred in 351. The following year brought the law that of the consuls one must be plebeian. Eleven years later, one censor must be plebeian. In two years more, in 337, the first plebeian sat on the prætor's bench. In 326, the tribunes of the people, who heretofore had been officers only of the commons, became regular magistrates of the Roman people entire. In 252, the seat of the pontifex maximus received its first plebeian occupant.

Two hundred and fifty years of intense conflict, in which the two great weapons of the people are the tribunate and the refusal to take up arms, have brought the full political privilege to all free Romans. The struggle has disciplined both liberty and authority. The citizenship of Rome, of whatever social rank, has been enriched and made strong for service by the sense of responsible power. The orders have mingled blood and fortune, and the state is more closely knit. The senate of ancient and proud patricians has been fertilized and vitalized by the assimilation of men whose wit and capacity in actual service have demonstrated their right to the highest public honors, until it has become the most dignified and most authoritative body of counsellors the world has ever seen. The Roman republic is not a perfect state. It will not succeed at home in quieting once for all the claims of the unfortunate many against the fortunate few. Abroad, it will find too great for its many-headed authority the task of keeping in order a world too large and too rapidly annexed. It will crack and crumble under the strain from within and without, and monarchy will have to be called to the rescue; but it will have achieved a wonderful work, and will forever remain the world's example of vigor and nobility of character in commonwealth and individual.

2.

THE CITY OF CATO

BEFORE we add to our character-study of the Roman state a character-study of the Roman citizen, let us look at the city which was the home of both. It is not a city easy to visualize. Of its actual members few survive, and fewer still are to be seen; the great city of the Empire destroyed, obliterated, or buried it deep under the foundations of the new. Of testimonials of the pen, almost as few survive; the ancient Roman writer knew hardly more of the city of his fathers than the modern student.

It was a city of generous dimensions. Something of the amplitude which distinguishes it today from the smaller cities of Italy, and from most of her larger cities, was to be noticed even then. The Tiber and its broad valley dividing the hills to east and west, and the hills themselves with broad surfaces, and the generous depressions between that once separated the primitive villages incorporated into historic Rome, all gave the city an ample frame. The city of the Four Regions had approached five miles in circumference. The so-called Servian wall, the probable amplification, after the Gallic raid, of the old defences of the Four Regions, attained a circuit of five and three-eighths miles. The Rome of 149, the year of Cato's death, had straggled far beyond its walls, and their towers in many places rose from thickly settled quarters that made them useless as a defence. Rome had become an unwalled town.

A firmly welded Italy and a distant frontier were her ample protection now.

As to the city's size in population, we may only speculate. Fabius Pictor, of Hannibal's time, set down the number of military age and condition in the reign of Servius as eighty thousand. This was when Roman citizenship belonged in large part to the city and its outlying lands. In 465, the number of Roman citizens not dependent is recorded by Livy as 104,714; in 458, as 117,319; in 319, as 250,000. How many inhabitants of all conditions in Rome itself are represented by these and other figures, it is not easy to estimate; the citizenship of Rome was no longer confined to Latin lands. At the beginning of the second Punic war, in 218, there were on the citizens' roll about 270,000 names; in 208, the number had sunk to 137,108; in 204, it was 214,000; in 188, it was 258,318; in 172, it was 269,015; in 156, it was 328,316; and finally, just before the third Punic war, it had diminished again to 324,000. These figures but faintly indicate the number of citizen-names in the city alone. If we build on their dim suggestion by comparing the area of twentieth century Rome, containing three-fourths of a million but spreading far beyond the walls, with the probably much more thickly inhabited area of the city at Cato's death, we may reasonably estimate the Rome of that time as containing, men and women, slave and free, some three to four hundred thousand inhabitants.

The center and heart of the city is the Forum. On the borders of its three acres of space are temples to Saturn, the god of sowing, to Concordia, in token of the harmony of the orders fondly believed to have been attained by the Licinian laws, to Castor and Pollux, the divine twins who brought the news of Lake Regillus, to Janus, god of war and beginnings, to Venus of the Cloaca. There are the basilicas of Porcius Cato, of Sempronius, and of Æmilius Paullus, rectangular buildings of nave and aisle and portico for the housing of the courts and legal business in general. At the northwest corner is the venerable senate, and, at its front on the Forum's edge, the comitium for assemblies and the rostra for harangues and announcements. On the northern and southern sides are lines of shops, the New and the Old. At its eastern end are the ancient round temple of Vesta and the fountain of Juturna, and, farther east, on the north slope of the Palatine, is the temple of Jupiter Stator. High on the Palatine, already the richest residence quarter, are the better mansions of the city, commanding wide prospects over Forum and hills. The temples of Jupiter Victor and the Great Mother of the Gods are also on the Palatine, the latter looking across the deep valley to the twin heights of the Capitoline, where the Mint and temple of Juno on the arx, and the temple of Jupiter Best and Greatest on the southern peak, seem almost to float in air above their low environment. Traversing the Forum from the temple of Jupiter Stator beyond its eastern end to the winding road that climbs the Capitol at the other end, is the vagrant Sacra Via. Besides these two, there are other outlets from the Forum: the Vicus Tuscus, through the dense Velabrum to the Tiber on the south; the passage that leads through the crowded, plebeian Subura on the northeast to the Clivus Suburanus on the Esquiline; the Argiletum, through the district of the same name, a quarter of small tradesmen near the senate.

To the south, between Palatine and Capitoline and

near their bases, the business of the too crowded Forum
has overflowed into cattle-market and vegetable-market.
A round temple and a temple in Ionic Greek are near.
Out of the dense plebeian quarters on the Aventine,
whose base is washed by the Tiber, rises the ancient
temple of Diana. To the north of the Aventine, in the
long valley whose farther limit is the foot of the Palatine, is the Circus Maximus. The Cælian to the east, the
Esquiline, the Viminal, and the Quirinal, to the north,
are a mingling of houses of rich and poor, with many
smaller shrines at corners of the streets, and here and
there a larger sanctuary.

Temple and public building in the city of the Republic were of rugged hewn blocks of native stone, the
houses of stone or wood frames and sun-dried brick and
tile, and, in some of the poorer quarters, of the primitive
clay and osiers. The tenement of two stories, and sometimes more, was beginning to appear. Many houses, in
obedience to a law of the Twelve Tables, were still isolated by narrow passages. Cramped and dirty alleys led
into crooked and unpaved streets ten or twenty feet
wide that found their way to the better but still winding
thoroughfares which left the city through the sixteen
gates in the old wall.

Outside the gates of the Esquiline was the burial-
ground of centuries. Beyond other gates were growing
suburban quarters. The Campus Martius, traversed by
the avenue that on leaving the city became the Flaminian Way, was beginning to fill on its eastern and
southern sides. Two bridges, the Æmilian, hardly completed, and the ancient wooden bridge by the Aventine,
led over the river to meadows and slopes at the base of
the Janiculum, fast becoming a populous district. The

Appian Way, already with many tombs on its borders, cut straight across the plain and through the vineyards of the Alban slopes and on to the south. The salt-carts jolted up the road from Ostia and the marshes and out of Rome on the opposite side by the Via Salaria to the towns in the mountains of central Italy. All roads now led to Rome.

There were docks and warehouses and shipping on the Tiber outside the walls near the Aventine, and naval yards at the edge of the Campus Martius. In 172, fifty ships of war were to be fitted from the out-of-date quinquiremes assembled there. The southern part of the city had been supplied with water from near the Alban Hills for over a hundred and fifty years through the Appian aqueduct. The Anio aqueduct, from the upper Anio fifty miles away, had supplied the northern quarters for over a hundred years. There were a few simple public baths, and the public bakery had appeared. There were no permanent theaters, though Plautus and Terence had lived, and Accius and Pacuvius were still composing.

It was already a city old and full of years. The stranger within its gates was taken to visit temples that had stood for centuries, and lesser shrines and altars and monuments whose origins were lost in the mists of unknown times. He saw the hut of Romulus on the Palatine, the cave of the Lupercal where the Twins were taken up, the Ruminal fig tree in the Forum, grown from a shoot of the original that sheltered them, the Sister's beam under which the Horatius who slew his sister was made to pass, the statue of Attius Navius, the augur who put the doubting king to confusion by cutting the stone with the razor, the marvellous horns in the temple of Diana on the Aventine that belonged to the Sabine cow whose sacrifice by the wily Roman priest retained the dominion at Rome, the statue of Horatius Cocles who kept the bridge in the brave days of old, the wonderful temple of Jupiter Optimus Maximus that was founded in the days of the kings, the Tarpeian rock, the pool of Curtius in the Forum where the hero spurred on his horse and leapt into the smoking chasm, the senate house from Tullus Hostilius' times, the rostra with the beaks of the rebel ships fixed to it two hundred years before.

It was a city honest and unadorned. The principal streets were paved, the temple of Jupiter was decorated with the crude archaic terra cottas done long ago by Etruscan artists, and other temples made some pretence to color in their upper members, and sometimes relieved their bareness within or without by the use of stucco, painting, statues, relics, and offerings of the devout. From the times of interference in Macedonia, Greece, and Asia, the spoils of war had begun to be seen in temple and public place. All this, however, did little to enliven the city as a whole. Cato in 195, when Greek art was beginning to be felt in the capital, already heard "too many people praising and admiring the ornaments of Corinth and Athens, and laughing at the antefixes of the Roman gods." Thirteen years afterward, the train of Prince Perseus of Macedon passed the jest at the expense of the Romans, "some on their ways and institutions, some on their achievements, some on the appearance of the city itself, not yet beautiful either in public or private places, some on certain of the leading men." In the next century Cicero was to contrast with Capua, a city "laid out on a very level site," Rome, "set on hills and valleys, with garrets hung aloft in the air, with avenues by no means the best, and with miserably narrow little streets," and was to ridicule the Latin towns outside of Rome in comparison with those in the Capuan neighborhood. Not much later, Augustus found eighty-two temples so worn with age as to need restoration, and Strabo made interesting comment on the tumble-down walls and houses of Rome.

It was a city swept by fires, undermined by floods, shaken by earthquake, and sometimes in the throes of plague. In 213, "a terrible fire raged unrestrained at Rome for two nights and a day"; everything between the southern base of the Capitoline and the Tiber was levelled with the ground; "and outside the gate the fire raged far and wide, consuming many buildings sacred and profane." In 192, "there were at the same time at Rome two very great terrors. The one was of long duration, but of less violence: the earth shook for eight-and-thirty days, through as many days all work was suspended for anxiety and fear, and a three-days supplication was held because of it. The other was no empty fright, but a real calamity for many people: a fire broke out in the cattle-market and for a day and a night the buildings toward the Tiber were ablaze, and all the shops with their valuable merchandise went up in smoke." Two years before, a certain Pleminius, in prison for many crimes against gods and men, "had suborned persons to set the city on fire by night in many places simultaneously, in order that the citizens might be thrown into panic by the tumult and the prison be broken open." The plot was detected, but the incident suggests the inflammability of the structures of the time. In 192 also, "the Tiber swept down with more damage than the

THE TIBER AT OSTIA

THIS IS THE SITE OF THE ANCIENT MOUTH,
NOW FOUR MILES FROM THE SEA

year before, and overturned two bridges and many
buildings, especially about the Porta Flumentana. A
huge mass of rock, started from its place by the rains
or by some quake of the earth too light to be felt elsewhere, crashed down from the Capitoline into the Vicus
Jugarius and crushed many people; the fields were overwhelmed by water, and flocks of sheep carried away, and
villas wrecked." In 189, the Tiber raged again: "in that
year there were huge floods; twelve times did the Tiber
inundate the Campus Martius and the flat parts of the
city." In 174, "the plague, which the preceding year had
attacked the cattle, was converted into an epidemic
among men. Those who were stricken could hardly survive the seventh day; those who did survive fell a prey
to lingering disease, especially the quartan fever. The
slaves were the ones to die in greatest number; their un-
buried bodies were a dreadful sight of ravage through all
the streets. Decent burial could not be managed for even
the free. Corpses untouched by dogs and vultures were
consumed by rotting; and all agreed that neither in that
nor in the preceding year had the vulture been seen anywhere devouring in such quantities cattle and men.
Priests of the people to die in that plague were Gnæus
Servilius Cæpio the pontifex, father of the prætor, and
Tiberius Sempronius Longus the son of Tiberius, de-
cemvir of sacred matters, and Publius Ælius Pætus the
augur, and Tiberius Sempronius Gracchus, and Gaius
Atellus Maximus the chief curio, and Marcus Sempronius Tuditanus the pontifex." In 173, a different danger threatened the city: "Such clouds of locusts were
suddenly carried over the sea by the wind into Apulia
that far and wide the fields were covered by their
swarms. Gnæus Sicinius the prætor-elect was sent to

Apulia with full power to act in rescuing the crops from this pest, and spent a considerable time with a huge force of men he drafted for the purpose of gathering the locusts up."

Such was the Rome of the citizen-soldier and ruler of the world of the time: a city rugged and sincere in aspect; a city indifferent to the graces of art, and disdainful of effect except in its temples and edifices of state; a city already ancient and historic; a city crowded with habitations and teeming with life, that sat like a queen in the midst of the plains and hills whose essence it was fast absorbing into its own life. The cities of Latium had dwindled or ceased to grow, and many were only memories. In 187, a delegation of Latins complained before the senate of the migration of their citizens to Rome and their enrollment on her censors' lists, and twelve thousand were returned to their native towns, the throngs of the alien-born being already a burden to the capital. Ten years later the senate was the scene of a similar protest; at the present rate, it was informed, the Latin towns would soon be empty, and the deserted fields would yield no soldiers.

The aspect of country as well as city was rapidly changing, but in opposite directions. The clearing away of groves, the erosion of plowed lands, and the constant drain of centuries of intensive tillage, had thinned and weakened the soil. The rise of urban opportunity for livelihood and pleasure had attracted the rustic to the city, and the growing importation of grain and other foodstuffs from distant and more abundant markets had compelled him to leave the farm. Annual tribute of a million bushels of wheat was exacted of Carthage at the end of the first great war. The ranks of the ancient peasantry had been thinned by death in the battles of their country. The small farmer, who during the earlier centuries tilled his own acres with the aid of his sons, had long been a renter and subordinate of the landed proprietor, but now the tillage of the soil was giving way to the pasturing of herds and flocks. The olive and the vine were planted by men of means on the choicer of the Alban slopes. The lands about the city were more than ever in the hands of the aristocratic rulers of the Roman state.

The Rome of Cato's last years, the Rome that had conquered Carthage, Macedon, and Syria, the Rome of assured imperial sway, the Rome that was soon to pillage Corinth and plow the ground where the Punic city stood, was already turning from provincial ways to the ways of the world. Her noblest and strongest sons she had left on the battlefields of a hundred years of momentous wars. Her veins had been all but emptied of the old-time pure and vigorous Latin blood, and into the void was fast flowing the blood of the nameless, the alien, and the slave. She was to assimilate and make it her own, and to go forward on her Eternal way; but she had passed a moment in her eternity that was never to occur again. The day of the citizen-soldier was all but past. The character which through singleness of purpose and self-domination had raised her to the pinnacle of power and usefulness was fast becoming a memory.

THE CITIZEN-SOLDIER OF ROME

WHO is this man who taught the nations of the earth at first to obey and respect, and finally to love, his mistress Rome? Let us look at him and know him well before he leaves the scene forever. We shall doubtless see him raised by the buskin to a stature more than real, and arrayed in a cloak of dignity too faultless for action in the rough turmoil of actual life; but we shall see him as he appeared to his regretful descendants of the later and less heroic days of Rome, and to the long succession of generations who have found in him the inspiration to manliness and patriotism. And who is the real man if not that part of him that lives on in the life of the race?

The Roman who has thus lived on was from the first a soldier. To secure and maintain his home in earliest Latium, the tribesman-warrior had perforce to live under arms. Earliest Rome was a city-camp. The Roman of the early Republic was bred to the use of horse and weapon, and trained to the maximum endurance of hardship. Whatever the trade or calling his ambition set before him, his boyhood instruction, whether formal or informal, was centered about the idea of military usefulness. Whatever ambition he entertained for serving the state in the civic capacity, the avenue to its achievement lay through the soldier's training and the soldier's career. The Villian law of 180, so regulating the order of office that its first important position, the quæstorship, could be held only after ten years of actual army service, or readiness for it if required, no doubt made formal the approximate practice of many years.

The spirit of the earliest men of the plain persisted through Monarchy and Republic. Remulus, the Rutulian foe of Ascanius, cries out to the Phrygian invaders of his country: "What god has driven you to Italy, what madness? Not here will you find sons of Atreus or a Ulysses the weaver of tales. A hardy race are we, from a hardy stock. Our new-born sons we carry to the rivers and harden them in the cruel cold of their waters; they pass their boyhood years in vigil for the chase, and ply the woodlands, and their sport is to rein the steed and send flying the level arrow from the bow of horn; yet, enduring in toil and acquainted with want, our young men subdue the earth with the mattock or shake cities in war. Our years are consumed in the wielding of iron; with the spear reversed we tire the flanks of our steers, and sluggish age does not weaken our souls or change our vigor; on heads that are white we set the heavy helmet."

The vigor of body and soul in the fighter of historic times is vividly pictured by Ennius, himself a soldier in the Sardinian campaign, whence Cato brought him to Rome: "Like rain the spears come flying upon the tribune from every side. They pierce his shield, the boss rings with their shafts, his helmet of brass resounds beneath their strokes; but, strive though his enemies may on every hand, no one can rend his body with the steel. The spears that ever surge upon him he shatters and breaks in pieces. His whole body flows with perspiration, his travail is great, his breath is failing. The Histri hurl their flying weapons and vex him sorely."

A less poetic and more intimate characterization of

the soldier is afforded by the speech of a veteran cam-
paigner in the Macedonian wars. He is speaking in the
year 171, seconding the consul's appeal to centurions
for prompt response to the senate's call: "My name is
Spurius Ligustinus, my fellow citizens; I belong to the
Crustumina tribe, and come of Sabine stock. My father
left me half an acre of land and the little cabin in which
I was born and reared; and that is my home today. As
soon as I was of proper age, my father gave me to wife
his brother's daughter, who brought with her nothing
but a free state and her chastity, and with these a capacity for the bearing of children which would have
suited a rich man's house. We had six sons, and two
daughters, both already married. Of our sons, four have
the toga of manhood, and two are still in the boys' præ-
texta. I entered the service under the consuls Publius
Sulpicius and Gaius Aurelius. In the army which was
taken across to Macedonia I served as a private against
King Philip; in the third year Titus Quinctius Flamininus as a reward of valour promoted me to centurion of the tenth rank of spearmen. After the defeat of
Philip and the Macedonians, and after we had been
brought back to Italy and discharged, I immediately
enlisted as a volunteer, and set out for Spain with the
consul Marcus Porcius. Of all commanders alive, there
is none a keener observer and judge of worth than he,
and those who have known both him and other generals
in long service know it. This commander thought me
worthy of promotion to first centurion of the spearmen.
The third time I served, which was the second time I
volunteered, I went into the army that was sent against
the Ætolians and King Antiochus. . . . Twice after
that I served in Spain. . . . For the fourth time within

a few years I was first centurion, four-and-thirty times I had prizes from my generals for valour, and received six civic crowns. I have twenty-two years of service to my credit, and am over fifty years old; but even if my years of service were not run out and my age did not excuse me, nevertheless it would be the just thing for me to have my discharge, Publius Licinius, because I could give you four soldiers in place of my single self. However, please understand this that I am going to say in regard to my case: as long as anybody enrolling an army thinks me fit for soldier's service, I shall never offer excuse. In what rank the tribunes of the soldiers judge me worthy to serve, belongs to them to say. I will see to it that no one in the army excels me in valour, which has always been my way of doing, as both my commanders and fellow soldiers can witness. And the right thing for you too, comrades, though you are within your rights in making this protest, is to continue the record of your younger days, in which you never opposed the authority of magistrates and senate, and on this occasion, too, to yield to the power of senate and consuls, and consider all posts honorable in which you can defend the state."

The Roman who made his country great was not only a soldier, but a citizen-soldier. If he was first of all a soldier, it was because he was also first of all a citizen. The state was his own affair, and the army as its instrument was equally his affair. Whatever the abuses that troubled the relations of order to order and of class to class, the Roman freeman was the equal of other Roman freemen. He had his vote in the assembly, when in capital danger he could appeal from king or consul to the mass of the citizenship, and in the end the way was opened for him without reserve to the highest honors of the state. Responsibility went with privilege. He helped to make the laws, it was his to guard them against abuse, it was his to fight for the state at home and abroad. He and his fellows in citizenship were the center and the flower of the army. They held the post of honor and the post of danger; the allies, not yet welded to single temper, were given the right and left. When disaster overtook the Roman arms, it was the citizen-soldier who first and most freely poured out his blood. Pyrrhus found him lying in line with wounds in front. Mago after Cannæ emptied whole measures of gold rings on the senate floor at Carthage, and, "to make the proof of the Roman disaster stronger, added words to action by saying that no one but those of equestrian rank, and even of them the most distinguished, could wear that token."

The citizen and soldier of Rome was farther distinguished from the men of other states of his time by being essentially a man of the country. In the earliest days of Latium he was shepherd and farmer, and to the latest days of the Republic still bore the stamp of his native acres. The Palatine was the hill of Pales, the shepherd's goddess; its northern gate was the Porta Mugonia, the Lowing-gate. Of the thirty-five voting tribes that finally made up Roman citizenship, thirty-one were rustic and four urban. More than a dozen religious festivals in the Roman calendar were of rustic origin. There were the Ambarvalia in May, when a procession of garlanded folk with olive branches in hand went chanting around the borders of the fields with the sacrificial bull and sheep and pig; the Fontinalia in October, in honor of springs and wells; the Saturnalia in December, for the ancient god of the soil; the Paganalia in the same month, for the seeding soon to come; the Lupercalia, to purify and fertilize the flocks, and the Terminalia, the festival of boundaries, in February; the Palilia and the Robigalia in April, to prosper the sheep and keep the rust and blight from the grain; the Vinalia in April and August, for thrifty vines; and others whose origins were in the mists of unknown days. The names of certain long-established families were derived from rustic possessions in plants and animals: there were the Fabii and the Lentuli, from beans and lentils; the Cornelii, from the cornel tree; the Porcii, the Equitii, the Juventii, from hogs and horses and oxen. The earliest money of Rome was stamped with the ox or the plow. Cincinnatus and his kind, when the business of the state was off their hands, were busy on their farms beyond the walls.

"The country was at that time the home of senators," says Cato in Cicero's essay *On Old Age;* "for it was while he was at the plow that the message came to Cincinnatus of his having been made dictator. . . . Curius and the rest of the elders used to be summoned to the senate from their farm homes." "When they praised a man for his good qualities," writes Cato in his work *On Agriculture,* "they used to praise him as a good farmer and a good worker of the soil. He was thought to be most amply praised who was praised in these terms . . . and those who are given to that pursuit are least liable to evil thoughts." "Those great men, our ancestors," says Varro a hundred years later, "were not without reason in esteeming the Romans of the country more than those of the city; for as those in the country who are in the villa are of less spirit than those who live in

the fields and engage in some work, so they judged those
whose home was in the town of less energy than those
who tilled the fields." When Horace wishes a contrast
in strong colors to the lax household morals of Augustan times, he goes back to the rustic soldier of the
Punic wars.

> The manly brood of rustic soldier-folk,
> Taught, when the mother or the father spoke
> The word austere, obediently to wield
> The heavy mattock in the Sabine field;
>
> Or cut and bear home fagots from the height
> As mountain shadows deepened into night,
> And the sun's car, departing down the west,
> Brought to the wearied ox the friendly rest.

Even in the later times when the city had drawn the
citizen-farmer away from the soil, his contact with it
was not lost. The wealth of the ruling class continued to
be the pastures and fields of the Campagna, the ambition of the humbler citizen never ceased to be the possession of acres of his own. When the Roman standards
were planted on foreign soil and the conquered lands
were sold or rented by the state, the noble found a field
for speculation and the nameless to some extent the
opportunity of winning a home. At the end of the second
Punic war, the state was owner of some two million
acres, a large part of it in the devastated areas. The
question of the disposition of public lands, or of the
hindrance of the large estate, or of confiscation and
division into smaller holdings, was always to the fore
in Roman politics. The senators and their kind were
forbidden by the feeling of their class, and almost by

law, to engage in ordinary traffic. An act of 218 forbidding the senator to own more than one ship, and that of ordinary size, suggests the desire to keep the men whose proper sphere was government away from the distractions and corruptions of the commercial career. It is probably true that no state and no body of public men have ever been less actuated by plain commercial greed than the Roman republic and the Roman senate. The absence of economic detail from the pages of Roman literature is not due entirely to the failure of its authors to realize the part of economics in history.

Both circumstance and sentiment thus kept the leading men of the city close to the soil. The management of the landed estate was at the same time dignified, salutary, and as profitable as a man should wish whose desire for wealth was second to his devotion to the affairs of his country. When he needed restoration of body or soul, it was on his estate that he found it. When he returned to the senator's seat or the bench of the prætor or the consular bureau, the aura of the countryside came with him and breathed freshness and sanity into the life of the state. The gravitation of the citizenship from farm and hamlet to the growing capital was accompanied by the same effect; the life of the country was projected constantly into the city, and for many generations neutralized the tendency to urban sophistication. The practical works of Cato, the soldier and statesman, and of Varro, the soldier, administrator, and scholar, and the exquisite country flavor of Virgil, Horace, and Tibullus, and of Cicero's *On Old Age,* are all alike witnesses to the rural imprint upon the life of Rome; for these men, even to Cato himself, were not men of the country first of all, but men of a city which

had never been weaned from the soil. The Rome of the
citizen-soldier was not a city sharply defined and standing apart from the Latin acres; it was a city whose roots
were deep in the soil and ever absorbing its fruitful
juices. The city and the country were one.

In a character thus blended of citizen and soldier and
rustic, it follows as the night the day that certain definite traits will appear. The Roman who subdued the
Italian cities and wealthy Carthage was frugal to the
point of abstinence. The life of his fathers had bred him
to it. His food was the rude bread and homely porridge
afforded by his grains, the fruits of his own garden and
orchard, the flesh of his beasts in sparing quantity, the
honey and oil of his bees and olives, and the temperate
draught of wine. He was hard-working. The toil of
generations of earnest men was in his blood; "industry
grafted into the souls of the Romans," writes Livy. He
was simple in his ways and ideas; simple, not consciously
or for effect, but by nature. The scant sum given to
certain informers of a plot against the city in 419 is recorded by Livy as "riches in the esteem of those times."
He had the rustic distrust of luxury. Almost from the
first, he was on his guard against the inroads of easy
living. The so-called law of Numa forbade the use of
wine to quench the funeral embers, and the tenth of
the Twelve Tables was devoted largely to sumptuary
restrictions. The wood of the funeral pyre was not to be
planed; not more than three cloaks or three fillets of
purple were allowed in either cremation or burial, nor
more than ten flute-players employed; the bodies of
slaves were not to be embalmed; expensive libations,
funeral dinners, and wreaths were forbidden, and the
erection of incense-altars; not more than one ceremony

was to be performed for the same deceased; gold was
not to be buried or burned with the dead unless as a
necessary part of the teeth. As late as 154, the first stone
theater, already half completed, was ordered down by
the senate. The whole life of Cato was a warfare against
the growing taste for indulgence.

The luxuries of the mind as well as of the body were
actively opposed. The citizen-soldier-farmer held art in
contempt; beyond its giving distinction to the buildings
that represented the greatness of the state, he did not
even understand its uses. Beyond the contribution of
practical knowledge to excellence in the ranks, at the
rostra and on the senate floor, and in matters of livelihood, he understood as little the nature of education.
All occupation that did not yield immediate and substantial results was unworthy in his estimation. The only
education that counted with him was that which taught
his sons to ride, to wield the weapons of war, to swim,
to endure hardship and toil, to read and write and cipher,
and to stand on his feet and deliver with effect his
thoughts on the welfare of the state. His sole object was
to render them serviceable to the republic and to equip
them with shrewd, practical common sense for the
affairs of every day. He saw that they learned the
Twelve Tables by heart, and exercised the most careful
supervision over their younger years, himself acting as
their tutor whenever possible, and making them his com-
panions at home and abroad in city or country as he
moved about his affairs. The niceties of written and oral
expression he hardly comprehended, and even despised.
Even in public address he scorned anything that savored
of finish. The first of the Roman orators to cultivate
smoothness of period, rhetorical rhythm, and the art of

presentation, according to Cicero, the master in all these things, was Marcus Æmilius Lepidus Porcina, consul in 137, and the fragments of the early orations support the statement. "Master the subject, and your words will come," was the favorite counsel of Cato; the best eloquence consisted in the straightforward utterance bound to come from thorough knowledge of the matter at issue.

Besides his rustic simplicity, abstemiousness, and hard common sense, the Roman citizen-soldier had also the immovableness of the unchanging country. He was immovable in the stern austerity of family life to which his race was bred. His power was absolute over all the household except his wife, who as the mother of citizens and the representative of the home was dignified by the law with a certain independence. He was capable, in times of patriotic exaltation, of condemning a son to death for breach of discipline. He was stern no less with himself than with the members of his house. He held himself to faithful observance of duty to the gods, to the spirits of his fathers dead and departed, to his living kin, and to the stranger within his gates; he had the highest ideals of justice and integrity, and of all the qualities that go to make the man. His definition of *virtus,* virtue, or manliness, was comprehensive and enlightened. Of course it included vigor and fearlessness; for the rest, Lucilius with characteristic wordiness no doubt reflects the views of the earlier times: "Virtue, Albinus, is knowing how to set the true price upon the things among which we live and move and have our being; virtue is for a man to know all true values. Virtue is for a man to appreciate what is upright, useful, and honorable, what is bad as well as what is good, what is useless, base, and dishonorable. Virtue is to know the end and measure of getting. Virtue is to know how to place their true value upon riches, to give to honor what is really its due, to be the enemy and assailant of bad men and bad morals, but to be the defender of good men and good morals, to magnify and wish them well and be their friends; and, besides, to hold the good of one's country first, the good of one's kinsmen next, and one's own good third and last of all."

He was as immovable in the face of the new as he was stern in his family relations and with himself. He was a conservative of the conservatives. He resisted not only change for the sake of change, but change that was grounded in reason. Novelty for him had no charm. The *mos maiorum,* the way of his fathers, was for him of the highest authority, in morals, in religion, and in politics, in matters public and private. His attitude in religion in this respect was extreme. His ceremonies and formulæ, once established and of the desired effect, were fixed. What had once been tested and found effective, he saw no reason to alter; in change there was peril. He preserved the exact wording, the exact spelling, of every formula, the exact movement of every rite. The song of the Salii, as they leaped and danced and clashed their sacred spears and shields to the glory of Mars, was conserved in this scrupulous manner until in the first Christian century it was practically a composition in a foreign tongue, and Quintilian declared it was scarcely intelligible to the priests who used it. The flamen of Jupiter was hedged about by commands and prohibitions whose meaning in many cases had long since been forgotten. He was forbidden to ride a horse, to look upon an army in battle array outside the city, to wear a ring which had not been broken and deprived of its nature as a bond, to wear a knot in any part of his dress, to touch leavened bread. His bed must have the posts daubed with clay where they touched the floor, and he must not be absent from it more than twice in succession. A man in bonds, in case he entered the flamen's house, must be freed, and the bonds must be removed by being taken up through the impluvium and then let down to the street. The ancient worship of Latin Jupiter on the Alban Mount was maintained throughout the centuries; the pilgrimages to Juno of Lanuvium still continued long after a less primitive and barbarous Juno sat on the Capitoline and Aventine. The Roman and the Roman state were in all things very religious. They lived in the dread and fear of portent and prodigy, especially in times of pestilence and war. The stroke of lightning, the croaking or flight of birds in some peculiar manner, the earthquake, the birth of a one-handed baby or the hatching of three-legged chicks, and the like, all set both individual and state to searchings of heart, to consultations of priest and Sibylline books, to festivals of prayer and purification. Ardea is omitted in the distribution of meat on the Alban Mount, and the Latin festival entire must be repeated; a falling timber topples a goddess over, and a day is added to the Ludi Romani; a man has repeated dreams of Jupiter's displeasure at some detail in the games, and the senate orders their celebration anew; the sacred pullets will not feed, and the battle must not be fought.

Such things as these lasted on in the city until Cæsar's time; his enemies obstructed his plans by "watching the sky," and by other uses from the hoary past, until he broke through custom and law by disregarding them. In the unchanging country, the lore of superstition never died. Livy himself, whatever his beliefs or disbeliefs, is not without reverence for the ancient survivals from the golden age of Roman character. "I am not unaware," he writes, "that, because of the same indifference which has brought with it the prevailing disbelief in signs from the gods, almost no prodigies are either officially reported or set down in the annals; but, as for me, somehow when I am writing the story of the olden time my mind takes on the cast of ancient days, and my conscience also forbids me to regard as unworthy of my chronicles the things that those sagest men of old thought worthy of the state's attention. At Anagnia that year two prodigies were reported, a torch seen in the sky, and a cow that spoke; she is kept at the public expense. At Minturnæ also in those days the heavens had glowed as with a blazing fire. At Reate there was a shower of stones. At Cumæ in the citadel Apollo dropped tears three days and three nights. In the city of Rome, two temple-keepers reported, the one that a serpent with a crest had appeared to several in the temple of Fortune, the other that in the temple of Fortune the First-born, the one on the hill, two prodigies of different sorts were seen, a palm that sprang from the court, and a rain of blood by day. . . . In the matter of the prodigies affecting the state, the Books were consulted by the decemvirs, who ordered the sacrifice of forty major victims at all the altars by all the magistrates together, and the wearing of chaplets by the people."

It was not that the Roman of these early times was entirely static in religion, for he was not. The beliefs and practices of the surrounding Latin tribes, of the more distant Etruscans and Samnites, of southern Italy and Greece, were not without their impress on the Roman mind, nor indeed without a degree of welcome; but the character of the citizen-soldier-farmer resisted sudden change. It was only what met his need by being in accord with his nature that was wrought into his faith and practice, and it was by a slow and living process. By 217, the great gods of Greece had all found homes in the city of Rome, and in 204 the Phrygian Great Mother was brought as a means of sustaining the popular courage; but the Homeric Twelve had to lose much of their Hellenism before they were more to the Roman than instruments of state, and the goddess from Asia was three hundred years in winning her way.

But it was especially in the capacity of citizen and patriot that the Roman was steadfast and immovable, and most of all when calamity and danger were at their greatest. "Adversity tames us," writes Cato to his son in the *Origines,* "and teaches us our true line of conduct, while good fortune is apt to warp us from the way of prudence."

Adversity did indeed discipline the Roman, but it never subdued him. Probably no people in all history ever passed through such a fiery trying-out as the Romans endured and survived in the war with Hannibal. "The most memorable of all the wars that have ever been waged," Livy rightly calls it. The two strongest nations of the earth, each at the peak of prosperity and power and skill in the practice of arms, and both inspired by a hatred almost greater than their strength, met in a life-and-death struggle of seventeen years in which "so varied were the fortunes of war and so doubtful the event that those who finally won were the nearer to destruction." At the Trebia in 218, the Roman fortunes seemed to hang upon the one shock with Hannibal's army, and the battle was lost. At Trasimene in 217, the Roman army was cut to pieces and scattered in the wildest rout over all Etruria. At Rome, after an anxious, uncertain day with the Forum thronged and the senate surrounded by the breathless, questioning population, "at length, a little before the setting of the sun, Marcus Pomponius the prætor appeared. 'There has been a great battle,' he said, 'and we have lost.'" This time the state seemed lost indeed; there was nothing between Hannibal and Rome. But there was no thought of yielding. An embassy from Naples with massive golden plate for the exhausted treasury was politely thanked for its generosity and pains, and the lightest of all the pieces accepted. Delegates from Pæstum received the same answer. The offers in money and men and ships by Hiero of Syracuse, the veteran ally of Rome, who "knows well that the greatness of the Roman people is almost more wonderful in adversity than in times of success," and that they "make use of no regular infantry and cavalry not of Roman and Latin stock," are partly accepted as far as men and ships are concerned, but the money is refused. For the first time the usual military pledge is supplemented by an oath not to retreat and never to step from the line "except for the purpose of picking up or seizing a pike, or of wounding the enemy or saving a citizen's life." Once more the army was re-created, the following year once more to be annihilated. Of the hundred thousand in the ranks at Cannæ, fifty to sixty thousand met death, the greater part of them Roman citizens, and among them eighty volunteers who were either senators or holding offices on which their seats in the senate followed. The remnant was dispersed in every direction, and the road to Rome again lay open. At the first receipt of the news, the senators themselves assumed responsibility in the absence of magistrates, and in person took measures "to suppress the tumult and panic in the city, to forbid women in the street and to keep them behind their own doors, to hush the family funeral-cries, to have messengers in every case taken straight to the prætors and to have the citizens await at home the news of their fortunes, and besides to station guards at the gates to prevent all going out, and to compel the people to look for salvation nowhere but to the city and its walls. When the tumult should have subsided, then the senators were to be called back to the senate house to consult on the protection of the city." Yet even now they refused to ransom the captured, and would not so much as receive the Carthaginian officer sent to negotiate. The dictator and master of horse put through a draft from the age of seventeen, and included some of the boys not yet in the toga of manhood. They ordered the forging of new armor and weapons, and the stripping of temples and porticoes of the old-time spoils of the enemy. When one of a body of prisoner-envoys sent to solicit ransom for himself and fellows refuses to return to the enemy on the ground that he gave an ambiguous oath, the senate orders him arrested and conducted back to Hannibal under guard. The Italians and Greeks to the south and the Gauls to the north go over to the Carthaginians, "yet these disasters and the defection of allies never moved the Romans to mention peace, either before the consul's arrival or after his return had freshened the memory of the crushing defeat they had sustained. Even at the moment of this crisis, of such great soul was the citizenship that all sorts and conditions of people went in crowds to meet the consul as he returned from the disaster of which he himself had been principal cause, and thanked him for not despairing of the republic. If he had been a general of the Carthaginians, he would have been spared no form of punishment."

"Hannibal was in Italy, the victor of Cannæ," Livy has Cato say; "presently he had taken Tarentum, Arpi, Capua; his movement upon the city of Rome seemed imminent; our allies had abandoned us; we had no soldiers for reinforcements, no naval allies to safeguard the fleet, no money in the treasury; slaves were being bought to put in the ranks on condition of their owners being paid for them when the war was over; against the same term of payment the contractors had said they would arrange for the delivery of grain and other supplies demanded by the uses of war; out of our private means we were contributing slaves to man the oars in numbers fixed according to the census; all of our gold and silver, following the lead of the senators, we turned over to the state; dependent women and children contributed their savings to the treasury." When at length, in 211, the long-expected comes to pass, and the dreadful Hannibal crosses the Volturnus, sweeps up the Latin Way through Frusino and Ferentinum and Anagnia and Gabii, and pitches camp on the Anio three miles from Rome, soon afterward to ride up to the very walls at the Colline gate, "two circumstances, one of great moment and the other slight, caused his hopes to fall: the one of moment, that while he in person was at the gates of Rome with his army he was told that sol-

diers had marched out of the city with colors flying
as a reinforcement for Spain; the slight one, that he
learned from a certain captive during those days that
the land on which he had his camp had been sold with
no reduction in price because of his presence. It seemed
to him so arrogant and insulting that a purchaser had
been found for the soil which he had seized in war and
actually had in possession, that he straightway called a
crier and had the silversmiths' shops about the Roman
Forum put up for sale."

Such were the constancy and endurance of the Roman under stress, such the solid, old-fashioned virtues
in general of the men who wrought and maintained the
city of Rome and the Roman state. "It was our way in
those times," says Livy of the comparatively recent day
of the Macedonian wars, "in the midst of reverses to
wear the countenance of success, and in success to keep
our souls within bounds."

But, in the appraisal of character, action too should
be allowed to speak. No race in the history of the world
has had a nobler gallery of hero-portraits than the Roman people. Who was the Roman? Let us look at the
long line of those remembered for deeds of daring and
devotion. If the colors are sometimes intense and the
lights high, this does not signify that the likeness is not
present.

Lucretia, first of all, is there, spinning the wool late
at night with her women, and dying by her own hand
lest any Roman woman should justify by her example
a life, however guiltless, that bore a stain. There is
Collatinus, who, Tarquin though he is, resigns the consulship and goes into voluntary exile in order to relieve

the new régime of all embarrassment. There is Brutus, who would have brooked

> The eternal devil to keep his state in Rome
> As easily as a king,

trying his sons for plotting against their country, and presiding at their execution. There is Horatius, the gallant defender of the bridge; and Mucius of the Left Hand, who holds his right in the fire to convince the Etruscan king of the Roman temper; and Clœlia, hostage in the Etruscan camp, who swims the Tiber with her fellow hostages, and brings them safe home through the rain of weapons. There is Menenius Agrippa, who narrates to the plebs in secession the story of the mutual dependence of belly and members, and there is the plebs that generously allows itself to be convinced. There are the Fabii, three hundred and six strong, marching out of the city on the voluntary mission of keeping the men of Veii in check, to be caught in ambush with not a man surviving. There is Coriolanus and his mother Volumnia, whose entreaties for the state turn back her rebellious son from assured revenge to exile and miserable death. There is Cincinnatus, leaving his plow in the field across the Tiber for the dictatorship and the rescue of a Roman army. There is Virginia and the resolute father who will have her dead but not dishonored. There is Marcus Manlius, who single-handed in the dead of night discomfits the Gauls on the rock of the Capitol; and the young Fabius, who, faithful to the religion of his family and the state, arrays himself in the priestly vestments and calmly walks through the astonished enemy's lines to the Quirinal, performs the wonted rite, and returns unharmed; and Cominius, who floats and swims his

way down the Tiber, gets into the city, and climbs the
Capitol to deliver the message of help; and the old and
feeble, refusing to enter and crowd the arx which will
scarce contain the city's defenders under arms; and the
dignified and venerable Fathers, in stately toga and
with scepter in hand, immovable and solemn in their
curule chairs, awaiting in the halls of their homes the
savage invader's coming.

We see there Camillus, too, scourging back into the
enemy's town at Falerii the master who would betray
it by handing over his pupils to the Romans. We see
the young Titus Manlius, short and compact and armed
with dagger, sword, and shield, who faces the leering
Gallic giant and cuts him down, and from the spoil of
the necklace wins the name Torquatus for his descent.
We see the same Titus Manlius, twenty years later consul for the third time, who has his son, returned the
moment before to camp victorious from a duel with a
taunting enemy, beheaded in the presence of himself and
the army for disobeying orders by fighting outside the
ranks, "a stern example, but wholesome for the youth
of generations to come," remembered long in the phrase,
"the Manlian discipline." We see Marcus Valerius the
boy tribune, who with the aid of a bird divinely sent lays
low a second terrifying warrior from the north and becomes Valerius of the Raven. We see Publius Decius
Mus, the tribune who rescues the entire army from sure
destruction in the Samnite war by volunteering to dis-
tract the enemy by leading a forlorn hope, and through
a cool head and a sharp wit returns in safety with his
little band; and, three years later, forewarned in a vision
that in the coming battle one side will lose an army and
the other a general, takes with him into the fight the

VIEW OF SENTINUM FROM SASSOFERRATO

THE SUPPOSED SITE OF SENTINUM IS NEAR THE ROAD

pontifex, duly to consecrate him at the proper moment, assumes the priestly robe, and calmly rides to death in the thick of the combat, to be found next day amid the heaps of the slain and covered with spears; and Publius Decius Mus the son, who forty-five years later repeats at Sentinum the deed of his father, with the proud claim that "this is the privilege of our house, to offer up our lives for the rescue of the state from peril"; and Publius Decius Mus the grandson, who in the war with Pyrrhus treads in the footsteps of sire and grandsire.

And there is Papirius Cursor, the ideal commander, a man who everybody agrees is worthy of all praise in war, excelling in vigor of spirit and strength of body, the nimblest and most enduring runner of his time, magnetic in his power with Romans and allies alike. There is Manius Curius Dentatus, at the simple sight of whom in his rustic dwelling as he prepared his frugal meal of herbs, the would-be bribers knew their hopes were vain; and Appius Claudius, authoritatively persuading the senate to make no peace with Pyrrhus, uttering such words of wisdom as, "every man is the architect of his own fortune," and even in blind old age commanding the respect, obedience, and love of all his household; and Gaius Fabricius, who magnanimously sends word to the Epirote king of a proposal made to the Romans by one of his intimates to poison him, and whose sterling nature is easily proof against Pyrrhus' offers of gold and power.

There is Regulus, sent by his captors to dispose the Romans to negotiation, but advising the wavering senate to continue the war, and proudly making his way through protesting friends and kinsmen to Carthage and the tortures of the cruel enemy to whom he gave his word; and old Duilius, admiral in Rome's first victory at sea, pursuing a homeward way through the streets of the city with the special honor of a torchlight and the strains of a flute.

There is the dashing stripling Scipio, who rescues his father at the Ticinus, confidently claims the privilege of the consulship while under legal age, saves the day in distant Spain, restores unharmed to her family and lover the beautiful Iberian reserved for him by a zealous soldiery, discomfits Hannibal on African soil, and, when charged with irregularity in the Asiatic war, draws forth his accounts and tears them in pieces before the people, and, proudly mounting the rostra in the midst of silence, says: "On this day, tribunes of the people, and you, my fellow citizens of Rome, I measured strength with Hannibal and the Carthaginians in Africa and won the day. And so, since this is a day when quarrels at law and wordy strife should be dropped, I shall go straightway hence to the Capitol to give holy salute to Jupiter Best and Greatest and to Juno, and to Minerva and all the other gods who keep ward over Capitol and citadel, and offer thanks for their having bestowed on me, both on this day and often at other times, the purpose and power of discharging well the people's trust. If it is true that from my seventeenth year to these elder days you have always in conferring office on me anticipated the legal age, if it is true that I have always done service greater than the trust demanded, come with me, citizens, you too who find it well, and pray to the gods for men like me to lead you."

Paullus is there, prodigal of his great soul unto death, who atones for the sins of his colleague at Cannæ; and gallant Marcellus, the sword of Rome, with tears for the fate of Syracuse, and honored in death by even the heartless enemy; and Fabius, the shield of Rome, with iron constancy under stress of criticism and calumny refusing to allow Hannibal the coveted opportunity for battle. And the sympathetic Flamininus is there, hero of Cynoscephalæ and liberator of cities. And Æmilius Paullus is there, stern old warrior victorious over Macedonian abroad and hostile citizen at home, riding resplendent in purple and gold in stately and hard-won triumph over Perseus and over himself; "for of his two sons, the only ones he had kept for himself at home to perpetuate his name and house and the rites of his fathers, the younger, at about the age of twelve, had died five days before the triumph, and the elder, of fourteen years, died three days after; who should have stood in purple-bordered robes beside their father in the triumphal car, looking forward to similar triumphs of their own."

And there were not only these, whose enlightened vision saw more clearly the reward of patriotic and manly deeds, and who lived and died under the eyes of the living and the dead, but there were the young men, untaught and even rustic, that filled the ranks of the legions, and looked with scorn upon death, "and often set out with quick and eager hearts to places whence they never expected to return." There was the Unknown Soldier.

And there was the Roman mother, daughter, sister, wife, and maiden betrothed. There was the Unknown Woman. If the history of human endurance could be written in all completeness, no chapter in it would be richer with inspiration than the story of Roman womanhood.

But above all there is the figure of old Cato the censor, the latest and most real of all the men that made the great republic, the man in whom the Roman of later days saw all the solid virtues of the past,—Cato bred in the country, a soldier at seventeen, with breast scarred over by honorable wounds before he arrived at years of manhood, a general who took more cities in Spain than the days he spent, who saw service in every land invaded by Roman arms, who disciplined his body with the soldier's regimen to the last, and kept his mental vigor unimpaired; Cato the industrious farmer and the keen and active citizen, who in young manhood, before residing in Rome, "early in the morning went on foot to the market-place and pleaded the case of all who wished his aid; then came back to his farm, where, clad in a working-blouse if it was winter, and stripped to the waist if it was summer, he wrought with his servants, then sat down with them to eat of the same bread and drink of the same wine"; Cato "who wrought with his own hands, as his fathers did, and was contented with a cold breakfast, a frugal dinner, simple raiment, and a humble dwelling,—one who thought more of not wanting the superfluities of life than of possessing them"; Cato of the dry-humored and pithy utterances, who said, "It is a hard matter, my fellow citizens, to argue with the belly, since it has no ears," and, "It is a hard matter to save a city in which a fish sells for more than an ox," and who would have had the Forum paved with sharp stones for the benefit of idlers; Cato who "used to say that he preferred to do right and get no thanks, rather than to do ill and get no punishment; and that he had pardon for everybody's mistakes except his own"; Cato the incorruptible, who took no part of the booty in Spain, "except what he ate and drank," who "strove to keep not only himself, but also his associates, free from all taint of gain," who preferred "to strive in bravery with the bravest, rather than in wealth with the richest, and in greed for money with the greediest"; Cato content with the enmity of the unworthy citizens he constantly impeached, and trampling revengeful accusations under foot; Cato the censor fearlessly rebuking vice and taxing luxury and degrading the unworthy; Cato the austere moralist, who expelled a senator "because he embraced his wife in open day before the eyes of his daughter," who "thought it more praiseworthy to be a good husband than a great senator," who allowed no business to "be so urgent, unless it had a public character, as to prevent him from being present when his wife bathed and swaddled the babe," who was himself "not only the boy's reading-teacher, but his tutor in law, and his athletic trainer, and he taught his son not merely to hurl the javelin and fight in armor and ride the horse, but to box, to endure heat and cold, and to swim lustily through the eddies and billows of the Tiber," who declared "that his son's presence put him on guard against indecencies of speech as much as that of the so-called Vestal Virgins, and that he never bathed with him"; Cato the unremitting enemy of easy living as a danger to the state, the scorner of the trifling Greek, the unrelenting foe of his country's ancient rival in Africa.

"But far above all the patricians and plebeians of the best known houses," writes Livy, "stood Marcus Porcius. In this man so great was the vigor of mind and soul that, in whatever station he had been born, he would doubtless have attained fortune. No capacity was lacking in him for either personal or public enterprise; he was quite as much at home in the business of the city as of the country. Some have risen to the highest honors of the state by knowledge of law, some by eloquence, some by glory in the field; but this man's talent was so wholly versatile that whatever he set hand to you would say he was fitted for that alone. In war he was of the greatest prowess, and famous for many remarkable fights; he was likewise, after he had risen to the great offices, a most able commander; likewise in peace, if you sought his counsel, he was most expert, if a plea was called for, most eloquent. Nor was he only of the sort whose tongue is powerful during their lifetime but leave no monument of their eloquence behind; no, his eloquence lives and flourishes still, perpetuated by writings of every kind. He delivered many orations both in his own defence and in defending and attacking others, for he wore down his enemies not merely by haling them into court but also by pleading the cases. He both attacked and was attacked with exceeding frequency, and you would have found it difficult to say whether the nobles pursued and pressed him harder, or he the nobles. Beyond all doubt he had a harsh temper and a bitter tongue to whose freedom he set no bounds, but his soul was uninfluenced by covetousness, he was a man of uncompromising righteousness, and held favor and money in contempt. In frugal living, in endurance of toil and dangers, he was body and soul almost of iron, of a sort that not even old age, the destroyer of everything, could break; in his six-and-eightieth year he defended himself in court, and himself made the plea in his case and wrote it out, and in his ninetieth year brought Servius Galba to trial before the people."

Such was the ideal of Roman character as clothed in flesh and blood, and posing in the robes and jewels of the tragic scene. That the heroic figure was ideal, is evident enough. Livy himself, the glorifier of noble deeds and noble men, was aware of it. "Details like these," he says, "which are better suited for display on the stage, which delights in the wonderful, than for sober credence, it is worth while neither to affirm nor to deny."

Perhaps it is the duty of essayist and historian to go farther than Livy, and to deny the perfect deed and the perfect character. If this is so, it is easy enough to point out how the Roman virtues were inevitably accompanied by the defects that were proper to them. If the man who built the Roman state was rustic, simple, frugal, abstemious, conservative, and practical, he was of necessity also to some degree rough, narrow, parsimonious, unimaginative, and unenlightened. If he was conscientious and strict in religion, he was also formal and inclined to superstition. If he was exact in justice and scrupulous in meeting obligation, he was also legalistic and could take advantage of the letter of the law. If he was always alive in the pursuit of the civic ideal, he was often quarrelsome and violent. If he was constant, stern, enduring, and a devoted patriot, he often forgot the lesser duty in the greater, and was harsh to friend and family and merciless to subject. If he was a great soldier and civilizer, he did not always resist temptation to shorten or ease the way to the goal by the use of unjust or brutal means. In times of real or of fancied stress he was not always nice in his choice of measures. Like other warring nations before and since, he could justify by supreme necessity the massacre of unarmed and unsuspecting men, as at Henna; hand over to soldiers for pillage whole captured towns, as in Macedonia; deliberately seize what was not his own, as at Messana; take advantage of a defeated foe, as in the annexation of Corsica and Sardinia; destroy a helpless and inconvenient rival, as in the case of Carthage; provoke wars for the sake of mines or lands, enslave and traffic in prisoners of war, and find pleasure in the blood of the gladiatorial fight for life.

It is easy, too, to throw upon the city of Rome some flashes of the light of common day, to reveal the motley crowd that helped to make up the life of the capital on unheroic days. Plautus, on a morning not more than a score of years from Hannibal's fall at Zama, will help us. "I'll tell you," says one in *The Weevil,* "where you can easily and quickly find any sort of man you choose, whether villainous or upright, honest or a rascal. If you want a perjurer, go to the comitium. If you want a liar or a boaster, you'll find him at the altar of Cloacina. For rich and spendthrift husbands, look about the basilica. In the same place you'll meet the faded prostitute and the man who will bargain himself away. The fellows that club together for dinners have a place of meeting near the fish-market. At the lower end of the Forum is the promenade of the respectable and the rich. In the middle, near the canal, are the big talkers. The impudent, the blabbers, and the malicious are above the Pool; they slander each other out of whole cloth, and have plenty that might with perfect truth be said of themselves. By the Old Shops are those who give and take for usury. Behind the temple of Castor you will find men whom you will trust to your own cost. In the street of the Etruscans are men who will sell their souls to you, and who will either themselves deceive, or find you the means to do it. In the Velabrum you will find the bakers, the butchers, and the fortune-tellers." The fortune-tellers, perhaps, whom Ennius also knew: "Superstitious prophets and impudent fortune-tellers, lazy, crazy, or forced by want, who see no path for themselves, will point out the high road to others, and from those whom they promise wealth will ask only a drachma. Let them only get that out of the pile, and they will let you have all the rest."

Nor need such men as Ennius himself and his friends be without the illumination that lends reality to the life of Rome. Scipio Nasica, calling one day on the poet at his home on the Aventine, is told by the slave girl at the door that her master is not in, though Scipio knows very well that he is. A few days afterward, Ennius in turn knocks at Scipio's door, to be surprised by his friend's calling from within that he is not at home. "What!" cries Ennius, "don't I recognize your voice?" "Oh, yes!" answers Scipio, "but when I called on you and the slave said you were not in, I believed her, and can't you believe me when I myself tell you I am not at home?"

Easiest of all is it to make Cato himself an example of the presence of alloy in the gold of Roman character. The old censor was not without the defects belonging to the qualities he so thoroughly represented. He was arbitrary in the use of the power his great office conferred. The faithful "watchdog of the treasury" was niggardly in the management of public finance. He enjoyed and never ceased from litigation. He was stubborn and unyielding. He despised the Greeks and their civilization, and recognized Greek letters only in extreme old age, and then grudgingly, with the excuse that it was for his son's sake. He promoted dissension among his slaves, the better to manage them, he sold them off when they began to weaken with age, to escape feeding useless property, and at the conclusion of dinner flogged those who had in any way been remiss in its preparation or serving. We are constrained to agree with Plutarch when he says of these and other examples of the vigorous hero's strictness and sturdiness that "whether these things should be set down to greatness of spirit or littleness of mind, is an open question." Even in personal appearance, he was anything but the usual type:

> With eyes so grey, and hair so red,
>   With tusks so sharp and keen,
> Thou'lt fright the shades when thou art dead,
>   And hell won't let thee in.

And yet, let realist and skeptic prove as they will that not all Romans were equal to the best, and that even the best were not ideal, their effort is in vain. The breed of which he was the last was already a legend in Cato's own time, and the old man was hardly dead when he too became a legend. The world has long since formed for itself the image of those times. It remembers the citizen-soldier for the best that was in him. In this instance it is not the good, but the bad, that is interred with the bones. It remembers Cato for his fearless and dogged aggressiveness against the enemies of public and private virtue. It remembers the Roman people for its plain and wholesome living and its stern, enduring heroism. It remembers the Roman senate for its grave and impressive demeanor and its magisterial wisdom and dignity, and agrees with Livy that "he who said it was composed of kings had the true impression of its appearance." In these judgments, soon formed, almost before the actors had left the stage, and long continued, the idealist world has seen the essential truth more clearly than the critical searcher after sordid fact. If it could formulate a reply to the skeptic, it would probably use again the measured speech of Livy: "But in matters as ancient as these, if what resembles the truth is accepted in place of literal fact, I shall rest content."

IV.

AUGUSTAN ROME

Non his iuventus orta parentibus
Infecit æquor sanguine Punico
  Pyrrhumque et ingentem cecidit
    Antiochum Hannibalemque dirum,—

'Twas not the sons of parents such as these
That tinged with Punic blood the rolling seas,
Laid low the cruel Hannibal, and brought
Great Pyrrhus and Antiochus to naught.

HORACE, Odes, III: 6: 33-6

Quid enim manet ex antiquis moribus quibus ille dixit rem stare Romanam? quos ita oblivione obsoletos videmus ut non modo non colantur sed iam ignorentur,—

For what is left of those morals of the olden time in which he said the Roman state was grounded? They are so far fallen away and forgotten that they are not only not cultivated, but are now not even known.

CICERO, De Republica, V: 2

Magnus ab integro sæclorum nascitur ordo,—

The great round of the ages begins anew.

VIRGIL, Eclogues, IV: 5

1.

A GREAT FAILURE AND A GREAT SUCCESS

TO pass from the Roman state and the city of Rome
and the Roman character of Cato's day to their
descendants of Augustan times is to come under a new
heaven and into a new earth where former things are
passed away. The one hundred and sixty years between
the destruction of Carthage in 146 and the end of the
first Roman emperor's reign in the year 14 of the Christian era is a period of great and spectacular movements,
of rapid and sweeping transformations, of tragic intensity. Three years before it began, the death of the
venerable censor removed from the scene the last great
citizen-soldier and the last disinterested champion of
the commonwealth against the assaults of multiplying
enemies without and within, carnal or of the spirit. At
its end, the accession of Tiberius marks the transition
of Rome beyond recall from a state composed of men to
a state envisaged in one single man.

The history of Rome the state in this period of change
is the story of a Great Failure and a Great Success. It
is the story of the gradual decay and falling apart of an
old organism, and the upward shoot of a new organism
from the midst of the rottenness of the old. It is the
story of the agony of death and the agony of birth.

The realization of persistent old Cato's will in the
levelling of Carthage with the ground and the literal
passing of the plow over the place that knew the city

no more removed the last great hindrance, real or fancied, in the path of Roman expansion and Roman security. The siege and sack of Corinth, in the same year, was not only the end of Roman effort to deal with the land of Greece as a protectorate, but the end of sentiment of any sort in the conquest and management of subject peoples; in so short a time had the gallant enthusiasm of Flamininus, proclaiming peace and freedom to Greece at the Isthmian games, and the still more real though sterner and more impartial devotion of the grave Æmilius Paullus, visiting famous Hellenic sites on the morrow of Pydna and nurturing his sons in Hellenic culture, passed to the hardness of the practical soldier Mummius, for the sake of final peace and order shutting the gates of mercy on mankind. The Roman territories, now comprising Italy to the valley of the Po, Sicily, Sardinia and Corsica, the Spains, Illyricum, Macedonia, Greece, the Punic portion of Africa, and footholds on the coast of Asia, come soon to include, through conquest, persuasion, and legacy, Asia, Cilicia, Syria, Bithynia, Pontus, and Hither and Farther Gaul. They surround the Mediterranean and make it a Roman lake, and Roman authority reaches far inland from vantage points on its shores.

But the onward march of the Roman legions was not all success. So vast was the expanse of Roman territory, so great was the rapidity with which province after province was carved out and annexed from the first imperial venture in the crossing of the strait of Messina to the subjugation of Gaul two centuries later, and so enormous was the amount of energy, material and moral, required by it all, that neither government nor character was able to keep pace. Roman possessions and Ro-

man spheres of influence made up a mighty empire, but
the Roman state was still the city-state of Rome, still
thinking and acting in terms of a city, still unconscious
of being the heart of a great and living body. The setting in order of the immense estate cried out for administrators who had seen the cities and learned the
minds of many men, but the supreme authority over all
this world of diverse tongues and diverging interests
still continued to be lodged in a council of some hundreds of men, not yet grown really cosmopolitan, of a
wisdom great indeed but not sufficient for the demand;
whose collective will was slow and uncertain, and whose
action was inexpert; and whose character, once the
compensation for mistakes of head and hand, had given
way with a rush before the assaults of temptation that
came with the flood of provincial wealth and the possession of opportunity. The senate of landed patricians,
proud, dignified, and untouched by greed for aught but
patriotic and family fame, had become, through death
in the wars for their country and through corruption
by the wealth which their houses wasted themselves to
conquer for the state, a senate of moneyed men and for-
tune-seekers embarked in the state career as a paying
thing. There were lands to be assigned, there was spoil
to divide, there was tribute to come in, there were offices
to fill, there were business openings, there were bribes
to accept. The instruments by means of which they
ruled the subjects of Rome were from their own ranks.
Their training was that of the senatorial career. They
had the practical education of young men destined for
the public service, they had, as a usual thing, the soldier's experience and the soldier's qualities, they could
manage an estate, they were possessed of the skill in

politics that helped them to office, they had the fund of
practical common sense and shrewdness that came of
mingling with the men who constituted the Roman
state; but they knew little of provincial administration
through actual experience until they had reached their
fields of duty, and the scant knowledge they acquired
during tenure of office was of little avail because their
experience ended with the year. Proconsul and pro-
prætor, with their trains of military and civil subordinates, looked upon the province as an opportunity. They
went out for one year among peoples whose speech they
did not understand and whose thoughts they could not
appreciate, relieved their blundering, plundering predecessors, blundered and plundered in their turn, and
came back to Rome as their predecessors had come, with
purses so filled as to endure the drain of possible punishment and still be far from empty. There were able men
among them, and men who retained their integrity; but
there were more who were either by nature or circumstance not competent, and whose honesty would not
bear the strain. When a Cicero went out in the spirit of
a governor to whom a public office was a public trust,
he became an example to grace the pages of history.

In a word, the great republic was without a civil
service worthy of the name. The corruption of governors entailed the corruption and disorder of the governed. The far-flung area of the Roman possessions,
from the Pillars of Hercules to Pergamum and from
Carthage to the Rhine, was without the uniform and
expert administration that alone could give it unity.
The remoter provinces were dependencies, not parts, of
the Roman state,—the farms of the Roman governors.
Their laws were uncertain, their taxes excessive and

capricious, their fortunes fluctuating from year to year. There were those not yet convinced of Rome's superior strength, to say nothing of superior righteousness. There were gaps in the reach of her authority. There were mobile neighbors and mobile boundaries. There was piracy on the sea and brigandage and insurrection on the land. Travel, communication, and commerce were slow, uncertain, and unsafe.

Corruption and disorder abroad were equalled and surpassed by corruption and disorder at home. Each was at the same time the cause and the effect of the other; provincial opportunity was a stimulation to election bribery, and bribery before the governorship, with the buying up of courts at the end of the term of office, provoked abuse in the provinces. The rank and file were themselves affected. The real tragedy of the republic occurred in the city of Rome. Rome was not only unable to govern her world of provinces; she was unable to govern herself. The century preceding the advent of Augustus was the era of revolution.

The seeds had long been lying in the ground, had often put forth shoots to flourish for a day and wither, and had often been resown. Now, however, with the assured supremacy of Rome in the Mediterranean, with the sight and the touch of riches to rouse the appetite for more, and with leisure for the masses to think of themselves and their wrongs instead of the dangers of the state, the ancient grievances of the weak against the strong, of the many against the few, of plebeian against aristocrat, of the poor against the rich, of the nameless against the noble, and especially of the landless against the landed, which had once blazed up in the driving out of the kings, again in the secession of the plebs, and

once more in the Licinian laws, and was ever smoulder-
ing even in times of greatest unity, flamed forth in the
fiercest heat of all. The times of the Gracchi brought at
last a strain which the fabric of the state could no longer
bear. The loosely constructed constitution of Rome,
whose foundations were in the elaborate system of
checks,—of consul upon consul, of tribune upon consul
and upon tribune, of censor upon citizen and senate, of
senate upon magistrate, of civilian upon soldier, and of
the sovereign people upon them all,—and whose stability was no longer possible when the Roman citizenry
had grown to immense proportions and extended to
distant lands, and Roman morals and patriotism no
longer retained their austere cast, gave way.

The arbitrary deposition of a fellow tribune by Tiberius Gracchus and the popular party sixteen years
after Cato's death, with the arbitrary passing of the
reformer's agrarian measure, was the first real act of
revolution. It provoked, and excused, other acts of violence, among them the deaths of both the Gracchi at
the hands of the opposing faction. From that time forth
the constitution ceased to be supreme. The Gracchi were
followed in a score of years by Saturninus, and Saturninus by Marius. Four times in less than forty years
had the people assailed their political enemies, and four
times failed to gain their ends; four times had blood
been shed and the time-honored traditions of government been set aside, and four times had both parties to
the conflict been left more passionate and reckless. The
quarrel became in Marius' and Sulla's time personal as
well as partisan, and thousands of persons were slain
without regard to law or precedent. The Rome of Sulla,
however temporary or unconfessed, was a monarchy.

The Roman republic from the Gracchi to Julius Cæsar was an irregular, disorderly, and futile succession of monarchies. The use of force supplanted the use of law and reason. The monarchs of the people armed the mob or seduced the legions; the monarchs of the oligarchy employed the armies of the state to carry their measures.

A more just name for it all is anarchy. The Roman arms were supreme abroad, but confidence in Roman righteousness and capacity was being destroyed. At home the Roman state had crumbled, and the Romans were rending each other. The course of government by consuls, senate, and people was run. The extension of the Roman realm had been too rapid and too great to be at the same time solid and well knit. The stately phrase in which Livy describes the task he has set his pen is equally fitting when applied to the state whose fortunes he regretfully records: "An undertaking of infinite labor, going back as it does more than seven hundred years, and from small beginnings growing to such size that now it threatens to collapse from its very magnitude."

This was the Great Failure.

But the Roman state was not to perish, though the days of republican Rome were numbered. Eternal Rome does not die; it only changes. In the midst of death there still was life.

The final blow that brought to earth the tottering constitution was delivered by Julius Cæsar. Obstructionists were brushed aside, new laws took the place of old, realities were regarded instead of forms, the senate was crushed and re-created, the foundations of a new structure were laid. The blind half-measures of narrow and selfish partisans gave way to the boldness and vision of a man of genius.

Augustus completed the structure which Julius designed and began. By the end of the emperor's reign of forty-one years, the Roman realm was compact, its limits definite, its administration converted into system. On the west was the stream of Ocean. On the south, the Atlas mountains and Sahara, and Syene in the upper valley of the Nile, marked the end of Roman dominion and desire. On the north, the Briton, the Dacian, and the Scythian were left in peace in their wilds beyond the Channel, the Danube, and the Pontus; beyond the Rhine only, the Roman eagles made unsuccessful advances toward the Elbe. On the east the limit was not established with scientific precision; the Roman standards traced a wavering line from Cilicia on the south to the eastern end of the Pontus, with Palmyra and other vassal states to mark and protect its course, and with Mede and Armenian, half hostile and half friendly to Rome, kept safely busy with their own quarrels beyond it. Order was created from the chaos of the old abuses. Governors continued to be sent, the more important responsible to Augustus himself, the less to the senate, but their terms of office were not always a single year, and the powers and duties of themselves and their official and commercial trains were better known. An expert civil service came into being, and the rights of the governed were recognized as well as the desires of the governor. The seas were clear and the roads were safe. Travel was easy on the great post-roads that led like arteries to the limits of Roman dominion. Prosperity followed in the wake of peace and order. The Greater Rome became a unit. For the first time, the mother city

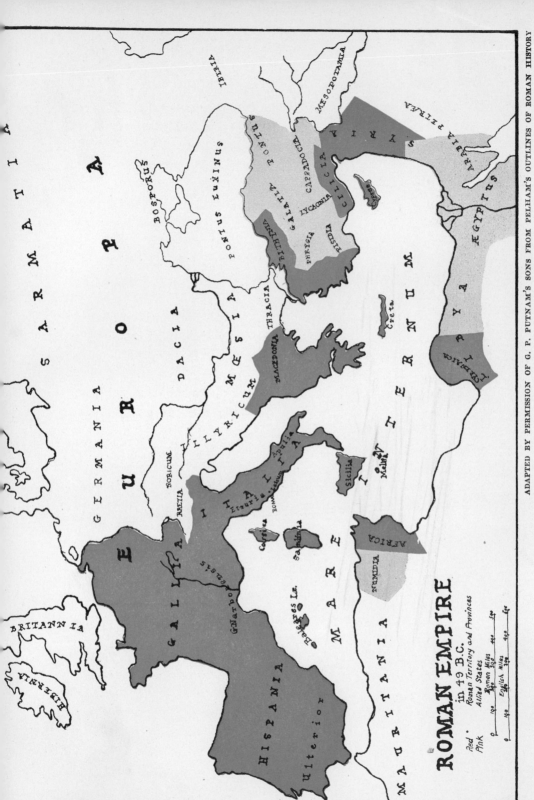

ROMAN EMPIRE
in 49 B.C.

Red · Roman Territory and Provinces
Pink · Allied States

THE ROMAN SWAY IN 49 B.C.

ADAPTED BY PERMISSION OF G. P. PUTNAM'S SONS FROM PELHAM'S OUTLINES OF ROMAN HISTORY

felt herself the capital of a state, and not the state itself. For the first time, the provincial began to feel himself an active part of the empire. Roman law and the Roman tongue were spread abroad, the sign of a better civilization. Something like mutual confidence, and even gratitude, began to be felt; Rome looked to the provinces for men and means, the provinces to Rome for justice and security. What Strabo said of thirty nations of Spain near the Tagus might have been said in substance of most of the Mediterranean world: "Notwithstanding the fertility of the country in corn, cattle, gold, silver, and numerous other similar productions, the majority of its inhabitants, neglecting to gain their subsistence from the ground, passed their lives in pillage and continual warfare, both between themselves and their neighbors. To this the Romans at length put a stop by subduing them, and changing many of their cities into villages, besides colonizing some of them better." "These provinces, so widely scattered, so numerous, and so fierce, which never knew respite from wars of first class magnitude," says Velleius Paterculus not long afterward, "Augustus brought to so peaceful a state that they were free from even acts of brigandage."

And what was true of the Roman realm at large was true also of the more intimate and essential affairs of citizenship in the heart of the realm at the capital. The two great factions of conservatives and radicals whose differences Julius Cæsar was kept by his tragic end from composing had been convinced by thirteen years more of war on land and sea of the need of an individual will to save the state. The universal hope was for peace and order. Even to his enemies, the emperor embodied that hope. The senate was given new character by the selection of men of stability in property and character. Its business was no longer the unwieldy process of ascertaining the will of a crowd of inexpert and interested politicians; matters of moment were considered in privy council, and the findings presented to a senate at large which had learned to have respect for business as well as politics. However cautious to avoid the appearance, however sincere in the attempt to share his authority, the emperor was really the senate.

The senate was not the only authority to be lost in the emperor. The consuls were still elected, but not with the fierce partisanship of the olden days. The emperor himself was really the consulship. The scandals of maladministration by proconsul and propraetor came to an end. The provincial governors were responsible directly to the emperor or to the senate that knew his will. The emperor was really the governor of the provinces, and in case of abuse the court that awarded punishment. The ancient quarrels between tribune of the people and aristocrat no longer spattered the pavements with blood. The emperor himself became the tribunate. Election riots and election bribery were things of the past. The choice of the senate or the appointment of the emperor took their place. The emperor himself in reality became the electorate of the four million citizens of military age revealed by the census of 28.

That the emperor was really the army is truest of all. There were no more rival claimants to military power; it was by annihilating such rivals that Augustus had made himself supreme. Nor were his efforts confined to the visible and the tangible. By his measures for the moral inspiration of Roman citizenship, the emperor became in a sense the morals of the state. As

pontifex maximus, he was already the religious head
of the state; but he became more. By reviving forms and
restoring temples, he not only encouraged religion; by
skilful use of the current of religious and patriotic sentiment and thought, he became religion itself. With
Augustus, descendant and heir of the Julius who had
been declared Divine, and whose temple in the Forum
stood as a constant reminder of the fact, began the worship of the Roman state in the worship of its emperor.

In a word, the emperor became the state. He did not
do it suddenly and without regard for opinion. In reality, he was the state from the moment his superiority
in arms was assured. In word and appearance, he never
baldly asserted the fact. He was never the emperor; he
was the Princeps Senatus, the First Man of the Senate.
The powers he already possessed were legally conferred
from time to time by people and senate, and without
display. The old offices were not abolished, the name
of the republic was not forgotten or neglected; indeed,
we may not disbelieve that the emperor purposed its
restoration. The content only was changed; the mould
remained unbroken. In the phrase of Seneca, Augustus
"clothed himself in the garment of the republic."

The process was not a success in every detail. There
were acts of the strong hand and the remorseless will.
There were imperfect instruments of the best of wills.
There were the irreconcilables who maintained that the
new régime was tyranny, and never ceased to believe
that the desired end could have been reached by clinging
to republican substance as well as form. There are still
today those who, forgetting that even the tyrant may
have sincere and worthy desires, refer to Augustan reforms as "organized hypocrisy." And there are, on the

other hand, those who, thoughtless of the century that followed, are prone to justify too readily the seizure of arbitrary power as means to an end.

Whatever the judgment be as to the emperor's personal merit, whatever the verdict as to the effect of the new régime upon universal history, it is not to be denied that at the end of Augustus' seventy-seven years of life and the forty-one of his formal leadership of the Roman state, the result was peace and order, and a revived faith in the destiny of Rome.

This was the Great Success.

THE BRIDGE OF AUGUSTUS AT NARNI

HERE AT NARNIA, SIXTY MILES NORTH OF ROME, THE VIA FLAMINIA CROSSED
THE NAR, THE MODERN NERA

2.

THE CITY OF BRICK AND THE CITY OF MARBLE

IF we look to the fortunes of Rome the city during these years, we shall find them reflecting the fortunes of the state at large. The history of the capital, too, is the story of failure and success. In extent, in appearance, in administration, and in its citizens alike, the city of Augustus presented a remarkable contrast with the city of Cato.

The three or four hundred thousand inhabitants of Cato's time, which had swelled to a possible half million at the beginning of the last century before Christ, were now approaching a million. The city which here and there had straggled loosely beyond the walls had widened still more. The wall itself had been built against and built upon until its course was no longer easy to follow.

The southern part of the Campus Martius was crowded with buildings public and private. Beginning at the base of the Capitoline, among the larger edifices and monuments from south to north were the theaters of Marcellus and Balbus, the portico of Octavia, the Circus Flaminius, the great theater and portico of Pompey, the baths of Agrippa and the Pantheon, the fountain of the Virgin aqueduct, the polling-place called the Sæpta Iulia, the temple of Isis and Serapis, the portico of the Argonauts enclosing the basilica of Neptune or the Admiralty, the amphitheater of Sta-

tilius Taurus, the obelisk of Augustus, the altar of
Peace, and, finally, the great mausoleum of the Julian
family erected by Augustus at the beginning of his
reign. Of the original area free for military exercises
and general diversion, but little remained.

Across the Tiber, spanned now by at least five bridges
instead of two, a populous living-quarter had grown up.
To the south, docks and warehouses had multiplied.
Small shipping came directly up the Tiber to the southern base of the Aventine; the larger craft dropped
anchor opposite Ostia, where they were lightened by
smaller vessels of parts of their cargo, and thus enabled
to reach the capital. To the north of the Aventine along
the river were the cattle-market and vegetable-markct,
and farther still, by the Campus Martius, the naval
yards.

The district about the Capitoline, the Palatine, and
the Forum was the heart of the city and the densest in
population. The Capitoline was majestic with towering
temples, the Palatine, in former times the residence of
Crassus, Catiline, Hortensius, and Cicero, was now the
home of the emperor, whose palace was part of a stately
group including the portico and temple of Apollo. To
the northeast, the expansion of the city was such that
Mæcenas converted the ancient burial-ground outside
the great dike of defence into a public garden, and the
dike itself into a promenade. Near by were the gardens
of Lamia. At the northern end of the city were the gardens of Lucullus and Sallust, later to become, like other
private parks, the property of crown and public. There
were the gardens of Agrippa in the Campus Martius.
Across the Tiber, to the north, there were the gardens
of Drusus, Cassius, Clodia, and others, all existing in

Cicero's time; at the extreme south, on the brow and slope of the Janiculum, lay the gardens bequeathed to the people by Cæsar, who had planned and begun a great number of beautifications and utilities whose realization was cut short by his death and accomplished by Augustus, and whose vision had also contemplated the diversion of the Tiber to the right as it passed Rome, the consequent annexation of the ground between its old channel and the new one at the base of the Vatican and Janiculum, and the construction of a canal to the south through the Campagna to the Pomptine marshes, a distance of seventy-six miles, to connect the capital with the sea independently of the Tiber, already too deeply silted at its mouth for the ready passage of larger shipping.

Roughly, the city already covered, though in places thinly, the area to be enclosed two hundred and sixty years later by Aurelian's wall. The whole was divided into fourteen regions, or wards, and surrounded by a customs-barrier with thirty-seven points of entrance. Seven aqueducts now, instead of the two of Cato's time, supplied the city with water.

But the transformation of the city's appearance was more remarkable than its increase in size. The city of the Republic had been of wood and tufa and sun-dried brick and stucco, with few ornamental features except those afforded by the more pretentious public buildings and temples, the honorary statues and monuments in the Forum, and occasional relics of the sculptural art of Greece. It had never been the way of the Romans to build pretentious residences. As Horace proudly wrote:

Scant were their private means; the public, great;
'Twas still a commonwealth, their state.
No portico, with private rod surveyed,
Assured one man the cooling shade.

The laws approved the house of humble sods;
'Twas only to the homes of gods,
The temples, reared with earnings of the nation,
They gave rich marble decoration.

Not only the native simplicity and frugality, but the necessities of war, and especially the uncertainties of civil war, retarded the city's progress in this respect. There were houses reputed wealthy on the Palatine, and Cicero in 68 is concerned about the artistic furnishings of his; but the character of the residences even in that pretentious quarter may be inferred from the nickname of "Palatine Venus," applied to Crassus because of the six columns of marble, the first to be used in a Roman house, which adorned his atrium; and the nature of ordinary dwellings is suggested by Strabo's remark that, notwithstanding the prodigious increase of the city, there has been plenty of "wood and stone for ceaseless building, rendered necessary by the falling down of houses, and on account of conflagrations, and of the sales, which seem never to cease . . . each owner knocking down and rebuilding one part or another, according to his individual taste."

This was the crude city which Augustus found of brick and left of marble. Since the city was not adorned as the dignity of the empire demanded, and since its condition exposed it to the dangers of flood and fire, the extent to which he improved and beautified it was such that he could with justice make the celebrated boast.

To a Roman who saw both cities, to Livy, for example, who was born four years after Augustus and survived him three years, the boast would have seemed almost literally true. For the first time in her history, Rome had come upon a period of quiet and assurance, and could look to the future with little apprehension. After the victories over Carthage and Macedon, the state had enjoyed a period of freedom from danger, but its quiet was the quiet of exhaustion; with a restoration of strength came the renewal of strife between citizen and citizen. When the city finally found herself free, after a century or more of anarchy, and when for the first time in five hundred years her will was summed up in a single man, she advanced with a great bound to the position of the first city in the world in wealth and magnificence as well as in power.

The hand of the emperor himself was foremost in effecting the transformation. On two bronze tablets beside his mausoleum in the Campus Martius, containing a detailed account by himself of the achievements of his reign, there was included a paragraph enumerating his improvements in the city. After mention of the senate house, the temple of Apollo on the Palatine, the temple of the Divine Julius, the temple of the Great Mother, and a dozen other buildings and monuments, he continues: "The Capitolium and the theater of Pompey, both of them works involving great expenditure, I restored without the inscription of my name. The water-conduits that in several places were old and ruinous I refitted, and doubled the water called the Marcia by letting into its channel water from a new source. I completed the forum and basilica of Julius, the latter between the temples of Castor and Saturn, and both of them begun and carried forward by my father (Julius), and also, when the basilica had been destroyed by fire, I amplified the ground and began it anew in the name of my sons (grandsons, Gaius and Lucius), providing for its completion by my heirs in case of my death. When consul for the sixth time, by decree of the senate I restored two-and-eighty temples of the gods in the city, neglecting no single one which needed restoration at that time. In my seventh consulship, I (re)built the Via Flaminia from the city to Ariminum, and all the bridges except the Mulvius and the Minucius. On private ground I built from the spoils of war the temple of Mars the Avenger and the Augustan forum. The theater near the shrine of Apollo I built on ground bought in large part from private citizens, to be named in honor of Marcus Marcellus my son-in-law."

"More than that," says Suetonius in his biography of the emperor, "he often urged other prominent men to adorn the city with new monuments or to restore and embellish old ones, each according to his means. And many such works were built at that time by many men; for example, the temple of Hercules of the Muses by Marcius Philippus, the temple of Diana by Lucius Cornificius, the hall of Liberty by Asinius Pollio, the temple of Saturn by Munatius Plancus, a theater by Cornelius Balbus, an amphitheater by Statilius Taurus, and by Marcus Agrippa in particular many magnificent structures." Among the last were the Pantheon, the baths of Agrippa, and the fountain of the Virgin aqueduct, all in the Campus Martius.

The city of Augustus was a magnificent spectacle. Its heart was solid and brilliant with pillared temples, basilicas, and porticoes, with arches and statues, all of gleaming marble from every quarter of the world. Where marble was not employed, there was the hardly less beautiful travertine, the fine-grained, creamy limestone from the great beds by the Anio near the Apennines. Where there were neither travertine nor marble, there was the durable stucco which covered and beautified the walls of kiln-dried brick and indestructible concrete of which the great masses of business houses and dwellings were constructed. The city had a regular, a massive, stable, reposeful look. Columnar and arched construction was everywhere present to the eye, and in the principal thoroughfares the upper lines of palace and apartment house kept an almost steady level of seventy feet.

But it was not a monotonous city. There were marbles of different colors, there were colors applied to frieze and cornice, there were tinted stuccoes, there was gilt and bronze, there were hundreds of little shrines at corners and crossways, with bright-hued flowers on their altars twice in the year at least. There was running water on every hand, in the great ornamental fountains of the aqueduct-heads, and in the smaller fountains and basins for popular use. There were sun-dials here and there. There was the alternation of gay shop front with stately temple and rich palace. There were breaks by market and square. There were the breathing-places of the city where public or private gardens refreshed the eye and the ear with fountain and stream and statue and trim gravelled walks that wound among verdure and flowers. There was not lacking the picturesqueness of the ancient and meaner parts that belong to great cities. The crumbled wall of Servius, half hidden among the crowds of houses, shot up in a tower here and there, and monuments to the age and heroism of departed times were never far away. The rise and fall of hill and valley, the winding river with its massive bridges, the abruptness of the central hills, were not the least aids to variety. The temples and palaces of the Capitoline and the Palatine were outlined in splendid relief against the sky, high in air above the general level of the city's roofs, with the sun shining on their columns and vari-colored cornices and giving sharp line to their lights and shadows.

But here let Strabo the geographer aid the imagination by giving his impression of the city of Augustus. "The Grecian cities are thought to have flourished mainly on account of the felicitous choice made by their founders in regard to the beauty and strength of their sites, their proximity to some port, and the fineness of the country. But the Roman prudence was more particularly employed on matters which had received but little attention from the Greeks, such as paving their roads, constructing aqueducts, and sewers to convey the sewage of the city into the Tiber. In fact, they have paved the roads, cut through hills, and filled valleys, so that the merchandise may be conveyed by carriage from the ports. The sewers, arched over with hewn stones, are large enough in some parts for wagons loaded with hay to pass through, while so plentiful is the supply of water from the aqueducts, that rivers may be said to flow through the city and the sewers, and almost every house is furnished with water-pipes and copious fountains. To effect which Marcus Agrippa directed his special attention; he likewise bestowed upon the city numerous ornaments. We may remark, that the ancients, occupied with greater and more necessary concerns, paid but little attention to the beautifying of Rome. But their successors, and especially those of our own day, without neglecting these things, have at the same time embellished the city with numerous and splendid objects. Pompey, Divus Cæsar, and Augustus, with his children, friends, wife, and sister, have surpassed all others in their zeal and munificence in these decorations. The greater number of these may be seen in the Campus Martius, which to the beauties of nature adds those of art. The size of the plain is marvellous, permitting chariot-races and other feats of horsemanship without impediment, and multitudes to exercise themselves at ball, in the circus, and the palæstra. The structures which surround it, the turf covered with herbage all the year round, the summits of the hills beyond the Tiber, extending from its banks with panoramic effect, present a spectacle which the eye abandons with regret. Near to this plain is another surrounded with columns, sacred groves, three theaters, an amphitheater, and superb temples in close contiguity to each other; and so magnificent, that it would seem idle to describe the rest of the city after it. For this cause the Romans, esteeming it as the most sacred place, have there erected funeral monuments to the most illustrious persons of either sex. The most remarkable of these is that designated as the Mausoleum, which consists of a mound of earth raised upon a high foundation of white marble, situated near the river, and covered to the top with ever-green shrubs. Upon the summit is a bronze statue of Augustus Cæsar, and beneath the mound are the ashes of himself, his relatives, and friends. Behind is a large grove containing charming promenades. In the center of the plain, is the spot where this prince was reduced to ashes; it is surrounded with a double enclosure, one of marble, the other of iron, and planted within with poplars. If from hence you proceed to visit the ancient forum, which is equally filled with basilicas, porticoes, and temples, you will there behold the Capitol, the Palatine, with the noble works which adorn them, and the piazza of Livia, each successive place causing you speedily to forget what you have before seen. Such is Rome."

And the splendid capital teemed with a life as crowded, as varied, and as picturesque, as the city itself. The menials of house and shop were astir at early dawn. The clients knocked at the door of early-rising patrons at cock-crow. High two-wheeled carts from vineyard and garden came laboring up to the customs-gates, paid the tax on their loads of produce, and rumbled into the city, where the markets were alive with slaves and plebeians at their morning trade. The streets that led to the Great Forum and the forums of Cæsar and Augustus adjoining streamed with magistrates and men of affairs and lawyers and clerks on their way to senate and shop and court. Everywhere was the confusion and din of a great city, though in the central parts there was no wheeled traffic by day. The turmoil of busy contractors with mules and workmen, and cranes swinging into place huge beams and blocks of stone, while funeral processions were mingling with trains of ponderous wagons, was maddening to the poet meditating the Muse.

At their posts in the streets and stations were the seven thousand police of the newly organized service. Soldiers and officers in uniform lent color to the throng, and prætorian guards were on duty before the emperor's

THE MAUSOLEUM OF AUGUSTUS

FROM THE OPPOSITE BANK OF THE TIBER;
THE CURVED ROOF ONLY IS VISIBLE

palace and the senate. A fire broke out, and the *vigiles* were soon on the way to the scene. Horace came sauntering down the Sacred Way toward the Forum, and was buttonholed by a bore, who released him only when forced by a court appointment in the near-by Julian basilica. A knot of bystanders gathered to witness the amusing scene. The pontifex maximus with Vestals and attendants passed through the crowd, which respectfully divided, and silently wound his way up the Capitoline to the temple of Jupiter Best and Greatest. The golden colonnade of Apollo on the Palatine was opened, and Horace and Propertius were there to see it, with its columns of richly colored marble from Africa and its statues of the many daughters of the ancient Danaus, surrounding the temple of shining marble and its wondrous doors of storied carving in ivory, its chariots of the Sun above the pediment, its statues of Apollo, Leto, and Diana, and Myron's four oxen that seemed to be alive. A chorus of white-robed boys and girls of noble parentage chanted the *Secular Hymn* in the temple on the Palatine, and passed through the Forum and up the steep to repeat it on the Capitoline. A procession of priests and victims and lordly dignitaries and stately members of the emperor's house moved up the Flaminian Way from the base of the Capitol to dedicate the altar of Peace at the north of the Campus Martius.

Men and women resplendent in bright-hued stuffs were carried in gorgeous chairs or conducted on foot to entertainment or social diversion by retinues of liveried slaves. There were pretentious dinners that lasted from mid-afternoon to early morning, in houses splendid with marble, bronze, and tapestries, and there were friendly reunions of genial spirits in quiet, flowery garden nooks and under opaque arbors, with eating and drinking and reminiscence to the music of brooklet and fountain. There were walks on the sunny dike of the old wall, through gardens that covered the once unsightly ancient burial-ground on the Esquiline. Mæcenas entered the theater after an illness, and was greeted by prolonged applause that was returned in echo by the hills across the Tiber. He sat and chatted with Horace between the acts.

On the sands of the amphitheater, wild beasts by hundreds were slain in the artificial chase, and men butchered each other to make holiday for the roaring mob. The Circus Maximus resounded with the cheers of scores of thousands as the daring driver grazed the posts and whirled on with glowing wheels in the dusty career. In the intervals between heats, Ovid flirted with the not unwilling beauty beside him. The great triumphal procession of the emperor approached from beyond the Palatine, with officers and guards in brilliant uniform, with standards and banners and trumpeters, with captives and spoils and prancing horses and glittering cars, and as the long victorious pomp wound down the Sacred Way,

> And through the bellowing Forum,
> And round the Suppliant's Grove,
> Up to the everlasting gates
> Of Capitolian Jove,

the men and women who had climbed to walls and battlements,

> To towers and windows, yea, to chimney-tops,
> Their children in their arms, and there had sat
> The livelong day with patient expectation

to see great Cæsar pass the streets of Rome, burst forth
in universal shouts of *Io triumphe,*

> That Tiber trembled underneath her banks
> To hear the replication of their sounds
> Made in her concave shores.

The solemn parade of Marcellus' funeral advanced
on the way to the Forum and thence to the tomb, with
somber music and dirge of hired mourners; and dancers
and clowns; and six hundred cars, each bearing an actor
wearing the wax mask and insignia of a distinguished
ancestor of the dead and each preceded by the appropriate number of lictors; and the tokens of the greatness
of the dead; and the funeral torches; and the dead himself, high on the funeral car and couch with face upturned to the sky.

The dead Augustus himself, on a day in August,
was borne up the Appian Way from Campania by an
escort of chosen men, to lie in state in the vestibule of
his home on the Palatine until his impressive carrying
forth on the shoulders of senators to the Forum, where
Tiberius, before the temple of Julius, and Drusus his
son, at the rostra of the olden times, pronounced the
last words of praise over the master of Rome and the
Roman world before his body was reduced to ashes.

THE OLD ORDER AND THE NEW

THESE people, the gowned and bedizened rich, the togaed nobles with their retinues, the nameless multitude in tunic and rags, that fill the streets of the imperial city,—who are they?

They are no longer the Romans of Hannibal's time. The eye of a Scipio Africanus, an Æmilius Paullus, or even a Cato, would be strangely bewildered were it to look on the motley throng that jostle each other in the midst of wealth and magnificence. It might recognize the form and essentials of the city of other times, but it would despair in the search for the old familiar types in the strange faces and strange demeanor of the new. The population has swelled, but changed. The old stock in large part has perished, and new blood has taken its place.

The old stock has perished. When Horace speaks of the young manhood of Rome made fewer by the sins of sires who have whetted the sword against each other instead of the Parthians, he is speaking literal truth. Within the hundred years preceding, there had been twelve civil wars, with their dreadful losses in the field and their still more dreadful, if not such numerous, losses in proscription. Three hundred senators and two thousand knights were on the death-list in the proscription that cost the Ciceros their lives. Four thousand seven hundred were doomed by Sulla on the overthrow of the Marian party. Marius, but a few years before, had hunted and butchered for five entire days the senators and other distinguished men who had sided against him. The victims in the proscriptions were picked men, men of the old stock; two Cæsars, two Crassi, and the orator Antonius were among those slain by Marius. Besides the civil wars, there had been in these hundred years the wars with Jugurtha in Africa, with the Cimbri and the Teutons, with the Italians in their struggle for the franchise, with Mithridates and the pirates, with the Gauls and the Britons and the Germans, with the Parthians and the Spaniards and the tribes along the Danube. And before all these there had been the great Punic wars. At Cannæ and Trasimene, the flower of the Roman citizenry had fallen by scores of thousands. The year after Cannæ, the senate was far below the normal three hundred, and the number of vacancies could not be legally filled. The war with Hannibal alone is thought to have consumed a third of the citizens; and its long drain of seventeen years was continued without intermission by the wars in Macedon, Greece, and Asia that lasted for fifty years, years marked not only by deaths in the field but by loss to the social fabric through the withdrawal from family life of the strongest and most fit.

The old stock fell away, and the new flowed in and mingled with the remnant. Who were the new? They were the strangers from allied cities in Italy and from the provinces who were drawn by the needs of the capital and their own desire for adventure. They were the artists and craftsmen and professionals and traders from Greece and the Orient. They were the discharged soldiers of both foreign and Italian blood. They were the men and women slaves of two hundred years of wars and kidnapping in every Mediterranean land. Ten thousand slaves a day is said to have been frequently the sale at Delos. A hundred and fifty thousand was the result of one campaign in Epirus. It was the regular thing for the captives of a conquered town to be sold with the spoil. Ninety thousand Teutons and sixty thousand Cimbri were sold as slaves after the victories of Marius and Catulus, and Cæsar made a like disposition of fifty-three thousand Aduatici. The number of these unfortunates in Italy at large and in the city of Rome may be estimated from the two great uprisings of 134 and 102 in Sicily, when two hundred and forty thousand slaves were said to have taken up arms, with the destruction on both sides in the five years of the second war of a hundred thousand men, and from the insurrection of Spartacus in 73, when two years of campaigning were necessary to subdue the seventy thousand rebels in Italy. It is estimated that in the most populous time of the city there were two hundred and eighty thousand slaves in Rome, about one to every five free men. Slaves in gangs performed the rough labor of the country estate, and the houses of the prosperous in country and city alike were filled with slaves. Slaves herded the cattle and tilled the soil, paved and repaired the roads and streets, reared the aqueducts and public buildings, were the city's carriers, street-cleaners, and errand-runners, its scullions, cooks, waiters, and valets, its actors and artisans and gladiators, and in many cases its artists, physicians, schoolmasters, and pedagogues. Their lot at the worst was worse than death, at the best a very endurable life. They could be free in all but name, they could purchase freedom from their savings, they could be set free for merit of their own or even for the sake of their owner's pocket. The more frugal and the more gifted did attain liberty in very great numbers, and became freedmen lightly attached to their former masters as clients, soon to sever these bonds and integrate with the mass of the free. They prospered and mingled in marriage among themselves and the humbler Romans and the free from the provinces, and their sons became the well-to-do, the respectable, the better class of the new to fill the place of the better class of the old that was constantly disappearing.

There was thus a great modification in the population of the capital. The patricians now were in large part the fresh creations of Julius Cæsar, who had found the original families so depleted as not to suffice for the proper filling of positions requiring patrician blood. The other nobles were of origin no less recent. The senate under Cæsar, with a membership of nine hundred, comprising soldiers, sons of freedmen, and even Gauls, had been a scandal to Romans of the old school, and Augustus himself had reduced the number and increased the property qualification. Even so, it was now an assemblage mainly of moneyed mediocrities. The middle classes were the plebeians, and the plebeians were the slaves, of a generation or two before, and both had been replenished by the immigrants and captives that had come to the city in pursuit of fortune or in the wake of war. Racially, the result was a cosmopolitan motley. "It is Rome you are dealing with, a city made up of the nations of the earth," wrote Quintus Cicero in counsel to his brother on the winning of votes. Socially, there were still the patrician and the noble élite, there were still the equestrian class and the plebs and the slaves; but they were not of the ancient mould.

Nor was their moral fiber of the old heroic type. The

stern consecrations of the men whose first thought was duty to the state had almost wholly passed. Rustic frugality and simple-mindedness had wholly passed. The ancient and intimate bond between the city and the life of the country had been dissolved. The Campagna was still fruitful, but belonged only to the few, and the vast acres with their population of overseers and slaves saw little of the Romans except as they came to sumptuous villas on a rich man's holiday. The life of the country was no longer projected into the life of the city; the life of the city was extended to the country. The common people not only had no connection with the soil, but were fed in large part at the state's expense on grain imported from distant provinces. The list of those receiving grain at nominal prices when the custom was introduced under Gaius Gracchus had swelled enormously by the time of Clodius, who made the distribution free, and under Cæsar was reduced from three hundred and twenty thousand to one hundred and fifty thousand. The few but already noticeable idlers of Cato's time, for whose benefit the grim old censor would have had the Forum paved with sharp stones, had grown into a monstrous rabble dependent for subsistence upon a government glad to purchase its good will and good behavior on these terms.

Whatever may be said as to the poverty of these recipients of bounty at the hands of the state, and of others who received their gifts from the rich houses of Rome, they enjoyed at least the luxury of that for which they did not render a return in labor or money. And the idle and luxurious poor were matched by the idle and luxurious rich. The day was past when a Fabricius struck a senator from the rolls for having more than ten pounds of plate. For two hundred years the city had levied upon the wealth of the world. In spite of disorders and wasteful wars, the Rome of Augustus found waiting a rich inheritance, and the moment that the question of mastership was settled the coffers of emperor and subject were overflowing with wealth.

The ease, indulgence, and luxury against whose first slight inroads the self-denying Cato had so persistently fought had at last broken down every defence. In 195, the old censor had seen danger in the women's desire for the repeal of the Oppian law, a sumptuary regulation of the second Punic war which forbade the wearing of costly dress and more than half an ounce of gold. The return of soldiers from Asia in 187 with dining-couches finished in bronze and upholstered in precious stuffs, with fancy ornamental tables, "which in those times were regarded as sumptuous furnishings," and with expensive tastes in dining, was called "the first invasion of the city by luxury from foreign sources." "It was from that time that the cook, the meanest of slaves among the men of old both in price and in employment, began to be valued, and what had been mere service began to be considered an art." In 169, the artificial chase in which the ædiles exhibited sixty-three wild beasts from Africa and forty-two bears and elephants was another sign of increasing luxury. Yet, had Cato's vision extended a century and a half beyond his death, he would have agreed with Livy, that "things like these, which in those times were conspicuous, were the merest seeds of the luxury that was to come," and would have been more than ever convinced of the dangers that lurked in prosperity. "I am greatly concerned," he says in the *Origines,* "lest the cheerful times we are now en-

joying bring on too much indulgence. Adverse fortune
tames us, and keeps us in the right idea of duty. Favoring fortune and the lightness of heart it brings are apt
to drive us from the course of good counsel and understanding."

And the effect of ease and indulgence was not only
the weakening, but the degradation, of character. The
Roman had always been practical, and more or less un-
sentimental and hard in dealing with men in his power;
but now the unquestioned possession of authority over
subject and slave, the freedom from effort and responsibility, with the frequent witnessing of the perilous
race, the pitiless slaughter of animals in the shows, and
the cold-blooded setting of man against man in the
sports of the arena, had changed hardness into selfish
cruelty. Worse than all these, there grew up the scandalous evils that affected the life of the home and undermined the foundations of the state. Times had changed
since Cato refrained from kissing his wife before their
daughter and from bathing with his son, and ejected
from office the brother of Rome's most popular general
for besmirching the name of the state by favors to a
harlot. A Clodius by amorous intrigue had violated
religion as well as the home of Cæsar, and escaped
punishment. A Clodia had flaunted her vices in the face
of society and been able to maintain a certain standing.
A Cæsar had been both profligate and pontiff. And now
an Ovid, who had set before the public *The Art of Love,*
could complain of exile in the tones of injured innocence, and the emperor's own daughter Julia could be
almost less an outrage in Roman eyes for being a
woman of the streets than her father for sending her
away to banishment.

Yet, with all its resignation to the seizure of power by a single man, with all its hardness and cruelty, with all its idleness and self-indulgence, with all its security and irresponsibility, the Rome of Augustus retained a conscience. There were still the poets and the moralists. They gathered up the feeling of the age about itself, and left it expressed for their own and after generations to read.

The world was tired of discord and war, and resigned to the idea that the peace it so gladly accepted was possible by no other means. The phrases of Tacitus, writing a short time afterward about the Augustans, are expressive of the truth: "the whole world weary of civil strife"; "they preferred security for the moment to ancient ideals and danger"; "he lured them all with the sweet prospect of peace"; "believing there was no other remedy for the divided state than rule by a single person." The philosophic resignation of Livy, the acceptance of the new by Horace and Virgil, dispossessed though they once had been, the almost total absence of conspiracy against the emperor, the rapid recovery of affairs, were all a great testimony that men were possessed by the desire for peace and stability. When once the desire was gratified and the result seemed permanent, resignation grew into relief and gratitude. The response of the poets to the emperor's advances, their words of praise, the coöperation of one-time enemies, the people's applause, the worship of the Genius of Augustus and the State, are not to be interpreted as mere adulation. The hand that so surely and so quickly created order out of the chaos of a century might well seem divine. The emperor himself and his party at times might well forget the darker episodes in the course of action by which they had reached their end.

For the feeling of the emperor and his friends was hardly that of triumph unalloyed. In the midst of success, their souls were possessed by a sense of disillusionment and skepticism. When Mæcenas had finished the ministerial duties of the day, he slipped off the garment of state and sought refuge in pleasure as the real end of living. Horace was sometimes afraid of being thought to take seriously his own preaching. Augustus himself, at the end of a long and laborious life, called in his friends to his bedside and asked them whether they thought he had played fitly the comedy of life.

If there was not always the skepticism of disillusionment, there was at least its sadness. The ample harmonies of Augustan literature are deepened and enriched by a strain of homesickness and regret. It is not the literature of an age that is satisfied with itself and at rest. It is the literature of an age that has triumphed, but has not triumphed in righteousness as its fathers triumphed in the citizen-soldier days. It is the literature of a city that looks longingly out to the unspoiled life of the fields and the mountain valleys, and back to the austere virtues of the olden time. This is the real meaning of the rich enthusiasm of the *Georgics*, and the gentle rustic moods of Tibullus, and the exquisite country touches of Horace. This is the meaning of Cicero in the generation previous, with his face turned backward to Cato and the great examples before greed for money and lust for power had transformed the Roman realms into civil battlegrounds, and of Lucretius, contrasting the present with the primitive past. And this is the meaning of Livy, the unconverted republican,

THE EMPIRE OF AUGUSTUS

and of Horace, the convert to imperialism. In the age
in which he lives, Livy "sees these modern times, in which
the very strength of a people now long exceedingly
powerful is working its own destruction"; he under-
takes his onerous task with the prospect of relief from
contemplation of the ills which his age has known for
so many years, of relief for at least so long as he loses
himself in reviewing the brave days of old; "either love
of the task he has undertaken deceives, or there has
never been a greater state than the Roman, nor one more
righteous or richer in good examples, nor a commonwealth into which greed and high living set foot so
late, or where humble means and thrift were so long
and so highly honored"; "in recent days, riches have
brought in avarice, and unlimited pleasures the impulse
toward indulgence in luxury and license to the ruin of
oneself and all that belongs to life"; let the reader attend, and see "what has been the life and what the character of the Roman people, and through what men and
in what ways, at home and in the field, its sway was
established and increased, and then let him follow on
and see how, as discipline gradually weakened, character first began to crumble, as it were, and to give way
more and more, until it started on a headlong rush to
ruin and brought us to these times of ours, when neither
our vices can be endured nor their remedies." "This
self-control, this regard for fairness, this greatness of
soul, that in those times belonged to the entire people,"
he says of a famous political event,—"where could you
find it now in a single individual?" Horace almost repeats the words of Livy's preface: "Fruitful of sin, our
times have defiled the marriage-bed, our children, and
our homes; this is the source from which came the stream

of ruin that has overwhelmed our country and people. . . . The generation of our sires, worse than that of our grandsires, has brought forth us their still more worthless children, soon to beget a progeny worse than ourselves."

This is the meaning, too, of Augustan reform. The age was under conviction of sin. It had reached the end it sought, and the end seemed good; but the memory of the means employed would not be gone, and it drove men on to attempt a return to the morals and faith of older and purer times. The woes of the present were the end of a long decline from rectitude and piety. "The sins of thy fathers, O Roman," chants Horace, "though guiltless thyself, thou shalt continue to expiate, until thou hast restored the crumbling temples and sanctuaries of the gods, and their images begrimed with black smoke. Humble thyself before the gods, if thou wouldst rule. From them comes every beginning; in them see every end. It is neglect of the gods that has brought many woes on mournful Hesperia."

This is the meaning, finally, of Augustus himself. Augustus was not alone and single-handed the masterful soldier, the legislator, the builder, the reformer of morals and religion. The man who placed himself at the head of soldiery, overcame his enemies and seized the state, who labored unceasingly and enlisted the talent of the times in the task of reconstruction, who kept to the ancient forms while destroying the ancient substance of the constitution, who used the same bedroom, winter and summer, for over forty years, who disliked pretentious palaces except as they contributed to the dignity of the capital, whose furniture was hardly choice enough for a private citizen, whose ordinary garments were made after the old manner by the women of his household, who ate but lightly and of plain food and was sparing in the use of wine, who worked far into the night, who was afraid of thunder and lightning, suspicious of omens and dreams, and restored the temples and service of the gods, who sternly banished his own daughter once for all and who was not himself free from the stain of vice,—this man was the personification of his age, of its weariness of talk and its despair of peaceful means, of its opportunism, of its pride, of its skepticism and disillusionment, of its regret and its lapses, and of its longing to get right again with men and gods.

Augustus the imperial master was the expression of the political conclusions of the age. Augustus the reformer expressed the conscience of the age. In the massive lump of disorder, selfishness, and cynicism, that conscience was the saving leaven. In the fields furrowed by war, it was the seed of a new Rome.

Rome did not die. The old city of the Republic crumbled, but did not fall. Out of it appeared a new and larger and more splendid Rome, not yet of perfect stature and beauty, but established in the mould of the city that was to come. The Roman state did not disappear. It was recreated from the ruins of the old, to become the greater Rome whose work was to complete with better method what the old had begun. Roman character did not perish from the earth. It lost in part the peculiar virtues of the men who thought and felt in terms of farm and family and city-state, but it lost also their narrowness and crudities.

Roman citizenship was being born again. To be a Roman from now on was to think in terms of the em-

pire, not of the city alone, to think in terms of the
human kind, not of race alone, to think in terms of eternity rather than time. The singer and chronicler of the
earlier days, and the poetry and prose of the later, had
crystallized the character of the brave days of old. They
had done not only that; they had amplified and created.
Now again they took the leaden metal of a rough age,
the character of a ruler and régime that were charged
with rising upon the ruins of ancient liberty, and trans-
muted them to the lustrous gold of an ideal to light the
way for another succession of the generations of men.
Men thought of the perils and escapes of the already
ancient city,—from the Sabines, the Albans, the Etruscan, and the Gaul, from Pyrrhus and Hannibal, from
Antiochus and from Cleopatra, from the even greater
savagery of civil war,—and saw in her the Eternal City.
They thought of the steady advance of the Roman arms
from Romulus to their own day and from the Seven
Hills to the four ends of the Mediterranean world, they
thought of the spread of civilization to barbarian lands,
and of the pacification of warring tribe and nation, and
saw in her the City of Destiny.

V.

GREECE AND ROME

Græcia capta ferum victorem cepit, et artes
Intulit agresti Latio,—

Greece, taken captive, took captive her rough conqueror,
and brought the arts to rustic Latium.

HORACE, Epistles, II: 1, 156-157

Sed quo sis, Africane, alacrior ad tutandam rem publicam, sic habeto:
omnibus qui patriam conservaverint, adiuverint, auxerint, certum esse in
cælo definitum locum ubi beati ævo sempiterno fruantur,—

But, that you may be still more eager in your efforts for the state,
Africanus, consider thus: that for all who have striven to protect, aid, and
increase it there is set apart in the skies a sure abode for blessed enjoyment of eternal life.

CICERO, Somnium Scipionis, 13

Quid dicam insulas Græciæ? quæ fluctibus cinctæ natant pæne ipsæ
simul cum civitatum institutis et moribus,—

What shall I say as to the islands of Greece? which, begirt by waves,
are themselves almost afloat, together with their institutions and morals.

CICERO, De Republica, II: 4, 8

HELLENISM AND ROME

A CULTIVATED Athenian, entering Rome for the first time in the closing years of Augustus' reign, would have been impelled to exclaim first of all at the size and splendor of the capital. Its distances especially would have impressed him. The descent from the Alban slopes into the plain, and the approach up the long, level arrowy stretch of the Appian Way, already bordered by tombs, through the infinite rolling fields of the Campagna; the towering temples and palaces of the Capitoline and Palatine, the massive colonnaded basilicas and temples of the Forum at their base; the profusion of ornament and color everywhere, the endless thoroughfares traversing hill and valley, the spacious gardens, public and private; the magnificent distance of the Flaminian road as it left the base of the Capitoline on its unswerving way through the buildings and monuments of the Campus Martius like a tramping Roman legion; the generous sweep of the broad Tiber and the answering sweep of the Janiculum and its greenery high above,—together produced an effect of amplitude and richness unmatched in any other city.

The stranger from Athens would have cried out next at the many features of Rome that reminded him of his own city. He might have noticed that Rome was situated upon hills in a plain not distant from the mountains and was fifteen miles from the sea, with Ostia as a port, as Athens was situated on rocky eminences in a plain rimmed on three sides by Hymettus, Pentelicon, and

Parnes and was five miles from the sea, with Piræus as
a port. He would surely have noticed that the Capitoline
with its arx and temple of Jupiter was in some sort a
parallel to the Acropolis and the Parthenon. He would
have seen everywhere the column, architrave, and pediment of his native city, in many cases constructed in
the very marble he knew at home. The Roman basilica
would have reminded him of the Athenian basilica by
its form as well as by its name, and the portico would
have reminded him of the stoa. He would have seen in
temple and square and garden and palace a great many
Greek statues and copies of statues. The theaters of
Pompey and Balbus and Marcellus, though not resting
on the rock of hillsides, would have reminded him by
their architecture and appointments in general of the
theater of Dionysus at the base of the Acropolis. If he
had attended a play in one of them, in company with
the thirteen thousand or so Romans who found seats
there, he would probably have been struck by the fact
that the stage setting, the costumes of the players, and
the matter of the play itself, were all Greek. He might
even have recognized the play as an adaptation of
Menander or Euripides. In the great law courts, he
might have been told that the pleader at the bar who
was speaking apparently with much straightforward-
ness and simplicity was an Atticist who patterned after
the Athenian Lysias, and that his more florid opponent
professed the style of Isocrates, but that Cicero, greatest
of all the Roman orators, a generation before had combined the excellences of all the styles.

Had he been invited to dinner by a prominent Roman, the Athenian would have noticed the pillared
atrium, the peristyle, and the triclinium, and commented

on the retention of Greek names here and elsewhere. He
would have been served by slaves with Greek names,
and entertained by dancers, musicians, or readers of
Greek education. The host and guests would have
graced their conversation with Greek phrases, and some
of them would have conversed with the stranger in his
own tongue. If a Horace and a Virgil had been present
and recited from their verses, his ear would have recognized Sapphic or Alcaic stanza and the long roll of the
hexameter, and he would have commented on the way
in which the content of their poetry, as well as its form,
kept him thinking of the ancient Greek lyric and the
Iliad and Odyssey.

"I feel really very much at home in your city," the
Greek might have said, politely. "There is so much in
your architecture and painting and sculpture, and so
much in your literature and history, that resembles our
own, and I find you speaking Greek so well, that as
soon as I get used to the bigness and variety of everything I shall feel as if I were among my own people
rather than among strangers."

After saying this, he might have added: "But then,
you *are* my own people. Your hills were settled by
Greeks, you know, even before Æneas and Romulus,
and Æneas himself was the son of a Greek goddess, and
Troy was of Greek origin if you go back far enough."

"Yes, you are quite right," the Roman might have
replied. "We are indeed kinsmen. Our origin is common, our languages resemble each other, and our purpose in history has been the same. If we Romans seem
to have appropriated your literature and art rather
than to have created our own, it is because our time has
been employed in conquering and organizing the world

and making the spread of a better civilization possible
rather than in attempting to do over again what you
have already done so well. With you, the emphasis has
been upon the creation of enlightenment; with us, it has
been upon the means of spreading and making it of
effect in the far parts of the earth; but our destiny is
the same. We are the two great instrumentalities of the
gods in the work of civilizing the world."

Quite naturally, the Athenian would not have forgotten the exquisite refinement of the Parthenon or the
graces of life in general in his native city, and would
have had his reflections as he looked on the art and
manners, and especially the amusements, of Rome. The
secret thoughts of the Roman would have been busy
with the contrast between the Greek character of his
day and that of the times of Pericles, and with the contrast between them both and the robust vigor of Roman
character. But the thoughts of both would have remained discreetly unexpressed.

In his judgment of Greek and Roman civilization,
the Athenian visitor to Rome in the time of Augustus
had incomparably the advantage of the average twentieth century visitor. The Greek could not only see the
superficial likenesses, but distinguish the essential differences. The modern who makes the acquaintance of ancient Rome, whether through its remains or through lecture and book, sees usually only the merest resemblances.
All his life he is led to associate Greek and Roman
things more or less without discrimination under the
term "classical," with the consequence that he has only
a dim idea that Greece and Rome are separate individualities, and that his ideas as to what constitute these
individualities are dimmer still. He has read and heard

of and seen the classical style in architecture, and sometimes it has meant pure Greek, sometimes Roman, sometimes Renaissance, and sometimes all at once. His thoughts of classical sculpture, painting, and religion are hardly more distinct. If he knows neither Latin nor Greek, the usual medium of acquaintance with Rome and Greece, or knows Latin alone, he entertains the loosest notions as to the traits that distinguished Rome from Greece and the Roman from the Greek.

Lack of opportunity to make real acquaintance with Greece and Rome, however, or failure to seize the opportunity, is not the only obstacle to a better appreciation of their differences. At best, the undertaking is not easy. Let it be the business of this chapter to attempt a division of the word of truth in a really difficult matter.

What glimpses of the sturdy Roman folk in their early stages are possible to us, when as yet they were subject to little more than local influences and the wider world was unknown and almost unheard of, arouse the curiosity as to what their civilization would have become had its course been allowed to run thus undisturbed to a natural end. In such a matter, however, conjecture only is possible, and is of little profit. Such was the number of influences which affected Roman civilization from its infancy up, and such the power of one of them, the Hellenic, that it is only with difficulty that its primitive character can be appraised, and there is almost no part of the finished product which may be called wholly native to the soil of Latium.

Long before Rome became an important factor in history, the cities of central Italy had known something of the civilization of the eastern Mediterranean. Phœ-

nician and Mycenæan had reached the shores of the
peninsula, and, directly or through other peoples, had
left their wares in the markets of the Latin towns. In
their wake, in the course of time, came the great west-
ward colonial movement of the Greeks. There probably
had been groups of Greeks in Italy as early as a thousand years before Christ, but the wave of colonization
reached dimensions only in the eighth century, not long
after the coming of the Etruscans and the founding of
Rome. In less than a hundred years, Cumæ became the
center of a Greek culture on the coasts and islands of
the Naples region; Tarentum, Metapontum, Sybaris,
and Croton were Hellenizing the south of Italy; Rhe-
gium and Zancle were on either side of the straits of
Messina; while Naxos and Catana, to the north and
south of Ætna, with Leontini and Syracuse farther
south and Gela and Selinus to the west, had gone far
toward making Sicily a Greek island. The influence of
Cumæ was soon strengthened by Pæstum, founded
from Sybaris; and the rise of Massilia, the later Marseilles, in 600, at the mouth of the Rhone, was a cardinal event for Rome.

It was not long before the crude city on the Tiber
began to receive from these Greek neighbors something
of greater importance than the mere pottery and stuffs
that found their way to her shops either directly from
their ships and wagons, or indirectly through Etruscan
traders. The alphabet of the Greeks came to Rome in
the earliest days from Cumæ. The Greek system of
weights and measures influenced the Roman. The so-
called Servian reform is thought to bear the marks of
Greek military and political life. The Diana of the
Aventine temple, said to have been an imitation of the

Greek Artemis at Marseilles, was the first image of deity known at Rome. The event was important; the Romans had taken from the Greeks, perhaps with some assistance from the Etruscans, their first lesson in the conception of deity under human form and endowed with human personality. The old formless gods of the field, the forest, and the sky were already beginning to recede from the city.

As time went on and the city increased, nowhere was the influence of Hellenism more effective or more manifest than in religion. At the beginning of the Republic, some four score years after the statue of Diana is said to have been placed on the Aventine, another strong impulse toward the imitation of Greek worship resulted in the first direct appropriation of a Greek cult. The bringing of Apollo and the Sibylline Oracles from Cumæ was the initial event in a series whose end was the naturalization at Rome of all the major deities of Greece. As the strange gods became well known, they were identified with the principal native Italian deities and the two pantheons were blended into one. The Zeus and Hera of Olympus became Jupiter and Juno of Rome; Poseidon and Athena became Neptune and Minerva; Ares and Aphrodite, Mars and Venus; Apollo and Artemis, Apollo and Diana; Hephæstus and Hestia, Vulcan and Vesta; Hermes and Demeter, Mercury and Ceres. By 217, the second year of the war with Hannibal, the process was complete. The Greek deitics had been Italianized in name, and no doubt to some extent in substance. The Italian deities had been Hellenized into gods made in the image of man and possessing personal attributes. The ancient rustic deities were no longer recognizable in them. They had be-

come the gods of a great state religion, with pillared and
pedimented temples and impressive statues, a stately
priesthood in gorgeous regalia, and solemn spectacular
processions moving through the crowded Forum to
public sacrifices before monumental altars on the hills.
Their brothers and sisters, the countless minor deities
of the earliest men of Rome, had faded from the public
life of city and village, and lingered only in the seclusion of the old-fashioned household, and in field and
hamlet remote from the forces of innovation. So far as
the visible life of the capital was concerned, the simple
and unpretentious religion of the olden time had largely
disappeared.

But the change during the first three centuries of the
Republic from simplicity to elaborate and showy form,
and from the many gods to the few, was not the only
transformation wrought by contact with Hellenism. In
the train of Greek religion soon came Greek philosophy.
The religion of Homer's gods, long questioned in their
own land, had given way among intellectual Greeks to
the speculations on the physical nature of the universe
and the moral nature of man whose evolution resulted
in the severe philosophic faith of Zeno the Stoic and the
defiant philosophic skepticism of Epicurus. The process
was repeated at second hand in Rome. Philosophic
thought revealed to the intellectual class among the Romans the fallacy not only of the old-time rustic beliefs,
but also of the newer Greek faiths. Ennius, in the early
second century translating with approval the blasphemous teaching of Euhemerus that the gods were only
glorified benefactors of times long past, was the rude
forerunner, first, of Epicurean lecturers from Greece,
and, finally, of Lucretius, denying both the immortality

THE RUINS OF OLYMPIA

TWO COLUMNS OF THE TEMPLE OF HERA,
IN WHICH WAS FOUND THE HERMES OF PRAXITELES

and the incorporeal nature of the soul, asserting the total unconcern of the gods with human affairs, and crying anathema on all religion. The Stoic, with his more pious teachings of ultimate truth regarding the nature of matter and the soul, was hardly less destructive of orthodox faith.

The cultivated portion of Roman society in the last century before Christ was not on the whole, however, contemptuous of the gods, or even irreverent. The thinking Roman still believed, but not in the usual sense. He believed in maintaining the existing régime because he respected the tradition of his fathers, and because he saw in religion a salutary institution for society in general and for the state. As to the content of religion as conceived by the ordinary uninquiring mind, the intelligent Roman was not only skeptical, but indifferent. It is true that he was only one among many Romans, and that the many, had they considered his attitude at all, would have regarded him as fallen away from the faith; but he represented the evolution of religion, and represented progress. The old faith appealed no longer to right reason or to cultivated sentiment. To the best minds, it had become an instrument of political and social control; to the best hearts, a chill and empty form. As the Etruscan and Greek faiths had filled the native Latin religion with a new life, so now a new faith was needed to fill once more with a fresh vitality the exhausted body of the old. That regenerating contribution was to come from the east, and the process had already begun.

The effect of Greek proximity on the religion of Rome was paralleled by its effect upon Roman literature and culture in general. If the effect is not so strikingly visible until comparatively late in the Republic, the reason is to be seen both in the more intimate nature of religion and in the fact that, with the Roman, religion was a practical interest affecting the state, while the art of letters and the other luxuries of the mind he had to be taught to appreciate.

Prior to the earliest actual contact of the Roman with the Greeks of southern Italy in the first decades of the third century, over two hundred years after the inauguration of the republic, the literary art could hardly be said to exist at Rome. Whatever prose there was consisted of such purely practical compositions as the laws of the Twelve Tables, the simplest public and private chronicles, treaties, and other documents of like nature. Poetry existed only in legal and religious formulæ descended from the earliest days, in the ancient hymns chanted by priests or sung in honor of dead ancestors, and perhaps in a rough form of drama. All of this was in the Saturnian verse native to Latium, a rude measure sounding somewhat like the familiar "The-queen-was-in-the-parlor-Eating-bread-and-honey."

So far, Roman literature was hardly an art. But with the taking of Tarentum in 272, at the close of the war with Pyrrhus, and the extension of Roman administration throughout lower Italy, there began a much more intimate mingling with the Greeks and a much greater familiarity with Greek art. Livius Andronicus, brought from Tarentum as a slave and employed as teacher and craftsman in letters at Rome, marks the visible beginning of Roman literature. His translations of the Iliad and Odyssey for schoolroom purposes, his adaptations of Greek comedy and tragedy performed on Roman holidays at the end of the first

Punic war when Roman officers had brought home from the Sicilian campaigns an enthusiasm for the hitherto unknown Greek stage, and his lyric sung by matrons in procession in honor of Juno on the Aventine, were all in Saturnians, and no doubt crude enough, but they represented the launching of a movement whose effects upon both letters and life were of great magnitude. In less than fifty years after the advent of Græco-Roman literature with Livius, the Saturnian measure as a literary form had practically disappeared, and in less than a hundred an extensive body of Roman literature in Greek form and with Greek content had come into existence, together with much that was really Roman. Ennius, the "father of Roman literature," had written tragedy and comedy and an innocent form of satire, and naturalized the hexameter in his epic, *The Annals of Rome*. Nævius had followed with tragedy and comedy in the Greek manner, but with satire and an epic on the second Punic war which were of Roman stuff. Pacuvius had devoted himself to tragedy alone; Plautus, Cæcilius Statius, and Terence, to comedy. There had been histories of the war with Hannibal composed by Fabius Pictor in Greek and Cælius Antipater in Latin.

In the meantime, Hellenism had found other ways of ingress. Marcellus, in 212, had captured Syracuse and carried rich spoils of art to Rome, to be placed in the temple of Honor and Virtue. Tarentum, recovered from Hannibal in 209, had made another contribution of like nature. Scipio Africanus had championed the cause of broader liberal culture in the education of Roman citizens. Titus Quinctius Flamininus, the hero of Cynoscephalæ, had brought back to the city in 197, in the treasures of the conquered Philip, the first art contribu-

tion of the eastern Greeks to the beautifying of Rome,
and had been elder brother to Greece in the campaign
of its liberation from Macedon. In the renunciation
of power over the Greek cities, the one magnanimous
act in the grand style by the conquering Roman state,
is no doubt to be seen the effect of the now more intimate contact of Roman nobles with the art and letters
of an intellectually superior race. Ten years later,
Fulvius Nobilior had brought home two hundred and
eighty-five bronze and two hundred and thirty marble
statues and placed them in the temple of Hercules of
the Muses, built especially for the purpose. Æmilius
Paullus had toured the great centers of Greece after
Perseus' defeat at Pydna in 168 and radiated fresh enthusiasm to the lovers of enlightenment, and had handed
on the torch to his son, the younger Scipio by adoption,
and through him to the Scipionic circle, including such
men as Terence the writer of comedy, Polybius the historian, Panætius the Stoic, Lælius the administrator
and philosopher, and Lucilius the satirist. Philosophers
and orators from Greece had visited the city, delivered
public lectures, and been received into the homes of
Rome's leading men. In the meantime, too, from the
defeat of Philip of Macedon, the necessities of diplomacy and administration had made Romans more or
less familiar with Greek lands and Greek ideals, and the
increasing number of artists, teachers, traders, and adventurers in general who came to Rome in pursuit of
fortune had contributed to the same effect. To all these
more or less enlightened sources may be added the less
liberalizing but intimate contact with the Greek and
Greek-speaking slaves that now began to throng the
streets of Rome.

The Hellenizing movement of the hundred years succeeding the attempts of Livius Andronicus did not
cease during the century of broils and wars that intervened before Augustus reduced the Roman world to
order. Sometimes its agents were not the disinterested
and generous kind that Flamininus, Paullus, and the
Scipios had been. The sack of Corinth in 146 filled the
public gardens and temple-museums of Rome with the
marbles and bronzes of fallen Greece. The Roman
governors, the commercial exploiter of art abroad, and
the dealer and dilettante at home, by fair means or foul
filled the private gardens, palaces, and shops. Not every
coarse and plundering Verres was matched by a refined
Lucullus, nor every extortionate Appius Claudius by a
Cicero who paid for the art that beautified his villas.
The effect, however, was identical in kind. The daily
sight of Greek art and the frequent discussion of Greek
literature and history familiarized the minds of thoughtful men with Greek ideas. The architecture of the city's
best buildings was as Greek in the impression it made
as the Græco-Roman drama that amused its public, or
the Græco-Roman gods that protected the state. Even
in education a change was perceptible. In spite of the
opposition of practical Romans of the sterner sort, the
Hellenic ideal of cultivation gradually possessed itself
of the minds of the upper class. Men like Scipio and
Lælius, whose vision was too broad for them not to
realize both the greater fulness of life and the greater
usefulness that were the gift of liberal culture, soon
rapidly multiplied, and the ideal of the broader education after the manner of the Greeks at length ceased to
be opposed, though its realization was always limited
to the comparatively few. It was not that the ideal of

Cato and the Roman fathers was discarded or despised; it was only supplemented. Practical training in the elements of reading, writing, speech, and numbers, and in the manly accomplishments, continued as before in all classes; but for all who desired and possessed the necessary talent and means there was added to this the study of Greek and Latin literature, the study of Greek philosophy and rhetoric under Greek masters at Rome, and a period of finishing in Athens, the great center of learning and the arts, or in some center of less fame made important by the presence of a great master; such as Rhodes, where Posidonius taught.

The most fruitful period in the history of Hellenism at Rome was the century of Cicero, Lucretius, Horace, and Virgil, and the greatest figure in it the orator himself. If a personality is needed to illustrate the effect in both intellectual satisfaction and usefulness of Hellenic culture at its best, none will better serve the purpose than Cicero. Nothing on Roman soil could have been more Greek than the education Cicero received after leaving Arpinum at an early age for Rome. Its curriculum, even where the content was Latin, was patterned after the Greek. Its masters were Greek rhetoricians and philosophers, some of whom could not speak the Latin language. The future orator learned to read, write, and speak as readily in Greek as in his own tongue. He used the Greek orators as models and the Greek essayists and poets as mines of intellectual richness. He even kept learned Greeks in his house, and the Stoic Diodotus died under his roof. He spent two years of his early manhood in study at Athens and other cities in Greek lands. Such was the enthusiasm which possessed him that from one of the most active and most anxious lives ever lived he still found time and strength to digest and re-create and transmit the riches of the Greek intellectual life, and thus to place the world of his own and succeeding times forever in his debt.

What Cicero was in prose to Greek thought in general, Lucretius in his poem *On Nature* was to the physical and ethical speculations of Epicureanism in particular; and what both were to Greek philosophy, Virgil and Horace were to the epic of Homer and the lyric of sixth century Greece, and Catullus, Ovid, and Propertius to the later, more ornamental, and less purely Greek poetry of the Alexandrian era, when the Hellenic art of Athens the Periclean capital had passed into the Hellenistic art of the great Egyptian city and other centers in the realms of Alexander's conquest. All these, with Cæsar and Quintus Cicero, the younger Ciceros, Asinius Pollio, Varius, Quintilius, Mæcenas, Augustus himself, and many a lesser poet and patron, were educated in the broader culture, and were saturated with the literature and other arts of Greece. Versifier, dramatist, essayist, and pleader followed the advice and example of Horace and thumbed the Greek exemplars night and day.

The age of Cicero and Augustus was not only the most fruitful period of Hellenism at Rome, but approached the climax and culmination of the Hellenizing movement. That movement may have reached greater numbers of Romans from Claudius to Hadrian, but it never again so vitally wrought on the Roman intellect. What the elder civilization had had to offer had been set before the younger. Whatever the appetite of the vigorously growing younger civilization had required had been seized upon, digested, and assimilated. Greek religion had entered into both the body and the soul of the religion of Rome. Sculpture and painting had contributed all that these arts at Rome could receive. The architecture of Rome had taken from the Greek as much as served its purpose. The rough prose of the rustic Roman had absorbed the substance and been inspired by the form of Greek oration and essay until the tongue and pen of Cicero rivalled the force and refinement of Demosthenes and Plato. Through the poetry of Horace and Virgil, the poetry of Greece had entered into the national life-blood of Rome. The speculative word of the moral philosophers of Greece had been made flesh in Roman living. The lessons of Greek political failure and success had contributed character to the Roman ideal of government. That the man at court or in the salon, the poet and the philosopher, the councillor and the administrator of provinces, should be masters of speech in both tongues, had become the rule of taste, if not of necessity. Rome had grown to the vigor of a world capital, Greece was in the pallor of decline. The life of the Mediterranean world which had centered in the Athens of Pericles, in another form now centered in the Rome of Augustus. The blood of Athens had not been lost; it had been transfused, and circulated now from another heart.

ROME AND HELLENISM

SUCH was the course of Hellenism in the city of
Rome. Such in the main was its course also in the
Latin-speaking centers of the empire at large which reflected the life of the capital. To pass thus in rapid
review the facts of its history, however, is to risk the
danger of believing that the Roman identity had been
transformed or swallowed up by the Greek. The popular mind, indeed, is accustomed to think of the two as
much the same; and there are also those who, even after
more intimate acquaintance, conceive of Roman art as
a barbarous imitation, of Roman literature as a pale
reflex of the Greek, of Roman religion as differing from
the Greek in only the occasional employment of Latin
names instead of Greek for the same deities, of Roman
civilization in general as bearing the relation to Greek
civilization of a poor copy to an inspired original, and
of Rome as at least a Hellenistic city, to be classed with
Pergamum, or Rhodes, or Alexandria, or Athens, or
other centers of Hellenic distribution after the conquests
of Alexander.

If we are to appreciate Roman institutions and Roman character and Rome's contribution to the world's
work, these conceptions must be modified. The contribution of Greece was incalculable, but Rome none
the less remained Rome, and the Roman did not cease
to be a Roman.

In the first place, Hellenism affected at first hand an

exceedingly small part of the population of Rome. The masses, so far as its intellectual and spiritual import was concerned, were all but unreached by the waves of influence whose force grew less in proportion as they radiated farther from their center among the wealthy and ruling classes. Plebeian in the city and rustic in the country, going about their daily life of commonplaces, still worshipped in the manner of their fathers the little gods of home and farm and flock, trained their sons and daughters in the practical affairs of life as their ancestors had done before them, and spoke no language but their own, and that not in the polished phrases of a Cicero, but in its natural vigor, direct, untortured, and idiomatic. They did not recline at exotic banquets, but sat at table and ate sensibly of what belonged to the season and the place. Their pleasures in the city were not those of the refined, but such as suited the taste of the multitude, for whom to the end the excitement of circus and amphitheater and the humor of the mime afforded charms in comparison with which the attractions of legitimate art were nothing. In the country, they continued in the simple festivities of the olden time. They saw Greek architecture and sculpture on occasion, and sometimes went to Greek plays in Latin, but even when not the prey to boredom underwent small change of character. Art had no problems for them, and letters were not necessary to their enjoyment of life. They were not schooled by Greek sages, living or dead, in the control of the passions, nor given to any philosophy beyond the homely good sense always native to the Italian people. The speculations of religious inquiry, the doubts of the skeptic, the exhortations of ascetic and reformer, did not trouble them. They did what tradition had taught them to do, and asked no questions.

Nor must those who belonged to the inner circles be supposed, except in the cases of the very few, to have undergone sweeping change. Whatever their culture, they remained on the whole the same practical, strenuous, and straightforward people. If their ideas of what was really practical in education were broadened, the extended training of the new education looked nevertheless to practical ends. If their sense of the beautiful was quickened by the presence of Greek art, the fact did not communicate to them either the ability to execute, or, very greatly, the desire. They were almost boastfully content that others should mould the figure of bronze or marble, win the palm in oratory or science; their mission, their art, was to bring to the world the blessings of peace under just and merciful rule. If contact with Hellenic culture reacted upon their manners, it did not insure them unerring judgment in matters of taste. Their attempts at refinement resulted too often in mere display. If acquaintance with Hellenic philosophy made them ever so skeptical of religion, they clung none the less to the forms of their fathers, and gave them up only after three centuries of resistance to the Christian faith.

Thus far, we have dealt with the failure of Hellenism to change the Roman individual. In the broader fields of the national life the persistence of character was still more marked.

If the spirit and practice of Roman government were modified at all by contact with the political life of Greece, it was in the direction of contrast rather than of likeness. The Greek continued to look toward the freedom of individual community and individual citizen; the Roman went on as he had begun, bending all his energies toward the consolidation of the whole and the regulation of individual conduct with reference to effect upon the whole. Lucilius, member of the philhellenic Scipionic circle, writing that "the part of virtue is to consider first of all the good of the state, next the good of one's kinsmen, and, third and last of all, oneself," is Greek in the use of hexameter, but deeply Roman in sentiment. The contrast between the two tendencies is reflected by the attitudes of Greek and Roman toward deity; the one characterized by a sunny familiarity and general elasticity of contract, the other by solemn formality and the sternest obligation on both sides. At the death of Germanicus, the stoning of the temples by his Roman lovers was grounded in the feeling that the gods had failed in their obligation. It may be conceded that in the finer arts the Roman possessed much less genius than the Greek, and that he made himself the benefactor of the modern world rather by transmitting to it the treasures of remote antiquity than by creating art of his own, but in the art of governing men he early displayed unquestioned genius, and soon outstripped his teachers by improving on their lessons. If Livy's account of the Servian reform is based on truth, it was the Greek who gave the Roman his first effective instruction in the organization and equipment of a citizen-soldiery; but the space of a few centuries sufficed for the younger people to become the foremost power in the peninsula, and finally to go beyond its borders and conquer and set in order the nation that had been its instructor. In administrative as well as in military science, Rome built up a system which for centuries held the world firm against the assaults of barbarism, which profoundly influenced its government after her fall, and which furnished the model for the organization of the greatest spiritual power mankind has ever seen. Most of all was the legal system of the Roman a creation of his own. At a time when his written language was still unwieldy and obscure, he had already begun to codify his laws; and the result of his thousand years of effort to adjust the relations of men one to another and to the general whole was a body of law which had been called into being by the living needs of people and state, which had been proved by the practical tests of time and constant use, and whose virtue was such that it continued to exist as the basis of the principal legal systems of Europe to modern times, and in many instances still constitutes almost the entire fabric.

But not even in the less original contributions of the fine arts and letters was the change wrought by the impact of Greek upon Roman so sweeping as is often supposed. The architecture of Rome, however plentiful its use of column and architrave in the marbles of Greece, is not identical with the builder's art of Athens, or even a close copy. By tradition, by the convenient presence of great quarries of marble, by physical setting, by the nature of architectural demand in a civilization of diminutive city-states, the Greek was kept faithful throughout to the column-and-lintel ideal of grace and beauty. The Roman, with no tradition but hillside wall and primitive hut, with suggestion from Etruria and Greater Greece, with a great variety of the coarser materials, with the needs of a city of hundreds of thousands and a realm going out to the ends of the earth, evolved the art of building giant utilitarian structures

upon immense foundations of mingled cement and
stone, with vault and arch to sustain and the Greek
orders to adorn. The essential principle of Greek construction is the rectangular; the column and beam are
what make it stand. What made the Roman building
defy the centuries was the partnership of massive wall
and vault; Greek column and architrave were inessen-
tial, and served only to beautify. The Greek impressed
the world with the single exquisite type of the temple,
so perfectly realized that later days have added nothing
to it, and with the lesser beauties of theater and portico.
The Roman accepted the temple, modified it in the direction of greater exuberance and mass, and gave the
round form and vaulted roof a greater currency. He accepted the theater, but with orchestra cut in two and
stage brought nearer the audience. He popularized the
portico. Beyond this, however, he practically created
the monumental aqueduct, the amphitheater and the
circus, the great law-court, the forum-group of public
buildings, the triumphal arch and column, the public
bath, the imperial palace, the wall and castle and city-
camp of the frontier, the bridge, and the road, itself not
undeserving of the name of architecture, and spread
them over all the world, to be useful in their own time
and to inspire the exquisite building of the Renaissance.

In the less practical arts of sculpture and painting,
he was less creative; yet even here he made contributions. For the purely Roman triumphal arch and
column, and for other monuments of the kind, he so developed and naturalized the historical relief and the art
of portraiture that they lost all oriental, if not Hellenic,
character. The stately processions on the altar of Peace
and the arch of Titus, the multitudinous campaign

scenes on the columns of Trajan and Marcus Aurelius,
are neither oriental nor Hellenic nor Hellenistic, but
the national art of Rome. The accurate realistic portraiture of Roman sculpture and Pompeian painting
claims kinship not so much with Greek art as with the
busts and portraits of the early Italian Renaissance.

Roman literature has lent itself in greater degree
than the other arts to the encouragement of exaggerated
views regarding the extent to which Hellenism possessed itself of Rome. Literature is printable, portable,
and easily scrutinized. When the enthusiastic discoverers
and printers of the Renaissance had made Greek letters
available as well as Roman, it required but a glance to
see that Cicero and Horace and Virgil were not the independent creators they had been thought to be, and
that Plautus and Terence and Seneca were even more
indebted to other hands. The fine old figures of the Romans began to look less Roman, and their periods and
verse to ring with a hollow sound. It was the scientific
study of literature, which began in the latter eighteenth
century and has not yet run all its arid course, that first
made known to the world the enormities of Roman unoriginality. The patient and mechanical comparing of
title with title, phrase with phrase, word with word,
syntax with syntax, concept with concept, was made to
reveal that the Roman dramatists had only plundered
from the Greek, that Cicero was a second-rate Isocrates
and his essays a dilution of Plato, Xenophon, and Posidonius, that the early Roman historian filled in his gaps
with Greek material, that Roman criticism was copied
from the Alexandrians, that Horace's odes were a
miscellaneous borrowing from the Lesbians and Euripides, and that Virgil was only an adaptation of The-

ocritus and Homer. The idols revered for centuries were found to have feet of clay. The masters to whom the world owed its ideal of Roman character stood revealed as little better than Greeklings.

The scientific study of literature has usually been true in detail, but often false in the conclusions it has caused to be drawn. There is a difference between mere borrowing and assimilation. The Roman essayist and poet did not plunder or plagiarize; they appropriated. Even in the drama, which in any country and at any time is the first form of literature to be indiscriminately borrowed, translated, adapted, and imitated, the Roman was not without effect. For better or worse, he helped to crystallize its rules, he enriched it by the doubling of plot and characters, gave it a native content in the præ-textata and togata, and inaugurated historical drama. He transmitted the drama of Greece in the Romanized form which in the Renaissance inspired the classical masters of Italy, Spain, France, and England, and developed the mime and the native Atellan play into the forerunner of modern Italian farce.

If in drama, however, the amount of direct transfer is so great as to excuse the charge of unoriginality, this is not true of the remaining forms of literature. Ennius used the hexameter, but his epic was the story of Rome. We have noted that Lucilius wrote in the same Greek form, and with others of the Scipionic circle stood for Greek culture, but there is little in common with the spirit of Greek literature in the strenuous and stern patriotism, the contempt for affectation, and the disregard for polish which characterize this son of Italian soil. It would be hard to find anywhere in Greek literature the militant hedonism, the stoical Epicureanism,

the religious unbelief, the fervent passion for calm and
quiescence that distinguished Lucretius, whose meter is
Greek, whose science is from Greek sources, and whose
philosophical system is Greek, but whom no one ever
thought of as anything but Roman, as no one ever
thinks of the passionate loves and hatreds of Catullus
as anything but Italian. Tibullus belongs only to the
landscape of the Roman Campagna and the Sabines,
Ovid and Propertius to the streets and drawing-rooms
of social Rome, Livy, Tacitus, and Juvenal to the imperial capital fallen from the faith of its fathers, Pliny
to the court-room and the respectabilities of middle-
class success, Martial to the cosmopolitan city whose
endless variety invited the spectator and provoked the
satirist.

The comparatively little internal and essential effect
of Hellenism upon either Roman literature or Roman
character is illustrated by Cicero's works and life. It is
possible that Cicero was less Roman than many others
of his time, and that his intimacy with the best thought
of Greek literature may be looked upon as the cause
which contributed most toward making him the lover
of the gentler aspects of life who in the intervals of
action enjoyed the library and the villa, his family and
friends, and who cared little for a coarse stage and the
rough sports of the amphitheater. Yet, "Rome's least
mortal mind" though he was, he was thoroughly Roman
in his absolute devotion to the state. He was an idealist
in everything pertaining to its welfare, his having served
it was his proudest boast, its downfall was his deepest
sorrow, and his resistance to its enemies in the time of
need cost him his life. However he may have failed in
vision, his patriotism was that of the good old times

when the citizen-soldier held no parley with the enemies
of the republic. The sentence in which he expresses his
anguish of soul at the overthrow of the old régime is
worthy to be placed beside the stanzas of Horace on the
return of Regulus to Carthage and death: "I have
mourned for my country longer and more deeply than
a mother ever sorrowed for her only son."

In spite of his broad and deep culture, too, Cicero
shared with his race the practical bent for which it has
always been noted. He was indeed broader than old
Cato in his conceptions as to what constituted the practical, but he was thoroughly practical none the less.
However much to his liking the Greek language and
literature, the methods of Greek masters, and his two
years of sojourn and study in Greek lands, he looked
upon them all primarily as means to the practical end
of becoming a finished orator and pleader and rising to
leadership in public life. He regarded all knowledge
and all accomplishments as tools to be used in achieving
his ambition. "The poets, too, must be read," he writes
in *On the Orator,* "one must know history, all teachers
and authors in the field of the liberal arts must be read
and thumbed, and, for the sake of exercise, praised, interpreted, corrected, adversely criticized, refuted. Every
subject must be discussed from contrary points of view,
and whatever in them seems capable of proof must be
brought to light. One must have a thorough knowledge
of common law, be well acquainted with the statutes,
be cognizant of all the past, be familiar with the ways
of the senate, the discipline of the state, the law of nations, treaties, conventions, the basic principles of government. One must also dip into every sort of urbanity
and acquire a certain charm of witty speech with which,

TUSCULUM AND THE ALBAN MOUNT

THE TUSCULAN VILLA OF CICERO WAS IN THE VICINITY

so to speak, like salt, to sprinkle all his discourse." In Cicero, the orator and stylist swallowed up everything else. It is true that, both as a student and in his later years, he loved the philosophical content of Greek letters, but his enthusiasm for its purely æsthetic qualities, at least in poetry, is open to question.

For other forms of Greek art aside from letters, Cicero cared little. What he has to say of them is not only so scant as to show that they had no appreciable place in his interest, but consists, almost without exception, of reference merely for illustration, and conventional in the extreme. The sculptures with which he adorns the Tusculan villa are shipped from Greece, but are valued more for their appropriateness than for intrinsic art value. The great names and the great works of the golden age of Greek art are mere commonplaces to adorn the pages of the stylist or the paragraph of the barrister. His acquaintance with them is only superficial, and his enthusiasm, in spite of repeated experience on Greek soil and contact with Greek art in Magna Græcia and Sicily, is less than his knowledge.

In a word, in his attitude toward art in general, in his roughness and directness of attack in the orations, in his occasional descent in them to coarseness, in his complete devotion to country, in his regard for knowledge and accomplishment as first of all a means to practical ends, Cicero represents thoroughly the spirit of Roman character; and even his more refined tastes and qualities are more reasonably accounted for as the legacy of a father fond of retirement and books than as the contribution of contact with Greek letters. And what is true of his character as a man is true also of his works. The essays on rhetoric are the summing up of Roman achievement in the art of speech. Despite their debt to the masters of Greece, the orations are a Roman product. The letters are a great searchlight playing upon the darkness of Rome the city and Roman lands and Roman character in an era unmatched for interest in the whole course of Roman history. The essay *On Old Age,* in spite of whole paragraphs from Xenophon and Plato, is the expression of Roman national and individual character, and the other moral essays are hardly less saturated with Roman experience.

What is said of Cicero's life and works may be said with as much truth of Horace and Virgil, in whose education Greek was quite as prominent, and in whose poetry there is even a greater abundance of the marks of Hellenism. Their debt to Greek letters is great indeed. Greece gave to them, as it gave to many others, the metrical conveyance of their poems, no small part of the substance of the poems themselves, a wealth of ornament, much of the richness of their intellectual furnishing, and a measure of their sureness in taste and execution. But the real Horace is an Italian poet, and a Roman. He is Italian by birth and experience, Italian in person, habit, and temperament, Italian in his love of Italy's natural charms and the life of her people, Italian in his homely wisdom. He is Roman in his pride in Rome's past and present, in his faith in her destiny, and in the intimate relation of his art to life. He is a national poet, the interpreter of Italian landscape and life, of Roman ideals as expressed in the Augustan régime, of the religion and philosophy of the simple householder in town and country, of the more sophisticated conclusions of the educated class. The *Satires* and *Epistles,* with such parts of the *Odes* as are most in tune with their mellow strain, are among the world's most original achievements in letters. The *Eclogues* of Virgil are indeed but youthful and frigid performances, like the great mass of Theocritean imitation throughout the ages; but the *Georgics* and the *Æneid* are tossed aside as bloodless imitations of Hesiod and Homer only by facile critics who have never felt the genial charm of Italy or been impressed by the grandeur of Rome.

Finally, in an account of the many details of Hellenic culture which entered Rome, it should not be forgotten that the process covered hundreds of years, and that the apparently easy invasion met in many cases a real resistance. If Hellenism had really gone far in the changing of Roman civilization, the slightness of its effect on the Latin language would be strange. In spite of original kinship, in spite of a borrowed alphabet, in spite of early religious and literary schoolmastering, in spite of later mingling of manners and speech in the streets of the capital, the language of the Romans resisted and remained itself. A greater contrast between individuals of the same family would be hard to imagine than that between the dignified and disciplined tongue of the Romans, in which every word and every syllable keep place in the ranks and the periods advance with the sure and steady precision of marching legions, and the elastic and supple Greek, which never hesitates to transgress at the bidding of impulse, with a sunny confidence that gracious breaking of the law will bring its own pardon.

The contrast between the two tongues is but a reflection of the contrast between the two races, and the resistance of the Latin language to Greek is a reflection of the resistance of Roman character and culture in general to Greek. With what opposition the encroachments of Greek religion on the soil of early Latium were met, witness is lacking, and we are left to imagine. Even supposing, however, that the religious ideas and the cults of Greece found easy entrance into the young state because of the toleration which seems never to have opposed a strange religion provided it threatened no moral or civic damage, and supposing that Greek architecture, sculpture, and letters received a ready welcome, there were other invasions of the Greek which were obstinately resisted. This was notably so in education, which was always of moral and civic import to the Roman. To the citizen-soldier of the early day, the Greek ideal of symmetrical development of all the faculties at once may have seemed appropriate for Greeks on the soil of Greece, but how it was necessary to his own ideal of citizenship he did not see. On the contrary, he could not understand how it could be other than dangerous. In his eyes, the speculations of philosophy and the subtleties of dialectic were hair-splitting and triviality, not to say immorality. To compose in Greek, to criticize Greek poetry, to appreciate the beautiful in statue and painting or architectural part, were not only beside the point, but weakened and corrupted manhood and unfitted Roman youth for the common sense duties of Roman citizenship at home and in the field. It was this belief in the dangers of individual indulgence in the non-civic accomplishments and in the free thought of philosophic inquiry that caused the public burning in 181 of the so-called *Books of Numa,* a number of rolls on pontifical law and the theory of wisdom discovered in mysterious chests of stone at the base of the Janiculum, the expulsion from the city of two Epicurean teachers in 173 on the ground that they were dangerous

to Roman youth, the decree of 161 forbidding Greek
philosophers and rhetors a longer residence, and Cato's
motion of 155 in the senate to dismiss from Rome, where
they had come on a political mission, the three philosophers at the head of the principal schools at Athens. It
was this spirit that prompted the tearing down in 150,
at the instigation of a Scipio himself, of the partly completed theater of Longinus, condemned as an encroachment of luxury because, like the Greek theater, it had
permanent seats of stone. It was this spirit that lay at
the root of Cato's stubborn hostility to Greek culture
in every form.

The opposition of Cato was so virulent that it seemed
to sum up and include in itself the hatred of all the old-
school Romans. With him and with his following, natural bitterness on grounds of moral danger to Roman
citizenship was intensified by political circumstance. The
Scipios, Flamininus, Paullus, and their like, who, partly
by attraction and partly by shame at the deficiencies of
their countrymen, had assumed the championship of
Hellenic culture and Hellenic cities, represented to the
censor not only the aristocracy, but the aristocracy who
had drawn Rome into the troublesome and expensive
business of a sentimental protectorate over distant and
unworthy lands. When reaction against the idealist
foreign policy gathered head, it was the Catonists who
gave it momentum. The blasphemous old patriot mocked
at all Greek culture, declared Socrates a monstrous
chatterbox who would have subverted the citizenry of
Athens, and predicted that the rule of Rome would be
at an end if she allowed Greek letters to infect her.

Perhaps Cato's taking up of Greek literature at an
advanced age is the sign of his at last having learned to

see the injustice of condemning at one stroke all things
that were Greek because luxury and sophistry had first
come to Rome with men from Greek lands. If this is
the case, it does not mean that he thought the better of
Greek character. Not only he, but Romans in general,
and even many of the philhellenic, retained to the end
their contempt for the person of the Greek. Nor were
their dislike and distrust directed to the contemporary
Greeks only, a conquered and humiliated race represented at Rome by slaves and fortune-hunting professionals and quacks and abroad by toadies and evaders
of the law; they thought of Greek character, ancient
and modern, as always the same.

"If there has ever been among our people any person
not disinclined to cultivation in those studies and not
without good will toward them," says Cicero of Greeks
and Greek education in the oration for Flaccus, charged
by Greek cities with extortion, "I think that I am such
a one now, and that I was still more in my days of
greater leisure. There are among that people many
good, cultivated, and decent men, who have not been
brought here to this trial, and many brazen, illiterate,
and worthless whom I see appearing, stirred up for
various reasons. This, however, I must say about the
race of the Greeks: I grant them letters, I grant them
skill in the teaching of many branches, I do not deny
them charm in conversation, acuteness of intellect, and
flow of eloquence, and, finally, if there is anything else
they lay claim to, I will not dispute them; but scrupulous good faith in the giving of testimony, that nation has never observed, and of the force, authority, and
right of the whole matter they have no idea. . . . One
of our own people on the witness stand, how he keeps

himself in hand, how he guards his every word, how fearful he is of saying anything in anger, or of speaking more or less than is called for! Do you suppose for a moment that they do the same? With them an oath is a jest, the giving of testimony a game to be played. . . . To pass over the Greece of today, long now shattered and ruined by its own counsels, let me say that the famous Greece of days past, once flourishing in wealth, authority, and glory, fell because of this one evil, the unlimited and unrestrained freedom of popular assembly."

Again, in his essay *On the State* he is thinking of Greek character in permanence: "What shall I say as to the islands of Greece, which, begirt by waves, are themselves almost afloat, together with their institutions and morals?" Livy entertains a like opinion of Greek lightness: "The Athenians, you see, were waging war against Philip with letters and talk, the only weapons with which they are strong." Virgil's tale of Sinon and the taking of Troy, his famous comparison of Roman and Greek in the sixth book of the *Æneid,* and the astute and evasive Ulysses of Roman literature, are all alike reflections of the Roman idea of the Greek. Augustus turned Greek phrases, but probably never thought of a Greek as a social equal. It is easy to imagine Greece and the Greeks all but absent from his thoughts and Julius Cæsar's as they were about the Roman task of setting in order a world in which the Greeks counted for little more than bystanders. Tiberius forbade Greek words and phrases in the senate records. The favor of Claudius was academic, the exhibitions and plunderings of Nero were less expressive of the love of Greece than the love of self, and Domitian in

Greek costume presiding at Greek games is suggestive
of the fad. Vespasian's endowment of Greek professors
and the education of his sons in Greek were probably
the tribute of the bluff old Roman soldier to a genius
he suspected rather than understood. Hadrian's enthusiasm was based on travel and study and real appreciation, but marked the culmination of the so-called revival under Claudius. Whatever the contribution of
Hellenism to life and letters under these emperors, it
can be regarded as only slight compared with that of the
times of Cicero, Virgil, and Horace.

We must conclude, then, in spite of the imposing
array of facts denoting the contact of Greek with Roman, that neither the character of the Roman nor the
character of Roman civilization was changed, if by
change is meant the loss of identity. The natural cleav-
age that exists between the east and the west in the
Mediterranean today was only less pronounced in ancient times. The Roman became in no sense a Greek,
and the march of Roman civilization through the centuries did not swerve. It marched with firmer and more
elastic tread, but it remained the tread of Rome. That
Hellenism contributed to Roman culture and character
is beyond dispute, but it did not contribute by taking
possession of Rome. It did not possess, but was itself
possessed. It did not swallow Romanism, but was swallowed up in Romanism. Its real contribution was not
external but internal, not to the members directly but
to the blood. It was one of the meats in the world-diet
from which Eternal Rome received nourishment and
strength for her task.

VI.

THE ROME OF THE EMPERORS

Nec ignoro ingrati et segnis animi existimari posse merito, si obiter atque in transcursu ad hunc modum dicatur terra omnium terrarum alumna eadem et parens, numine deum electa quæ cælum ipsum clarius faceret, sparsa congregaret imperia ritusque molliret et tot populorum discordes ferasque linguas sermonis commercio contraheret ad colloquia et humanitatem homini daret, breviterque una cunctarum gentium in toto orbe patria fieret,—

I am not unaware that I am open to the charge of being ungracious and slothful if I speak thus casually and in passing of the land which is at the same time the fosterling and the mother of all lands, chosen by the will of the gods to add glory to heaven itself, to gather into one fold the scattered nations of the earth, to humanize their religion, by the mingling of speech to draw into one communion the discordant and barbarous tongues of the many peoples, to confer enlightenment upon the human race, and, in brief, to become the one parent-land of all the nations in the whole world.

PLINY, N. H., III: 39

Ut enarrabilis gratiæ per totum mundum diffunderetur effectus, Romanum regnum divina providentia præparavit,—

That the working of unspeakable grace might be spread abroad throughout the whole world, Divine Providence prepared the Roman empire.

LEO THE GREAT, A.D. 440-461

1.

THE GRANDEUR THAT WAS ROME

FOR good and ill, the collective vigor and wisdom of Augustus and his staff of soldiers and statesmen, together with the irresistible movement of events which modern men call nature and evolution and the ancients thought of as Fate or Destiny, had given definite shape, and almost definite limits, to the Roman empire and the city of Rome, and determined the traits of Roman character. The history of the two centuries that follow is only the story of how the shape of empire and city was modified, and the limits fixed, and how the Roman character comported itself.

The bounds of the Augustan empire, maintained and stabilized by Tiberius, who had been a chief instrument in their definition, were first extended by Claudius. Britain, on whose remote and secluded shores no invader's foot had been planted since Cæsar's visit ninety-seven years before, again felt the power of Roman arms in A.D. 43. The Claudian conquests of seven years, almost undone by the great rebellion of Boadicea in 61, were confirmed and carried farther into west and north by the generals of Vespasian, Titus, and Domitian. Marked under Hadrian by the drawing from the Solway to the Tyne of the great rock wall seventy-four miles long, with its ditches and dike and roads, and its turrets and mile-castles and twenty-three permanent camps, whose remains form one of the modern world's most picturesque and moving monuments, again extended for an interval of time by the wall of Antoninus

Pius from the Clyde to the Forth, these conquests were kept secure in the peace and comforts of civilization until, three centuries later, the decaying empire itself was obliged to detach the hands now clinging in desperation to Mother Rome. In similar manner, through the spacious solitudes of the gap between the waters of Rhine and Danube ran the great palisade of Hadrian, and, a century later, the long two hundred and thirty-two miles of wall and fosse from Rheinbrohl to Regensburg, with its fifty-eight camps, a definite line protecting the Roman Peace from the assaults of crude and unstable barbarism. On the Rhine itself, the Roman cities of Colonia and Mogontiacum, now Cologne and Mayence, became the capitals of lower and upper Germany, whose limits reached beyond the stream. On the lower Danube, Trajan in the two campaigns that ended in 106 reduced to submission the land of the Dacians, now Roumania, and completed the march of the long line of defence from Scotland to the Black Sea. Farther east and south, the fluid boundary of Augustus in Asia, at first made firmer by Nero's achievement of friendly peace with Parthia on terms of the Armenian protectorate, and then established for the moment on the Tigris by Trajan's annexation of the protectorate, and of the Tigris and Euphrates valleys, was definitely fixed by Hadrian's drawing of the line back to the Euphrates; though Mesopotamia did not cease to be the aim of imperial ambition. On the south, from the ancient seat of the oldest civilization, divided into upper and middle Egypt and the Delta, the Roman border, protected by camp-city and desert, ran an irregular course along the south of the long and narrow fringe of fertility, planted with three hundred Roman towns, whose

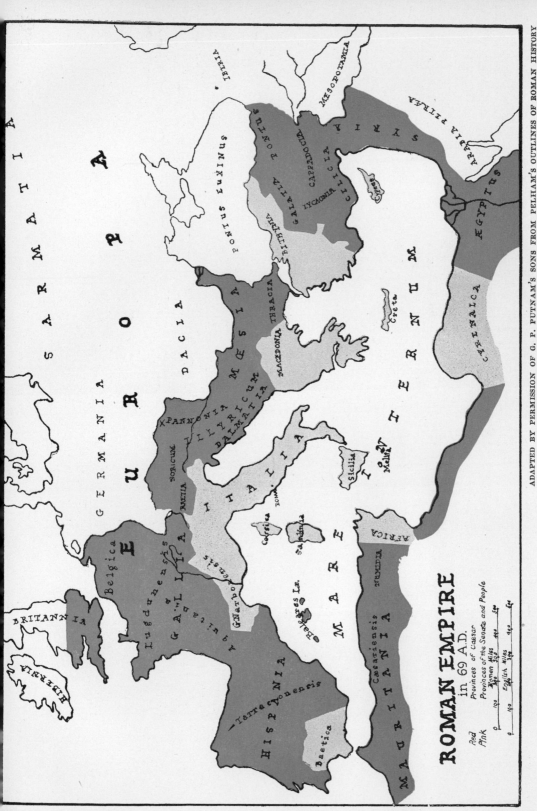

ROMAN EMPIRE
in 69 A.D.

Red — Provinces of Caesar
Pink — Provinces of the Senate and People

Roman Miles
0 100 200 300 400 500

English Miles
0 100 200 300 400 500

SARMATIA

EUROPA

GERMANIA

BRITANNIA

HIBERNIA

GALLIA
Belgica
Lugdunensis
Aquitania
Narbonensis

HISPANIA
Tarraconensis
Baetica

MAURITANIA
Tingitana
Caesariensis

AFRICA
NUMIDIA

MARE INTERNUM

ITALIA
Roma

Corsica
Sardinia
Sicilia
Malta

Baleares Lr.

RAETIA
NORICUM
PANNONIA
ILLYRICUM
DALMATIA
DACIA

MOESIA
MACEDONIA
THRACIA

Pontus Euxinus

BITHYNIA
PONTUS
GALATIA
CAPPADOCIA
LYCAONIA
CILICIA

Cyprus
Creta

SYRIA
ARABIA PETRAEA

AEGYPTUS
CYRENAICA

MESOPOTAMIA

ADAPTED BY PERMISSION OF G. P. PUTNAM'S SONS FROM PELHAM'S OUTLINES OF ROMAN HISTORY

THE ROMAN SWAY IN 69 A.D.

western end was Tangiers and the coast. Carthage, again arisen, was the world's third city, Alexandria the second. Across the straits, the Spains and Lusitania, with capitals at Tarraco, Corduba, and Emerita, and Gaul, with its thriving and cultured cities in the Rhone valley and its widely distributed Roman posts, brought the empire's limits to the western ocean.

The empire shaped by Augustus may thus be said to have reached substantially its limits under Trajan, to have settled itself solidly into them under Hadrian, and thenceforth, with the exception of incursions into Mesopotamia, to have made its sole task the maintenance of boundaries and the tutelage of the civilization which was working out its destiny within the protecting lines. It was no idle or unimportant task. The empire stretched from the Spains to Mesopotamia, three thousand miles, from the Tyne to the upper Nile, from the sands of the Sahara to the wilderness of Scythia.

Nor was the task meanly performed. Already bound by ties of gratitude and pride at the end of Augustus' reign, the diverse and widely sundered parts of the empire, ever knitting more closely as the rich blood of Rome coursed through their members, became by the end of the second century the world's foremost example of unification. Its two great languages existed side by side, each making conquest in its proper sphere, the Latin penetrating Hellenic lands as the language of administration, the Greek making way in the west as the language of culture. Its administration was uniform in type and firm, yet varied and liberal to suit the needs of nature among its diverse peoples. It had upwards of fifty thousand miles of magnificent highway, and they that went down to the sea in ships were assured of paths

unhindered. Its travel and commerce were more fluid
and easy than ever again till the age of steam. Its manners and methods were Roman everywhere in the north
and west and south, and penetrated only in less degree
the ancient east. The Roman building remains are alike
whether in England or on the Sahara's edge, at Rome
or Athens, on the Nile or on the Rhine. The camp-towns
of Amboglanna and Timgad, the villas at El-Djcm or
in Belgium, are all of the mark of Rome. Its aqueducts
were ministers to every city of size. The remnants of
more than seventy amphitheaters are known, and hardly
the humblest town was without its theater, baths, and
forum after the fashion of Rome. There were upwards
of five hundred memorial arches and gates, and countless other honorary monuments, dotting its length and
breadth as the signs of triumph in peace and war. The
temples, shrines, and altars of Roman gods were everywhere, and the religions of all the varied and polyglot
nations were welding into one. Mobile trader and soldier spread the faith of the humbler classes; teacher,
lecturer, philosopher, and publisher mingled the intellectual currents.

In a word, the ancient world had been Romanized in
material ways and means, in manners, in thought, in
religion. Nor was it Romanized by mere force. The
hold of the empire was not the throttling grasp of the
tyrant, though its firmness allowed no question. Many a
land, indeed, like Greece, passed more or less willingly
to Roman control; but in other cases the results were
like. After the first bitterness of conquest or annexation
had passed, and Roman rule could be known by its
fruits, the imperial government concerned itself as little
as it might with detail, leaving the subject nations to

ROMAN BRIDGE OVER THE GUADIANA AT MÉRIDA

THIS WAS AUGUSTA EMERITA, FOUNDED IN 23 B.C.,
CAPITAL OF LUSITANIA AND CALLED THE SPANISH ROME

ONLY PARTS OF THE BRIDGE ARE FROM ROMAN TIMES

follow their own established customs wherever these did not conflict with its own necessities.

"It governed from on high and afar," says Franz Cumont, writing of how Belgium was Romanized, "and the tyranny of central authority, the despotism of state, and the interference of bureaucracy, were much less during the first centuries of the Empire than with most modern nations. The Cæsars limited themselves to maintaining order and security, and to the exaction, in return, of military service and the payment of taxes. . . . No violence had constrained their subjects to abandon native customs, beliefs, or language."

Belgium was only a type. Proud in the consciousness of its own superiority, the state relied only upon the spread of its civilization for the transformation of conquered peoples, who acknowledged the moral conquest and submitted their wills in a spirit of conciliation which no enslavement could ever have secured. Rome gave them peace by ending their wars of ravage among themselves, and assured them prosperity by opening up the ways between them and the outer and richer world. It educated them.

"In the lands governed by Rome," says Haverfield, "instruction was better under the Empire than at any other time from its fall to the nineteenth century." The survival of Latin in Portuguese, Spanish, French, Sicilian, Sardinian, Italian, and far away Roumanian is the most eloquent proof of the power of Roman civilization. Even Greece, whose superior language and culture remained themselves, received and acknowledged the benefits of Roman rule. Whatever liberties it lost were probably more than counterbalanced by freedom gained. "For see," writes Plutarch, "that if we enumerate the greatest blessings which polities enjoy,—peace, liberty, material prosperity, populousness, and harmony,—as far as peace is concerned the communities have nothing to desire from their politicians: every Greek, every barbarian war has departed from us and vanished; as regards liberty they have as much as the rulers accord to such communities, and perhaps as much as is good for them. Good seasons and populousness are blessings to be sought from the gods."

The rapidity as well as the thoroughness with which assimilation took place is witness to the potency of Roman culture. The Belgians, "bravest of all the Gauls because farthest removed from the civilization of the Rhone province," within two centuries of the day that Cæsar overcame the Nervii, had adopted "the speech, the government, the manners, and even the religion of Rome. Prosperous cities and villages were being administered according to the laws of a race of jurists. Villas in which could be found all the refinements of luxury rose in countrysides made fruitful. An extensive commerce brought to industrious populations the products of their neighbors' activities, and even those of the far away Orient. And an ardent spirit of loyalty rendered thanks to the emperors for all these benefits assured by their protection." Not an inscription in Celtic or Germanic has been found in all Belgium; as in Britain also, Latin, and always correct Latin, is the language of the stones. "At the time when idolatry disappeared, it is doubtful whether in all the extent of the Gallic prefectures there existed a single temple where ceremonies were celebrated according to ancient local rites and in the native idiom."

If a farther testimony to the appeal of Rome is

needed, it may be seen in the ease with which the Roman
Peace was kept among its hundred million citizens and
subjects. The standing army employed in all the vast
realm three thousand miles from west to east and two
thousand from south to north, including the most diverse lands and nations, was a bare three hundred thousand men, and these were distributed in permanent
city-camps along the infinite reaches of the great circumference rather than at points within, with duties which
at many places and times were civic rather than military.
All Gaul was held by one garrison of twelve hundred
men at Lyons. There were in Asia five hundred towns
without a single garrison. The cities of the empire conformed to the Roman type. Wherever the Roman
standards had been planted, the organization and institutions of Mother Rome were repeated, and one more
living cell was added to the great organism. Rome was
not mistress of the world; she was its heart. When we
contemplate the extent and variety of the lands whose
destinies were shaped by her, and reflect on the peace
of centuries, disturbed only by border warfare and the
momentary conflicts of emperor unseating emperor, and
contrast the ancient state of these lands with the modern, the word of Gibbon no longer savors of exaggeration: "If a man were called to fix the period in the history of the world during which the human race was most
happy and prosperous, he would, without hesitation,
name that which elapsed from the death of Domitian
to the accession of Commodus."

It is against this imperial background that the city
of Rome must be set if its proportions and character
are to be appreciated. The Rome of the emperors was
no longer the city-camp of regal and early republi-

can days whose ambitions aimed no farther than at the building of Latium and Italy into a compact unit; nor the victorious city-state of the late Republic, unwieldily exploiting her provincial farms; nor even the Rome of Augustus, the responsible mistress of a wearied and submissive world. City and empire had completed the process of growing into one. By the time of Hadrian's death, Rome was the capital city of a unified and solid state of which she herself was an organic part. Distant and diverse cities shared and repeated the life of Rome, and Rome was compounded of the empire's life.

Just as the empire had been but slightly extended or altered in outline from Augustan to Hadrianic times, but had settled into its mould and taken permanent shape, so the area covered by the city was not greatly changed, but only established within the limits which were to define its form for eighteen hundred years. The outline of Rome was indeed not to be given the concrete-ness and precision of the line of a walled town until a century and a half from Hadrian, but the limit that divided city from suburb and country in the time of the early emperors was no less definite. That line was the customs-limit of Augustus, enclosing the fourteen re-gions of the city and protecting its merchants against the easy prices of outside rivals. Extended by Vespa-sian at his survey of the year 73 to include the outer parts of the Esquiline, it was pierced by thirty-seven gates, a few of which may have been the gates of the ancient Servian wall where the barriers touched its course, while the far greater number were architectural street openings through the line where it ran outside the wall. It was this customs-limit, marked by stone pillars at intervals between the gates, which in the main determined the course of the wall when Aurelian's engineers closed in the open city with its monumental fortification.

And, just as the changes in the great organism of the empire were not in the pushing forward of boundaries, but in the enrichment of life within the far-flung lines of the Roman army along wall and stream and desert, so the changes in the city itself were less those of outline and extent than those of character. The Rome of the first two hundred years of the Empire grew ever more wonderful to look upon, its population multiplied, and its life progressed from change to change.

The Rome which Augustus had repaired, restored, adorned, and amplified, whose limits he had determined, whose streets he had lighted and policed, whose life he had set in order and enriched, was not without its imperfections. The new city was heir to a city already ancient and long neglected. Its legacy was not only the time-worn temples and public architecture whose restoration was more or less unhindered, but crowded quarters threaded by narrow streets and crooked alleys like cañons, where tall living-houses were decayed and crumbling, and where ownership was in dilatory hands, and the only renovation was that performed by speculators who bought up and wrecked the buildings whose fall was imminent, or that which was forced by their actual tumbling to the ground. Before the city could really become "the golden Rome possessing the treasures of all the world," it needed purification in its meaner parts.

Such purification the city received. Its agent was fire. The Rome of ancient times did not enjoy the immunity from fire of the modern Italian capital. Its crowded sections of tenements largely built of wood, its market districts packed with shops and magazines containing easily combustible wares, its frequent public buildings with frames and roofs of timber, its inadequate means for the fighting of fire, the cramped spaces that hindered the use of the means, were invitations to destruction. At least seven great fires occurred in the two hundred years preceding Augustus, some of them raging for days before they burned themselves out or could be stopped. Their breaking out was usually either about the Forum or between the southern base of the Capitoline and the Tiber. How many lesser conflagrations there were in the same districts, or how many in districts of less importance, can only be imagined. Nor did the service of the seven thousand men equipped by Augustus after disastrous fires in the year 6 of the new era insure a greater safety. The reign of Tiberius, in addition to several of smaller dimensions, saw two great fires, one on the Cælian in 27, the other in 36, causing more than five million dollars damage, on the Aventine and reaching to the Circus Maximus. There were heavy losses under Caligula and Claudius, and even after the great fire of Nero there are widespread conflagrations recorded under Titus, Domitian, Antoninus Pius, Commodus, Maximinus, Aurelian, Carinus, and Maxentius. The fire of Titus in 80 ravaged the Campus Martius for three days and three nights. One of the fires in the reign of Antoninus Pius destroyed three hundred and forty living-houses. Aulus Gellius in the same reign witnessed the outbreak of another in a many-storeyed tenement on the Esquiline, saw the fire spread to all the neighborhood, and heard a bystander remark that the high rents at Rome would long since have led him to invest if only there had been means of protection against the continual fires. The fire of Commodus began near the temple of Peace to the northeast of the Forum and swept the neighborhood as far as the great libraries on the Palatine. Sometimes the fires were due to accident, sometimes to armed conflict in the streets. The Capitol was burned when the Vitellians stormed it in 69; a street fight between people and prætorians in 237 brought on a fire that levelled a large section to the ground. The sufferings of single buildings are a reflection of the general fortune. The Pantheon was burned in 80, struck by lightning and burned again in 110; the temple of Jupiter on the Capitoline was burned in 83 B.C., in A.D. 69, and in 80; three times in the course of a century the Circus Maximus was partly ruined, and once perhaps completely.

There were of course other means of purification. Frequent floods of the Tiber and occasional earthquakes hastened the disappearance of old and unsightly structures, and became the allies of natural business enterprise. But Rome was a capital city and the seat of absolutist princes, and it was to the emperors and their wealthy circle of friends that the city owed its character. Piso won the praise of Augustus for building his palace as if Rome were to last forever. The popular belief may not have been true that the hand of Nero was responsible for the greatest of all Rome's fires, which broke out in July, 64, and for nine days and nights converted the city into a sea of fire; sparing entirely only its heart in the Forum and Capitoline and the four outlying regions to the south, northeast, and east, and across the Tiber; destroying utterly three, and reducing the remaining seven to blackened and smoking wastes out of which, like islands, rose the parts that as if by miracle had escaped the general fate; but the charge was the reflection of what had been many a prince's and courtier's thought as he looked on unsightly obstacles to the beautification of the capital.

From Nero Rome began anew. To the great monuments of the Augustan city that had escaped annihilation, there now began in the Forum and on the Capitoline and in the Campus Martius, and in lesser number on the circumference, the accretions public and private which by the first decades of the third century made Rome the most magnificent capital in the world's history. Broad and straight thoroughfares took the place of many a crooked, narrow street whose course had remained unchanged since the burning of Rome by the Gauls four hundred and fifty years before. Palaces for the richer and middle classes and apartment houses for the lower order, built about courts and stairways, and showing many windows on the streets, made the newly built residential parts resemble modern Rome in dimensions and general character, and far surpass it in splendor without and within. The Augustan limit of seventy feet, reduced by Trajan to sixty, gave the long lines of blocks a solid and reposeful, as well as regular, appearance. The inner regions were solid masses of giant buildings; the outer were grand with monuments that rose in the midst of greater spaciousness.

There was hardly an emperor or prominent man of wealth who did not actively have at heart the pride of the city. To the palaces of Augustus, Tiberius, and Caligula on the Palatine, were added those of the Flavian emperors and of Severus, until the ancient hill was a vast pile of palaces and temples, a magnificent sight from any direction, but especially from the Appian

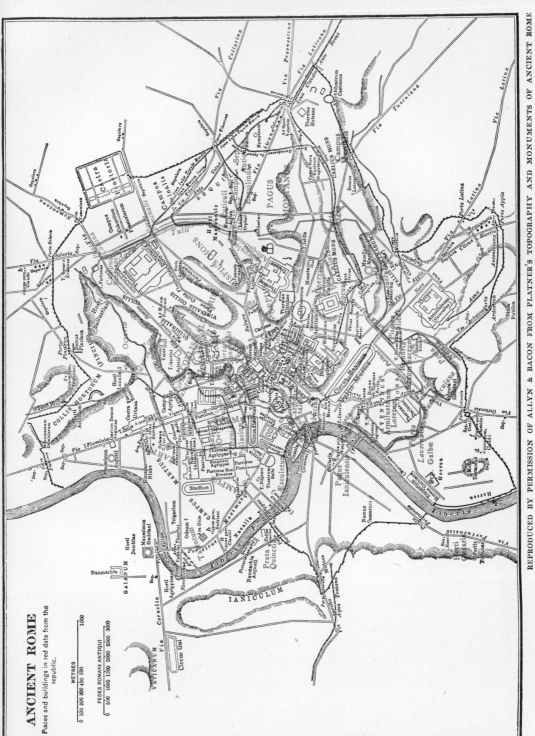

PLAN OF ANCIENT ROME

REPRODUCED BY PERMISSION OF ALLYN & BACON FROM PLATNER'S TOPOGRAPHY AND MONUMENTS OF ANCIENT ROME

ANCIENT ROME

Places and buildings in red date from the republic.

METRES
0 100 200 300 400 500   1000

PEDES ROMANI ANTIQUI
0   500 1000 1500 2000 2500 3000

Way, where the huge portico-façade of Severus' Septizonium was the great object in the vision of those who
approached the city from the south. The Coliseum, seating fifty thousand persons, rose in one part of the
Golden House and Park of Nero after Vespasian came
to the throne and restored the space to the people. To
the Great Forum and the two fora of Julius and Augustus were added the fora of Domitian and Vespasian,
and, most splendid and impressive of all, the forum of
Trajan. The baths of Titus, Trajan, and Caracalla
were added to those of Agrippa and Nero. The mau-
solea of the Flavians and of Hadrian were added to that
of Augustus. The temple of Peace was reared in Vespasian's forum, the temple of Vespasian at the head of
the Great Forum, the temple of Antoninus and Faustina at its northern edge, the great temple of Venus
and Rome by Hadrian near the Coliseum. There were
elsewhere sculptured columns a hundred feet high in
honor of Trajan and Marcus Aurelius, and a monolith
of red granite fifty feet high in honor of Antoninus
Pius. Besides arches to Augustus, Tiberius, and Claudius, there were the arches of Titus, of Hadrian, of
Marcus Aurelius, of Septimius Severus. There were
miles of porticoes to shelter from sun and rain, and
scores of porticoed enclosures for business and pleasure.
There were great bridges that brought the number to
eight. There were a dozen aqueducts, many of them
carried on monumental arches above the ground. The
five aqueducts of the last days of the Republic poured
seven hundred thousand cubic meters of water daily
through the pipes and fountains of Rome. The eleven
waters of two hundred and fifty years later must have
doubled and tripled the amount. The four aqueducts of

modern Rome, which is probably the most abundantly
watered of the world's cities, have a daily flow of four
hundred and fifty thousand meters. "If anyone," says
Pliny for Vespasian's time, "will take the trouble to cal-
culate the abundance of the waters in public, in the
baths, reservoirs, artificial streams, palaces, gardens, and
suburban villas, and the distances they come, the arches
built to carry them, the mountains tunnelled through
and the valleys levelled up, he will confess that the whole
world has produced nothing more wonderful."

For the most part, it is only of the prominent examples of all these kinds of buildings that knowledge has
survived. The smaller, and not always the less beautiful,
were countless in their total. There were minor public
baths to the number of eight hundred, there were four
hundred temples, there were thousands of shrines and
fountains at the corners and sides of the streets. The
best and most beautiful building material the world
afforded was seen in profusion on every hand. The
streets were laid with monumental pavement of basalt
from the stream once sent forth from the Alban crater.
There were rugged and vigorous peperino and creamy
travertine in the arches of aqueducts and the walls of
forum and amphitheater. There was the fine white
marble of Luna near Carrara, the creamy-golden and
purple-veined marble of Numidia, the black-streaked
grey-green marble of Euboea, the sparkling translucent
marble of Paros, the ruddy and black mottled Africano,
the variegated Phrygian, and more than a hundred other
kinds from every part of the Roman dominion, in column and architrave and in the heavy veneer of walls
and floors, in ornament within and without. It is estimated by Lanciani that at least four hundred and fifty

thousand columns of marble found their way to Rome
through Ostia. There was stucco as hard and as fine as
marble itself. There were porphyry and granite, and ser-
pentine and alabaster, and other decorative stones of
every color and from every place.

In and on and about these colossal and splendid and
varied buildings, sacred and profane, there were to be
seen in street and square, in park and promenade, in
temple-museum and private palace, the spoils, unwilling and willing, of two hundred years of conquest and
two hundred years of benevolent domination. And, not
least, like a green girdle around the majestic city of over
a million men, lay an immense chain of parks, some in
the natural state, some carefully landscape-gardened,
the acquisition of the reigning families for the city by
gift, inheritance, purchase, and confiscation throughout
the two hundred and fifty years that followed on Julius
Cæsar's death and the bequest of his gardens on the
other side of Tiber.

To complete the wondrous picture, we need only to
look down upon the wide and peaceful fields of the Campagna, by this time little touched by the plow but alive
with flocks and herds and dotted by hundreds of pala-
tial villas with luxuriant gardens, and to see running
their unswerving way through the clear sunlight of summer to the city's portals, the eleven great highways,
with their richly variegated border of splendid tombs in
the shade of pine and cypress, over whose smoothly
jointed basaltic pavement rolls the traffic of all the
world's roads that lead to Rome.

Such was the city two centuries after the days when
it came to pass that there went out a decree from Cæsar
Augustus that all the world should be taxed. Its mar-

bles and ornamental stones, from every possible quarry, its reliefs on column and arch that told of triumphs in every distant border, its architectural styles that were reminiscent of Etruria, Greece, and of Egypt and the east, its commerce from every strand, its museums, temples, libraries, palaces, and gardens, rich with the art and letters and relics of every civilization, its shrines that sheltered the religions of every land, made the imperial capital the visible representative of all the world.

It was no less the representative of temporal than of physical space. The great structures and restorations of Hadrian's times were already mellow with age. The monuments of Augustus were the venerable remains of an already distant past. The still remoter monuments were hoary with antiquity and carried the imagination back to the heroic days of the early citizen-soldier, and beyond to the primitive huts of shepherds on the hills. Rome was the capital of the world in space, the capital of the world in time, the Universal and Eternal Mother.

OF ONE BLOOD ALL NATIONS

SO, too, were the Roman people the cosmopolitans of time and of space. The fortunes of the Roman stock paralleled the fortunes of the city of Rome. The old had almost disappeared, the new had taken its place and in its own turn become old, the newer still was an inundation that all but overwhelmed what had gone before. The heroic Fabians, Fabricians, Æmilians, and all the others of the score or so of the noble houses that for three hundred years had supplied the major part of the greatest consuls of Rome, were gone. The Cornelii alone remained, yet with ambiguous title to nobility; Sulla's ten thousand slaves had taken the name at their emancipation. The forty-five patrician senators of Cæsar had diminished to one in Hadrian's time. Of the twenty-five families raised to patrician rank by Augustus and Claudius, nineteen had died out by the time of Nerva, in less than a hundred years. Vespasian had recruited the aristocracy from Italy and the provinces, as Claudius had from Gaul. Only one generation after Nero, half of the nearly four hundred senatorial families recorded in 65 had disappeared. The violent deaths that had thinned Roman blood in the broils and battles of the later Republic were continued in the terrors of the early Empire. Three hundred knights and thirty-five senators perished under Claudius; in Tiberius' latter years, we are told that not a day was without its executions; the poisonings and secret dagger-thrusts of Nero's and Domitian's times, the judicial murders, the forced suicides, and the less illegal penalties, with conflict in the field when imperial succession was at stake, contributed their part; and all these causes of death depleted first of all the purer Roman blood.

What violence did not accomplish was consummated by vice and the decay of the family fortunes. Augustus, Tiberius, Nero, and Vespasian had all subsidized or pensioned prominent houses, and the gaming-table and orgy often undid the imperial charity. Aristocratic poverty refused to rear or beget children, or even to marry. Aristocratic vice compelled the childlessness that poverty had volunteered. Violent death and voluntary childlessness and unrestrained vice were the conflagrations of racial Rome. They left standing only the ruins of the ancient Roman stock.

Against and into and around and over these human ruins, and out of their torn-down fragments, the Roman people of the Empire gradually built itself. The city was ever destroying, but ever renewing its life by reaching out for new material. It had long ago absorbed the population and life of the surrounding plain, and taken to itself the life of Italy; now it was blending into one the peoples of the world. Cicero's Rome, "made up of the coming together of the nations," had become the Rome of Petronius, "the inn of the universe." The Roman army was no longer composed of Latin and Italian farmers, but of men from distant parts of the empire paid to bear the arms of their mistress. At the most, they were officered by men of peninsular or Roman blood. The tradesmen and artisans that occupied her shops and streets, the innumerable slaves that thronged the palaces of the rich and the homes and business places of the middle class, her teachers and doctors and artists, the soldiers and sailors in her garrisons and on her galleys, her writers of history and poetry, and even her emperors, represented all quarters of the Roman world. Septimius Severus was an African of Berber origin, Trajan was a Spaniard, Hadrian derived from a colony in Spain, Vespasian was a Sabine mountaineer. Of all the men of letters achieving fame, exceedingly few were born at Rome, and many came from outside the borders of Italy. The available names of slaves and freedmen at Rome are seventy per cent Greek; in Latium outside of Rome they are sixty-four; in Cisalpine Gaul they are forty-six. It is estimated that ninety per cent of the permanent population of Rome were of blood not purely Roman. From slavery to freedom, from freedom to citizenship, from citizenship to prosperity and prominence, from prominence to nobility; from foreigner and provincial to native-born, from native birth to established family standing, from established standing to ancient stock; from poverty to means, from means to wealth, from wealth to aristocratic poverty, from aristocratic poverty to extinction by voluntary or forced sterility,—this is the way in which the people who filled the streets and the dwellings of Eternal Rome went on in the process of everlasting change.

Yet it need not be supposed that Rome was not a city of Romans. The physical city of wood and tufa and sun-dried brick and stucco had been changed and enriched by the use of other material and other methods, but the presence of marble veneer and Greek members did not make of Rome a city of the east. The coming of Greek and oriental blood could fertilize and modify the life of Rome, but the Roman people in essence were slow to change. To suppose otherwise would be to forget the assimilative power of Rome. The tenacious and enduring character that Romanized the world would hardly yield and disappear in its native city. For both ill and good the Roman type was wrought upon, and its features changed, but it never ceased to be of a Roman stamp. The citizen mingled of Roman and foreign blood remained a Roman. The population mingled and shifted, perished and was renewed, but the Roman ideal lived on. It may have touched little the lives of the multitude, but it always wrought upon the best minds and the best souls, and the cosmopolitan mass was never without a leaven. The Italian provincial needed only days to make him as much a Roman in spirit and thought as the Roman-born themselves. The cultivated provincial from farther distance required but a longer time. Plautus from Umbria, Ennius from Calabria, Lucilius from Campania, Horace from Venusia, Cicero from Arpinum, Livy, Virgil, Pliny, and Catullus from the north of Italy, Mæcenas and Persius from Etruria, Juvenal from Aquinum, are never thought of as other than Roman. Terence, Fronto, and Severus from Africa, Martial, Quintilian, the Senecas, Trajan, and Hadrian from Spain, Antoninus Pius from Lyons, are not less Roman than Lucretius, Julius Cæsar, and Augustus. They may differ one from another in blood, and all from the Romans of centuries before, but in essentials they conform to type. They are alike in language and manners, alike in their conception of virtue individual and public, alike in their pride in the city that represents to them the welfare of the world, alike in their faith that Rome is the City of Destiny.

They were alike, too, in being cosmopolitan. The Roman of the better classes was a citizen of the world. If he was not himself the mingling of Roman with foreign blood, he was at least in daily contact with men of alien descent or birth, had continually before his eyes the products of art and industry from other lands, and in many ways was in touch with the empire's universal life. There was not only the continual residence in the capital, and the continual coming and going of the nations of the earth on errands of business and pleasure, but great numbers of Romans themselves travelled, or were employed abroad in the administrative duties of government or commerce. The city of Marcus Aurelius or Severus contained more of the world and knew the world far better than the city of Augustus, and the world of their times contained more of the city and knew it better than the world of Augustus' time. The blood of the provinces had flowed to Rome, and the blood of Rome to the provinces. If Rome was the less a city of Romans, the world was the more a Roman world. The edict of Caracalla in 215, giving the franchise to all provincials, crowned the long process of Romanization. The world was doing its business in the Roman way, defending itself with Roman arms, employing the Roman tongue, thinking the thoughts and praying the prayers of its Roman organizer.

A WEB OF MINGLED YARN

THE citizen-soldier of olden days had been proud of his country's achievements in the field, and of his own contribution to the common fund of courage and endurance that established it in the foremost place among the nations of the earth. Repeated triumphs over barbarous peoples, and the steady extension of Roman boundaries almost without his willing it, had waked in him the consciousness that he was a chosen instrument. The gods were his protectors and warrant; he was to rule the world. His face was turned toward the future. The Roman of the Empire, on the contrary, was not called upon to take his place in the ranks and fight for Rome's existence. The vision of his ancestors had been realized. Destiny had been fulfilled, and Rome was mistress of a world made into one invincible power, and blessed with peace, prosperity, and justice. His pride was the pride of success already accomplished, and his faith was warranted by actual fact.

And yet, with all his pride and with all his faith, the Roman of the Empire was content neither with himself nor with his times. Through all his thoughts and words there ran a strain of regret. Now that his race had a past and a literature and monuments of its own, the history of his fathers entered more than ever into his education. Now that autocratic rule had removed from his shoulders all responsibility in field and forum, he both lacked the blessedness of self-approval that comes of action in a righteous cause and was free to indulge in contemplation. He looked back upon the simplicity, the incorruptibility, the self-sacrifice, and the heroisms of the day when Rome was really a commonwealth; he looked about him upon the motley throng of hybrids and aliens of which the Rome of his own day was composed, upon the complexity of its life, upon its idleness and aimlessness, upon its selfishness and servility; and was uneasy with the sense that, after all, the only greatness was the greatness of character, and that Rome's real glory was in the past.

The Rome of the emperors, unlike the Rome of the citizen-soldier, is vocal. It stands condemned out of its own mouth. It is more than vocal; it is vociferous. A stinging sense of unworthiness impels it to shout abroad the imperfections of its own times in contrast with the virtues of the olden times. The result has been two character-paintings, in the one of which are seen no shadows, in the other no lights. The world in general has taken the Rome of the emperors at its word, or what is usually supposed to be its word. It has accepted the Roman of the Republic as an ideal of virtue, and the Roman of the Empire as an example of utter depravity.

If, after the usual manner, we are to accept the judgment of the city during the first two centuries thus passed upon itself, we must see the Rome of the emperors, with Tacitus, as "the cesspool of the world," and, with Lucan, as a city "filled with the dregs of all mankind." We must see it, with Juvenal, a city of fires and tumbling houses where crowd and confusion by day and noises and riot by night make life a horror; where it is unsafe to go out to dine without first having made a will; where upstart freedmen and Greeklings are pushing greedily aside the last remnants of the genuine

Roman stock, whose tissue is rotten with vice and decadence. We must see in it a city of men spoiled by riches and power, at ease in sedans and followed by endless trains of clients and attendants, or lolling on the dinner couch and thinking themselves disgraced if not surrounded by throngs of slaves, who are "flogged for a murmur, a cough, a sneeze, or a sigh," and put to death by hundreds if one of their number is caught in crime.

We must see in it a city of mad extravagance and criminal self-indulgence. Caligula wastes twenty million dollars a year, and makes away with half a million, the tribute of three provinces, in a single day; Lollia Paulina, his wife, possesses a headdress of pearl and emerald valued at twenty-one millions. Nero dissipates eighteen millions without a thought, and pays a hundred and seventy-five thousand for the Egyptian roses at a single dinner. His Golden House, a square mile of pleasure-grounds and palaces, is at last "a home fit for a man." Poppæa bathes in the milk of five hundred asses, and her mules are shod with gold. Domitian gilds the temple of Jupiter on the Capitoline at the cost of a million. Marbles and metals, furnishings and table dainties, are gathered at enormous expense from all quarters of a slavish world. There are songbirds at three hundred dollars, and a dish of them at five thousand; there are nightingales' tongues; Æsop the actor's son dines at a million by drinking down a pearl. Apicius kills himself because only half a million of his fortune remains. Kriton, physician to Plotina, knows twenty-five different pomades and essences. In days when the price of a freedwoman's mirror exceeds the dowry of a bride in the good old republican times, emancipated dames in

towering heads of other women's hair have their sickly
children drowned like kittens, and reckon the years by
husbands instead of consuls. Vulgarity and meanness
are quite as common as extravagance. Hosts who once
were slaves gabble at dinner of the rarity and cost of
dishes and service, and guests who are served with different wines according to rank backbite in their presence the entertainers whose favors they accept.

We must see in it a city crowded with idle poor whose
vices are as bad as those of the idle rich. Shameless hundreds of thousands receive the dole from patron and
emperor, grumbling as they accept. They praise or
slander, applaud or hiss, protect or waylay, cringe to or
insult, for hire. Their murmurs for "bread and games"
have brought them sixty-six days of games and spectacles in Augustus' times, and under Marcus Aurelius
a hundred and thirty-five.

We must see in it a heartlessly cruel city. For the
amusement of an idle population, hundreds and thousands of noble animals are slain in the artificial chase.
Strabo sees a Sicilian bandit dropped into a cage of
savage beasts. The use of gladiators, begun in 264 B.C.
as a funeral function and quickly secularized, has possessed itself of the Roman people and become a business. The captive in war, the slave, the criminal condemned to death, the swordsman under contract, are
compelled to face their fellows on the sands. Six thousand rebellious gladiators and slaves are crucified in 71
B.C., and their hanging corpses, one to every fifty yards,
line the road from Rome to Capua. Five thousand pairs
are brought on in the one hundred and twenty-three
days of Trajan's triumph over the Dacians. The chattering, pitiless mob is outraged by an awkward stroke,

and grants or refuses its favor to the prostrate fighter at the impulse of merest whim. It delights in the mortal dangers of the charioteer; when its favorite color loses, you would think the city mourning a second Cannæ.

We must see in it a city rotten to the core with depravity and vice, a city in which honor sells itself for nothing and violence knows no law. Seven Cæsars out of twelve meet their end by assassination, and every holder of the throne to the time of Marcus Aurelius is the object of conspiracy. The hired informer is everywhere; no man is safe from his neighbors, friends, or family—a chance word, a smile, a glance, may furnish the pretext for his denunciation and death. Religion is a mockery; in the streets of Croton, and probably in Rome, you can find a god more easily than a man, and yet the Romans are godless. The temples of the newly arrived superstitions from Egypt and the east are little better than assignation-houses. Marriage is a farce, or, at best, a social and economic convenience. Adultery is taught by manual. Both sexes are prostituted, and every class. The wives and daughters of emperors are guilty with the rest. The women of noble families dress in stuffs that display instead of conceal. No one longer cares for poetry unless it is indecent. The pursuit of rich and childless men and women for the sake of places in their wills has become an established profession.

Such is the usual indictment against the Rome of the emperors. The formal truthfulness of these details is hardly open to question. The whole line of literary witnesses,—Livy, Horace, Persius, Ovid, Lucan, the Senecas, the Plinys, Petronius, Martial, Juvenal, Tacitus, Suetonius,—widely diverse in station, experience, blood, and temperament, some of them enemies, some of them friends, of the imperial régime, agree in condemning substantially the same abuses.

For those who are in search of the whole truth, however, it is not enough that such details should be individually true. They must not only be true in themselves, but truthfully representative of the total life of the time. Before accepting them as such, let us inquire more carefully both into their nature and into the nature of their interpretation.

It should be remembered, first of all, that the testimony on which the general judgment is based refers in much the greater part to the spheres of power and wealth. The figures upon which it centers our attention are Tiberius, Julia, Caligula, Agrippina, Nero, Domitian, Faustina, Commodus, and the high social circles that actively and passively conformed with the morals and manners of the imperial house. It should be remembered, farther, that of these it is almost wholly those of the first century who give the Rome of the Empire the reputation it bears. Our witnesses present the worst details of the worst classes at the worst time of the Empire, as they also present the best features of the best men in the best times of the Republic.

The character of the testimony also should not be forgotten. Who are our witnesses? They are the contemporary historian, writing with moral intent and with face turned toward the heroic days of his fathers; the poet-idealist, setting the actual present below days past or to come; the satirist, of purpose magnifying the ills at which he strikes; the epigrammatist, finding in the sins and follies of men the target of his neatly driven shafts; the biographer, mingling gossip with history to make his pages lively; the philosopher, contrasting the actual with his ideal of renunciation; the partisan, unwilling to confess either virtue in the present or imperfection in the past. And, of all these, it must be added that some are fresh from simple and unspoiled rearing in provincial towns and for the first time behold the grossness of the age in the capital city, while all measure their own times in the town by the standard of rustic morals in the brave days of old. Exaggeration and prejudice inhere in this kind of testimony. Its painting is in nothing but black and white, and takes no account of background. The exceptional, the piquant, the startling, the scandalous, all in high relief, are its material.

But not even this far from perfect testimony reaches directly the average person of modern times. The Rome of the emperors, distorted once by moralist and satirist and partisan, is distorted again by those who interpret their witness. From what are twentieth century ideas of Roman society formed? From the commentaries of ancient and modern writers, who illuminate the text of Latin authors with exhaustive assemblage of references to the unusual; from the sermon, which from the early Christian orators down has systematically darkened paganism to make Christian times the brighter; from the historical novel, with its calculated and superficial use of the sensational; from the moving picture, with its exploitation of the horrible; from the brief and glittering commonplaces of essay, editorial, and platform lecture.

Farther still, these interpreters find quick and effective allies not only in prejudice, but in time and distance; for time and distance, just as they make the good seem better, magnify the worse. Our own passions, extravagance, and immoralities, known at first hand in all their environment, are divested of half their power to alarm. *Tout savoir, c'est tout pardonner,* is true in essence, if not in letter. Placed at a distance in space and time where they had no background of ordinary manners to give them proportion, ours might seem as deadly as the corresponding abuses of ancient Rome.

We need not wholly condone the faults of this harlot that sat on the Seven Hills. They were grievous enough, but they were not entirely unrelieved. The web of life in Rome under the emperors, as in other places and in other times, was of a mingled yarn, good and ill. There were, indeed, suspicious Tiberius, mad Caligula, conceited and self-willed Nero, tyrannical and heartless Domitian, and decadent Commodus, but the Rome of the Empire is after all more truly represented by the business-like Augustus, whose hand was on every lever of the monster machine of state; by Claudius, in his silly and ponderous way improving the legacy that suddenly came to him; by Vespasian, the rugged old soldier frugal to parsimony, "restorer of temples and public ceremonies," and making sentimental pilgrimages to the mountain home of his boyhood; by sane and vigorous Trajan, beneficent and public-spirited; by Hadrian, on foot and bareheaded at the head of his columns, rebuilding the monuments without inscribing his name, perfecting the civil service, knitting together the Roman world, desiring "to see himself all that was to be seen, to know all that was to be known, to do all that was to be done"; by Antoninus, called "Pius" because of devotion to his aged father; by Marcus Aurelius, self-controlled and self-denying, the philosophical saint; by the better sides, instead of the worse, of even the vicious emperors and their vicious friends.

We need not wholly deny the sincerity and the competence of our witnesses, but we should recognize that even they, if their total testimony is taken, are by no means wholly hostile. Their very existence is proof that the Rome of their condemnation was not wholly depraved. They were not alone in their protest, but were the product of their times. Their utterance was the crystallization of the general sentiment, and their audience was the common run of intelligent men. Juvenal did not say for himself alone, "Surely the path of a tranquil life lies only through virtue," and "Virtue is the sole and only title to nobility," and "The very greatest reverence is due to boyhood." The ideals of a Tacitus or a Seneca were not confined to themselves. The idealist, the satirist, the philosopher, all had their audiences. Art is a social product. They represent the active conscience of the age. That the conscience was shocked by vice, excess, and crime is itself an indication of health.

Nor are we left without positive witness as well as negative, direct as well as indirect. There were still compassion, love, devotion, and heroism, even in the darkest reigns. When the pages of first century literature are searched for evidence of virtue as they have been searched for that of vice, they soon reveal the presence of much that helps to redeem the age. The amphitheater at Fidenæ, not far north of the city, collapsed in the reign of Tiberius, killing and maiming fifty thousand persons. The amphitheater is the symbol of Roman hardness and inhumanity, yet the downfall of this one converted it into a monument of compassion and generosity. "The palaces of the nobility were thrown open to the sufferers," says Tacitus, "physicians and medicines were provided for them, and the city during those days gave itself over to the custom of its inhabitants in the olden time, who used after great battles to take charge of and care for the wounded without pay." Of the perilous times of 68 and 69, when Nero died and three emperors successively rose and fell, Tacitus can write: "The time was nevertheless not so sterile of virtue that it did not afford also its good examples. Mothers accompanied their sons as they fled, wives followed their husbands into exile, kinsmen were daring, sons-in-law constant, slaves held to their fidelity even in the face of torture. The supreme trials of fortune, death itself, were bravely met by great men in a manner which won them praise equal to that bestowed on men of old." The younger Pliny surely was possessed by high ideals, and lived among attractive and virtuous people; the elder Pliny was a monstrosity of devotion to letters and science, who never lost a moment of time, and consulted over two thousand volumes in preparation for his *Natural History,* itself a hundred and sixty volumes of close notes. Exclude from the epigrams those aimed at meanness, vice, and extravagance, and Martial is the illustrator of a great city filled with people of every sort, busy in the struggle for a livelihood and appreciative of the ordinary joys of life.

But there are other witnesses besides these writers of poetry and prose whose testimony should be heard. There are the shapeless and at first sight unconciliating walls and floors of the private house, with the wilderness of minute objects of daily use taken from them which fill the museums,—lamps, vases, urns, kitchen ware, remnants of foodstuffs, fragments of clothing and shoes, toilet articles, tools, crockery, votive offerings. There are wall-paintings and reliefs, illustrating in a

thousand details the life of the men who had them executed. There are tens of thousands of inscriptions from
the neighborhood of Rome alone, which tell of the life
not only of emperor, official, and courtier, but of the
artisan, the common soldier, the merchant, the sub-
official, the priest and sacristan, the imperial slave, the
husband, the wife, the child, the brother, the sister, the
comrade-in-arms, the comrade-in-toil. There are these
witnesses not only in Rome and Italy, but in the most
remote provincial towns, to which life flowed from the
capital, and from which life flowed in turn back to the
capital to freshen and reinvigorate the blood of Rome.

When we have thus examined more attentively the
usual testimony of letters, and have listened also to the
less vocal witness of material things, we see the Rome
of the emperors in a less repulsive aspect. Its life is more
kaleidoscopic, more universal, more recognizable, more
human. We discover that it is almost a modern city,
and find ourselves accounting for its mixture of good
and evil as we account for that of life in our own times.
We recognize the cruelty of the amphitheater, but we
think of the bullfight in Spain and the prize-ring and
football field in English-speaking lands, and realize
that ancient brutality also was tempered by art and
sportsmanship. There were not only spectators who
without conscience enjoyed the deadly game, but also
men like Cicero, whose taste was offended by it, and
those like Seneca, Pliny, and Tacitus, who abhorred or
despised it. There were not only the swordsmen fighting
for life and butchered to make a Roman holiday, but
those who elected the career for its rewards of money
or fame. The gladiator who was "the sigh of the girls
at Pompeii," was close kin to many a hero of the mod-

TOMBSTONE OF MINICIA MARCELLA

WE ARE TOLD OF HER DEATH
BY PLINY, IN EPISTLES V. 16

ern ring and field. We recognize the excesses of the
circus-loving populace, but remember the modern delight in the race-track and the perilous feats of the tent,
the insane betting of England and America, and the
Continental lottery. We recognize the triviality and
aimlessness of those who spent half their daylight and
more than half their dark in the pleasures of bath and
dinner, but remember the innocent features of both, and
the varied and salutary diversions of the baths. We
realize the presence of vice, but reflect that the satirist's
denunciations are more of ambition, greed, and luxury
than of the deadlier sins, and that the same charges in
the same vocabulary are found three centuries later in
Jerome's denunciations of Christian laxity. We recognize the hardness of slavery, but realize both from ancient evidence and modern experience that its inhumanity was tempered by kindness and the presence of
opportunity. We remember the organized charities of
Trajan in behalf of the deserving destitute, the unfortunate debtor, and the orphan. We recognize the para-
sitic idleness of the crowd, but realize that ruler and
aristocrat had always with them the problem of the
helpless unemployed, from the time of the Gracchi
down, and that the spirit of charity and justice played
a part, as well as selfishness. We recognize the evils of
despotism, but remember that the strong man had been
begotten by need and brought forth in the throes of the
state for its own salvation. We recognize the emperor's
vices on occasion, but realize that under normal conditions he was the busiest and most earnest man in the
Roman world. We recognize his occasional rapacities
and extravagance, but remember the size of his realm
and the relativity of values. The public receipts in

Cicero's time were ten millions of dollars; Augustus'
budget of thirty millions was less than five per cent of
the budget of New York City. We recognize com-
plaisance under abuse of power, but reflect that the
best men differed as to means of preserving the state,
and that the triumph of any means involved the acceptance of bad along with good.

And not only are our thoughts corrected and our
judgments tempered by this greater amplitude of evidence, but our visual imagination is made clearer. We
see not only Rome the capital, but the one thousand
one hundred and ninety-seven smaller cities said by
Ælian to be in Italy, the twelve hundred in France, the
three hundred in Africa, and the other innumerable
little images of Mother Rome. We see not only the
disorder and bloodshed of the "Year of the Three Emperors" in the capital, but the provinces undisturbed in
the peace and quiet assured by the great machine of
administration even when the throne is in question. We
see not only poison and the sword and dagger at work
in palace and forum, but advocate and judge conducting
cases in the courts according to due process of law, and
little boys in the schoolroom at break of day thumbing
their sooty Horaces and Virgils under the eye of the
bawling master, and women of the people filling bronze
pots at the five hundred fountains of Rome. We see not
only the hundreds of thousands being entertained in
amphitheater, circus, and theater, but other hundreds of
thousands who indulge in the simpler pleasures of the
spacious garden and promenade, or make excursions to
field or inn beyond the gates. We see not only Agrippina and Claudius, and Nero with his mistresses, but
Pliny writing love-letters to the young wife who is

bound to him in ideal companionship as well as in law.
We see not only the careless Romans walking the streets
with eyes vacantly on the ground, but the stream of
tourists with astonished gaze uplifted to monuments,
climbing the marble steps to palace and hill, and ascend-
ing the spirals of Trajan's and Marcus Aurelius' columns. We see not only the imperial purple and glitter,
the brilliant uniforms and dress of officer and noble, but
the press of the tunic-clad throng who swarm like ants.
We see not only the dinners and assemblages of the
rich, but the meetings of the men who do the hard work
of Rome, the guilds of the workers in wood and iron,
the carders and fullers of wool, the shoemakers, the
tanners, the porters, the potters, the paviors, the dealers
in goods and supplies, the clothmakers, the mechanics,
the boatmen of the Tiber, the drivers, the men of the
city's more than two hundred bakeries and almost two
hundred public magazines and over eight hundred
baths. We see not only the palace, the basilica, the portico, and the public monument, but streets and alleys
and shops and blocks of houses that look very much like
those of modern Rome. We see not only the triumphal
procession of the emperor with all its symbols of the
glories of this world, but the religious trains of Isis, the
dancing and whirling priests of the Great Mother, the
mystic celebration in the dim grot of Mithras, and the
secret assemblage of those who have sworn to be faithful
unto death to the God of Galilee.

We may go still farther, and detect in all this welter
of life in the Rome of the emperors, so much of which
was really bad and so much of which is made by partial
evidence and prejudice to seem more vicious than it was,
some features that warrant us in speaking of actual

progress in the great essentials of human experience. Back of all the scandalous conduct rightly and wrongly charged against women lies the fact that women have gained in freedom for good as well as ill, and in the upper circles have attained to something like real emancipation. The jades and freaks of Juvenal's satire are more than offset by the noble-minded women of Seneca, Tacitus, Pliny, and Plutarch, and by the representative hundreds the memory of whose old-time virtues is preserved on stones like that of Claudia:

Stranger, slight is the boon I ask: stop thou, and read;
Here is the tomb,—alas, not fair!—of a woman fair.
The name her parents gave to her was Claudia;
She loved her husband faithfully with all her heart.
Two sons she reared: the one she leaves behind on earth,
The other in the earth she laid away to rest.
Of charming speech she was, she was of gracious step.
She kept the house; she spun the wool. I have said. Pass on;—

or like that of another, who possessed "purity, loyalty, affection, a sense of duty, a yielding nature, and whatever qualities God has implanted in women." It is not too much to infer, from the total evidence, that in the middle class, at least, "female morality was probably as high as it ever was, as high as the average morality of any age," and that "the ideal purity, both in men and women, in some circles was actually rising." The memory of the citizen-soldier virtues and of the old-fashioned matron of the Republic was still made flesh in many a Roman family.

And back of the splendor and extravagance of the times may be seen the workings of a keener intelligence, a more compassionate heart, a more generous hand, and

a spirit more quickly responsive to God. Claudius and
Nero were enthusiastic lovers of Greek letters and art,
Vespasian first endowed instruction in Greek and Latin
rhetoric, with pensions at the end of twenty years, Hadrian was the most liberally educated of men, Antoninus
Pius honored and supported professors of rhetoric and
philosophy in all the provinces. Nor was the intellectual
life a merely barren product. Since its beginnings a
thousand years before, Greek philosophy had advanced
from physical speculation to ethical inquiry, from ethical inquiry to the formulation of systems, and now in
Marcus Aurelius and Roman Stoicism passed from
speculation to exemplification in life. What had been
purely intellectual and had led to skepticism of the old
religion, was now itself charged with the warmth of
living faith. Magnate and emperor were open-handed
toward capital and province, and the empire was dotted
with monuments inscribed to them by appreciative cities
and men. The blessedness of pity, the claims of gladiator and slave and subject, the ugliness of the abuse of
power, the obligation of man to man outside the law, the
beauty of living for others, were daily growing less
unfamiliar to Roman sentiment. The ideas that revenge
is wrong, that sin is in the thought, that a noble man is
his own ancestor, that the golden age is in the living
future and not in the dead and helpless past, that the
Kingdom of God is within and lies in a tranquil soul,
that God is one and the same in all lands under whatever names He may be worshipped, that the soul is to
the body what God is to all creation, that "the true worshipper of the gods is he who acts like them," that it is
"better not to believe in a god at all than to cringe before one who is worse than the worst of men," that "to

look for a form and shape in a god is a mark of human feebleness of mind," that penitence and self-sacrifice are means of drawing near to Him, were daily growing less unfamiliar to Roman thought. "Seneca, often one of ourselves," is Tertullian's appreciation of the better life of paganism as preached by the Stoic of Nero's day. The ethics of Cicero are soon to find a place in the body of Christian doctrine. Fellowship in the economic and funeral guild, mystic communion in Mithras, and spiritual aspiration in Isis will some day be transformed, along with the web of paganism, into the fresher web of Christian life.

The Roman world was getting together. It had already gotten together in visible empire. It was knitting now into the empire of the spirit. The visible empire was already passing its prime. Its pace was soon to slacken, its step to falter, its body to suffer dissolution and decay. But Rome was not to die. It was to be perpetuated in the life of the spirit.

VII.

THE FALL OF THE PAGAN EMPIRE

Exaudi, genetrix hominum, genetrixque deorum:
  Non procul a cælo per tua templa sumus. . . .
Fecisti patriam diversis gentibus unam:
  Profuit invitis te dominante capi;
Dumque offers victis proprii consortia iuris,
  Urbem fecisti quod prius Orbis erat,—

Hear, O mother of men and mother of gods:
Not far from the skies are we when in thy sacred abodes.
Thou hast made of diverse nations a single fatherland:
The reluctant, with thee to rule, have found it gain to be vanquished;
In bestowing upon the subdued equal rights in thy law,
Thou hast made a City what before was a world.

RUTILIUS NAMATIANUS, I: 47-50; 63-66

Fiunt, non nascuntur, Christiani. Auratum squalet Capitolium, fuligine et aranearum telis omnia Romæ templa cooperta sunt, movetur urbs sedibus suis et inundans populus ante delubra semiruta currit ad martyrum tumulos,—

Christians are made, they are not born. The gilded Capitol is foul with neglect, cobwebs and grime cover all the temples of Rome, the city is moved to its depths, and the surging people pass the half ruined shrines to hasten to the tombs of the martyrs.

JEROME, Epistle CVII: 1, 4

THE CRUMBLING OF EMPIRE

THE very culmination of the empire's greatness marked also the beginning of its visible decline and disintegration. Marcus Aurelius himself, the last in the succession of the five good men under whose rule the ancient world attained to its climax of prosperity and happiness, was the first emperor constrained to defend the Roman frontier by active and long-continued service in the field.

The ruler in whom was at last realized the Platonic ideal of philosophy governing the state had been on his throne but a year when the Parthians broke through the Roman lines in the east. Four years of campaigning by Avidius Cassius reëstablished the lines and put the ancient foe in his place; but no sooner was this break repaired than a second and far more serious one occurred in the north. Impelled by the pressure of still more distant barbarians, the Teutonic and Slavic nations between the headwaters of Danube and Rhine come crashing against the wall of Hadrian, and roll over it in a mighty inundation which does not spend itself until it has swept into Italy at Aquileia and beyond to the line of the Piave. The plague and the Parthian war have weakened the Roman armies and emptied the Roman treasury. In the face of the greatest alarm since the coming of Hannibal, the emperor fills the depleted ranks of the legions with gladiator and slave, and ministers to financial need by sacrificing the imperial jewels. A first war of eight years and a second of two, between which occurred the revolt of Avidius Cassius in the east, were necessary before the Marcomanni and Quadi in Bohemia, and the Slavs to their east, were again reduced to obedience; and at their end, before the conquered territory could be organized into provinces, the emperor died in camp, far from the city and the life of which he had known so little for the nineteen years of his devoted reign.

The barbarian rush through the broken dike between Rhine and Danube, and the rebellion of Avidius Cassius, were both foreshadowings of the approaching doom. The soldiery that under Cassius had failed to unseat the father, on the death of Commodus, the weaker son, became dictators of the throne. The prætorians of Rome who supported the able Pertinax soon took the life of their too virtuous master, and sold the throne to the wealthier and less exacting Julianus. Niger in Syria, Albinus in Britain, Septimius Severus on the Danube, were raised to the purple by armies quickly schooled in the lesson of violence, and the race for the throne was to the swift and strong. Severus kept his seat for the natural term of life, but Caracalla his son was murdered by Macrinus the prætorian, Macrinus was dethroned and slain by Heliogabalus and the legions, and Heliogabalus was slain by mutinous guards who declared in favor of Alexander Severus. From the latter's death at the hands of the soldiers in 235 to the rise of Diocletian in 284, the empire was a prey to the distraction from within which was one day to result in permanent division, and to the assaults from without which were finally to cause its fall. The strong hand of Septimius Severus checked for a time the inroads of Parthian and Pict and Scot; the weaker hand of Alexander

Severus was all but unable to maintain the empire in Asia against the Persian power now rising from the ruins of Parthia, and at his death the impact of Germany was again being felt along the Rhine. In vain the strengthening of the great dike and the concentration of rulers upon the army; in 251 the threats that had so long been ringing in Roman ears were realized. The Goths on the Danube ravaged Dacia and crossed to Macedonia, defeating and slaying the emperor Decius. The Franks accomplished the passage of the Rhine and swept over the now Roman civilization of Gaul. Nine years later, the Persians vanquished and captured the emperor Valerian. Egypt was in the hands of a rebel, and refused the grain supply. The Germans and Goths pushed across the Rhine and Danube in quest of places in the sun of the Roman provinces and Italy.

The empire was all but lost, when out of the disorderly rise and fall of haphazard princes a succession of abler men emerged. Marcus Aurelius Claudius in 268-270 confounded and destroyed the invading hordes of Goths; Aurelian in the next five years recovered Gaul and Britain, drove back the Germans once more, and overthrew the kingdom of Queen Zenobia, carved out of Roman territory in Egypt and Asia Minor; and Probus, after the one-year reign of Tacitus, confirmed Aurelian's victories.

But Aurelian's restoration of the Roman lines was not entire; he withdrew the Romans from beyond the Danube, abandoned Dacia to the Goths, and made the broad stream once more the frontier as it was before Trajan's day. The soldiery continued to dictate the rise and fall of the emperors. The reign of Carus, who followed after Probus, was brief, and the empire was divided by Carinus and Numerian, the latter soon to be the victim of a prætorian, the former to be slain by his own officers when Diocletian, his brother's successor by choice of the army, met him in battle the following year. And Roman fear of the vague and terrible north was confessed and kept ever present by Aurelian's eleven miles of gigantic wall.

The hundred years succeeding the death of Marcus Aurelius had thus seen the first actual abandonment of Roman territory, the growth of occasional border anxiety into permanent fear for the integrity of the empire, the undisguised neglect of the senate as authority, the rise of a military despotism based on the passions and greed of officers and men, the degradation and decline of population, the exhaustion of the treasury, and the springing up of the dread and fear of barbarian kings in the city which for the six centuries since the Gallic raid had not been entered by a foe except of its own citizenship. They had seen the cessation of monumental building, the utter debasement of sculpture, already coarse in the second century, the disappearance of letters except in law, the discontinuance of inscription and memorial. From the Severi to Diocletian the silence of the stones is all but unbroken. The art of the column of Marcus Aurelius and the arch of Severus is clumsy and crude; that of the arch called Constantine's would be unworthy of the Middle Age.

The suddenness of this descent is even farther beyond belief than its depth. In what causes must we seek the explanation of both?

The sagest of Americans is credited with the saying that in the hands of good men the worst form of government will succeed, and that the best will fail in the hands of the bad. The more ancient of the Greek philosophers, after having collected and studied two hundred and fifty constitutions and observed the mortal nature of states, had formed the conclusion that constitutions, like men, were subject to natural and inherent causes that led them from youth to prime, from prime to age and decay, and from decay to death. Both Franklin and the men of Plato's and Aristotle's stamp might have formed the same conclusions regarding the wider and more universal constitution called society.

The Roman form of government under the Empire, and Roman society from the beginning to the end, were weakened and imperilled by serious faults. Whether we regard these faults as inherent or as accidental, they were so deeply grown into the fiber of Roman life that ultimate decay was not to be avoided; the flaws were fatal, and remedy was futile. It was a society which was eaten into by human slavery, with all its consequences in moral and economic degradation. It was a society whose base was force, with all its consequences in cruelty and wrong. The conduct of the state depended upon the will of a single man. The election of this man lay neither with people nor senate, but either in the accident of birth or the will of a predecessor or the selfish interest of an army. The loose confederation of widely separated and widely different nations that composed the state was held in subjection to central authority by a bureaucracy constantly becoming more unwieldy and expensive, and always contained some member whose only compelling bond was force. The rule of autocrats destroyed initiative and the sense of responsibility in the individual, while long prosperity, with freedom from the disciplinary duties of war, had softened his temper.

For two centuries of the Empire these forces of death were neutralized by other forces of life. The solid efforts of the better emperors from Augustus to Vespasian and Titus gave the arts and industries of peace throughout the Mediterranean world the opportunity denied through all previous ages by war and incoherence. The virtues of the Five Good Reigns obscured for nearly another hundred years the vices lodged in the fiber of society and state; but with the sudden removal of effort on the part of good and able men at the death of Marcus Aurelius, the diseases in spite of which the empire had prospered as never before began to rage with all the vigor of uncombated evil. The worthlessness and viciousness of Commodus revived the assassination of emperors; the purchase of the throne by Didius Julianus taught a greedy and degraded soldiery once for all the lesson of power and profit; the success of the worthier Septimius Severus confirmed the appeal to arms as the means of election to the throne. From now on, doubled perils beset the Roman world; to the weaknesses and vice inherent in state and society were added the weaknesses and vice of rulers. In the story of Rome's decline, too much responsibility can hardly be laid upon the fifty years of anarchy in high places that followed the death of Alexander Severus, years of waste and non-productiveness in man and every resource of society.

It is not necessary, nor would it be justified in truth, to regard either subject or ruler as lost to good intentions. The average emperor no doubt had the good of the state at heart, and the average citizen faced in all

seriousness the problems of life. Both struggled on as
best they could under heavy burdens. The times were
out of joint. The Roman world was wearing out. Moral,
social, economic, political, racial, and military exhaustion were marching hand in hand with equal step to
bring the day of dissolution.

The day of dissolution was deferred by the timely
rise of able men. Aurelian and Probus reëstablished respect for the throne at home and fear of the Roman
arms abroad. The firm hand of Diocletian at first united
the freshly sundered empire, and then with wise pro-
vision divided it. Under the two Augusti, with capitals
at Nicomedia in the east and Milan in the west, and
the two Cæsars, with capitals at Sirmium on the Save
and at Treves and York, remodelled into twelve dioceses and ninety-six provinces, the state took on new
life for the struggle against barbarism from without
and decay from within. United again by Constantine,
it was held together by force of arms under Constantius
and Julian, once more divided, and became a unit again
for the last time under Theodosius the Great.

But the day of dissolution was only deferred; it could
not be escaped. The division of the empire which had
first taken place in the times of Severus became the
norm instead of the exception. The emperor became not
only absolute, but an oriental despot with all the ceremony and splendor of eastern monarchs. The army was
no longer recruited from Italy, or even from the more
enlightened of the remaining provinces, but from the
semi-barbarous races. Partly from a settled policy of
self-protection, partly from necessity, the emperors
created innumerable paid positions that emptied the
pockets of the people. The taxes became enormous, the

coinage was debased. The movements of armies and fleets in the wars of succession were the ruin of trade. The leading citizens in the once self-governing and lightly burdened cities and towns were gradually weighted with heavier and heavier responsibilities to the central government until in the later fourth century to be a member of the common council meant the total sacrifice of fortune and happiness. Men of modest means were ruined; the little landowners lost their holdings and became serfs to the soil, which gathered itself into monstrous estates. The demarcation of social, industrial, and professional groups became so sharp that men and women were hopelessly enslaved to the position or occupation to which they were born. The Roman government and Roman society became a machine instead of an organism.

And in and upon this aged and halting world of men two special forces were at work. In it was the silent and solvent force of a new religion that had grown to be the center around which gathered all the protest of nature against the selfishness, the violence, the cruelty, and the injustice of an outworn pagan society, and was destined to be the conveyance, if not the cause, of the change from old to new. Upon it was working the less invisible and less quiet force of a vigorous northern world that clamored and pushed for entrance into the Roman lands. Adventure and bloodshed were less the aim of the intruders than escape from the enemy behind and a share in the greater peace and plenty of the Roman realms. From the time of Hadrian on, Pict and Scot and German and Goth and Slav again and again broke through the walls or crossed the streams that separated them from the land of civilization. The spacious Roman border towns of the second century had been changed in a hundred years or so into walled towns where everything was sacrificed to protection against the invader. The prisoners taken by the emperors in their campaigns and added as slaves to the population of Italy, the natural mingling and seeping through along the border, the reception of volunteers and the hiring of mercenaries in the intervals of peace to fill the ranks of the army, the granting of lands within the border as the best means of insuring quiet,—all this, in the course of two hundred years, had obscured the line that bounded the Roman lands, had Teutonized the Roman armies, and had familiarized the Romans of Italy with the Teutonic presence. The convenient dates of 313 and 476 for the triumph of the Church and the fall of the empire are misleading. In reality the Roman world had fallen asunder long before Odoacer dealt the final stroke; the edict of Constantine was only the recognition of a success long since assured. Neither the victory of Christianity nor the end of the western empire was a cataclysm or even a sudden change. By need and by process of nature the old grew gradually into the new.

THE FLIGHT OF THE EAGLES

IN like manner, the year 330 in the history of Rome the city marked only the formal end of a process long in operation. The arrival of the court at Byzantium and the rise of Constantinople may have been of a sudden and artificial nature; the departure of headship from Rome and the descent of the ancient capital from its high estate was a matter of degrees.

The history of Rome's relation to the rest of the realm is the story of a levelling process. Under the Republic, the city is the mistress of a subject world, and enjoys, with Italy, the privileges and immunities of the conqueror. Under Julius Cæsar and Augustus she becomes the responsible capital, and part of the empire of which she is the leading city. When Caracalla grants citizenship to all the Roman world, one more distinction of Italy and Rome from the rest of the state is removed. When at last under Galerius the land-tax, from which Italy had been immune since the tribute was removed from her in 167 B.C. as a result of the prosperous wars with Macedon, was again laid upon the peninsula, the process of levelling before the law was complete. So far as privilege was concerned, Rome was like other cities.

But the loss of privilege was not the only change that diminished the power of the city. In the early days the authority and dignity that lodged in the senate remained inseparable from Rome because the senate was composed of Romans. With the coming of the Empire, this authority passed largely to the emperor, and inhered no longer in the capital. However considerate the treatment of its imperial masters, from Augustus on the senate became more and more a symbol rather than the reality. At the beginning of the third century, every pretence on the emperor's part was dropped, and absolutism stood frankly and brutally confessed. Septimius Severus does not consult the senate regarding his election, nor ask its favors; he announces his accession to the throne, and henceforth the successful claimant is confirmed by acclamation after the event. The senate keeps up the forms of the ages, and continues to deliberate and to recommend, but the exercise of real power is only for the briefest intervals or in matters of little moment.

The decline of the prætorians, too, was a loss to the city's importance, though a loss of the coarser kind. At their creation by Tiberius for the most part Roman and all Italian, their ranks were later opened to Spaniards, Macedonians, and Noricans, and finally by Severus to recruits of every blood. His second Parthian legion, newly and permanently encamped in its guarded and watchful position on the slope of the Alban Mount, could only remind the city of its lessened authority. When Galerius entirely abolished the prætorians, now become little better than urban police, with the disappearance of the makers and unmakers of emperors for three hundred years vanished also the last sign of the military importance of Rome.

And the passing of authority from senate to emperor not only made authority detachable from Rome, but made it mobile. From now on, the capital went with the emperor. With Trajan, Rome began to see less and less of the imperial retinue. Hadrian's court was almost peripatetic. Marcus Aurelius governed from the distant frontier, and from Severus' time the emperors were rarely in residence on the Palatine. The city which had been the center of Latium and the center of Italy was far from the usual seats of trouble in the east and north when Roman rule had covered the Mediterranean. Diocletian's capital was Nicomedia in Asia Minor; he visited Rome but once, and paid no attention to the senate. The court of the western Augustus, Maximian, was at Milan. The courts of the Cæsars were at York and Treves and at Sirmium beyond the Alps. Not a single rescript is dated from Rome in the time of Symmachus.

When, therefore, Constantine in 330 removed the seat of government to Byzantium and built the city of his name, he did not inaugurate so much as mark the decline of Rome's importance. She had in reality long been a provincial capital, and now became it in name. The senate had long been possessed in fact of only local authority; it now became the common council of the leading city of the province of Italy. Whatever its pretensions to being the capital of the west, the real seat of government was in the north. When Honorius in 403 came for a time to occupy the Palatine, the now venerable pile had known no imperial tenant for nearly a hundred years.

Thus, after a thousand years of existence as the center of the military and political life of her realms, did the city on the Seven Hills see her glory depart. The Roman eagles looked down on the broad waters of the Bosporus now, instead of on the eddying current of yellow Father Tiber, and Rome was governed, when legislation other than local was needed, from Ravenna

WALL OF SEPTIMIUS SEVERUS' CAMP AT ALBANO

HERE THE SECOND PARTHIAN LEGION WAS STATIONED

or Milan. The tide of the world's business rolled far from her, and she was left to her own devices. Constantine had deserted her, and with him many of her first men; the dead emperor's body, in spite of Roman entreaty, was laid away at his own request in the new capital instead of the old. Nineteen years after his death, his successor, Constantius, in the brief visit of 356, trod her streets for the first time and the last; fresh outbreaks on the Danube called him suddenly away, and from the Danube the pressure of the Persians called him permanently to the east.

Not only were the interests of the rulers elsewhere, but the lands of their birth and the cities of their preference. Julian probably never saw Rome, and his command of the Roman tongue was but one detail in a training almost wholly Greek; the name of Virgil, so far as may be seen, was never written by his pen; and he was capable of the un-Roman utterance that Alexander could have conquered Rome. From Trajan on, few were the emperors born within the borders of Italy. Few, too, were the Italian-born among the men of letters of the later Empire. Ammianus Marcellinus, historian of the times, was a Greek of Antioch, and learned the Latin tongue as a foreign language; Macrobius was a Greek; Claudian, court poet of Theodosius and Honorius, was a native of Egypt; Ausonius was a citizen of Bordeaux, with blood half Gallic; Sulpicius Severus also was a Gaul; Prudentius was a Spaniard; and the Christian orators and essayists were in large part African. It was nothing new for the literary art to come from the provinces; but now, for the first time, the artists were no longer Roman by either birth or adoption. Ammianus is hardly Latin; Ausonius is hardly less modern French than ancient Roman; in Commodianus the old classical prosody and syntax are already breaking up; Julian is altogether Greek; Augustine and Jerome belong more to the Middle Ages than to classical times.

The greyness of old age was upon the city. Her literature was becoming the work of alien pens; her art was barbarous in design and execution; her emperors born in other lands, nursed at other breasts, and almost unaware of her existence; her political power faded to a shadow; the ranks of her defenders recruited from all soils but that of Italy; her citizens of family and fortune, like those of the empire at large, burdened with taxes and civic duties requiring their all; her population, like that of all the realm, rapidly decreasing; her tradesmen, artisans, and professionals in the throttling grip of caste; her landholders abandoning the estates that now entailed impossible obligations; her impoverished environs infested by brigands and fever; her dwindling rural population of small farmers, slaves, and barbarian colonists declining into serfdom; her growth in building at an end; her already decaying monuments requiring the shield of the law to prevent their total dismemberment; even her time-honored religion barely tolerated, and fast approaching the hour of extinction.

But the ancient capital not only suffered the humiliation that came with loss of power and prestige; she was beset with actual dangers. The threat of Hannibal in the second Punic war, the threat of the Cimbri and Teutons in the last years of the second century before Christ, the threat of Antony and Cleopatra at Actium, was repeated in the alarming rush of Slavs and Germans over the Alps in Marcus Aurelius' time, and lived

again in Aurelian's day, when the irresistible wave of
the Alemanni surged once more across the bulwarks of
Italy and rolled to the banks of the Metaurus before it
could be stayed. The city which for more than five hundred years had felt secure without the protection of
walls now suddenly woke to a vivid sense of danger. The
capital in the heart of Italy, as well as the towns that
held the watch on the Rhine and Danube, now frowned
with battlements and towers. With haste that was born
of fear, Aurelian and the Romans reared the great wall
which still bears his name, following the outer limits of
the Fourteen Regions, utilizing in their eagerness the
walls of garden, amphitheater, prætorian camp, and
aqueduct, building into its mass the tombs and houses
that lay in its path, pushing it through the beautiful
gardens of the imperial domain that girdled the city; a
giant defence whose size and beauty were in keeping
with the importance of the city it enclosed, but whose
presence was a monument to alarm and insecurity.

And there were other perils than those from the barbarians beyond the borders. The ruin of ancient monuments was being hastened by the hand of violence.
There were seven acts in the fourth century against the
plundering of tombs for the sake of their marbles, with
penalties ranging from confiscation of property to
death. Already Constantine complains of the neglect
that is bringing on decay, and himself transports from
Rome to Byzantium eight mighty drums of porphyry
for the famous Column, and takes with them the very
Palladium that so long has assured the ancient capital
of safety. From Gratian to Honorius there are edicts
requiring the repair of ancient buildings and forbidding

private seizure of public spaces and edifices. There was
the peril of fire. The reign of Commodus, in 191, and
the reign of Carinus, in 283, saw conflagrations of considerable magnitude that were the more devastating
because of the tardiness and want of taste in restoration and repair. There was the peril of pestilence. In
Marcus Aurelius' reign it not only ravaged the east,
but in Italy is said to have swept off half the population. There were the straits, if not the serious peril, of
famine. After Constantine's removal to the east, the
grain ships of Egypt sailed for the Bosporus instead
of the Tiber mouth. A great famine troubled the latter
days of Gratian. When Gildo revolted and seized the
province of Africa, supplies were again endangered, and
the Roman populace in great anxiety. "We eat or
starve at the will of the Moor," wrote Claudian. And
there was the peril of the new religion, which exulted
in the downfall of ancient temples, and was helping
to kill the ancient society by withdrawal from it or by
transformation of its fiber.

The effect of these humiliations and dangers may be
felt in the literature of the times. What a picture of
Rome is this that Claudian paints when in *The Gildonic
War* he represents the city under the threat of famine:

"And now Rome, filled with fears and worn by long
deprivation, was hastening with rapid pace to the
threshold of Olympus. Unwonted the expression on her
face; not such as she wears when dictating law to the
Britons, or when she makes bend before her fasces the
fear-struck Indians. Her voice is quavering, her step
slow, her eye sunken, her cheeks hollow; barren hunger
consumes her members. On her wasted shoulders she

can scarce support the ruinous shield. The crevices in the broken helmet betray her hoary hair, and the spear she wearily drags is eaten deep with rust. When at length she reaches the heavens, she prostrates herself before the knees of the Thunderer, and thus begins her sorrowful plaint."

The ancient pagan city is hardly less humbled and broken in the page of Symmachus, where she pleads with Valentinian the Second and Valens to restore to the senate the altar of Victory, on whose final banishment, as a sign of their triumph, the Christians were bent:

"Imagine that Rome is before you speaking on this wise: 'Excellent princes, fathers of your country, have respect for the years at which I have arrived in the practice of these sacred rites. Leave me to the ways of my ancestors; I have not had cause to repent of them. Permit me, since I am free, to live in accord with my wonted customs. This religion brought all the world under my laws; these holy ceremonies drove Hannibal from my walls and kept the Gauls from the Capitol. Was I saved only to be outraged in my old age? Even could I see the good in what others think proper for me to learn, it is too late now; it would be shameful to change, at my day.' "

These passages are only two; both are the stuff of rhetoric, and Symmachus was taken to task by the Christian poet Prudentius for thus representing Rome; yet the fact that they were written at all is eloquent of the condition to which the city was reduced. What they signify may best be realized by attempting to think of Virgil, or Livy, or Pliny, as writing them. To the men of the earlier day, the thought of Rome as aught but the proud mistress of the world was not possible. It was possible to men of the late fourth century only because the pagan city was aged and weary unto death.

3.

MONUMENTS AND MEN BEFORE ALARIC

IN a moment more a Christian emperor will pronounce the doom of the ancient faith, and the northern kings the doom of the ancient capital. Before the curtain falls on the last act of the pagan city and the pagan culture, let us look at Rome as it appeared to the last of the ancient Romans, and at the ancient Romans as they appeared to the observer and to themselves.

The two centuries following the accession of Septimius Severus in 193 had no great building periods like those of Augustus, the Flavians, and Hadrian, yet they were not without their striking additions to the dignity and beauty of the city. Her princes still delighted to do her honor. Severus erected the monumental arch in the Forum, the Castra Peregrina for his foreign guards, and the palace and the Septizonium on the Palatine. The Silversmiths' arch, between Capitoline and Palatine, was erected in honor of the emperor and his family. Caracalla's baths, to the south of the Palatine, were the largest and most completely equipped up to their times, including huge vaulted chambers, hot, cold, and tepid, gymnasia, promenades, clubrooms, and athletic grounds, with even a Mithræum in the basement. Decius in 249-251 constructed baths on the Aventine. The slight but not unpleasing arch of Gallienus, erected in 262 by the emperor's admirer Marcus Aurelius Victor "on account of his bravery, surpassed only by his piety," still stands on the Esquiline to give life to the memory of this ruler as preserved in Gibbon: "In every art he attempted his lively genius enabled him to succeed; and as his genius was destitute of judgment, he attempted every art, except the important ones of war and government. He was a master of several curious but useless sciences, a ready orator, an elegant poet, a skilful gardener, an excellent cook, and a most contemptible prince."

Aurelian was not without thought of the city's grandeur when he reared the great wall of brick and concrete twelve feet thick and running in places to the height of sixty feet, whose loop-holed galleries and parapet crowned by nearly four hundred towers made it one of the most impressive monuments in the ancient world, as its mighty remnants are among the most impressive in the modern. In the vigorous and splendor-loving emperor's temple to the Sun, on the Quirinal, the city was dignified by another marvel of giant architecture. The bridge of Probus completed the arching of the Tiber, now monumentally spanned at nine points. On the high plateau where Quirinal and Viminal come together arose the baths of Diocletian, twice the size of Caracalla's and of even greater splendor, enclosed by huge walls and towers and apses and domes, and containing theater, promenades, and assembly halls, besides athletic and bathing conveniences for over three thousand persons. The ruined fragments of its principal mass today are housing Michelangelo's church of Santa Maria degli Angeli, one of the largest in Rome, the Museo Nazionale, one of the most important in Italy, and a number of philanthropic and educational institutions; two of the domed halls that rose at its cor-

THE WALL OF AURELIAN

FROM OUTSIDE THE OSTIAN GATE;
THE PROTESTANT CEMETERY IS BEYOND THE WALL

ners are occupied by a girls' school and the church of San Bernardo; and the print of the great semi-circle that formed the middle of its southwest side is to be seen in the curve of the Piazza dell' Esedra. Maxentius, the candidate of Rome for the purple, added in 309 the great circus outside the walls on the Appian Way, probably the third in size of these places of amusement, and erected a temple to Romulus, his son, on the Sacred Way beyond the eastern bound of the Forum. The monster basilica beyond it begun by him was finished by Constantine after the battle at the Mulvian bridge in 312. The arch of Constantine, in 313, a compound of Domitian's and Trajan's times and his own, and the enormous baths on the slope of the Quirinal where it overlooked the forum of Trajan, were the last of the remarkable buildings of Rome.

By the end of the second century, popular usage had probably fixed on the fourteen regions the names by which they are designated in the two catalogues or breviaries of the city in the time of Constantine which are known as the *Curiosum* and the *Notitia*. A review of them under the new nomenclature will farther aid the imagination in reproducing the Rome of the later day. Region I. was known as Porta Capena, from a venerable remnant of the Servian wall, then thought to be nine hundred years old; Region II. as Cælimontium, from the spacious southeastern hill; III. as Isis and Serapis, from a temple to the Egyptian deities; IV. as Templum Pacis, from the great building in Vespasian's forum; V. as Esquiliæ, from the broad plateau on the east; VI. as Alta Semita, High Lane, from the long, straight thoroughfare, once perhaps a primitive path, that ran the length of the Quirinal to the north-

east and out of the city; VII. as Via Lata, or Broad
Street, from the avenue that traversed the Campus
Martius and became the Flaminian Way as it left the
gate for the far north; VIII. as Forum Romanum; IX.
as Circus Flaminius, from the old race-course to the
south of the Campus Martius at the northwest base of
the Capitoline; X. as Palatium, the hill of the Cæsars'
palaces; XI. as Circus Maximus, where the immense
rows of seats filled all the space between Palatine and
Aventine; XII. as Piscina Publica, or People's Reser-
voir, where the common folk had access to a pool or
basin for washing; XIII. as Aventinum, the western
elevation of the Aventine where it overhung the Tiber;
XIV. as Transtiberim, the more or less spacious separate quarter across the river containing the circus of
Caligula where now is Saint Peter's, and to the south
the gardens of Cæsar.

Around all this, pierced by thirteen monumental
gates that marked the egress of the great highways, ran
the ruddy, towered battlements of Aurelian's fortification. There were three hundred temples, twenty-eight
libraries, eleven great baths, and ten basilicas. There
were twelve porticoes in the Campus Martius alone
whose aggregate length of sheltered promenade was
four thousand six hundred yards. There were eleven
fora. There were aqueducts and branches to the number
of nineteen, many carried on imposing arches of hewn
stone. There were the nine bridges that spanned the
four hundred feet of the Tiber. There were the great
theaters, amphitheaters, and circuses, with an occasional
stadium or odeum. Everywhere was bronze and marble
ornament. There were three thousand seven hundred
and eighty-five statues in bronze even after Alaric. In

spite of oppressive conditions, and perhaps because of
them, there were still some citizens enormously rich,
and their palaces were establishments of marvellous
size and splendor. "Every house is a town," exclaims
Ammianus, "and Rome includes a myriad of cities."

The heart of the city, as ever, was most imposing of
all. The giant pillared edifices of Palatine and Capitoline, soaring aloft in relief against the sky, were
splendid in material and brilliant with ornament that
caught the light. The impression made by them is reproduced by Claudian on the occasion of Honorius'
visit to Rome and occupation of the Palatine:

"Behold, new honor dignifies the Palatine as with
joy and gladness it receives the divine tenant. . . .
Rearing aloft its crown, with the Rostra far below, the
royal pile looks forth upon countless sanctuaries and
countless sentinel gods encircling it. How fair a sight,
to behold yonder beneath the gable of Thundering Jove
the graven temple doors and their Giants in space above
the Tarpeian Rock, to look upon statues soaring amid
the clouds, and upon the high air dense with thronging
temples, and everywhere the terrain a forest of columns
adorned with beaks from many a conquered ship, and
palaces reposing on foundations mountain-high which
the hands of men have upreared, adding still to Nature,
and arches unnumbered, rich with the glittering spoils
of war! The eye is blinded and bewildered by flashing
metal and the gleam of gold on every hand."

The poet has this part of the city also in mind when
he addresses its savior, Stilicho: "Look about upon the
Seven Hills, how with the gleam of gold they rival the
rays of the sun, and upon arches clothed with the spoil
of battle, and upon temples reared to the clouds."

In spite of her decline in power and population,
Rome was still the most splendid city of the world. But
it was not only the incomparable richness and profusion
of her buildings and monuments that made her great.
To the impressiveness of size and splendor was now
added in all its fulness the impressiveness of age and
historic interest. The monuments of Constantine and
Diocletian and Aurelian themselves were already becoming venerable when Claudian wrote. The monuments of Augustus were four hundred years old, and
spoke of the founding of the empire. There were other
monuments whose origins went back to the times of
consuls and kings, or disappeared in the mists. That
some of them were decaying from natural causes, that
some had suffered from fire and flood, that others were
repaired or restored, that many were being neglected
and some despoiled, that there were abandoned buildings covered with ivy and vacant spaces grown to weeds
and shrubbery, increased the city's hold upon men's
imaginations and affections. Ammianus carried away
the impression of her as a venerable city now entering
upon old age, withdrawing to enjoy the more tranquil
pursuits of life, leaving to the Cæsars as to her sons, like
a parent thrifty, provident, and well-to-do, all the responsibilities of rule.

"Her people," he writes, "from its first cradlings to
its last years of childhood, a period including about
three hundred years, engaged in successful wars about
her walls; then, having entered upon years of adoles-
cence, after many anxious trials in the field crossed the
Alps and the sea; risen to proud youth and manhood,
it brought back laurels and triumphs from every quarter of the limitless circle of the world; and finally, arriv-

ing at the turn of the years toward old age, and conquering often merely by the power of its name, it has retired to the more tranquil things of life. And so the venerable city, after bending the proud necks of undisciplined races and spreading abroad her laws, the everlasting foundations and stays of liberty, like a thrifty parent, provident and well-to-do, has surrendered to the Cæsars, her sons, so to speak, the administration of her property rights. And although the tribes are quiet and the centuries are no longer at variance, and there is no more warring over the ballot, but the peacefulness of Pompilius' time has returned, yet in all parts whatsoever of the world she is acknowledged as mistress and queen, and everywhere the grey hairs and authority of her Fathers are held in regard, and the name of the Roman people is respected and honored."

Rome was the parent who for centuries past had watched over the world with maternal care. The succession of curious visitors which had begun with the confirmation of Roman dominion in the days of the Republic swelled to a broad stream of grateful and reverent pilgrims when once peace was thoroughly established and citizenship had spread to distant parts of the empire. As early as 193, a custodian's lodge existed near the column of Marcus Aurelius. The original of the *Notitia* and *Curiosum* was probably a little guide to the monuments of Rome in the first century. Rome was still the center of the world's interest; her political and military influence had waned, her spiritual influence was increasing. When Stilicho, after the discomfiture of the Goths at Pollentia in the reign of Honorius, held his triumph in Rome, and Constantius chose it for the scene of his triumph in 356, it was not because the old capital actually figured in the life of the empire. Constantius' capital was in the east, and his headquarters in the west were at Milan. Honorius' capital was Ravenna rather than Rome. The Christian pilgrim was already swelling the stream of visitors. Rome had become the sentimental instead of the actual capital of the pagan world. In her material decadence, she was in the transition stage from her ancient supremacy in the world of arms to her mediæval supremacy in the realms of the spirit.

If we wish farther to visualize the city as she approached the end of her pagan life of a thousand years, and to appreciate more fully the effect of her age and monumental splendors, no words can better convey the impression left by them than the account which Ammianus Marcellinus gives of the triumphal entry of Constantius into Rome in the year 356:

"As if the temple of Janus were closed and all his enemies laid low, he was eager to visit Rome, intending to celebrate a triumph because of Magnentius' destruction, though he lacked the right, inasmuch as the blood of the slain was Roman. . . . He wished to display to the city an endless procession, with standards stiff with gold and brilliant guards and retinue, though the people, who were now in peace and quiet, at no time either expected or desired this or any such spectacle; not knowing, perhaps, that certain of the old-time emperors had been content in time of peace with lictors . . . and that many of them had made themselves illustrious by splendid deeds in order to hand down to posterity the memory of glories earned by their own achievements.

"Accordingly, after long and elaborate preparation, in the second prefecture of Orfitus, he passed through

Ocriculum, elated by his great honors, escorted by a
formidable array of marching columns, making his
progress as if in order of battle, while from every direction the eyes of all were fixed upon him and never left
his face. And when he drew near the city, as he contemplated with serene gaze the senate paying their respects, and looked on these figures, reverend because
they were the likeness of the old patrician line, he did
not think, like Cineas the famous ambassador of Pyrrhus, that a multitude of kings was assembled together,
but that here was the asylum of the whole world. And
when he had turned from them to the people, he was
astounded to think in what throngs the whole human
kind had come streaming together from all quarters to
Rome. And as if he would have terrified with the sight
of his arms the Euphrates or the Rhine, with standards
going ahead on either side he himself came on, sitting
alone in a golden car. . . .

"And also, saluted as Augustus by voices of happy
omen, though the hills and shores were filled with thun-
derous clamors, he did not move a muscle, but preserved
the same unchanging countenance he was wont to show
in his provinces. For, very short though he was, he
bowed his body when riding under the high gates, and
as if his neck were fixed bent his gaze straight before
him, turning his face neither to right nor left; and, as
if the statue of a man, when the rolling wheels shook
him, he was never seen either to nod, or to spit, or to
wipe or rub his mouth or nose, or to move his hand. . . .

"Then, having entered Rome, the home of empire
and of all virtues, when he had arrived at the Rostra,
and saw before him that most famed scene of ancient
power, he stood speechless with amazement, his eyes

dazzled by the multitude of wonders that assailed them wherever he turned. After addressing the nobles in the senate, and the people from the tribunal, he was escorted amid resounding applause to the Palace, where he enjoyed himself as he had desired.

"And often, as he was conducting the races, he expressed his delight at the piquant speech of the common people, who were neither presumptuous in their ways nor yet lacking in the sense of their native liberty. He himself, too, maintained a bearing of due respect toward them; for he did not, as was usual in other cities, allow the contests to be finished according to his own preference, but, following the custom, left them to various circumstances.

"Then he went the rounds of the city, visiting the summits of the seven hills and the various places on their slopes and in the level parts, and the suburban districts also. Whatever his eyes first rested upon, he felt sure must excel all the rest. There was the temple of Jupiter on the Tarpeian Mount, as much greater than other temples as the heavenly is greater than the earthly; baths built up like whole provinces; the great pile of the amphitheater, a mass reared solidly in Tiburtine stone, to whose summit human vision found it hard to reach; the Pantheon, like a whole region, rounded and polished, and reared on vaulting of wondrous height; the lofty monuments whose summits, ascended by winding stairways, supported effigies of former emperors; and the temple of the City, and the forum of Peace, and the theater of Pompey, and the Odeum, and the Stadium, and, intermingled with these, the other ornaments of the everlasting city.

"But when he came to the forum of Trajan, a struc-

THE FORUM AND COLUMN OF TRAJAN

THE BASILICA WAS IN THE FOREGROUND,
AND THE GREEK AND LATIN LIBRARIES
ON EITHER SIDE OF THE COLUMN

ture unique under all heaven, which, to my thinking,
even the gods would agree to call wonderful, he was
rooted to the spot with amazement as he contemplated
those gigantic edifices, which are neither to be described
by words nor again to be attempted by mortal men. And
so, compelled to lay aside all hope of undertaking anything of that kind, he said that Trajan's horse alone,
which was located in the middle of the court and bore
the emperor himself, he would imitate, for he could do
that.

"The prince Ormizda, to whose departure from Per-
sia we have referred above, happened to be standing at
his side, and answered, with well-bred wit, 'Sire, you
will first have to order the construction of a stable like
this, if you can, so that the horse you have in mind to
make may succeed to as broad a realm as that of the
horse we are now looking at.'

"He himself, being asked what he thought of Rome,
replied that the one thing that delighted him was to
learn that there, too, men died.

"And so, after he had seen a multitude of things to
his amazement and stupefaction, the emperor complained of Fame as either powerless or spiteful, because,
though she always exaggerated, she had failed of showing forth what was at Rome; and, deliberating a long
time as to what course he should pursue, he determined
to add to the ornament of the city by erecting in the
Circus Maximus an obelisk, of whose origin and form
I shall speak in the fitting place."

To the orientalized despot from the eastern center of
the empire, plainly the western capital was a foreign
city whose splendors were an utter surprise. He was
probably quite as ignorant of the qualities of Roman

character in his own and more ancient times as he was of the actual city. The soldier-historian who describes his visit, however, was one of the many whom the spirit of Rome had seized upon and made its own. We can do no better than to look to him for a judgment of Roman society.

In the two extended passages where he tarries in his narrative to speak of the Romans of the time, it is true that he becomes for the moment satirist rather than chronicler, and sees actual Rome against the background of the ideal Rome of the past, the Rome that had grown to greatness because Virtue and Fortune, commonly at variance, had in her case made a treaty of eternal peace; but his tone is that of the just and truthful observer, anxious both not to seem prejudiced and not to be misunderstood: "And since in my opinion strangers reading my words may wonder why, whenever my pen is turned toward setting forth what is going on in Rome, nothing is told of but seditions and shops and other low matters like them, I shall touch briefly upon the reasons for this, never of my own will departing from the truth." He is anxious not only to tell the truth, but to leave a truthful impression. He not only guards against exaggeration by the use again and again of "sometimes," "often," "many," "certain ones," "there are some who," and like words, but states expressly that it is the few whose worthlessness detracts from the city's greatness. "But this splendor and magnificence of the whole is marred by the tasteless trifling of the few, who do not stop to consider where they were born, but, as if privileged to give the rein to their vices, have fallen into error and wantonness." It is not hostility, or very greatly even indignation, that prompts his words, but rather a mingling of contempt and mild amusement, together with the sincere regret of an admirer of Rome and her traditions.

Ammianus sees the faults of both high and low. The common people and the nobles alike are filled with vanity, always attempting to prove an ancient origin or to keep up appearances. They are insane over the circus, and entirely given to gambling. All friendships at Rome are cool, but those formed over the dice are the only ones with any degree of affection. Some persons, indeed, repudiate the name of gambler, and call themselves "dice-players," but the difference is that between thieves and robbers. The people are lax not only in habit but in manners. Ampelius, the prefect of the city, might have made himself illustrious by correcting the riotous living of the times, but his good intentions were not supported by firmness of purpose. He had resolved that wine-shops should remain closed until the fourth hour of the day, that no one should provide warm water for the common people up to the same hour, that there should be a time-limit for the sale of meats, and that no respectable person should be seen eating in the streets. "Unseemly practices like these, and others of a worse nature, have through long neglect and connivance run riot with so little hindrance that not even the famed Epimenides of Crete, could he in some fabulous manner be called back and return to our times, would be equal alone to the task of purging Rome; under such a burden of shameful and incurable corruption are many laboring."

When Ammianus distinguishes classes, he will speak first of the faults of the upper class and then of the failings of the common people. In his eyes the higher rank is the worse. The vanity of those who compose it is beyond all bounds. Some, who pretend to famous ancestry, go about putting on airs and calling themselves Reburri, and Fabunii, and Pagonii, and Geriones, and Dalii, Tarracii, or Perrasii, and other high-sounding names, to prove the antiquity of their families. You may see them making a show by riding in a carriage higher than the ordinary, or by going about perspiring under a great weight of mantles so delicately textured that the wind blows through them, to which they call attention by wiggling their bodies or by waving the left hand, so that the long fringes and embroideries may be seen. Some of them are as magnificent as if they were being led to execution. When they are lolling in their painted boats on Lake Avernus, "if a fly lights on the silken fringe of their golden fans, or the least ray of the sun breaks through a hole in the awning above them, they complain because they were not born in the land of the Cimmerians." When they come forth from the health-giving waters of the bath at some resort, they dry themselves with napkins of the finest texture, and then open their presses, whence each one takes out with care garments so delicate as to be transparent, and enough to clothe eleven persons; and finally, after selecting some of them and wrapping himself up, takes his rings from the hand of his slave, to whom he has entrusted them to keep them from the moisture, and goes away. Again, "some, though holding only an ordinary office, stalk along the streets with neck stiff and head erect, and giving only a side glance to old acquaintances as they pass, so haughty you would think it was Marcus Marcellus just back from the capture of Syracuse!"

There are some, too, who fancy they can be remem-

bered forever by having gilded statues of themselves
set up, "as if they would reap a greater reward from
senseless brazen images than from the consciousness of
just and honorable deeds." They would do better to
follow the example of Cato the censor, "who, asked
why he had no statue when so many others had, replied, 'I prefer that good men should be in doubt as to
why I have not deserved this favor rather than that
they should go about asking how I had obtained it.'"
"Others, assuming a grave air, praise endlessly their
ancestral acres, though no one has inquired, exaggerating the yearly product of their rich fields, which they
boast of possessing in abundance from the rising to the
setting sun, not being aware that their ancestors, as a
result of whose deeds Rome has reached her present
magnitude, were conspicuous not for riches, but because
through hard-fought wars they overcame by their valor
every enemy that faced them, differing from the common run of soldiers neither in fortune nor in living nor
in quality of clothing."

Their vanity is equalled only by their arrogance and
triviality, and they can fawn and flatter despite their
arrogance. One of your overdressed rich will enter the
public baths with fifty servants and begin to bawl out,
"Where are my men?" If he and his kind see suddenly
some old jade, they all dash up and begin to caress and
wheedle her, praising her as the Parthians would a
Semiramis, or Egypt a Cleopatra. "And these things
they are guilty of,—they, in the days of whose ancestors
a senator was disgraced by the censor for having dared
to kiss his wife in the presence of their own daughter!"
Women drive through the streets with whole armies
of slaves in their trains, arranged in squads and com-

panies according to occupation, with the rear brought up by a multitude of horrible eunuchs old and young, a sight that makes the onlooker curse the memory of the ancient queen who began the practice of thus treating youth. And wherever you turn, your eye finds numbers of women with frizzled hair, who might, if they had married, by this time have been mothers three times, polishing the paving-stones with their feet until they are weary, whirling and tossing in imitation of the innumerable figures put on by players in the theater.

There are "whirlpools of banquets, and a variety of voluptuous allurements," which Ammianus, for fear of growing too lengthy, will pass over; but he will mention those who career through the wide spaces of the city, recklessly urging their horses on over the upturned pavement of silex as if they were the post, dragging behind them squadrons of slaves that look like bands of robbers. It is these that the women drivers imitate. In such a city sober men and persons with brains are of no account. Learning and letters are held in honor no longer. "Instead of the philosopher, there is the singer; in the place of the orator, the teacher of the art of drawing a laugh is employed. Libraries, like tombs, are closed forever. Organs to be played by water-power are manufactured, and lyres so huge that they look like carts, and flutes, and ponderous apparatus for stage exhibitions." When the city was threatened by famine, all the strangers were sent packing, and the few who practiced the liberal arts were thrust out without a moment's breathing-time; but the actresses in the mimes, and their assistants, real or feigned, and three thousand dancing-girls, without a question asked, remained, with all their following and all their dancing-masters. Stran-

gers are no longer welcome in the city and protected
by the patronage of citizens, as in the olden time; now
no one from outside the walls is desired who is not rich,
without children, and unmarried. These are warmly
received, and fawned on, flattered, and courted by those
who expect to be mentioned in their wills. Roman society knows nothing good except what brings profit.
The social secretaries of the rich make a practice of
falsifying their masters' dinner invitations to sell to
obscure and unknown strangers.

Hypocrites and snobs abound. When you meet and
salute them, they offer you in the most extravagant
manner their hands or knees to kiss, thinking this all you
need for perfect happiness; and, even if you have done
them a favor and put them under obligation, they
consider you well repaid if they inquire what baths or
waters you visit, or where you are living. In their houses
you meet chatterboxes who make it a business to praise
their master's every word and act, and to admire the
lofty pillars and walls of inlaid colored stones in their
houses. "Often, too, at their dinners the scales are sent
for, and the fish and birds and dormice on the table
are weighed, and their size repeated again and again,
and boasted of as hitherto unequalled, to the weariness
of those present; especially as there are thirty secretaries by, taking all these figures down in their note-
books, until you would think nothing lacking but a
schoolmaster." If a stranger has been invited to dinner,
to kill his host's brother would be a less serious offence
than to refuse; for a senator who, after much weighing
of the case, has given an invitation, if the guest does
not accept, takes on as though he had lost his whole
estate.

Your reception at the hands of these snobs varies according to occasion or the mood of the entertainer. If you are a stranger with some pretence to standing and enter the home of a wealthy, puffed-up grandee to pay your respects, "at first you find yourself received as if your host had been longing to see you, and are asked question after question, and compelled repeatedly to lie, until you begin to wonder why a great man like that who has never seen you before should so load with attention a little fellow like yourself, and to feel sorry, as you think of this supreme advantage, that you didn't come to Rome ten years before. But if you rely upon this affable reception and do the same thing the next day, why, there you are, unknown and utterly strange, with your insistent host of yesterday all at sea, and for a long time trying to figure out who you are or where you are from. And, supposing that you are finally recognized and admitted to his friendship, and then pay him your respects with assiduity and devotion for the next three years, if you are then absent for the same number of days you will come back and have him meet you exactly as usual, never once asking where you have been in the meantime."

In religion they are superstitious and inconsistent. "Many of them, while denying the existence of higher powers in the heavens, will nevertheless refuse to go out on the street, or to dine, or to think they can safely take a bath, before they have carefully consulted the almanac and found out, for example, where the planet Mercury is, or what part of Cancer the moon is in as she passes through the sky."

They are as inconsistent in other matters. Some of them will give a slave three hundred stripes for being

slow with the hot water, and on the other hand condone
the offense if he has purposely killed a man. They try
to escape diseases, which are so violent in the capital
that the physician's art is helpless before them, by making it a rule for no one to visit a sick friend, and not
even to admit back into the house a slave who has been
sent to make inquiry, until he has taken a bath. They
are thus afraid of contagion that has merely been looked
upon by the eyes of another. Yet, with all these precau-
tions so carefully taken, let them be invited to a wed-
ding, where gold is waiting for them in the hollow palm
of a right hand, and, though their bodily powers are
broken, they will muster strength if they have to go as
far as Spoletum.

These are the ways of the nobles, says Ammianus;
this is enough about the senatorial class. Now he will
speak of the idle and lazy common people, some of
whom, shoeless as they are, boast of high-sounding
names, and call themselves Cimessores, Statarii, Semi-
cupæ, Serapina, Cicimbricus, Gluturiorus, Trulla, Lu-
canicus, Pordaca, Salsula, or the like. These men "spend
all their days in wine-drinking and gambling, in the
brothels, and in the pleasures of the public shows. The
Circus Maximus is their temple and home and rendez-
vous, the sum of their hopes and desires. You may see
them in the market-places, at the street corners, in the
public squares and assembly-places, gathered in groups,
disputing and quarreling, some taking one side, some
another." Some of them pass the whole night in the
wine-shops, some lie hidden under the awnings of shady
nooks about the theaters. They quarrel over their games
of dice, noisily snuffling and drawing the breath back
through the nose. Or, what is the greatest of all their

delights, they are from sunrise to sunset, rain or shine, gaping at drivers and horses to detect their good or bad points. Old greybeards among them may be heard crying out that the state will fall if a certain driver does not win in a coming race. Before sunrise on the day of the races you may see them rushing to the circus with a speed that would do justice to the horses themselves. They are torn in pieces by the violence of their excitement, and most of them cannot sleep for anxiety. "And it is very wonderful to see the innumerable common people, their minds glowing with the ardor of excitement, hanging upon the event of the races. These things, and others like them, will not permit the doing of anything serious or worth mention at Rome."

There may be in these judgments something of the exaggeration that inheres in the satirical, but we hear them pronounced with little doubt as to their essential truthfulness, and find them confirmed by other evidence. When we learn that it was usual for the masters of the first houses to have an income of over a million dollars, and for families of the second to enjoy three hundred thousand, and reflect that the city was a capital filled with grandees and retired officials and moneyed men, and that slavery still existed, the vanity and triviality witnessed by Ammianus seem probable enough. When we read that the senator Probus spent a quarter of a million on the shows provided by his son, a prætor-elect, and that Symmachus, with at least three palaces in Rome or near it, and fifteen country seats in Italy, spent four hundred thousand on a similar occasion, and that Maxentius gave a series of festivities which lasted seven days and cost eight hundred thousand, it is no longer surprising to hear of the craze of

the people for spectacles. There had been one hundred
and thirty-five days of the year given to public festivities of some sort in the time of Marcus Aurelius; in
Ammianus' time there were one hundred and seventy-
five, whose entertainments the ambition or liberality of
rich men and rulers on the one hand, and the demands of
the people on the other, made as varied and as osten-
tatious as possible. Seventy-five years before the time
of Constantine, between four and five thousand gladiators had fought in the course of a single year; even after
the reign of the Christian emperor, who forbade it, the
sport lasted on a hundred years. Ten days were assigned
to it, sixty-four to the circus, one hundred and one to
the theater. The favorite sport, however, was the race.
To make real the absorption of the Romans in them
before their occurrence and their frenzied excitement
while they were in progress, would require a greater
pen than Ammianus possessed. Perhaps they can be
better imagined as we read of whites and greens and
blues and reds and purples; of twenty-two to twenty-
four races in one day in Caligula's time; of glittering
processions with the brightly colored cars and jockeys
of the different factions, and the president of the day,
and priests and deities, and bands of trumpeters; of the
great tiers of seats containing a hundred and fifty thousand vociferating people, with the great loggia on the
side of the Palatine for the imperial dignitaries and at
times the emperor himself, and boxes for senators and
grandees; of drivers winning races into the thousands
and worshipped by the populace; of Diocles, who won
five thousand two hundred and fifty-one, with purses
amounting to a million eight hundred thousand; of one
man who threw himself into a driver's funeral pyre;

of Christians yielding to the popular craze and justifying themselves by Elijah's example. And finally, when we remember that the emperor's dole of wine and oil and pork was a custom that had been continued for half a millennium, it is easy to believe that the common people were idle and lazy and without pride.

Of the worst feature of Roman character Ammianus says little except by implication. The change which had set in with the first day of the empire had reached its consummation. The Roman of these latter days was almost without trace of the heroic pride and sense of responsibility that constituted the greatness of Roman character in the formative days of the state. Whether or not it was bound under any condition to disappear, the monarchy encouraged its rapid decline and in the end accomplished its destruction. The worst result of tyranny was not that it robbed the citizen of his privileges. The crowning wrong of the empire as an institution was its taking from him his duties. The emperor fed the people, thus fostering and perpetuating their idleness. The emperor maintained a personal standing army, and discouraged men of property and position from entering the service lest rivals rise against him; in the later fourth century, senators had been excluded from the legions, and ordinary citizens were forbidden to carry weapons. Mercenaries of foreign birth soon came to make up the army; a Gaul in Tiberius' time declared that its only real strength was in the foreign contingents. The emperor absorbed all the old-time political powers, and thus removed the great goals of civic ambition. He made the laws, and charged himself with their interpretation and execution. The wisdom of the citizen in their creation, as well as his strength in their upholding, was no longer demanded. The emperor's administration thought for the people, and the citizen body was stripped of all obligation except to obey. Education became a matter of purely personal interest instead of a preparation for active civic life. Eloquence was an accomplishment for the school instead of an instrument to use in the public career. The round of artificial and arid exercises in rhetoric, the barren trifling with the philosophers, the almost absolute lack of science, did much to separate the mind and sentiments from the realities of life and to render useless the talent that may have existed. The qualities of the citizen-soldier had begun to lose tone before the beginning of the first century; by the fourth they had died from lack of exercise. The end of the third century after Augustus finds the Roman citizen designating the state by *regnum,* the word best hated in Rome for a score of generations, and the end of the fourth finds him resorting to evasion, desertion, and self-mutilation to escape the call to arms against the Goths.

Keeping equal pace with the change in the spirit of citizenship went the change in race and position. The mingling of slave and free and native and foreign, the rise of the humble and the fall of the proud, the interchange between capital and province, had run their course. The old stock and the old names were all but gone. The names that provoked the satire of Ammianus are the sign of the great change. The nations had belonged to Rome; now Rome belonged to the nations. Gibbon is extreme, but represents the truth: "The nation of soldiers, magistrates, and legislators who composed the thirty-five tribes of the Roman People, was dissolved into the common mass of mankind, and con-

founded with the millions of servile provincials who
had received the name, without adopting the spirit, of
Romans." The mediæval Roman was at hand.

And the mediæval religion was at hand. The faiths
of the nations had mingled as well as their bloods. The
old stock of the gods had dwindled and changed, and
all but disappeared. It was not in the name of Jupiter,
Juno, Apollo, and Minerva that paganism stood against
the new religion, but in the name of Isis the Egyptian,
Cybele the Phrygian, and Mithras the Persian, and the
hosts of their lesser brothers and sisters. It was no
longer Roman common sense, or Romanized Hellenic
philosophy, or even the reasoned myths of neo-Platonism, that supplemented religion and supplied the spur
to conduct, but astrology and the grosser superstitions
of Egypt and the east. These oriental faiths and superstitions had once been the captives and slaves, so to
speak, of Roman religious life. Like the actual slaves,
they had risen first to freedom, and finally, through in-
termingling and evolution, to respectability and mas-
tery; but, like them, too, they were compounded with
the old into something that was no longer of the ancient
Roman world, but was already in transition to the world
of the Middle Age. With the Christian faith, they represented the hope of eternal life; but the dross was too
much for the gold.

It must not be thought that the age was without stirrings of the ancient spirit. Ammianus, Syrian Greek
though he is, and a stranger in the city, measures men
and manners by the standards of Cato and the days of
heroic citizenship. Julian the Hellene is hard with himself in the manner of Marcus Aurelius. The accomplished Symmachus, orator, stylist, and gentleman, in-

carnates once more the public spirit of the ancient
patrician families. In Nicomachus Flavianus, a last defender of the faith against the militant new religion, the
proud and aristocratic spirit of the state religion revives
for a brief moment before the final agony. Pedantic
Macrobius appreciates and preserves for us from
Cicero's *Republic* the sonorous language and sublime
sentiment of *Scipio's Dream*. Vettius Agorius Prætextatus, the capable pagan prefect of the city, teaches the
rioting factions of the Christian Church to keep order
and respect the law of the land, if not of their religion.
Among the hosts of the Most Distinguished, Most Perfect, Egregious, Illustrious, and Respectable into which
bureaucratic society had crystallized, there were many
who imitated and emulated the few whose names and
sentiments are known to us. Among the throngs who
lived for Bread and the Circus, and among the greater
throngs who wrought for an honest livelihood and lived
the eternal average of human life, there were many possessors of the ancient heritage. The rapid increase of
the Church itself was an indication of the presence of
worth, and when toleration became assured the Christian as well as the pagan was proud of the grandeur
that was Rome.

It was not a society in which all was ruin. It was a
society which in the matter of morals thought well of
itself. Apollinaris Sidonius, bishop of Auvergne, con-
gratulating his generation in about 460 on being more
decent than their ancestors, is no more sincere, and it
may be no more truthful, than the pagan guests in
Macrobius' *Saturnalia* when they pay the same compli-
ment to the end of the preceding century. It was a so-

ciety whose greatest fault was lack of spirit. It was not so much vicious as tired and wornout.

It was a society which could still feel pride in the city's past and present. To the Roman, as well as to men in general, Rome was the "venerable mother" of Ammianus, who had "spread abroad her laws, the everlasting foundations and stays of liberty"; the "mother of arms and justice" of Claudian, "who has extended her sway over all mankind, the first to cradle them in law; who, beginning in narrow bounds, spread to the twin Poles, and setting forth from her little realm reached abroad her hands wherever shone the sun; . . . who alone has taken to her bosom the conquered, and cherished the human family under one common name as mother, not as queen, and has called the subdued by the name of citizen and bound them from afar with the bonds of love. To her peace-bringing ways we owe it that the stranger may feel every land his own, and men may change their abode at pleasure; that to look upon Thule and to visit places that once were dread is but pastime; that we may drink of Orontes or Rhone; that we all are of one great family."

It was a society strangely confident of the city's future. Rome was still to the men of those perilous times the Eternal City,—"Rome, destined to live as long as men shall be," once more in the phrase of Ammianus. Some alarm at the frequent approach of the northern invader they may have felt, but at each escape the old security and confidence returned. Their own and the city's weakness was not a reality to them as it is to us. Their imagination refused to conceive of the downfall either of the empire or of Rome. She was the city of Claudian, "the city as everlasting as the Pole," "to whose reign there never shall be an end." She was the city of Symmachus' pride; it was from *her* Alps to *her* Ocean that the Rhine flowed, and from the couch of rising Aurora to the goal of the setting sun she looked upon nothing not her own. The Goths themselves were struck with awe, and for a moment withheld their hands.

The men of these late autumn days were nearer right, and nearer wrong, than they knew. The sceptered sway they dreamed of as eternal was already crumbling, soon to perish utterly. The Roman armies had long been training in their own ranks the men who were to accomplish the downfall of Roman rule. The spiritual sway which was destined to replace the material, and which as yet they saw but as through a glass, darkly, was far along in its evolution.

VIII.

THE RISE OF THE CHRISTIAN EMPIRE

Cruciate, torquete, damnate, atterite nos: probatio est enim innocentiæ nostræ iniquitas vestra. Ideo nos hæc pati deus patitur. Nam et proxime ad lenonem damnando Christianam potius quam ad leonem confessi estis labem pudicitiæ apud nos atrociorem omni pœna et omni morte reputari. Nec quicquam tamen proficit exquisitior quæque crudelitas vestra; inlecebra est magis sectæ. Plures efficimur quotiens metimur a vobis; semen est sanguis Christianorum,—

Crucify us, torture us, condemn us, wear our bodies out,—your injustice to us is the proving of our innocence. It is for this reason that God permits us to suffer these things. For recently by condemning a Christian woman to the brothel rather than to the beasts, you admitted that among us a stain upon woman's honor is considered worse than any punishment or any death. And yet all your far-sought cruelties do you no good; they are but an attraction that add to our sect. The more we are cut off by you, the more we spring up. The blood of the Christians is their seed.

TERTULLIAN, Apologeticus, 50

1.

THE CITY OF THE DEAD

THERE were really two empires. There was a sinking empire, and there was a rising empire; an empire whose tissue was slowly decaying and beginning to fall apart, and an empire which was steadily growing in the strength of youth; an empire within an empire. Just as with the bulb, even before the outer sheath is far along in decay, there is already growing within it the new life which will increase by feeding on the old plant until it bursts the rotten fiber asunder, so in the heart of Roman pagan civilization at the moment of its greatest ascendency there was already beginning to swell the new organism which was destined to consume the body of the old, but to reproduce its form in a new substance.

There were two cities in Rome, just as there were two empires in the Roman world. There was a great city in the process of decay, and there was a city just springing into life; a visible city, and an invisible city. The remains of the one are to be seen above ground in the ruins of temple, palace, basilica, aqueduct, and amphitheater, in all the host of monuments testifying to its power and pride. Of the other, all that survives is below ground,—the long corridors of the catacombs, with chapel and sarcophagus, niche and inscription, to tell of its humility in life and its hope in death.

The city of the earliest Christian living left no traces of itself among the great monuments inside the pagan

city. Its life was obscure and retiring, its citizens poor
alike in worldly goods and standing. Their own humble
abodes were at the same time their homes, their temples,
and their schools. The gloomy dungeon of the Tullianum at the head of the Forum, and the ruinous walls
of the Coliseum looking down on the sands of its gigantic arena, are the only material monuments within
the limits of Rome itself which bear witness of the relations between the two cities, and their tale is eloquent
only of separateness and opposition.

But Pale Death summoned with impartiality both
rich pagan and poor Christian. In the vast city of the
ancient Roman dead which girdled the city of the Roman living the Christian was represented as well as his
pagan neighbor. Nothing in the Roman Campagna is
more impressive than the two long lines of ruined se-
pulchral magnificence which stretch along the miles of
the silent Appian Way; yet all the great pagan burial-
places that border the highways radiating from the
city will rival neither in impressiveness nor extent the
cemeteries of the Roman Christians which lie not far
away, unseen and unsuspected, beneath the brown
reaches of the Latin plain. In a wide circle about the
city at a distance of from one to three miles, but more
numerous to the northeast and to the south, repose some
forty communities of the ancient Christian dead, in
galleries sometimes six one below another and reaching
seventy-five feet into the earth, whose total length would
amount to more than five hundred miles.

The visitor to Rome who knows of the catacombs
only through sermon, popular lecture, and romance,
and who has formed the idea of a district rugged with
rocks and caverns to which the Christian population in

masses fled for refuge during times of persecution, emerging only after the danger was past, may be surprised on first approach to them. He is conducted into the cloister of a church, or the garden of a country inn, or the grounds of a villa beyond the walls, and descends to a cemetery as he would to a cellar; or he enters the portals of one in the side of a bank of tufa by the highway; or, more commonly, he turns through a roadside gate and emerges in a peaceful meadow in the rolling farm-fields of the Campagna, hardly aware that he is treading historic ground.

The catacombs are for all that none the less impressive. On the twenty-second of November, pilgrim and sightseer pass through the gate of Saint Sebastian and traverse the mile and a half of the New Appian Way which leads to the catacombs of Saint Calixtus, seventeen hundred years ago their superintendent and afterwards bishop of Rome. The twenty-second of November is Saint Cecilia's day. With the stream of other visitors they pass through the gate in the wall of brick which borders the way, and find themselves in a level field. There are a few eucalyptus, pine, and cypress trees, and beds of roses. A short distance from the ancient oratory of Saint Calixtus, which stands near the entrance, in the midst of the roses and the shrubbery they see the stream of humanity continually disappearing into a portal, as continually to reappear at another portal but a few rods away.

They descend by a flight of twenty or thirty steps into the bosom of the rolling landscape of the Campagna, and stand in the home of the Christian dead. Guided by the light of serene candles, the throng moves quietly along over the uneven path through the long succession of high corridors and cross-corridors, with shoulders brushing against walls of dark-brown tufa which are often less than a yard apart. On the right and left, and above their heads in the face of the walls, are the innumerable niches in which the dead, enveloped in tunic and winding-sheet with coating of plaster, were laid to await the resurrection. Most of the niches are now agape, long since profaned and despoiled by greedy or curious hands, or even by the pious in quest of relics; but many of them, too, are faced as on the day of entombment with the marble slab, set in with mortar, which is still allowed to keep the trust confided to it. The name of the dead, sometimes his years, are inscribed on the protecting slab, with many a phrase expressive of simple faith and practice: "Lucilla sleeps in peace"; "Regina: live in the Lord Jesus"; "Vincentia, in Christ: pray for Phœbe and her Verginius"; "Anatolius placed this for his well-deserving son, who lived years seven, months seven, days twenty: may thy spirit rest in God: pray for thy sister"; "Constantia, in peace, who lived years fifty-one"; "Utulius Calligonus: gentle soul, live ever in the Lord"; "Agape: live forever"; "Atticus: sleep in peace, secure in thine own salvation, and pray earnestly for our sins." Many a phrase is ungrammatical, many a word spelled by the unlettered Muse, many a line rudely cut. Many an epitaph is in Greek. Many a sacred symbol is cut into the stone, to testify more eloquently of faith and hope than the words they stand beside. There are the dove and the olive branch of peace; the cross; the monogram of Constantine; the anchor of faith; the ship of steadfastness breasting the waves of life; the vine; the fruitful branch; the tree of life; the Alpha and the Omega; the mystic

THE CATACOMBS OF SAINT CALIXTUS

THE DESCENT IS NEAR THE SMALL BUILDINGS
AMONG THE TREES

fish, whose spelling in Greek resolves into the initial letters of Jesus Christ, Son of God, Savior.

At the end of a corridor or one of its short branches, or at an intersection, a widening and deepening of the space marks a tomb of the great, perhaps of a martyr, or a chapel for the gatherings of anniversary days. Here the slabs which cover the niches may be more elaborately inscribed, the wall may be stuccoed, and still show, in dull and faded fragments, almost incoherent, the remains of sacred story told by the brush of the painter; or sarcophagi may be ranged along its base, with uncouth sculptures attempting the same narration. Here, stands the Good Shepherd with the lost lamb upon his shoulders. There, Moses smites, and living waters gush from the rock. There, is Noah and the ark. There, the whole story of Jonah. There, are Abraham and Isaac, Adam and Eve, Tobias, the Last Supper, the Holy Family.

The stream of pilgrims from many lands moves turbidly on until it enters and fills to overflowing a chapel more brightly illuminated than the rest. Here, in the year 821, eleven hundred years ago, were found the mortal remnants of Cecilia, who suffered for the Name toward the close of the second century. On the chapel floor lies the marble statue representing her prostrate figure as the headsman of Marcus Aurelius left it after the vain attempt to slay. Masses of flowers cover the pavement, the air is charged with their odors, a funeral hush is over the assembly.

The hush deepens. A voice rises in the solemn chant, and begins the service commemorating the passion of the Roman daughter in Christ of seventeen centuries and a half ago. As the strains of the chorale rise in answer, strangely faint in the breathless chamber so far removed from the light of day, they add to the sense of reverence and compassion already reigning, the sense of awe at thought of the ages that have passed since these corridors first heard the chant for the blessed dead who died in the Lord.

The catacombs were neither the natural rock formations of popular imagination nor the enlarged quarries sometimes supposed by the antiquarian. They were simply excavations for burial purposes, the gradual growth of some three hundred years, in the great mass of soft tufa and volcanic ash that form the bed of the Campagna. Their beginnings as Christian cemeteries go back to the later years of the first century, but even before that the nucleus of more than one of them already existed in the great roadside crypts that received the dead of distinguished Roman families, ready for Christian use when their owners became converts to the new religion and extended the privilege of their private burial-places to the humbler brethren of the Church communities. They were therefore hardly in use during the earliest persecutions; nor were they used at any period, except in rare instances and for the shortest time, as places of refuge. Life in them was confined to the ceremonies of interment and to anniversaries of the dead, especially the martyr dead. The romantic stories of their all being connected, and of their extending under the Tiber, or to the mountains and the sea, are without foundation.

The growth of the catacombs in the second century was still gradual. In the eyes of the law they were only private cemeteries, and their patrons were never wholly safe from molestation. By the beginning of the third, however, a change had taken place. The catacombs had evolved into corporation burial-places held by the different parishes in the city, and the Christians, though still under the ban as regarded religion, were allowed as burial guilds the usual rights of the well-known pagan corporations. From that time on they were freely used, and their growth was rapid throughout the century. After the edict of Milan in 313, with the removal of all danger from interference with burial or from violation of tombs, and all necessity of secrecy or separateness, their use diminished, until at last their excavation was practically discontinued, and surface burial became the rule, with the rank and file of the Christian dead laid away in trenches walled with brick, sometimes containing lines of bodies ten deep. In the later fourth and early fifth centuries, burial in the catacombs was a rare occurrence, and usually due to the desire to rest in holy places near the remains of the saints who had died for the faith, and whose tombs had multiplied in the times of persecution. By the time that burial there had ceased altogether because of unsafety, and had been transferred to the deserted spaces nearer the city walls or within them, the catacombs had become noted for the visitations of pilgrims.

2.

THE BLOOD OF THE MARTYRS

THUS, just as the towering ruins within the city walls represent centuries in the life of pagan Rome, the mazes of corridors, chapels, and niches in the catacombs outside represent centuries in the life of Christian Rome. At Rome least of all was paganism quickly supplanted. The new religion from the first attracted many adherents, and in the end its effect amounted to revolution; but a process which required for its consummation a length of time almost as great as that from the discovery of America to the present day can hardly be called by a name denoting sudden change.

There were no doubt Christians at Rome as early as the reign of Claudius (41-54), though there is no direct evidence to prove it. Under Nero there is abundant proof of their presence. The letter of Paul to the Romans in 58 makes it clear that a Christian community of importance existed in the city, though the statement in *The Acts* that "the brethren came to meet Paul as far as The Three Taverns," a station twenty-five miles out on the Appian Way, may mean that it was very small. The presence of the apostle, however, who "dwelt two whole years in his hired house, and received all that came in unto him," and his "preaching the Kingdom of God, and teaching those things which concern the Lord Jesus Christ, with all confidence, no man forbidding him," had their effect, and later under Nero the community swelled to appreciable numbers, though its members were not understood, and in the minds of the Romans were confused, if not identified, with the Jews, of whom there were upwards of fifty thousand in the city, and to whom Paul had addressed his efforts. If we are to believe the historian of the time, it was not their peculiar beliefs which drew to them the attention of the emperor, but rather their general reputation as people who shrank from the rest of society because of hatred of the human kind; a reputation which the Jews, clannish and uncompromising, devoted only to religion and trade, and despising the Roman people, had already established for themselves. Not even this, however, would under ordinary circumstances have brought his cruelty upon them; it was only because he found it convenient to divert from himself the charge of having set the great fire that he noticed them and singled them out for punishment. The Christians were made the scapegoats of the emperor, and the people were not unwilling to see the fall of the most disagreeable sect of the time.

"And so, for the purpose of putting an end to rumor," writes Tacitus, "Nero charged with the crime and inflicted the most unusual punishments upon those whom the people commonly called *Christiani,* and who were hated for their criminal conduct. The author of this sect, Christus, was put to death in the reign of Tiberius by the procurator Pontius Pilate; and the deadly superstition, repressed for the time being, had broken out not only in all Judea, the original home of the evil, but even in the city of Rome, where all things atrocious and shameful flow from every direction and find favor. And so those were first brought to trial who confessed the charge, and then, as a result of their evidence, an immense number were convicted, not so much because they were charged with being incendiaries as because they were guilty of hatred of the human kind; and as they perished they were made to afford sport for the people by being covered with the skins of wild beasts and torn in pieces by dogs, or by being affixed to crosses to be set on fire, so that when the daylight had failed they might furnish light for the night as they were consumed. . . ."

By the time of Domitian the distinction between Jew and Christian had become clear. The Christians were not only like the Jews in their claims to being the chosen of God, but were unlike them in spreading their religion among the Gentiles with a fervor hitherto unknown. The persecution of Christians, which under Nero had been almost an accident, now appeared in the light of settled policy on the part of the throne. Domitian's persecution, however, was neither extensive nor very violent. It ceased, too, before the end of his reign; for the emperor had satisfied himself that there was less danger from the new religion than was supposed. Among those believed with good reason to have died for the Name were two members of the most noble families of the city. One was Flavius Clemens, son of Vespasian's brother and cousin of the emperor Domitian himself; the other was Acilius Glabrio, consul in 91 with the future emperor Trajan. Flavia Domitilla, the wife of Flavius Clemens, and his niece, of the same name, were banished. The catacombs of Saint Domitilla, to the south of the city, probably took form around the private cemetery of this family. Acilius Glabrio, many persons of whose name were placed in the cemetery of Saint Priscilla, was possibly the founder of the catacombs on the Via Salaria which bear the name of that saint.

It is doubtful whether the policy of Domitian was either based upon a clear idea as to the danger that lay in Christianity or was universally applied. The first known ruling which had a universal bearing on the treatment of the Christians is the rescript of Trajan. It is addressed to the governor of only one province, but represents the emperor's attitude toward all his realms.

Pliny the Younger, Trajan's governor in Bithynia from 111 to 113, finds himself in doubt as to the disposal of Christians brought before him, for he has never before conducted trials in which they were involved. Are the young and the old to be treated alike, and the weak and the strong? Is renunciation to be rewarded by pardon? Are Christians to be punished merely because they profess the religion, or is the ground of action to be instead the abominations which actually form part of its practice? What weight is to be attached to anonymous denunciations?

Up to the present, Pliny has followed this mode of procedure: "I have asked them whether they were Christians. On their confession of the fact, I have asked them a second and a third time, with threats of punishment. If they have persisted, I have ordered their execution; for I have had no doubt that, whatever they confessed, their pertinacity and their inflexible obstinacy at least ought to bring punishment upon them. There have been some afflicted with the same madness whom, because of their being citizens, I have taken steps to have sent to Rome for trial. . . . When those who have denied that they either were or had been Christians have called upon the gods in my presence, and have gone through the forms of worship, with incense and wine, before your likeness, which, with the images of the gods, I have ordered brought in for the purpose, and in addition to this have cursed Christ,—none of which acts those who are in real truth Christians can be brought to perform,—I have thought them deserving of discharge. . . . Some have said that they were Christians, and then presently denied it, saying that they had been but had ceased to be. . . . They have affirmed, moreover, that the worst crime, or rather mistake, of which they had been guilty, had consisted in their custom of coming together before dawn on stated days to sing together a hymn to Christ, as if to God, and to bind themselves by an oath not to commit theft, robbery, or adultery, and not to deny a deposit when called upon. After this, according to their statement, they had been wont to separate. They had been accustomed to come together again to partake of a meal, common to all, and without blame; but they had discontinued even this after the edict in which, in obedience to your instructions, I had forbidden the existence of secret societies. . . . I have been able to discover nothing except a distorted and exaggerated superstition. . . . The matter seems to me to demand consultation especially on account of the number of those who are in danger. For many, of every age, of every rank, and of both sexes, are being called into jeopardy, and will continue to be in the future. Not merely cities, but villages, too, and country districts, have been thoroughly infected with the contagion of this wretched superstition."

The emperor is so clear, concise, and unhesitating in his reply that he seems to be communicating a policy which has been carefully thought out, whether by himself or by his predecessor Nerva, or even by Domitian. "No definite rule, to apply in all cases, can be laid down," he answers. "The Christians are not to be sought out. If brought before you and found guilty, they are to be punished; but on this condition, that whosoever denies that he is a Christian, and makes good his assertion by performing acts of worship to our gods, is to have full pardon, however greatly suspected in the past. Anonymous charges are in no case to be admitted as evidence."

The ruling of the emperor is plainly a compromise. In Trajan's mind the Christian offence is political rather than moral, potential rather than active, enough of a crime to justify punishment when forced on the state's attention, yet not enough to admit of stern initiative on the part of a conscientious government.

Such a policy was satisfactory to neither party, and the weakness of its logic was apparent especially to the Christian. Tertullian, two generations later, sees in it not compromise, but contradiction: "O self-contradictory verdict, which says they are not to be sought out, because they are innocent, and yet orders them to be punished as criminals; which spares while it rages, which shuts the eye to crime and yet chastises it."

Whether the ruling of Trajan represents a new policy, or merely the formulation of a policy already in existence, it affords us the means of understanding the imperial attitude toward Christianity from Trajan up to the end of his century. Hadrian, it is true, laid down in his rescript the principle that no Christian was to be punished unless guilty of actual crime or misdemeanor, thus seeming to make impossible the conviction of a Christian simply on the ground of his profession of the

Name; and it is true also that under Marcus Aurelius
in some cases the Christians were sought out; but this
did not result in any wide divergence from the principle of Trajan. Notwithstanding the rescript of Hadrian there continued to be instances where mere profession was regarded as a crime and punished, but in
the main, even under Marcus Aurelius, the practice was
not to seek the Christians out. The attitude during the
whole of the second century, in spite of occasional variation, was essentially that of Trajan.

It is apparent that such an attitude could not inspire,
and would not admit of, a general persecution. It is
equally plain that under this policy no Christian could
feel assured of safety from informers and officials, and
that his peace, and even his life, depended upon the
good will of his pagan neighbors and the faithfulness of
his Christian friends. The straight and narrow path of
the Christian life was also the path to possible martyrdom. While there were no general or even widely reaching persecutions during the second century, there were
cases constantly arising in every part of the empire,
especially in the east, where Christianity had taken root
earlier and grown more rapidly. Occasionally, as in
Bithynia under Trajan, and in Gaul under Marcus
Aurelius, the severity became acute in a single district.
The law against the Christians was always ready at
hand, like any other law. Whether it was enforced or
not depended upon circumstance. A hundred different
causes, from the genuine alarm of prefect or emperor
at the Christian's undermining of the state's authority
to the spite of a neighbor or the desire of the rabble for
an afternoon of excitement in the arena, might result
in the blood of the martyrs. "If the Tiber rises to the

walls," cries Tertullian, "if the Nile does not reach the fields, if the skies are rainless, if there is an earthquake, if a famine, if a plague, immediately rises the cry, 'The Christians to the lions!' "

But the beginning of the third century brought with it a change. The Church had grown enormously. Tertullian, in Africa, had already made his defiant boast of Christian numbers: "We are of yesterday, and we already fill all that is yours,—your cities, your islands, your fortress-towns, your municipalities, your meeting-places, your councils, your very camps, your tribes, your public service, the imperial palace, the senate, the forum. We have left you nothing but your temples. . . . Without recourse to arms, and without rebellion, but by merely disagreeing with you, we could have fought you by the ill will engendered through keeping separate from you; for if such a multitude of men had broken away from you and removed to some distant corner of the world, your rule would surely have been put to shame by the loss of so many citizens, whatever their character, and would have suffered from bare desertion. Beyond doubt, you would have been terrified at your solitude, at the silence in everything, and at the stupor of a world as if dead. You would have had to look for subjects to rule over; more enemies would have remained than citizens."

Justin and Irenæus had said before Tertullian that no corner of earth, even among barbarians, was without its prayers in the name of Jesus crucified. "They take root and spread like noxious weeds," said their enemies. "Their places of reunion are multiplying everywhere." They had grown not only in numbers, but in strength of organization, and now more than ever presented themselves to the eyes of the government in the guise of a state within a state. There were sixty bishops in Italy alone. The new cult must either be forced to assimilate with the state or be utterly destroyed. Local persecution, depending for its frequency and severity upon the character of governor and populace rather than upon the emperor himself, continued to be the normal condition; but it was supplemented by outbursts of general persecution directed by the now alarmed and angered administration. The persecutions during the reigns of Severus and Caracalla (193-217) are the first which may be called general, though they centered in Africa. Under Maximin (235-238) came another, lasting less than two years but characterized by great cruelty. A third, under Decius (249-251), and continuing under Gallus (251-252), was aimed especially at the heads of the Church, in the effort to weaken its organization. At this time there were in Rome forty-six priests, seven deacons, seven sub-deacons, forty-two acolytes, fifty-two exorcists, readers, and doorkeepers, and the Church maintained over fifteen hundred widows and needy, all representing a total of from thirty to forty thousand faithful. After a few years of tranquillity, Valerian (253-268) instituted another, which raged in 257 and 258. Finally, most thoroughly organized, most sweeping, long-continued, and bloody of all, came the great persecution of Diocletian at the turn of the century.

By this time the Christians are variously estimated to have formed from one-twentieth to one-half of the empire's population, and enjoyed the feeling of confidence that comes from numbers and importance. They

MAP OF THE CATACOMBS

REPRODUCED BY PERMISSION OF DESCLÉE, LEFEVRE & CO., FROM
MARUCCHI'S ÉLÉMENTS D'ARCHÉOLOGIE CHRÉTIENNE

were in the army, in the civil service, and even at court.
At Rome there were forty or more basilicas and about
thirty cemeteries. At Nicomedia, in the very view of
the emperor's palace, stood one of their most important
churches. Whatever the case in the west, in the east
the dawn of toleration seemed at hand. But Diocletian
and his colleagues, in three edicts of 303 and the following year, deprived Christians of the rights of Roman
citizenship, ordered the arrest of bishops and clergy who
would not give up their books and sacred scriptures, and
the application of every means of coercion to turn the
obstinate back from the traitorous faith.

This was the deepest dark before the dawn. Ten
years after Diocletian's first edict of persecution, the
edict of Milan gave equal rights to Christianity with
paganism. Then began the long century of the gradual
downfall and destruction of the pagan cult. The conversion of Constantine and the favoring attitude of
Constans and Constantius inspired the Church with
confidence and rapidly swelled its membership. Paganism lost its prestige; not even the attempt of Julian to
restore the ancient worship produced a permanent
effect. The positive enactments against it, which had
begun with the measure of Constans and Constantius in
341 ordering the cessation of sacrifice under penalty, increased in number and effectiveness in the second half
of the century until their culmination in the sweeping
laws of Theodosius, which deprived paganism of its
temples and forbade all worship, both public and private. The short revival under the rebel Eugenius in
394, when for a few months Rome was the scene of a
brilliant series of pagan festivals, was the dying gasp

of the old religion. From that time forward, paganism was dead in the eyes of the law, and existed, where it had not utterly disappeared, only in the secrecy of the pagan home.

3.

THE WAY MADE STRAIGHT

THUS, after a life of a thousand years, had Roman paganism run its course, and Christianity taken its place.

Great as were the changes which had occurred, however, the process cannot be called a revolution. It was rather an evolution, long, painful, and agonizing, but wholly natural and necessary; as natural and necessary as the springing of the new plant from the bulb of the old. It involved decomposition, but also recomposition. The old decayed only to live again in the new under different form. If the change was momentous, it was more because of the rearrangement of the old than because of the creation of what was new. The thing that had been, it was that which was to be; and that which had been done was that which was to be done; and there was no new thing under the sun.

In the first place, Christianity was a natural step in the process of religious evolution at Rome. The old Roman religion in its earliest and animistic stage had included belief in a countless multitude of divine beings; not only every object, but every act, was immanent with spirit. In the passage of time, as attention became centered upon the more remarkable, the number grew less. Animism passed into polytheism. However long they lingered elsewhere, in the formal worship of the state comparatively few of the gods of the earliest times survived. The introduction of the principal deities, first of the neighboring Latin and Italic tribes, then of the

Etruscans, then of the more remote nations of Italy, and finally of Greece herself, while increasing the number of gods worshipped by the state, contributed nevertheless to the same concentration upon the few more remarkable cults. By the time of the late Republic, the greater number of the native Roman deities had faded into obscurity, and were known only in a few surviving ceremonies and in the lore of the antiquary.

Nor did the process of restriction cease with this. The identification and blending of newly received gods from abroad with similar deities already in existence at Rome tended also to lessen the number of the deities known to the Roman world from the earlier time. Etruscan gods were found to be identical with Roman gods. With less difficulty still, Hermes and Mercury, Aphrodite and Venus, Zeus and Jupiter, Artemis and Diana, and others of Olympic stature, were seen to be not only akin, but the same. Greek philosophy, coming in the wake of Greek religion, hastened the growth of the belief that deities of greater or lesser resemblance were the same under different guise. Not only the gods of Italian and Greek lands were thus interpreted, but those from farther afield. Phrygian Cybele, Carthaginian Virgo Cælestis, Greek Demeter, and Roman Ceres or Ops were only different manifestations of a single spirit. "The Phrygians," Isis is made to say in Apuleius as she reveals herself to her devotee, "the Phrygians call me at Pessinus the Mother of the Gods; the Athenians call me Cecropian Minerva; in Cyprus I am Paphian Venus; I am Diana Dictynna to the archers of Crete, Stygian Proserpina to the Sicilians; at Eleusis I am the ancient Ceres. To some I am Juno, to others Hecate. It is only the Ethiopians and the

Arians, illumined by the dawning light of the sun, and Egypt powerful in her ancient lore, who honor me with the rites that are really mine, and call me by my true name, the queen Isis."

With the great Stoic movement of the first and second centuries and its lofty reasoning, and with the neo-Platonism of the second and third, which attempted through philosophic and poetic reinterpretation of the old religion to purge it of its grossness and absurdities, the development of polytheism toward monotheism, already long in process, increased with special rapidity. The result was that the world, however unwilling to accept the One God of the Christians, was familiar with the conception of monotheism before the triumph of Christianity. Seneca, indeed, had written of the universal divine principle without employing the time-honored names of the ancient gods.

Farther, besides its preparation for monotheism, the pagan Roman world had also learned to comprehend deity as a person. The Etruscan had contributed something, but it was the Greek who gave the Roman his first effective lesson. Into the world of early Roman gods, vague and formless and impersonal, had come the deities of Olympus, possessing human shapes and attributes, appearing among men and being seen of them, and partaking of their joys and sorrows. But greater still was the contribution of the Orient. To the Greek lesson of the personality of the divine, the faiths of Egypt and Asia added the lesson that mortals might in some way raise themselves to the plane of deity, be filled with the god, partake of his nature, and receive rewards in the here and hereafter. The priests of Cybele, whirling in the dance, fasting, scourging themselves into the

divine frenzy, and renewing life in the baptism of blood;
the faithful of Isis, with their rites and purifications
and their prayers to the Mother; the brethren in Mithras, with their belief in atonement, and their perpetual
conflict with the principle of evil,—all these are manifestations of the mysticism communicated to Roman
religious life by the oriental faiths. The Greeks taught
the Romans the personality of God; the Orientals
taught them the possibility of the spiritual relation between man and the divine.

To this must be added the gradual emergence of the
belief in a happy immortality. This was no faith that
sprang into existence suddenly with the advent of Christianity. Egyptian, Assyrian, Greek, and early Roman
had known of existence beyond this life. At first confined to the tomb or its neighborhood and dependent
on the preservation of the body or its symbol and on
earthly goods or their symbols, it was an existence in-
secure and insubstantial, sometimes more unhappy,
sometimes less, but never wholly blest, not always everlasting, and not assured to all. The Eleusinian mysteries, the mysteries of Mithras, the communions of
Isis and the Great Mother, the communion of the stars
in the elaborate doctrines of neo-Platonism, all opened
the way to a happier life beyond the tomb for the more
select, while vulgarized astrology, with the arts of sor-
cery and magic, extended the hope to the common
crowd. The decay of the oracle, of divination, and the
critical spirit encouraged the success of astrology,
which, with magic, came in the train of the oriental religions. Its teaching of the cosmic year and the coming
destruction of the world by fire and flood suggests the
Christian belief regarding the end of the world. The

essential doctrine of magic, which was a sort of degenerate physics, as well as of astrology, which was perverted astronomy, was the solidarity of the universe and the sympathy of matter and spirit. Astrology discovered or interpreted cosmic influences; magic undertook to nullify them. Both were scientific inasmuch as they were founded upon observation of nature, but enjoyed power because they were really faiths. But the conditions of immortality were complicated, the end was hard to attain, and both its nature and duration hardly free from doubt. Men hungered and thirsted for the Kingdom of Heaven, but lacked the simple, single means of winning to it.

When, therefore, the Christian religion, the last great oriental faith of ancient times, arrived on the scene of Roman affairs, it found the ideas of monotheism, of the personal nature of the divine, and of the possibility of divine communion, not altogether unknown, and rapidly becoming clearer and more consistent. Whatever the morals of the pagan worshipper, the pagan religions were making straight the way of the religion of Christ. Even in the centuries of conflict with it, the trend of their teaching continued the same, and thus contributed to the ease with which the pagan world in the end, when the contest was proven hopeless, transferred itself to the new faith. The philosophical movement from Horace to Seneca and Marcus Aurelius was a parallel to the Christian movement, and in the event its ally. The doctrines of the atonement, of mediation, of baptism, of regeneration, and of immortality, did not shine with the same clear outline in the pagan faith as they did in the Christian, but they were more or less widely diffused, and Christian doctrine on that account presented the less that was strange.

What is said of these faiths in the pagan world may be said in the same manner of its morals. So far as knowledge was concerned, there was no lack of ethical truth among educated pagans. Neither the principles of the Ten Commandments nor those of the Sermon on the Mount were unknown to the world. Socrates and Plato knew that good should be returned for evil. The letters of Seneca so abound in the spirit of Christian ethics as to have been suspected of dependence upon the teachings of Paul. Cicero's words on immortality are exquisitely beautiful. The *Meditations* of Marcus Aurelius, the *Manual* of Epictetus above all, read at times as if a Christian had been their inspiration. If the pagan did not live according to the measure of his knowledge, the same thing has been true of men in more enlightened ages and under less hostile circumstance.

Christianity therefore introduced into the Roman world no wholly new moral truth, for the civilized world, so far as intelligence was concerned, was already in possession of the truths that were urged upon men by the new religion. It wrought nevertheless powerfully upon the ethics of its converts. It insisted that moral truths were to be lived, not merely known. It tightened the bond between morals and religion, which throughout pagan times had been so loose that the two were all but separate. Cæsar might be pontiff and profligate at the same time, but the convert to Christianity was to sin no more. Again, it placed the strongest emphasis on those moral duties which were not included in the law of the land. The Christian was obliged not only to obey, but to love the Lord his God with all his heart; he was not

FRAGMENTS OF BUILDING AT ELEUSIS

THE WHEAT HEADS ARE SYMBOLIC OF DEMETER THE EARTH GODDESS,
WHOSE MYSTERIES CONFERRED IMMORTALITY

only to pay his debts and to steal no more, and not to do murder, but he was to do to others even so as he would that they should do to him, and to love his neighbor as himself. Still farther, by its diffusion among the common classes of men and women, Christianity popularized the truths upon which its emphasis was laid.

Thus far of Christianity as a step in the orderly evolution of religion at Rome. In the second place, the organization of the Church was likewise the result of evolution. The extension of Roman boundaries, the perfecting of Roman administrative system throughout the empire, the establishment of universal peace, the elaboration of the means of communication, and the Romanizing, in greater or lesser measure, of all the subject nations, made easy the spread of ideas and movements. Throughout the world, lightly but authoritatively joined together under the imperial sovereignty, diverse according to locality, and having no clear creed in common except that of the supremacy of the Roman state, existed with its thousands of gods the Roman cult. In the path thus made easy, Christianity followed, extended itself throughout the vast empire, and, aided by the possession of a positive and universal creed, developed an organization whose unity finally grew to be stronger than that of the state itself. Let us recall the word of Leo the Great, spoken before the fall of the pagan empire: "That the working of unspeakable grace might be spread abroad throughout the whole world, Divine Providence prepared the Roman empire."

In the third place, the social effect of Christianity was also only the consummation of an evolutionary change. Roman citizenship had originally been confined to patricians. It spread first to the plebeian class at Rome, then to the Latin tribes, then to all Italy, and finally, under Caracalla, to all free subjects of the empire. The pagan poet of the late Empire calls all nations of the earth one family, and all citizens of the empire brothers, children of the common Mother Rome. Christianity completed the process by making all human beings, bond or free, brethren of one family; children, if they desired it, of the Universal Father and of the Mother Church. To prove from the inscriptions of the catacombs that Rome was a slave state would be difficult. The Christian stones recognize no slavery but bondage to Christ.

THE MEETING OF THE OLD AND
THE NEW

THE triumph of Christianity was thus only the last stage in a long evolution, the completion of a natural process in the religious, moral, political, and social life of the ancient civilization. Its advent was noiseless and unnoticed, its growth slow, sure, and steady, its triumph fully assured only after the first Christian emperor had been dead for half a century.

But why, if the process was natural, were there three hundred years of constant opposition, with frequent violence and shedding of blood? Two facts account for this. The first is, that the change from old to new involved the dissociation of religion from the state. The second is, that it required the association of religion with conduct. The one meant the enmity of the government. The other meant the hostility of the individual pagan.

With the pagan Roman, religion was a department of the state; its office was to secure the favor and avert the displeasure of deity by the proper performance of the rites established by tradition. This did not mean alliance of religion and state. Religion was not outside the state, and a separate entity, but inside, an integral part of it, like the army, or the judiciary. Paganism was imbedded in the state. When the Christian attacked the old religion, or refused obedience to it, or respect, he was guilty of something more than disregard of belief or custom; he was guilty of disaffection, of *læsa maiestas,* and became an enemy to the government.

On the other hand, morality was united to Roman religion by only the loosest tie. When the Christian, in obedience to his religion, put its precepts into practice not only by living them, but by condemning both in word and attitude the conduct of his pagan neighbor, he raised up against himself, in addition to the enmity of the state, the hatred of the individual Roman.

The intensity of the bitterness felt against the Christians by pagan society was not due merely to Roman cruelty, nor yet merely to the instinctive prejudice always entertained by men against their fellows who will not conform. The violence of the repressive measures adopted on occasion by the Roman government was inspired much less by passion than by reason. Before the pagan is wholly condemned for his treatment of the Christian, the manner of thought and feeling of both should be judicially examined.

If Christianity had involved merely a belief in one god as a god only of its own sect, the pagan government would have examined into its nature, satisfied itself that it meant no danger to the state, and authorized its presence at Rome just as it had authorized the admittance and maintenance of cults from its very foundation. The Roman government was nothing if not tolerant. Let any religion whatsoever be shown not to be subversive of the morals of the citizen or the authority of the state, and its right to unmolested freedom among the other cults of Rome remained unquestioned. The state was concerned neither with the belief, nor with the morals, nor with the practices of any religion except in so far as they made for a good or bad influence on the state itself.

But Christianity was something more than merely a

monotheistic faith. It not only believed in its own God, but disbelieved in every other god. It was exclusive,—in the eyes of the pagan, intolerant. It denied the virtues, if not always the existence, of all gods but its own. The Christian God was a jealous god; the Christian was to worship no other gods but Him, and was to make no graven images and bow down before them. What was more, His will was supreme in earthly as well as in heavenly matters. The Christian was to render obedience to earthly powers, to be sure, but he was to remember that God was the ruler and creator of all, and superior to all. He was to render unto Cæsar the things that were Cæsar's, and unto God the things that were God's; but his real citizenship was in heaven, and the moment the duties of his earthly and his heavenly citizenship came into conflict, it was the former that must yield.

It was quite natural that the emperors should become cognizant of this peculiar sect, which withdrew itself from participation in the religious functions of the state and thus expressed a disbelief in a necessary part of government. They were surprised. To refuse formal honor to the state gods was not only nonconformity with the traditions of a thousand years, in itself an offence of the first magnitude to the conservative Roman, but it was to endanger the existence of the state by default in its compact with deity,—the compact whose faithful observance had given Rome dominion over the world. Let the Christians believe as it suited them, but let them not refuse to participate in the forms which were as much a part of patriotism as military or diplomatic service, or other branch of the state's activity.

Surprise was quickly followed by irritation. The

Christians were obstinate and would not reason. The government also was obstinate; when cases of disobedient Christians came to its notice it not only began to insist on formal recognition of the state gods, but prescribed the cursing of Christ. The test recorded in Pliny's letter was the sure means of detection employed by the imperial agent: "When those who have denied that they either were or had been Christians have called upon the gods in my presence, and gone through the forms of worship, with incense and wine, before your likeness, which, with the images of the gods, I have ordered brought in for the purpose, and in addition to this have cursed Christ. . . ." For the Christian to refuse the first was treason to emperor and state. To curse Christ was treason to his own religion. He did not hesitate in his choice.

And yet the irritation on the part of the government did not early reach an acute stage. In spite of the attitude of the Christian toward the gods, and even in spite of the calumniation of his private life, the emperors and their advisers must have noticed that the new sect was peaceable and law-abiding in ordinary matters, that, in spite of what rumor said of them, crime was never actually proven against its members, and that conspiracies against the government were never discovered among them. For all of the first and second centuries, at least to the reign of Marcus Aurelius, their danger to the state must have been a matter of theory rather than real conviction.

In the course of time, however, conviction came. Surprise and irritation grew into anger, and then into alarm. Under the stress of both, the government abandoned its policy of punishing only those who were brought before its courts, and began to seek the offenders out. For the first part of the third century it clung to the idea that Christianity could be discouraged by the punishment of individuals, or by the destruction of its leaders and consequently of its organization; but finally gathered all its strength for a supreme effort to stamp the heresy out of existence,—only to find that its strength was not equal to the task.

Frequent, however, as the general persecutions were during the last hundred years of the struggle, bitter as was the hostility while they were in progress, great as may have been the loss of life caused by them, the sum of misery they brought on the Christian population was probably no greater than that experienced during the periods before and between, when persecution was dependent upon the initiative of the private citizen instead of the agent of the throne. It was after all in social rather than in governmental relations that the greater cause of animosity lay. Had persecution depended upon the initiative of the Roman governor alone, there would have been far less severity than was actually the case. In time of general peace he punished only such as he was obliged to discipline because they were brought before him, and to them he gave every opportunity within his power to save themselves by denial of the fact or by recantation. He was merciful so far as he could be under the law, and looked upon its victims as obstinate self-destroyers who would not be saved, and deserved their fate.

"Only offer a few grains of incense; appease Jupiter and be our friend," says Maximian to Saint Victor, who has already appeared before prefects unwilling to condemn, and now is brought before the emperor; and

Victor contemptuously refuses the proffer of reconciliation and dashes the altar to the ground.

Even in time of general persecution, when the prefect was under orders to leave no Christian unsought, he no doubt in many cases winked at offence, and exercised a lax authority. During those periods, as well as in times of greater quiet, it was after all the populace, filled with prejudice, passion, and the love of excitement, who were the real cause of most of the arrests and executions; for the Christian was obnoxious to the individual pagan not only because he was disaffected as a citizen, but because both his views and his conduct were offensive in social relations. The case was irritating enough to a pagan even when the Christian was partly understood, but it was doubly so when he was not understood at all, which was more often true. His religion was something positive, involving conduct as well as form. It bade him not only worship his own God, but have nothing to do, directly or indirectly, with other worships. He was to withdraw from the world and its affairs, to come out from among them, and be separate. If he took the extreme attitude of Tertullian, as he often did, he considered himself bound to keep absolutely free from the touch of paganism. If he was a carpenter, he could work on no pagan temple or shrine; if a sculptor, he could fashion no heathen image of any kind, destined though it might be for nothing more than the decoration of a building; if a schoolmaster, he was not to teach the names of heathen gods; if a shopkeeper, he was not to sell incense or images. He could hardly without qualms of conscience be present at the pagan ceremonies of the marriage or burial of a friend or relative. He could not take part in the festivities of the public holiday. In short, paganism was imbedded in society as well as in the state. Such was the number of pagan functions, so intimate was their connection with the life of the community, and so fraught was the old religion with the venerable memories of all the past, that the consistent Christian was compelled either to separate himself from his neighbors or to offend at every step. His very presence, however modest his demeanor, however benevolent his feeling, was a challenge. He was not only different from his pagan neighbors and from all his ancestors,—and nothing could be more offensive than the slighting of the *mos maiorum,*—but his religion, if he believed in it, compelled him to say by attitude, if not in actual words, "I am holier than thou."

Exasperating as were both attitude and words in ordinary circumstances, they were maddening when the Christian was carried away by the zeal for making converts, or for winning the crown of martyrdom. "We are called to serve in the shining company of the angels," say two soldiers in Spain, throwing down their arms. "There Christ commands His cohorts, clothed in white, and from His lofty throne condemns your infamous gods, and you, who are the creatures of these gods, or, as we should say, these ridiculous monsters." The literature of the early Church is full of the spirit of martyrdom. The possibility of his end by the sword of the executioner or on the sands of the amphitheater was kept ever before the convert's eyes. To meet the trial well when it came was all-important to himself because of the great reward, and all-important to the Church because endurance to the end was a powerful means of propagation, and renunciation before the pagan public the worst of blows to the cause. There were letters and addresses that were really manuals of martyrdom, and the life of many a convert was a conscious and formal training for the martyr's end.

The pagan attitude is thus not hard to understand. Given the conditions, his contempt, resentment, and hostility were natural enough. To describe the appearance of the Christian, he used the words *lugubris* and *mæstus,* "solemn-faced" and "gloomy," and when he attributed to him *odium generis humani,* "hatred of the human kind," it was his interpretation of the humility, self-denial, and separateness of the convert. The love, the faith, the hope, and the calm which lay behind the exterior, he could not see. How could a person be happy who denied himself the ordinary pleasures of life? How could he love mankind if he withdrew from its midst and condemned its innocent pleasures and activities? How could he be a lover of the state when he denied and hated the worship of the gods who had brought it to greatness, and when he prejudiced its welfare by refusing so slight a thing as conventional observation of its rites?

The pagan saw in the Christian not only a gloomy fanatic, but an absurdly presumptuous fanatic. Here was a sect which at one stroke did away with the whole religious system of an ancient state, and presumed to know all the thoughts and intentions of the One God whose worship they had set up in its place. And this, too, in spite of a membership composed of "fullers and cobblers." Philosophers had been deliberating for centuries on the great mysteries of creation, and were still unable to call the facts of existence by any other name than mysteries; yet a handful of men and women from the dregs of the populace, unstudied, ignorant, and totally unlettered, were ready in a moment to deliver themselves on questions which for all the ages had baffled the most penetrating minds. When Christianity was still obscure and almost unknown, such reflections were something to rouse indignation, not to say contempt; when it had reached greater dimensions and was more talked about, they could beget more violent emotions.

But these misunderstandings were not the worst that were bound to arise. The Christian, in addition to the charges of gloom, hatred of the social order, and fanatical conceit, incurred suspicion of active treason and actual crime. Arguing from the cruelty of the times, from the existence of secret societies of really sinister intent, and from the immoral practices of certain of the ancient cults, the pagan suspected the secret assemblies of the Christian of deeds which would not bear the light. In the minds of many, the not unnatural suspicion developed into conviction, and became an integral part in their judgment of the Christian community.

"Is it not enough to make one groan," says Cæcilius in the *Octavius* of Minucius Felix, an essay written toward the latter part of the second century, in a speech intended by the Christian author to epitomize the pagan view of Christianity,—"is it not enough to make one groan, I say, when the Athenians expelled Protagoras of Abdera for his discussion of divine matters and publicly burned his writings, though his words were in the spirit of wisdom rather than irreverence, to hear the gods assailed by these abandoned, outlawed, and desperate creatures, who gather together the more ignorant from the dregs of the population, with credulous women by reason of their sex an easy prey, and make of the common people impious conspirators that assemble in the dead of night, and with both appointed fastings and meats not fit for human beings bind themselves together not by any legitimate rite but by sacrilege; a sect shunning the light and lurking in the dark, mute in public and garrulous in the nooks and corners? They look with contempt upon our temples as tombs, abhor the gods, mock at their sacrifices, pity our priests,—if the wretches have the right to pity!—and, half naked themselves, despise the honors of office and the purple. O astounding foolishness, presumption beyond belief! They have no concern for torment in this life, while they fear the uncertainties of a life to come; while they fear to die after death, here and now they do not fear; for the truth is, that a false hope charms away their fears by holding before them an ever vivid consolation.

"And now, just as the viler a thing is the more rapidly it spreads, the abandoned ways of this superstition are day by day insidiously creeping through the whole world, and their abominable meeting-places for unholy union are multiplying more and more. This is a conspiracy that must be annihilated root and branch. They have secret signs and marks of recognition, and are a prey to mutual passion almost before recognition takes place. There exists among them in general, too, a kind of religion, as it were, of lust, and they call each other promiscuously brothers and sisters, so that it is not uncommon for their lewdness, through the employment of this sacred name, to become incestuous. Thus does their vain and senseless superstition glory in its crimes.

"There must be some foundation of truth underlying all this, or sagacious rumor would not utter about them tales shameful to the last degree and not to be repeated before decent people. I am told that they have consecrated the head of an ass, most vile of all beasts, and that under the impulse of some silly belief or other they actually worship it,—a worthy religion, and fitly sprung from such character as theirs. Others say that they worship the genitals of their representative and priest, thus adoring as it were the creative power of their Father. Perhaps this is not true, but at any rate it is a suspicion which accords well with their secret rites at dead of night. And as for the tale that their worship consists in the adoration of a man who was put to death as a criminal, together with the cross of wood on which he died, those who tell it are only attributing to them the kind of altar that accords with their abandoned and criminal character; for they worship what they deserve.

"I pass now to their initiation of converts, as horrible as it is well known. An infant, so covered with meal as to deceive the unsuspecting, is set before the novice who is to be initiated. The novice is drawn on by the covering of meal to pierce what is before him by strokes whose harm he does not suspect, and thus the babe is slain by blind and hidden wounds. Its blood,—O horror!—they thirstily lick up; they tear it asunder, fighting over the division of its parts. This is the sacrifice with which they bind themselves together; by this complicity in crime they are pledged to mutual silence. Rites like these are more horrible than any sacrilege.

"And of their banquets everybody knows; they are talked about the world over, a fact confirmed also by the words of our friend from Cirta. On the day set for the celebration they assemble for the feast, together with their wives, children, sisters, and mothers, persons of both sexes and all ages. There, after a long drawn out repast, when the banqueters have begun to glow and the heat of impure passion, stimulated by wine, has set them on fire, by tossing a morsel of food just out of the reach of a dog tied to a candelabrum, they provoke him to leap and spring and thus to overturn and extinguish the light; and when that, the only witness, has been removed, in the shameless dark they rush together at random in the embraces of unspeakable passion, all guilty of incest at least as far as conscience is concerned, if not in actual fact, since whatever may happen in the case of a single one is really what the whole of them desire.

"I pass over many facts, and advisedly; for even those I have mentioned are all too many, and the truth of all of them, or of most of them, is proven by the very mystery in which the shameful superstition is enveloped. For why should they take so much trouble to hide away in the dark and to keep from view the object of their worship, whatever it is? What is honorable ever rejoices in being known to all; it is crime that loves secrecy. Why is it that they have no altars, no temples, and no statues that are known? Why do they never dare to speak openly, never venture to congregate freely?—unless it is that what they worship and keep suppressed is something for which they ought to be punished or of which they ought to be ashamed."

Cæcilius passes from these crimes and immoralities of Christian practice to the absurdities of Christian belief, employing the ridicule in which every pagan found a ready weapon.

"Then too, whence, or if you please who, or where is that god of theirs, alone of his kind, solitary, forsaken,

whom no free people, no governments, whom not even
Roman superstition knows? To be sure, the lonely and
pitiable nation of the Jews also worships a single god,
but they do it openly, in temples, before altars, with
victims and according to definite rites, though his
strength and effectiveness are so slight that he, together
with his own race, is a captive among the Romans, who
are only mortals! But more, what absurdities, what
monstrosities, do the Christians frame in their imagination! That god of theirs, whom they can neither point
out to others nor themselves see, is engaged, according
to their belief, in carefully inquiring into the morals,
into the deeds, and, finally, into the words and secret
thoughts of all men,—running hither and thither, of
course, and everywhere present. They will make him
out petty, restless, even impudently curious; for he is
at hand to see every act, he is abroad in every place,
though he can do no good to individuals because of
being bound to attend to the whole world, and cannot
suffice for the whole world because he is engaged with
individuals.

"But what shall I say of their prophecies threatening
the whole earth, yes, the universe itself, stars and all,
with destruction by fire? as if the everlasting fabric of
nature, based upon divine laws, could be disturbed, or
as if, even supposing the bond of all elemental things
ruptured, or the framework of the heavens sundered,
the great edifice by which all creation is contained and
girdled could be crumbled into ruin. And yet, not content with a madman's belief like this, they add to it by
trumping up old women's tales. They say they are to
be born again after death, even from ash and cinders,
and, prompted by an assurance which to me is a mys-

tery, actually believe in their own lies. You would think they had already lived again. Double perversity and double nonsense, to threaten with destruction the heavens and the stars, which we leave at death as we find them at birth, and at the same time to promise to themselves, beings who, in like manner as they have entered upon existence, must also leave it, eternal life after annihilation in death! That, of course, is why they abhor the funeral pyre, and condemn cremation; as if any bodily frame, even if kept from the flames, would not be resolved into earth just the same after the passing of years and generations, and as if it made the least difference whether wild beasts tore it asunder, or the sea engulfed it, or the earth covered it, or fire consumed it. Any manner of disposition of the dead would be pain to the body if it retained the senses; and if not, its consumption by fire would be salutary because of its very quickness. Deceived by this mistake, they promise themselves after death, as a reward for their own goodness, an everlasting life of bliss, but to all others as a penalty for their wickedness, eternal torment. I could say much in regard to this, were I not in haste to finish. I have shown now that they themselves are unrighteous, and I care to go no farther. And yet, even if I should allow that they were righteous, it is a fact that both guilt and innocence, in the opinion of most men, are attributable to fate. You yourselves hold that view; for, just as others find in fate the reason for everything we do, you find it in your god. Thus those who belong to your sect do so not because of their own will, but because they are elect of God; and so you fashion a god who is unjust, inasmuch as he punishes men, not for what they will to do, but for what fate compels them to do.

"And yet I should like to ask whether they are to rise again without bodies, or with them,—and with what bodies, the same, or new ones? Without? That, so far as I can see, would be neither mind nor soul nor life at all. With the same body? But that has already been dissolved, long ago. With another? In that case it is a new creature that is born, and the former being is not reconstructed. And besides, think of the length of time that has elapsed, and of the innumerable generations that have arrived and passed in the stream of existence: and has there been a single one who has returned from the shades, even on leave for so much as a few hours, like Protesilaus, to give us a precedent on which to ground a belief? All those figments of an unhealthy imagination, all those silly consolations invented by lying poets to lend charm to their song, you, credulous fools that you are, have clumsily refashioned and ascribed to your god.

"You do not even allow the present to teach you how vain is the promise and how fruitless the vows in which you are deceived. Miserable that you are, while you are still in this life consider what awaits you after death. Part of you, the greater part, and, according to your claim, the better, are suffering from poverty and cold, are wretched from hard labor and hunger, and your god allows it, pretends not to see, and is either unwilling or unable to come to the aid of his own; so weak or so unjust is he. And you, who dream of immortality after death,—when you are shaken by danger, when you are burning with fever, when you are torn by grief, do you still not realize your condition? do you still not recognize your fragility? In spite of yourself, wretched that you are, you stand convicted of impotence, and yet will not acknowledge it.

"But I pass over the merely ordinary. Look, set before you are threats, punishments, torments, and crosses not indeed to be worshipped but to be endured, and even the flames which you both predict and fear,—and where is that god of yours who can aid those who are entering upon life a second time, but not those who are in this life? Do not the Romans command, do they not rule, without your god? Do they not enjoy as their own the whole world, and are they not masters over you? But you, in the meantime, in suspense and anxiety, abstain from honorable pleasures, refuse to go to the games, take no part in the processions, will have nothing to do with feasts in common apart from your own, or with contests in honor of the gods, or with the meats which remain from the sacrifices, or the wine left after libation at the altars. Thus it is that you stand in fear of the gods whom you deny. You set on your heads no garlands of flowers, you never grace your bodies with perfumes. You reserve your unguents for funerals, you deny the floral wreath even to the tomb. Pale and trembling with fear, you are worthy of compassion,—but on the part of our gods; for the fact is, poor souls that you are, you neither live a second time nor do you enjoy the present life.

"So henceforth, if you have any remnant of wisdom or modesty, cease to scrutinize the regions of the sky and to pry into the destinies and secrets of the universe. It is enough for men to contemplate what is under their feet, especially when, like you, they are untaught, uncultured, rude, and rustic, and not only have no idea of human affairs, but are much less qualified to discuss the divine."

Such was the attitude, and such the logic, of an unimpassioned philosophic pagan discoursing with a Christian friend. The attitude of the untaught mob when passion had taken the place of logic may be imagined.

5.

THE OLD AND THE NEW IN COMPROMISE

WHEN we remember the widely different ideals of pagan and Christian, and the magnitude of the change required on the one hand in the relations of religion and state, and on the other in the relations of religion and morals, and when we remember the misunderstandings bound to arise, and the exaggerations in opinion and conduct which were their consequence, it seems not only natural that the struggle should have been long and bitter, but surprising that the change was accomplished without a greater agony.

Had either side held inflexibly to the extreme position it occupied when the conflict was at its fiercest, the struggle would indeed have been both longer and more deadly, and its end would have seen the victor exhausted and pagan civilization utterly blotted out. But it is not in the way of nature for one civilization to supplant another without being affected by it. The pagan culture was not wholly bad, nor the Christian wholly good. Each party contained the same elements, only in different proportions, that composed the other. When the smoke of battle rolled away, and Christianity found itself the victor, it was not unalloyed triumph which it celebrated, though to its own eyes it may have so appeared. Triumph it was, but the triumph of compromise as well as of conflict. However vigorously the Christian might have been inclined to deny it, the result was rather a blending of the two religions than the super-

seding of one by the other. If the Church grew by receiving pagans into its fold, it also received, at the same
time with them, pagan ideas. If paganism gradually
yielded to the Church, the Church in turn was gradually
modified by paganism. If the new society transformed
the old by breathing into it a new spirit, the old society
gave to the new of its culture and institutions. The
Church gained in membership and breadth, but lost in
intensity; it lost in ideals, but gained in practice. It was
not until later that the results were fully manifest, but
the process began from the very first.

It may indeed be that during the two hundred and
fifty years of persecution the Christians departed little
from their ideals. The constant threat of danger and
death under whose shadow they lived, the actual bursting of the tempest over their heads from time to time,
the sense of loneliness and weakness while they were
yet few, their insignificance and lack of worldly prosperity, were the fiery furnace that burned away their
dross. Additions to their number were likely to be from
among the simple, the chaste, the strong and courageous,
and the steadfast. The glitter of worldly fame could not
attract, they had no wealth to corrupt them. Their only
temptation, to renounce the faith in time of danger,
had its source outside their ranks.

Yet it is all too easy to forget that the Christian of
the early Empire had his defects. His ideas were often
crude and imperfect. If the Disciples themselves were
unable to comprehend the fulness of the Gospel as it
came from the lips and acts of the Master standing
before them in the flesh, it is hardly reasonable to suppose that in every case the Christian Roman fully understood his faith. The fear of hell-fire and the hope of

celestial reward were motives more easily comprehended
than the doctrine of love and sacrifice. The martyr's
great stay as he faced the lions was the hope of eternal
happiness. The virtues of the poor and unworldly often
went hand in hand with improvidence. The imminence
of the Second Coming, so strongly believed in for many
generations, and the expectation of the end of the world,
with the injunction to take no thought for the morrow,
encouraged a disregard for the practical obligations of
life. The importance of citizenship in heaven made citizenship on earth a passive rather than an active duty.
Denunciation of the state that was holding civilization
together, renunciation of social and family ties, flight
from the trials of the world to the life of contemplation and barren asceticism, were elevated into supreme
virtues. Nor was the Christian's religion undefiled by
superstition, bred as he was, before conversion, to the
grosser ideas of magic, astrology, and the popular
paganism.

These were not the only respects in which the Christian did not forsake entirely the ways of the world. The
new civilization and the old had common ground in enlightenment as well as in ignorance. From the first,
among the converts at Rome there were rich and noble
families through whom was preserved the contact between the Christian life and the finer manifestations of
paganism. In spite of the early Christian's condemnation of the world and all its attractions, every form of
pagan culture began at the very beginning to insinuate
its way into the Church.

Among the first forms of the old culture to make its
allurements felt was the art of letters. The *Octavius,* the
earliest Christian work in Latin that has reached our

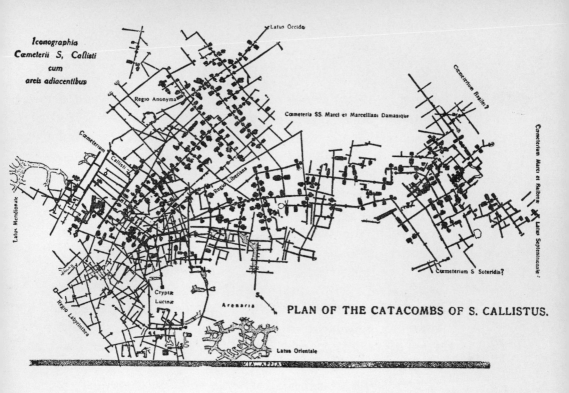

PLAN OF THE CATACOMBS OF S. CALLISTUS.

PLAN OF THE CATACOMBS OF SAINT CALIXTUS

time, is the essay of a Christian at the end of the second
century who knows the whole range of Greek and Roman letters and says almost nothing of the essentials of
the Christian doctrine. While Tertullian is engaged in
heated denunciation of every form of pagan culture,
condemning his flock for participation, however slight
and indirect, in anything that has to do with pagan religion, and crying that all that men need is the blood of
Christ, others are yielding to the siren of pagan beauty
in literature, philosophy, and art. Lactantius, a hundred
years later, is so much the pagan stylist as to be called
the Christian Cicero. Jerome, even in the days of repentance and fasting, cannot give up his pagan books.
In the delirium of fever he finds himself before the aw-
ful Judge, who thunders at him, "No, thou art not a
Christian; thou art a Ciceronian; for where thy treasure
is, there is thy heart also"; but even after his scourging
and return to earth is unable to resist the charm of the
classic authors. Augustine attributes his conversion to
the great pagan orator and essayist. Ambrose, converted pagan prefect, makes use of Cicero's philosophical and ethical content as he writes his Christian trea-
tises. The art and morality of pagan literature are
conserved, and enter into the new literature. It is the
same body with another spirit. It is faith that is the
inspiration of the new, but it does not and cannot escape
the charm of the old ideal of beauty. It was only the
Christian born in the faith and of uncultured parents,
or the convert devoid of all taste, who continued to rail
at the culture of the old society.

What was true of pagan literature was true of other
arts. It was especially true of painting. So far were the
Roman Christians from resisting the seductions of

pagan form that their painting not only shows the same characteristics and the same changes period by period,— its greatest excellence in the early second century, and its gradual decay from that time forward,—but borrows pagan motives and pagan figures. The Good Shepherd in the catacombs is not the bearded Christ of later time, but a smooth-shaven and shapely figure from pagan art. The pagan-born artist, when he entered the Church, could not leave behind him the appreciation of the manner and content of pagan painting which had grown into his nature in earlier years. Called upon to represent the Savior as the Good Shepherd, he simply chose from pagan art the familiar figure of Mercury carrying the lamb, adapting if not transferring it entire. Called upon to symbolize the power of Christ to draw to Him the souls of men, he took from a pagan canvas an Orpheus playing the wonderful lyre. The Cupids and Psyches and winged genii of paganism, the peacock, the vine, the ship, the anchor, and other innocent motives useful in the bodying forth of Christian doctrine, he transferred with hardly a change to the new art.

Sculpture was at first adapted to Christian use in a less degree; for, while the Christian painter could execute his commission in the safe seclusion of the catacombs, the art of sculpture, which required the workshop, could hardly exist thus hidden away. For the first three centuries, the sarcophagi of the Christian cemeteries are of an art almost entirely pagan, though the reliefs that adorn them present such motives as were common to both religions, and gave no offence to the Christian believer. It was only after the edict of Milan that sculpture, too, began to adapt or borrow as painting had long since done.

The architecture of the Church also rose from the forms of pagan building. Accustomed to the plan of the private dwelling, in which it first held its gatherings, and to the sight of the great law courts which were called basilicas, and acquainted with the type of mystic building whose best-known example is the recently discovered underground basilica near the Porta Maggiore in Rome, it finally developed for its own peculiar use a form which is reminiscent of both basilica and house, but especially of the former. If not directly derived from the basilica, the church was nevertheless so like it as to take its name.

Even in the domain of education the Christian came in time to adopt not only pagan methods but pagan matter. Shrink as he might from contact with works whose every page was filled with the names of false gods, condemned as he was by conscience and often by his spiritual head, he was nevertheless impelled by taste and by necessity to use them; he could not resist their allurement, and he had nothing to put in their place. The youth of Rome still continued to be trained in Horace and Virgil, Cicero and Terence, even though their instructors were Christians. When Julian attempted the restoration of paganism, his measure forbidding the use of the pagan authors in Christian schools was almost equivalent, so far as letters were concerned, to the banning of instruction itself.

But Christian civilization was indebted to paganism not only for the arts and culture in general. The new religion itself was not unmixed with the old. In both doctrines and ceremonial, it came to have much in common with the pagan religion. The resemblance between the doctrines of Christianity and those of the oriental religions especially was striking; above all, the parallels between Christianity and its great rival, Mithraism. The communities of each identified the object of their adoration with light and the sun; each had legends of the shepherds with gifts, of the flood, of the ark; in the art of each were found the fiery chariot and the drawing of water from the rock; each employed bell and candle, holy water, and the communion; each taught the doctrine of the constant warfare between good and evil, the mediation of the Word emanating from the divine, the atoning sacrifice, the resurrection of the flesh, the immortality of the soul. Isis had her early morning meetings, her rites of purification, and her forgiveness of sins. Vesta had her nuns. The Great Mother's worshippers had their days of fasting, their festival of the return of Attis from death, with its Easter hilarity. The baptism of blood in the *taurobolium* could bring eternal regeneration to the devotee. In ethical teaching, Christianity presented so little not known to ancient morals that its enemies could assert that it offered nothing novel and was only pagan philosophy employed anew.

Still farther, when toward the end the mass of the many religions at Rome had been wrought upon by neo-Platonism and the oriental faiths, they approached the consistency of a single religion with a fairly distinct theology. Christianity found itself confronted by a more or less unified faith, whose doctrines included the adoration of the elements, especially the cosmic bodies; the reign of one God, eternal and omnipotent, with messenger attendants or angels; spiritual interpretation of the grosser rites yet surviving from primitive times; the presence of the soul on earth to be proved before its final return to the universal spirit; the existence of an abysmal abode for the evil against whom the faithful must keep up unceasing struggle; the destruction of the universe, the death of the wicked, and the eternal happiness of the good in a reconstructed world. The religion of Symmachus was almost as much like Christianity as like the religion of Augustus.

The Christian ethics and creed, it is true, were so superior to those of pagan teaching that the Christian could claim that the two faiths had nothing in common; but the formal resemblances were so many and striking that the pagan was never at loss for a pretext to maintain that the old régime had as much to offer as the new.

But, however distinct or however indistinct the line between early Christian society and pagan society in Italy, the mingling of the two into one received a great impulse when Christianity triumphed by winning first the toleration and next the support of Constantine. With the disappearance of danger, the number of converts increased; with the conversion of the emperor and the active favor of the government, they became a throng. The membership of the Church was swelled enormously. Self-interest and the Christian life were no longer opposing forces. The pagan cult became "a fashion rather than a faith," supported at Rome in the main by the ancient aristocracy. When, with the confiscation of its property and the prohibition of sacrifice, it ceased publicly to exist, the rank and file who had clung to the ancient religion up to the last found their way into the Church in such numbers that assimilation was no longer possible. The victors were in danger of becoming captive to the vanquished, who brought with them into the Church the ideas to which their pagan childhood had bred them. The number of adherents who

were Christians only in form, who could comprehend
nothing beyond form, increased rapidly. Astrology and
magic persisted unabashed. Christian poets addressed
Christian emperors in the language of Horace and
Virgil addressing Augustus. One hundred years passed
after the edict of Milan before the law excluded unre-
pentant pagans from public office. The gladiatorial
shows and the theater were still the delight of the Romans in the last years before Alaric. It was impossible
for the spiritual leaders of the Church to destroy the
world of pagan spirits existing in the minds of the people. The gods of paganism lived on, with the difference
that now they were regarded as evil spirits banished to
hell, whence they emerged to tempt the faithful on
earth. The Genius of the Roman pagan became the
Guardian Angel. The places of Hercules, Diana, Castor
and Pollux, and other divine protectors of cities and
individuals, were taken by the saints. Devotion to the
Great Mother and other female deities was now transferred to Mary the Mother. The old pagan holidays
were replaced by Christian festivals: the Robigalia became the Major Litany, the Ambarvalia the Minor
Litany, the Lupercalia was transformed into the Purification of Mary, the feast of the resurrection of Sol
Invictus into Christmas.

To say that Christianity absorbed much of the literature, art, and religion of paganism is not to say that for
this reason it became less in worth or effect. The best
parts of the old were worthy of weaving into the fabric
of the new, and necessary to it. The vision of the Christian who despised pagan culture, and regarded its accomplishments, æsthetic and intellectual, as the voices
of sirens or the snares of the devil, was distorted. To

assimilate and to inspire was the mission of Christianity, not to divide and destroy.

Nor was the Church as a whole unaware of the mission or unwilling to perform it. "The Church," writes de Broglie, "destroyed nothing, adopted everything, by imperceptible degrees correcting and reforming, placing the victorious sign of the cross on all the monuments and infusing into all the laws the penetrating warmth of the Christian inspiration." Whatever the more intransigent early Christians who were not under the spell of the capital may have thought or done, by the time of Augustine reason had so far modified the attitude of the Church that it recognized the value and usefulness of the old culture and the monuments to the life of the new.

But the Church did more than to retain the good parts of the pagan world. It retained also some of its bad parts. It became larger, more prosperous, and more cultured, but it became also more worldly. Its organization completed and its liberty assured, it began to lose something of its lowliness and modesty. Its bishops could depart so far from the life of humility and self-denial that Prætextatus was able to utter his famous gibe, "Make me bishop of Rome and I'll turn Christian without delay." Jerome and Dion of the Golden Mouth are satirical against the vanities of Christian women who go about in tight sleeves, creaking shoes, powder, paint, perfumes, and jewelry, and gowns whose pictured embroideries and artful exposure of nudities attract the eyes of men. Even clerics are vain of their clothes and hair, and wear jewelry and scents. Ammianus in the same times notices the luxury of the clergy at Rome, who, once they have established themselves in office, "are to enjoy life free of care, enriched by the offerings of matrons, appearing in public with their carriages, dressed gorgeously, giving feasts so luxurious that their tables surpass those of royalty." Jerome inveighs against the shameful trickery of priests who cultivated widows and the rich for their property. Valentinian enacted a law forbidding the solicitation of legacies by priests, or even their acceptance, except from relatives, and caused it to be read in churches. Ecclesiastics and monks were forbidden to enter the houses of the rich or to accept bequests from religious women. Feasting and unrestrained drinking by Augustine's time had made the anniversaries of martyrs and saints a scandal that called for legislation. The communion had to be relieved of worldliness by the setting apart of the agape for the less worthy. The superstitions of relic and amulet in the worship of martyrs, the belief in healings and exorcisms, grew up within the Church, and provoked the entrance of pagan superstitions from without. The loaves and fishes were often the motive of the convert, among both the humble and the great. Constantine himself, in the famous edict, gives frank expression to the idea that profit is to attend his act; he "has resolved to accord to the Christians and to all others the liberty to practice the religion of their choice, in order that the divine power of Heaven may be propitious to us and to all who live under our sway." The Christian who felt himself inspired to live the life of the ascetic and saint was obliged to separate himself from the Church community as well as from the world.

Unfortunately, there was a worse form of worldliness than that of the love of pleasure or gain. While the Church was yet in the throes of persecution and crying bitterly for toleration, it had itself begun to be intolerant; and when finally the dread of persecution was entirely removed, it immediately fell a prey to fiercest dissension. By 180 the Christian dogma was practically complete, and heresies were multiplying,—Manicheism, Montanism, Novatianism, the Donatists, the Circumcelliones. By the time of Constantine, the question of Christ's divinity threatened to divide the Church. Now the Arians and now the Athanasians tyrannized, and whether the one or the other was in the ascendency made little difference in the heat of passion with which the contest went on. Not even the council of three hundred bishops at Nicæa and the triumph of Athanasius resulted in peace. Julian allowed full freedom of worship to the Christians, Ammianus tells us, because he knew that if left to themselves their dissensions would increase and he would need no longer to fear them; he had found out from experience that there were no wild beasts so hostile and so deadly to mankind as many of the Christians were to each other. After the death of Liberius at Rome, the quarrel of the rival bishops Damasus and Ursinus culminated in a fight which left one hundred and thirty-seven Christians dead on the floor of the building in which they had fought,—and the building was a Christian church. It must have been an edifying sight to the pagan Roman, especially to an enthusiastic supporter of the ancient religion like Prætextatus, who was prefect of the city and restored order by sending into exile the defeated Ursinus, and who no doubt preached to the rioters who remained a pointed sermon on the practice of the Christian virtues.

Intolerance toward each other, which found some

excuse in the heat of conviction, was accompanied by intolerance of other religions. The consciousness that his was the chosen religion, and the assurance he felt of the falseness of all gods other than his own, made the Christian from the first intolerant in thought. It needed only the removal of restraint, and his intolerance found vent in words. By the time of Augustine it is the Christian, instead of the pagan, who is hard put to it to find words to express his opinion of the adversary, and it is the pagan instead of the Christian who is the fool, the madman, the beast. Finally, unquestioned power was all that was needed to make him intolerant in action as well as in thought and expression. The old pagan conservatism that distrusted and disciplined the Christian now passed to the Church, which distrusted and persecuted both the pagan outsider and the dissenter within its fold. How fortunate for the peace of the world it was that paganism at the end was so listless, so amenable to reason and the milder forms of legislation, is suggested by the fate of Hypatia, torn to pieces by the Christian fanatics of Alexandria.

But these were the human defects of the Church's divine qualities. The great movement as a whole represented the highest ideals and the noblest practice. Christianity had emphasized fraternal and divine love, and bound men together in God. The pagan had made all free men citizens of the empire; the Christian had taught them in very practice that the Kingdom of God included even the slave. His religion had frowned out of existence much that was cruel and selfish. It had greatly humanized the conditions of slavery, and added an impulse to its decay. It had laid a new emphasis on conduct in the present life, and given the world hope by teaching the possibility of blessedness in a life to come. Its good qualities were essential, its bad qualities the accidents of human imperfection. Even Ammianus turns away from his satire to note "the unwavering faith with which, impelled by religion, the Christians endured excruciating torments, and came forth even to glorious death." Bitter as he is against the pampered clergy of Rome, he knows that they are not the real product of Christianity, but that one is to look for that to "certain bishops in the provinces, who are commended as pure and chaste to the eternal deity and his true worshippers by an extreme frugality in the matter of both food and drink, by the meanness of their dress, and by the fixing of their eyes on the ground."

And finally, when the barbarians came down upon Italy, the Church alone stood the shock and remained immovable. While all about was the din of horrible tempest, she only, says Ambrose, offered to all the shipwrecked a tranquil haven where they found safety. The time had passed when the Church saw in the empire her mortal enemy, and in the city of Rome another Babylon, the scarlet woman drunken with the blood of the martyrs, the harlot that sat on the Seven Hills. Christian and pagan alike were patriots who believed in the greatness and the destiny of the empire. Pagan Claudian saw in Rome the symbol of the unification of mankind under a common mother, benevolent and beneficent; Christian Prudentius saw in her the symbol of the unification of mankind under Christ. Both loved her and prayed for her salvation with equal fervor. Both saw in her already, though but darkly, the Spiritual Queen of days to come.

And so Christian Rome, having gathered up from the

ruin of pagan Rome what fragments of good she found, with many fragments of the evil which clung to them, moved on toward the gloomy vistas of the Dark Age.

IX.

THE DARK CENTURIES

O Roma nobilis, orbis et domina
Cunctarum urbium excellentissima,
Roseo martyrum sanguine rubea,
Albis et virginum liliis candida:
Salutem dicimus tibi, per omnia
Te benedicimus, salve, per sæcula,—

O Rome of noble name, Queen thou of all the earth,
City of cities thou, far above all in worth,
Red with the blood of the martyred ones shed for thee,
White with the lilies of virgin lives led for thee:
Hail thou, O holy one, our knees we bend to thee,
Praises and blessings, O world without end, to thee!

From a tenth century hymn sung by pilgrims
at the first distant sight of Rome.

THE CLOSING IN OF NIGHT

THE night of a thousand years did not descend suddenly upon Rome. There is no day or hour or year which may be said to have marked the passage from day to darkness.

There was indeed a moment when it seemed that the night had fallen. The protection of the strong hand of Theodosius had hardly been removed by death in 395 when the barbarian movement began once more with the revolt of Alaric, king of the Visigoths, against Arcadius in the east. For the moment pacified, he nevertheless at last turned his roving arms against Honorius in the west, and in 401 crossed into Italy.

The alarm that had seized on Italian and Roman hearts in the times of Marcus Aurelius, of Claudius Gothicus, of Aurelian, of Julian, and of Valens, once more swept over peninsula and city, and was once more allayed by successful confronting of the foe. The defeat of Alaric by Stilicho at Pollentia and Verona in 402, however, brought relief that was only temporary. The triumphal visit of Honorius to Rome in 404, the first of its kind since Constantius came down the Flaminian Way in 356, the jubilation of the populace, and the boastful panegyric of Claudian, were followed, in only one year, by still more lively alarm when Radagaisus with two hundred thousand Germans and Celts advanced to Fiesole before the Romans could stay his progress. In 406, Vandals and Suabians crossed, once for all, the barrier of the Rhine, and lodged in Gaul.

For the first time since Cannæ, the slaves were called to aid in the defence of their Roman masters. Provincials throughout the empire were exhorted to take up arms against the common invader.

The excitable pen of Jerome records the feelings of the Christian who was also a lover of the Roman empire: "My soul shrinks from reciting the ruins of our times. For twenty years and more, the blood of Rome has been poured out daily between the city of Constantine and the Julian Alps. In Scythia, Thrace, Macedonia, Thessaly, Dardania, Dacia, Epirus, Dalmatia, and all the Pannonias, the Goth, Sarmatian, Quade, Alan, Hun, Vandal, and Marcoman lay waste, pillage, and drag away. How many matrons, how many virgins of God, how many of the free-born and noble have been used for the mirth of these beasts! Bishops have been seized, elders and other officials slain, churches overthrown, horses stabled at the altars of Christ, the mortal relics of the martyrs dug up. Everywhere are lamentations, everywhere groanings, and on every hand the image of death. The Roman world is tumbling in ruins. . . ."

But the misfortunes of the city had not yet reached their climax. In 408, Alaric once more marched his men into Italy, this time to the very gates of Rome. Bought off with gold and silver and furs and silks and spices, but still not satisfied with these and the concessions of territory and honors that went with them, he returned in 409 to enforce the payment of arrears and to repeat the demand for lands. Again for the time being pacified, in the following year he besieged the city for the third time. On the night of August 24, 410, the Gothic chieftain and his soldiers burst through the Porta Salaria, and for three days had their will with Rome, while its inhabitants fled in every direction.

The world was aghast at the violence done the city which now for the first time since the Gallic descent of eight hundred years before felt the hand of a foreign invader. Jerome, hermit in the Holy Land, receives at one time the news of all these sieges and of the capture. His grief is overwhelming. "A terrifying rumor comes to me from the west," he writes from Bethlehem, "that Rome has been besieged and her citizens' safety bought with gold; that, once despoiled, they were again beset, so that after losing their substance they might yield up life as well. My voice is stopped, and sobs cut off the words as I try to speak. Captive is the city which once took captive all the world; yea, it perished from famine ere touched by the sword, and few were found to be rendered captive. Maddening hunger drove to the use of meats unspeakable; they tore their own members, the one the other, mothers not sparing the sucking babe, and consuming again the fruits of their own bosoms. In the night was Moab taken, in the night its walls fell. O God, the heathen are come into thine inheritance; thy holy temple have they defiled; they have laid Jerusalem on heaps. The dead bodies of thy servants have they given to be meat unto the fowls of the heaven, the flesh of thy saints unto the beasts of the earth. Their blood have they shed like water round about Jerusalem; and there was none to bury them."

From Scripture the grieving saint passes to his beloved Virgil. The woes of Rome recall the woes of Troy: "What voice could tell of that night's destruction and of its deadly woes, or what tears equal its sorrows? The city of old, the queen of the world for many

years, is fallen to ruin, and the lifeless bodies of men lie
thickly scattered in its streets and homes, and everywhere is the spectre of death."

But the world without and the Romans within soon
forgot or grew accustomed to the thought of the city's
downfall. The language of Jerome is declamatory, and
its author saw from afar and with vivid imagination.
Of the actual witnesses, none has left his testimony, and
of those who, like Jerome, were not at hand but have
left us their impressions, some saw Alaric's deed
with the eye of despair, and some saw in it only the
act of a brigand in a world at peace. The city soon recovered. Aided by the stimulus of the emperor's edict
in 412, directing governors to send the fugitives back,
the Romans returned. Rutilius Namatianus, leaving
Rome in 417 after his prefecture of three years, looks
back from his boat on the Tiber to a city still proud in
monuments and power, still resonant with the cries of
the crowd for their favorite charioteer, still unaware, so
far as words of his can tell us, that its days are numbered.

The pleasant age of Theodosius and Stilicho, of
Prætextatus and Symmachus, of Ausonius and Claudian, of Jerome, Ambrose, and Augustine, was the late
and deceptively genial afternoon of Rome. The coming
of Alaric was a storm-cloud that burst and covered the
earth with darkness, but passed and left the sun still
shining.

The sun was lower in the sky, however, and shone
with fainter light. There were other obscurations, and
at each one's lifting the shadows were longer. The catastrophe of 410 was not the first step, nor the last, though
it was the most alarming, that led to the fatal end. The

desertion of Dacia by Aurelian, the settling of 100,000 Bastarnæ in Thrace by Probus, the establishment of 300,000 Sarmatians in Pannonia by Constantine, the admission of the Goths into Thrace by Valens, the planting of German captives on the farms of the Po valley by Theodosius, the crossing of the Rhine by the Vandals and Suabians in 406, the sack by the Goths in 410, the settlement of the Visigoths in Gaul in 418, the crossing of the Pyrenees in 422, and of the straits of Gibraltar in 429, by the Vandals, and their completion of the African conquest in 439, the abandonment of Britain in 446, the descent of the Huns in 451,—were all blows that racked the frame of the empire, prepared it for dissolution, and brought the frontiers nearer the ancient capital. The vulnerability of the city and the unheroic cast of her citizens and army became as apparent to all mankind as the hollowness of the empire's shell, and henceforth neither veneration for Rome nor fear of Roman stayed the enemy's hand.

The children who saw the sack of Alaric were still in their prime when in 455 Genseric from Africa answered the call of a wronged and revengeful empress, and again devoted the unresisting city to a pillage of fourteen days that gave the name of Vandal its everlasting reputation. In 472, the German Ricimer, son-in-law of Anthemius and for a dozen years as patrician the real ruler of Rome, besieged for five months the starving and pestilential city, whose capture made it once more the prey to robbery and murder. A few years more of the insubstantial authority of emperors who were rulers only in name, while barbarian armies remained encamped on Italian soil, and the resignation of Romulus Augustulus on August 22, 476, confessed the entire dependence of Italy and Rome upon the invader's will.

Not even yet, however, had the darkness wholly fallen. Odoacer the Visigoth, patrician of Italy for thirteen years, desiring not the destruction of Rome but the comfort of his people, was followed by Theodoric the Ostrogoth, enthusiastic lover of Rome, the city of his adoption. The patriciate of Odoacer was the twilight, the thirty-seven years of Theodoric's reign the afterglow that was almost like the return of day. When, after Theodoric's death in 526, the dissensions of his successors gave hope to Justinian in the east that the west might be recovered, the darkness deepened indeed. Belisarius, having taken Sicily in 535 and Naples in the following year, entered the gates of Rome on December 9, 536. At the end of the struggle that drove the Goth from Italy, the city had suffered so unspeakably from famine, pestilence, assault, and desertion that the Rome which emerged to be ruled from 552 to 567 by Narses, Justinian's exarch in Italy, was a vast and empty mass of tumbling ruins among which dwelt in misery the merest handful of despairing men.

The death of the exarch and the practical disappearance of Byzantine authority from Rome may be called the final coming of the night. The City of this World had perished utterly; the City of God now sat on the Seven Hills, and even its citizens despaired. Pope Pelagius, on April 13, 556, had already written the bishop of Arles entreating him to send clothing and money, saying that poverty and need had become so great in the city "that not without pain and anguish can we bear to see the friends we once beheld as they enjoyed prosperity and high position."

But let the eye of the mind look upon Gregory the Great, as on the third of September, 590, he addresses the pitiful remnant of the Roman people assembled in the already ancient basilica erected by Constantine over the tomb of Peter:

"Our Lord desires to find us ready," says the grave preacher, "and shows us the misery of the worn-out world, in order to divert our love from it. You see how many storms have heralded its approaching overthrow. If we do not seek God in quiet, trials the most dreadful will teach us to fear His approaching judgment. In the extract of the Gospel we have just heard, the Lord forewarns us that nation shall prevail against nation and kingdom against kingdom, and that earthquakes, famine, and pestilence, horrors and signs from heaven are in store for us. We have already been visited by some of these disasters, and of others remain in dread. For, that nation rises against nation and subdues the land by fear, our own experience, more forcibly than even gospel history, might have taught us. We have heard from other quarters that countless cities are destroyed by earthquakes; while we ourselves suffer incessantly from pestilence. True, we do not yet perceive signs in the sun, moon, or stars, but changes in the atmosphere lead us to suppose that such signs are near at hand. Fiery swords, reddened with the blood of mankind, which soon after flowed in streams, were seen in the heavens before Italy became a prey to the Lombards. Be alert and watchful! Those who love God should shout for joy at the end of the world. Those who mourn are they whose hearts are rooted in love for the world, and who neither long for the future life, nor have any foretaste of it within themselves. Every day

the earth is visited by fresh calamities. You see how few
remain of the innumerable population; each day sees
us chastened by fresh afflictions, and unforeseen blows
strike us to the ground. The world grows old and hoary,
and through a sea of troubles hastens to approaching
death."

The history of Rome from the closing in of night in
the times of Gregory the Great to the return of the
popes from Avignon in 1377 and the breaking of the
new day is the history of the nations of the earth inter-
fering in the affairs of Italy. Scarce one of the peoples
in former days conquered by Rome is lacking from the
list of those who now returned and made captive their
captor.

The border inroads of Marcoman and Quade and
Alan and Thracian and Scythian and Sarmatian had
been succeeded by the wilder invasions of Vandals and
Suabians and Goth and Hun, resulting at last in the
Gothic occupation of Italy and Rome for nearly a century. This had been followed by the return of Byzantine
rule over Rome from 535 to 568, and its prolongation
in Ravenna until 754. In the wake of the Byzantine, and
finally displacing him entirely by the capture of Ravenna, came the Lombard presence in Italy from Alboin
in 568 to Desiderius at Pavia in 774. The Franks, whose
rise out of the ruins of Roman civilization in Gaul about
the Meuse and the lower Rhine had begun with Clovis
in 486, and who had interfered in Italy's affairs once
in 536 to 558, and again in 576 to 590, on both occasions
as allies of the Church, in 754 entered into active agreement with the pope. The creation of a patrician of
Rome in Pepin was followed in 774 by the end of the
Lombard rule, and on Christmas of the year 800 by

the crowning of Charlemagne on his fourth beneficent visit to Rome, and by the founding of the Holy Roman empire, to endure for a thousand years.

After the hundred troubled years of the Carolingian protectors, during which Saracen, Byzantine, and Lombard all contended against each other and the successors of Charles for the control of southern Italy and Rome, and after nearly another hundred years, during which the uncertain throne of Italy and the Holy Roman empire was occupied successively by Guido and Lambert of Spoleto, 891 and 894, Arnulf of Carinthia, 896, Lewis of Provence, 901, and Berengar of Friuli, 915, Rome saw the strange rise of the notorious Theodora, adventuress and senatrix, with her equally notorious daughters, Theodora and Marozia, and of Alberic and Hugo, their partners in daring and tyranny, the scandals of whose rule provoked the invitation of the Saxon Otto the First to the city, where he was crowned on February 2, 962. The Saxon line, 962 to 1024, saw the rival claims of emperor, pope, and feudal lords to the city of Rome, the rise of the communes of Italy, and the invitation of the Normans to aid against the Byzantines in the south, resulting in their lodgment there.

The Franconian period, 1024 to 1125, included the great struggle between Gregory the Seventh and Henry the Fourth, the humiliation at Canossa, the taking of Rome in 1084 by Gregory's ally, Robert Guiscard the Norman, the thirty years' war of the Investitures, the preaching of the First Crusade by Urban the Second in 1095, the appearance of the Franciscans and Dominicans, and the rise of the barons in the Roman Campagna, with the springing up of the great families of the Colonna, the Frangipani, and the Pierleoni.

To the Franconians succeed the Hohenstaufen, during whose tenure of the throne, 1125 to 1254, the communes reach their height, and the great figures of Frederick Barbarossa and Frederick the Second appear in their hundred years of vain attempt to dominate the communes and to set the authority of the empire free from the need of papal confirmation. Their presence, dividing Italy into factions of Ghibellines and Guelfs, is followed by that of Charles of Anjou, brother of Saint Louis of France, who, during the time from his invitation by the pope in 1265 to his death in 1285, accomplishes the death of Manfred and Conradin, the successors of Frederick the Second as claimants to the lordship of Italy.

Finally, four years after the exile of Dante, while Italy is fragmentary because of the communes, and seething with quarrels between pope and nobles and Guelf and Ghibelline, the Gascon Clement the Fifth removes the papal capital to Avignon in 1305, and the end of the long descent to darkness is reached.

During all this time the city of Rome is a prey not only to the vicissitudes of the larger struggle of monarchs coming and going over the land of Italy, but to the miseries of bitter local antagonisms. The murder and rapine of rival emperors and Goth and Vandal filled the fifth century. In these quarrels Rome was still strong enough to be one of the parties; but the sixth century found her helpless, as Goth and Byzantine contended over her dying body. The end of the Goth and the triumph of the Byzantine left her a mere dependency ruled from without by an agent from Ravenna, and from within by the ever-growing power of the bishop of Rome. The coming of the Lombard resulted in a

MEDIÆVAL TOWER AND WALL AT TERNI

TERNI WAS ANCIENT INTERAMNA,
SIXTY-FIVE MILES NORTH OF ROME

third claimant to authority. But the power of the Church increased with the steadiness of purposeful things. When Gregorius Anicius, who had resigned the prefecture of the city in 575, became Pope Gregory the First in 590, the pope was already a greater ruler of Rome than the exarch of Ravenna or the king of the Lombards, both of whom continued to interfere in the city's affairs; as when Isaac the exarch despoiled the Lateran palace, the papal residence, in 638, or Justinian the Second attempted the arrest of Pope Sergius in 691 and of John in 701-705, or the emperor of the east in 726 insisted on the destruction of images.

When the fall of Ravenna and the Byzantine rule in Italy had left the pope and the Lombard face to face, and Charlemagne had become the active ally of the Church, the affairs of Rome assumed suddenly a larger importance. The crowning of emperor by pope implies the approval of pope by emperor. Rome became the capital of the greatest partnership in the world's history. As the eternal is greater than the temporal and the spiritual transcends the material, so was she also the major partner. She disposed of that which was material as the soul disposes of the body. She went farther; she not only bestowed the crown, but wielded an earthly power of her own. The original holdings of the Church, consisting of landed estates in the Campagna and ecclesiastical property in the city and called the Patrimonium, acquired by purchase and by gift and testament of the faithful, had so grown during the century, especially under the patronage of Pepin, that at the coming of Charlemagne the pope was one of the richest property-holders in Italy. With the administration of these estates there had gradually come into

being an authority so great that the pope was already
king in all but name when the great Frank confirmed
and extended the possessions of the Church into an
actual state.

But the conferring of the crown by Rome and the
approval of the ecclesiastical state by the emperor were
not simple matters. There were emperors who claimed
the empire without the consent of the Church, and there
were popes who insisted on the supremacy of the
Church. Emperors resorted to force of arms, and popes
employed the formidable weapon of excommunication.
There were rival emperors set up by popes, and rival
popes set up by emperors. The ninth and tenth centuries were filled with wars and broils. Now that the
seat of the bishop of Rome was a throne, there were
those who desired it for the sake of secular power alone.
There were favors to receive and to confer. There were
animosities to gratify.

Nor was this all. To the uncertainty as to who was
the emperor and what was the empire, there was added
the ambiguous position of the municipality of Rome.
The limits of civil and ecclesiastical authority were
never wholly distinct. There were those who rebelled
against the temporal authority of the pope, and among
the rebels themselves there were vigorous antagonisms
between nobles and common people. In the course of
time, as the civic consciousness developed, the conflict
between patricians and people came to overshadow the
issue between the city and the Church. Now the people
ruled, and now the nobles; now one faction of the nobles
ruled, and now another faction supplanted it. The pope
from the Lateran approved now one, now the other, and
made their quarrels the stepping-stones to his own ambi-

tions. The absence of the popes at Avignon and the revival of the ancient Roman spirit in Cola di Rienzo made still more uncertain the state of the city.

Such is the briefest possible account of the vicissitudes of Rome from the beginning of the fifth century to the end of the fourteenth. Such is the background without which the physical and moral fortunes of the Eternal City for their thousand years of eclipse can hardly be appreciated. These ten centuries are not a period, but a succession of periods. They were not a dark age except as their ignorance and lack of pride made them so. They formed a procession of years bright with exciting movement. They were above all a period of mutation; of mutation so frequent, so varied, and so rapid that to review them is to see the lively changes of the kaleidoscope. They were centuries of violence. Their history is the record of quarrels personal and factional, of riots, insurrections, rebellions, and wars. A year may pass, but not a decade, without its larger appeal to arms. An hour may pass, but hardly a day, without its personal conflict. It is a world of gigantic collectivism and petty individualisms.

2.

A THOUSAND YEARS OF RUIN

AND what were the physical fortunes of the city during these centuries?

The visitor to modern Rome who comes upon arches and columns sunk two-thirds of their height in the soil, or who finds the Forum an excavation thirty feet deep, its floor covered by the minute fragments that represent a score of famous imperial structures none of which now rises above its foundations, or who from the southern brow of the Palatine contemplates the valley where stood once the gigantic banks of seats containing a hundred and fifty thousand cheering Romans, is struck with amazement at the utter ruin of the ancient city. The disappearance of statuary, or of the lesser monuments and smaller private houses, he can easily imagine; but what power broke into pieces the invincible masses of Roman concrete that formed the foundations, walls, and vaulting of the Circus Maximus and the baths of Diocletian? Whither have disappeared the temples of solid marble and travertine, the veneer and ornament of palace and basilica, and the millions of cubic yards of masonry; and how came the pitiful remnants of all the city's magnificence to be so deeply buried?

As he reviews the vicissitudes of the city's history, he finds the answer in a variety of causes. He finds it, first of all, in the devastation, direct and indirect, of the wars and broils of a thousand years. He finds it in the natural decay and neglect of time, and in earthquake, flood, and fire. He finds it in the ignorance, indifference, and self-

THE LATERAN CLOISTER

ishness of thirty generations of men who laid barbarous hands on ancient Rome to build a mediæval and a modern Rome. Rome was not a Pompeii or a Herculaneum, overwhelmed at a moment's notice and for eighteen centuries conserved intact for the eyes of modern scholars; but a great city over which no friendly mantle was spread to protect it against the assaults of nature, or against the still more destructive hand of the miserable population that found shelter in its ruins through the ages when darkness covered the earth and gross darkness the people.

Again and again was the city martyred by siege or capture. War may not have been attended always by the overthrow of monuments, but if it did not cause their ruin directly, it caused it indirectly by decreasing the number and pride of the population and magnifying its poverty. The threats of Alaric in 408 extorted a million dollars from Rome. In the three days' sack of August, 410, palace, temple, and bath were rifled of their treasure, statues and monuments were overturned or mutilated, the palaces of Sallust's gardens and the adjacent buildings inside the Salarian gate, through which the army entered the city, were destroyed by fire, and other districts also suffered, while it could be reported that the dead were more than the living could bury. The testimony varies, however, and the statement of Augustine that surprisingly few senators were slain, and that the city was spared because of its churches and the Christians, probably means that whatever destruction of life and property took place was that inseparable from the seizure of movable treasure.

The fourteen days of Genseric's ravage of the city in 455 was another systematic plundering in which all portable objects of value, including a half of the gilt-bronze tiles of the temple on the Capitoline, perhaps the golden seven-branched candlestick and other precious spoil brought by Titus from Jerusalem, and the remnants of wealth in the palaces of the Cæsars, with many captive citizens, were collected with business-like method and taken by ship to Carthage. Of the five months' siege by Ricimer in 472, when the soldiers of the emperor Anthemius were reduced to eating leather and the population suffered in proportion, no destruction of the monuments is reported. The many repairs and restorations of Theodoric at the turn of the century might be taken to signify the suffering of the city in these three captures; but the work of Theodoric, which is to be traced in many parts of the city and included the Palatine, the Appian Way, the walls of Aurelian, and an attempt to drain the Pomptine marshes, with the appointment of curators and special police for the protection of monuments, was perhaps due more to natural decay and to danger from the Romans themselves than to actual destruction by Goth and Vandal.

But the times of the great Ostrogoth passed. On December 9, 536, ten years after Theodoric's death, Belisarius with his five thousand men entered the gates and prepared the city for defence against the successor of the king. During the struggle of twenty years between the Byzantine and the Goths, first commanded by Vitiges and then by Totila, Rome was five times taken. The siege of Vitiges alone, the hardships of which began in March, 537, saw sixty-nine engagements in the year and nine days before the Gothic king received his final defeat at the Mulvian bridge and withdrew along the Flaminian Way with what was left of one hundred and fifty thousand men. Seven camps had encompassed the city, the aqueducts were cut by the enemy, the Campagna became a morass, the baths were emptied of their life, the fountains ceased to play, and the waterless era of five centuries began, during which the city resorted to the primitive uses of river, well, and cistern. It was then that the mills of the Janiculum ceased to grind and the floating mills of the Tiber took their place, to grind the city's grists for a thousand years. The mausoleum of Hadrian, assaulted by the Goths, gave up the profusion of sculpture that adorned its balustrades and terraces, to be broken and hurled in fragments upon the swarming besiegers, who left on the earth about the famous emperor's tomb some thirty thousand dead.

Recovering their strength under Totila, three years later elected king, and returning eight years after the first siege, they were more successful. The efforts of Belisarius to relieve the city were of no avail. On the night of December 17, 546, after long intercepting of the Roman supplies, Totila's men rushed through the Porta Asinaria, still standing today beside the gate of Saint John, and entered a city whose streets and gardens were filled with graves, whose palaces contained no plunder, and whose temples only were inhabited by the few hundreds of despairing Romans left behind by the fleeing garrison after the horrible siege, famine, and desertion of a year and a half. Overthrowing one-third of Aurelian's wall, the irate chieftain stripped the impoverished and empty city once more of its now scant spoil, took prisoner with him the senators, ordered the remnant of the common people to leave, and abandoned his conquest to desolation and solitude. For more than forty days the city was without inhabitants; and, though Totila yielded to entreaty and spared the monuments, such was the terror of the time, and such the persistence of its memory, that remote generations, ignorant of the real cause of the city's destruction, attributed all the ruin they saw about them to the Goths.

The forces that accomplished the utter downfall of the city, however, were more gradual, and belonged to a later time. Depopulated and neglected though it was, the Rome over which Totila and Belisarius fought was not yet the heap of ruins which later centuries were to look upon. The care of the emperors of the fourth century had been revived and surpassed by Theodoric, whose words indicate a city still great: "the city which is indifferent to none, since she is foreign to none; the fruitful mother of eloquence, the spacious temple of every virtue, comprising within herself all the cherished marvels of the universe, so that it may in truth be said, Rome is herself one great marvel." Cassiodorus, the minister of Theodoric, is enthusiastic in praise of the city and its monuments, making special mention of its "dense population of statues," and of its equestrian monuments, which he calls its "abounding droves of horses." In 549, Totila held the races in the Circus Maximus, and Narses in 554 celebrated the last triumph of ancient Rome amid the applauses of a population that may have numbered forty thousand. At a time perhaps as late as this, there were said to be in the city three thousand seven hundred and eighty-five bronze statues of emperors and other distinguished men. Even at the end of the century, in the opinion of the historian of Rome in the Middle Ages, Rome was richer in monuments than all the modern capitals of Europe combined.

But this is not to say that the city of Gregory the Great presented the same aspect as the city entered by Alaric. If Vandal and Goth had not been altogether merciless, there were other causes of ruin. They existed in nature. There was the beating down of rain and sun, the alternation of heat and cold, the sweeping of wind and the whirling of dust, the tremor of earthquake, the sure pressure of the root in the crannied wall, the not infrequent fire, the undermining of foundations by the torrents that furrowed street and hillside with every violent storm, the bursting of the Tiber at flood over and through its ruinous banks, the seeping of its waters beneath the aging structures of the lower districts. The record of thirty floods of the Tiber for the first five hundred years of the Christian era, an average of one for every sixteen years, suggests the extent of nature's aid in bringing about the downfall of the ancient city. The number set down for the succeeding thousand years is nearly as great, and the havoc wrought was the greater because of embankments no longer kept in repair. In 1598, at noon of Christmas day, there was water twenty feet deep on the floor of the Pantheon. The damage done by floods in the fifth and sixth centuries was no doubt increased by such earthquakes as that of 422; and the ruin caused by fire was not inconsiderable, unless conditions differed greatly from the days of the Empire, when great conflagrations swept the city again and again.

Such forces as these alone would have wrought dark changes in the course of two hundred years, especially when aided by neglect. The monuments had begun to decay a hundred years before Theodoric, but when the terrible suffering and depletion of the wars between his successors and the Byzantines had passed, neither men nor means longer existed even to contend with the forces of natural decay, to say nothing of restoration or construction. What the Visigoths, the Vandals, the Ostrogoths, and the Byzantines did not contribute to the ruin of Rome directly, they contributed indirectly so far as they aided in the ruin of the times. The column to Phocas, who reached the Byzantine throne through the murder of an emperor and his five sons, still stands at the head of the Forum where it was placed in 608, and, but for the statue that once surmounted it, is still intact. It was the last monument of ancient Rome,—a stolen column upon a stolen base, supporting perhaps a stolen statue. The wall of Aurelian, a world too wide for the shrunken population, enclosed a desolate area where the empty and crumbling temples and mansions of the glorious past outnumbered the wretched make-shifts of a spiritless present. Diogenes, holding the city for Belisarius in 549, had sowed fields of grain within the city walls.

But "unswept stone, besmeared with sluttish time," might of itself have endured as a witness to remote generations of the civilization that placed it there. Neither mere neglect and decay nor the attacks of Goth and Vandal were the immediate causes of the city's ruin. The hand of the Roman himself, and in times of peace, was the great destroyer. For over a thousand years the fallen and crumbling remains of classic times were a vast and inexhaustible quarry, of whose rich material alike prince and pauper availed themselves.

The dismantling of ancient structures by the ruling class goes back at least to 203, when the portico of Octavia was restored by Septimius Severus with mate-

rial from buildings of the time of Titus. Alexander
Severus in 223, and Decius in 250, repaired the Coliseum with miscellaneous fragments taken from other
damaged buildings. The wall of Aurelian contains the
ruins of many an ancient structure. The famous arch of
Constantine, erected or reconstructed in 315, is really
an arch of Domitian, with most of its sculptural ornament transferred from monuments of Trajan's time.
The church of Saint Peter was hurriedly built by the
first Christian emperor into a part of Caligula's circus,
and finished with columns assembled from every part
of the city. The same emperor also transported columns
of porphyry from the old capital to the new.

Only a score of years after Constantine, an emperor
found it necessary to legislate against the spoliation of
public buildings. One of Majorian's chief efforts in
behalf of the city was the edict of July 10, 458, through
which he was "determined to remedy the detestable
process which has long been going on, whereby the face
of the venerable city is disfigured." "For it is too plain,"
the edict continues, "that the public edifices, in which
all the adornment of the city consists, are being everywhere pulled to pieces at the suggestion of the city officials, on the pretence that the stones are wanted for the
public works. Thus the stately piles of our old buildings are being frittered away, and great constructions
are ruined in order to effect some trifling repair. Hence,
too, it arises that private individuals engaged in house-
building, who are in a position to curry favor with the
city judges, do not hesitate to supply themselves with
materials from the public buildings, although these,
which have so much to do with the splendors of the city,
ought to be regarded with civic affection, and repaired

rather than destroyed. We therefore decree that no buildings or ancient monuments raised by our forefathers for use or beauty shall be destroyed by any man; that the judge who orders their destruction shall pay a fine of fifty pounds of gold; and that the clerks and other subordinates who have fulfilled his orders shall be beaten with clubs and have their hands struck off,—those hands which have defiled the ancient monuments which they ought to have preserved. The buildings which are altogether past repair shall be transferred, to adorn some other edifice of a not less public character."

The year before this, Avitus, dismissing his Gothic soldiers from Rome in order to relieve the famine, sold bronze from the public monuments to pay them. The not yet calloused citizens were outraged by the act, and the law of Majorian was probably its direct consequence.

Less than half a century afterward, Theodosius employed a night watch to prevent the theft of statues, now valued as material rather than art. The stormy times of Belisarius, Narses, and the Goths witnessed the use of many a monument for purposes of defence. The mausoleum of Hadrian, remaining a fortress after the attack of Vitiges, no doubt continued to lose its ornament and marble facing. The emperor Constans the Second, on his visit from Constantinople in 663, despoiled the Pantheon, already a Christian church, of its roof-tiles of gilded bronze. In the hundred years that had intervened, many a building partially ruined in the Gothic wars was farther dismantled by citizens and city, now reduced to the last degree of poverty. The plundered palaces still standing were adapted to the needs of the privileged, their restoration or repair accomplished by the use of other decaying buildings.

As for the common people, they found shelter as best they could in the ruinous dwellings in which they were born, and, when these no longer served, in the vaults and nooks of circus, theater, and temple, among the falling ruins of palace and portico, or against the walls of basilica, bath, and forum. The clay-pits beyond the Tiber, the tufa-beds of the Campagna, the forests of Italy, the world's quarries of granite, porphyry, and marble, had long since ceased to send their contributions to Rome. Whatever was built anew was built at the cost of the ancient city. Stone-cutter, lime-burner, mason, carpenter, and smith laid hands on what they could get, their only control the need of the moment. Even in the comparatively enlightened times of Theodoric, it had been necessary to protect the statuary. From this it may be imagined what must have been the fate not only of ornament, but of temple, palace, and all their kind, in the centuries when neither people nor ruler held them longer in respect, or even knew their meaning.

"What is there in this world to gladden us?" cries Gregory the Great six hundred years after Augustus made Rome splendid with marble and bronze. "All around is mourning; all around is sighing. Cities are destroyed, fortresses levelled to the ground; farms laid waste; the earth reduced to a desert. No husbandman is left in the fields, scarcely a dweller remains in the towns, and still the remnant of mankind is daily stricken. The chastisement of divine justice knows no end, because the debt of sin, even under such punishments, is not wiped away. We see some led into captivity, some maimed, others put to death. We are forced to recognize the position to which Rome, once the mistress of the world, is reduced. She is bowed down by pain unfathomable, by depopulation, by the assaults of the enemy and the weight of her own ruins."

Let the imagination picture the Rome in which these words were uttered, and then let it essay to see in the same way the Rome of the latter tenth century, when for four hundred years more the decaying city has been quietly consuming herself. If the words of the great but despairing pope are an exaggeration for their own time, they would hardly be so for the city of the barons.

And yet the process of disintegration was for a long time slow, for men, hopelessly sunk as they were in poverty and exhaustion, were neither actuated by great ambitions nor possessed of great energy. There came a time, after the passing of the darker centuries, when the hitherto peaceful destruction of the city was hastened by the raging of armed conflict among her citizens. The riots by which the streets of ancient Rome had too often been made unsafe did not cease with the fall of paganism. The bloody encounters of optimate and democrat had been succeeded by those of pagan and Christian, and these by battles between pope and anti-pope. Following these, with the removal of danger from Lombard and Greek, and with the acquisition of temporal power by the head of the Church, had come the rebirth of municipal consciousness and the rise of the communes. The pope's pretensions to power over civil Rome were met with opposition, and the everlasting struggle began between the city and the papal throne. The powerful families of mediæval Rome sprang into prominence, transformed by the growing feudal system into a proud nobility whose princes sided now with pope and now with emperor and now with the people, and now fought fiercely among themselves. The neighboring cities and lands were their fiefs, given and taken away by pope or emperor as the conflict varied. The Campagna, the Albans, and the Sabines were dotted by dark fortresses, and Rome bristled with massive towers built into or from her ruins.

The destruction of the ancient city, already hastened by the building of strongholds within and without her walls, now received the greatest impulse of all. Responding to the call of Gregory the Seventh for help against Henry the Fourth, who had the pope shut up in the mausoleum of Hadrian, called since the time of the first Gregory the Castello Sant' Angelo, the Norman Robert Guiscard swept rapidly up the Latin Way from the dominions he held in fief from the Church, encamped before the city three days after the retreating emperor had deserted it, and on the morning of May 28, 1084, burst through the Porta del Popolo and the Porta di San Lorenzo, fought his way against the Ghibelline defenders through the blazing Campus Martius, and liberated his feudal sovereign. The third day after, attacked and endangered while engaged in merciless plundering, he added to a sack more savage than that of the Vandals a fire more destructive than Nero's.

The rapidity with which the city fell into ruin before this catastrophe was as nothing compared with that of the centuries which followed. The fire had swept the Campus Martius and the Lateran neighborhood, and had no doubt widely devastated other quarters. The face of the city suffered a great change. The Palatine had long been empty and abandoned; now the Cælian and the Aventine gradually lost the little population that had remained to them. The Forum, which had probably continued up to this time to be a popular meeting-place, was deserted, to become the Campo Vaccino of later times. The people gravitated by degrees into the Campus Martius, where water was more abundant, and concentration easier. What fire and violence had overthrown was utilized in the throwing together of other buildings, and the already great heaps of ruin were made still greater by the levelling of what decay and time had weakened. A new Rome arose in the great bend of the river where once had been the field of Mars, and the old Rome was the quarry and kiln from which its substance came.

And it was not only the bare necessities of shelter that wrought ruin among the blackened monuments. The great families whose strongholds had long since begun to cast dark shadows over city and Campagna now dominated the life of Rome. The city became the prey of impetuous princes whose fierce quarrels, originating in private dispute and taking the color of Guelf or Ghibelline partisanship, filled the streets with disorder and danger, and whose marauding made the Campagna unsafe even for the holy visitors to Rome. Their towers rose by the hundred within and without the city. Some of them were lofty fortresses of brick like the still surviving Torre delle Milizie, into whose walls were transferred the brick and marble of ancient Roman buildings; some were the ancient monuments themselves transformed into places of defence.

Circuses, amphitheaters, and theaters, palaces, porticoes, temples, and triumphal arches, and the very tombs of the ancient great, were made to serve the purposes of war. One gigantic fortress of the Orsini rose from the ruins of Pompey's theater, another stood nearer the Tiber, and the region of the Vatican was under their control. The theater of Marcellus afforded shelter first to the Pierleoni, later to the Savelli, and finally to the Orsini. The Margani and the Statii held the Circus Flaminius. The Colonna lodged one of their greatest strongholds in the mausoleum of Augustus. The Coliseum, damaged by earthquake in the early thirteenth century, was claimed alike by the Frangipani, who dominated Cælian and Palatine, and the Anibaldi, who controlled the Lateran quarter. The Septizonium, the arches of Titus and Constantine, the Janus Quadrifrons, and the towers of the Circus Maximus, were all in the hands of the Frangipani. The Savelli held the Aventine. The Savelli and the Gætani at different times fortified the mausoleum of Cecilia Metella on the Appian Way. The tomb of the Plautii at the Ponte Lucano on the road to Tivoli suffered a similar transformation. When the senator Brancaleone, in 1257, gave order to destroy "the towers of the nobles, fortresses for the oppression of the populace, prisons for debtors, dens of infamy and violence," there were some three hundred towers in the city, besides the three hundred still rising from the wall of Aurelian. How great was the destruction of the monuments in the tearing down of the more than one hundred and forty towers against which the outraged people rushed at his command, may be imagined. The barons in their erection had dismembered ancient Rome. The people in the demolition of them dismembered it a second time.

But the wearing of the elements, the work of Gothic, imperial, papal, feudal, and civic enmities, the appro-

priations by rich and poor for uses public and private,
were not the only agents of destruction. The effect of
the Church's rise is not to be forgotten. During all the
centuries, as the Church invisible grew gradually out
of the heart of pagan society, so the visible capital of
the Church grew out of the pagan capital. As the material City of the Cæsars fell, the material City of God
was rising.

Before the official recognition of Christianity by
Constantine, the meeting-places of the Christians in
Rome were in most cases either private houses adapted
to the simple needs of the time, without ceasing to be
the possession of individual owners, or the less convenient and less frequently used special chambers in
the catacombs. With the removal of the ban, the scant
number of churches other than these was increased by
the free building of formal places of worship, the
earliest of them being on the city's outskirts at the en-
trances of prominent catacombs, the later in the city
itself side by side with the temples of paganism, and at
last sometimes within their very walls. Among these
earliest churches of diverse origin were those of Santa
Pudenziana and Santa Prassede, developed from private houses, and the Constantinian churches, which included San Giovanni in Laterano, originally in the
palace of the Laterani, nobles implicated in the conspiracy against Nero, San Pietro in Vaticano, built
out of ancient ruins on the reputed spot of the apostolic
martyrdom, San Paolo Fuori, outside the walls on the
Ostian Way, where the Saint's death took place, San
Lorenzo, outside the walls on the road to Tivoli, Santa
Agnese, outside the Porta Nomentana at the catacombs
of the Saint, Santa Croce in Gerusalemme, to the east

beside the Castrensian amphitheater, and Santi Pietro
e Marcellino, another catacomb church on the road to
Labicum. Besides these, most of them rising soon after,
but some perhaps even before, were Santa Maria Maggiore, on the Esquiline, Santa Maria in Trastevere,
across the Tiber, Santa Cecilia, in the same quarter, San
Clemente, near the Coliseum, beneath which are house
remains and a temple to Mithras, Santa Maria in Cosmedin, near the Palatine and Tiber, built over and into
the remains of a temple or other public edifice, Santa
Sabina, on the Aventine, in honor of a martyr of Hadrian's time, Santa Prisca, also on the Aventine, Santo
Stefano Rotondo, on the Cælian, Santi Giovanni e
Paolo, built on the same hill over a patrician residence
of the fourth century, San Crisogono, across the Tiber
where the emperor Anthemius was killed in 472, San
Martino ai Monti, built into the house of a presbyter on
the Esquiline, Santa Susanna, on the Quirinal, in honor
of a martyr of Diocletian, Santa Lucina, near the Augustan monuments in the Campus Martius, and San
Marco, near the Capitol at the head of the Via Lata.
The church of Santi Cosma e Damiano was lodged in an
ancient building at the northeast corner of the Forum
in 526-530, the senate a century later became the church
of Sant' Adriano, and a few years before, in 610, the
Pantheon had become Santa Maria Rotonda.

These were the principal churches that rose out of
the desolate and empty city of about the end of the
Gothic wars. With them were many monasteries and
convents. The three thousand virgins of Jerome's time
no doubt increased in number. In the time of Gregory
the Third, who died in 741, there were four monasteries
about Saint Peter's alone. What the erection of all

these sacred edifices meant to the ancient monuments
is easily imagined. The process may not always have
been purely destructive. It frequently caused the peaceful occupation and preservation, especially soon after
the fall of paganism, of civic buildings, and, from the
beginning of the seventh century, of here and there a
temple; but even with the conservation of buildings as
a whole went the destruction of details in the erection
of pillars, pulpits, altars, choirs, and crypts, and in the
general rearrangement of interiors, while many a church
was built entirely from the ancient remains that rose
on every hand.

The revival of spirit on the part of the citizens and
the papal court in the times that followed the fire of
Robert was only the cause of farther destruction. The
building activities of the Church were as great as those
of the people and the nobility. Not only were churches
restored and built, but the church tower began to rise.
The church bells were ringing at least as early as
Paulinus of Nola, before the times of Jerome and Ambrose, and from 740 on were in common use in monasteries. The first bell-tower in Rome, in the atrium of
Saint Peter's and overlaid with silver and gold, was the
gift of Pope Stephen the Second, erected in gratitude
for his success with Pepin in 754. Its kind soon multiplied, especially when, at the approach of the feudal
period, they could serve also the purposes of lookout and
defence. By the time of Brancaleone's senatorship, from
among the three hundred towers of the barons inside
the crown of three hundred towers on the wall of Aurelian there rose another three hundred by the side of
church and monastery. Tall, square, of dark, ruddy
brick, most of them with horizontal crowns, and with

small windows divided by slender columns carrying round arches, they added to the belligerent picturesqueness of the city.

The erection and restoration of churches, with the development of the taste for decoration in marbles and fine stones, increased the already great demand upon the ancient remains. Inscriptions and statues, as well as the marble blocks of the larger monuments, found their way into the hands of lime-burner and marble-worker. The whole neighborhood of the Flaminian circus was known for its lime-kilns, and was called the Calcarario. Nearly every ruin of importance had its permanent or temporary kiln. The Forum Magnum and the imperial fora, the mausoleum of Augustus, the baths of Agrippa, the Julian basilica, the temple of Vesta, and many others, were thus equipped. A kiln of unburned statuary, ready for firing, was discovered in the palace of Tiberius. Cords of statues awaiting conversion into lime were found in the precincts of the Vestals. On the floor of the Julian basilica alone there were two kilns.

The activity of the marble-workers, though finer, was not the less destructive. From the middle of the twelfth century to the end of the thirteenth, marble-cutter, architect, mosaicist, and sculptor drew upon the materials of Rome. It was the age of the Cosmati and their school, so much of whose beautiful work is still admired in the older churches. Floors were laid not only with cut slabs, but with the inscribed marbles entire of antiquity. Two hundred inscriptions were thus used in the church of the Santi Quattro Coronati, and nearly a thousand in San Paolo Fuori le Mura. Tombs, altars, and pulpits were hewn out of ancient pedestals, columns, and blocks, while the choice colored marbles, granites, alabasters,

serpentines, and porphyry which had come to the city
of Augustus and his successors from every part of the
world, were cut and polished for use in the mosaics and
other decorative work which make the churches of
Rome the richest in the world. The Aracœli, within and
without, is an example of the method of the time; its
floor is a vast and vari-colored carpet of slabs and mosaic
in every kind of ancient stone, and the staircase of 1348
that leads to its lofty doors, one of the most imposing
in the world, is composed of one hundred and twenty-
four marble steps from various ancient monuments.

Nor did the work stop with Rome. The beautiful
material which the capital had drawn from the uttermost parts of the earth now began to be pulled from its
resting-places in the walls of temple and bath, or lifted
from its bed in the accumulating soil, and sent on a
second mission of beautification. Constantine had carried columns away to Byzantium, Theodoric and
Charlemagne had transported Roman marble to Ravenna and Aix. The cathedrals of Pisa, Lucca, and
Monte Cassino were built largely of it. The Normans
at the end of the eleventh century carried it off in quantities to use in the cathedral at Salerno. Later, the Sardinian monastery of Our Lady at Tergu, the church of
Saint Francis at Civitavecchia, the cathedral at Orvieto,
and many a church in the nearer vicinity of Rome, were
beautified from the same source. Westminster Abbey
itself has its Roman marbles.

The ancient city was inexhaustible. Such was the
facility with which marbles could be obtained that the
marmorata, or marble-wharf, whose activities had
ceased in the fourth century, leaving within its precincts
by the Tiber below the Aventine a vast store of material

not even now exhausted, was not exploited until the twelfth century, and then perhaps rather in the search for the rare than because of any lack. The great buildings of antiquity were gradually consumed in a process which for centuries was part of the life of every day. There were exceptional times when fire or feud wrought havoc more swiftly than usual, and there no doubt were also times when the stirrings of pride prompted measures on the part of pope, municipality, or emperor, and the destruction was for the moment stayed or kept within bounds; but, for the most part, sentiment for what was ancient was a thing unknown, and the privilege of utilizing was freely granted to those who could pay, or secured without cost by those who had other ways of obtaining their desires.

It was in this manner that the transformation of Rome in the century or two following the fire of Robert in 1084, though representing a revival of building enterprise, only rendered the desolation more apparent. The city of the Dark Age, huddled in the low Campus Martius and about Saint Peter's across the Tiber, had first left empty the southern, central, and eastern regions, and then consumed them. A poet of a hundred years before the fire had made the downfallen city cry: "I was resplendent, and celebrated through all the world . . . and as I once strewed it with delights now I sprinkle it with tears." Hildebert of Tours, making a visit to it in 1106, twenty-two years after the coming of the Norman, laments: "Equal to thee, Rome, there is nothing, all but utterly in ruins though thou art; how great thou wert whilst yet unharmed, in thy fragments thou dost show. Long ages have overthrown thy proud state; the citadels of Cæsar and the temples of the gods lie prostrate in the mire. . . . Woe, and alas! The city is fallen, and while I gaze upon her ruins and ponder her fate, I can only say, Rome hath been. Yet neither the flight of years, nor flame, nor the sword, have availed to destroy to the uttermost the glory that I see. So much still remains, so much is fallen in ruin, that neither the part still standing may be levelled, nor the part already in ruins be again raised up." "In comparison with its ancient state," adds William of Malmesbury as he comments on Hildebert's poem, "Rome seems now a little town."

And outside of the decayed city enclosed by Aurelian's wall, the Campagna rolled to the mountains and the sea. Ravaged by Goth, Vandal, Byzantine, and Lombard, its aqueducts in fragments, its drainage choked, it had sunk into a solitude of ruined farms and pastures which, like the city, was saved from absolute death only by the life of the Church. Belonging largely to the patrimonies of Saint Peter and the pope, and an important factor in the rise of the temporal power, after its long decline it had begun in the tenth century to revive. The towers and strongholds erected for defence against the Saracens and for the protection of farms against the brigands of local origin grew under the feudal system into the towers and castled villages held by retainers of pope and emperor.

More than seventy of these are known to have existed. There still remain in the Campagna today some fifty-seven villages whose origin goes back to the Middle Age, and forty-four farm or pasture holdings with "tower" entering into their names. By the thirteenth and fourteenth centuries the Savelli were at Aricia and

Albano, the Conti at Valmontone, the Orsini at Monte Rotondo and Marino, the Caetani at Sermoneta and Fondi, the Frangipani at Astura, the Anibaldi at Cave and Molara, and the Colonna at Palestrina, Paliano, Genazzano, and Olevano.

In spite of its rise in prosperity, however, the Campagna was beset with dangers from armed men and from fever. When the hosts of Barbarossa melted away under the pestilence in August, 1167, it was not the only time when the scourge of the Campagna proved the friend as well as the foe of Rome. "Rome, devourer of men, bends the necks of the proud," wrote Saint Peter Damiani; "Rome, fertile in fevers, is most rich in the fruitage of death; the fevers of Rome may be trusted to keep their faith."

In 1198, we are told, the population of the city and the Campagna numbered about thirty-five thousand. A man of forty was hard to find, a man of sixty impossible. In 1230, a flood of the Tiber, described as one of the most destructive yet experienced, swept the Leonine part of the city and the Campus Martius, carried away a bridge, and drowned some thousands of people. Terrible famine and pestilence immediately followed. Eleven years later, a priest writes from Rome to a member of the clergy who contemplates attendance at a council there: "How can you enjoy safety in the city, where all the citizens and the clergy are in daily strife for and against both disputants? The heat is insufferable, the water foul, the food is coarse and bad; the air is so heavy that it can be grasped with the hands, and is filled with swarms of mosquitos; the ground is alive with scorpions, the people are dirty and odious, wicked and fierce. The whole of Rome is undermined, and from the catacombs, which are filled with snakes, arises a poisonous and fatal exhalation."

This is the language of exaggeration, but in essence it conveys the truth regarding its time. The Rome of the papal absence, however, sank still farther in the decay of both men and monuments. The prostration of the city by the Normans was but momentary as compared with the long misery of seventy years during which the papal court remained at Avignon. In the early twelfth century, the vigor of a reviving age at least caused a reaction in its affairs; but by the fourteenth century not only had Rome consumed itself by the destruction of the pagan remains, but the Christian city into whose walls they had passed was itself crumbling with decay. Hadrian the First, the pope of Charlemagne's first visits, had already made extensive repairs in various churches. The atrium of Saint Paul's at the time was grazed by cattle. The portico and interior of Saint Peter's were in need of restoration. The history of the Lateran buildings is characteristic. The palace of the pagan Laterani, donated to the bishop of Rome by Constantine, the residence of the popes from 313 to 1305, when Avignon became their seat, and the Christian analogue of the pagan Palatine, was besieged and sacked by the exarch of Ravenna in 640, was in need of repair in Charlemagne's time, and in 1099 was again in ruins. The near-by Lateran basilica, also the work of Constantine, and, like the palace, built largely of pagan remains, collapsed in 897, was rebuilt by Sergius the Third after having lain seven years in ruin, was once more in a ruinous condition after the visit of the

Normans, and was a second and a third time destroyed
by fire, on May 6, 1308, and in 1360.

The absence of the popes was the darkness before the
dawn. At the time when Petrarch was composing his
odes and Cola di Rienzo was dreaming among her
fallen monuments, Rome was more hopelessly sunk in
misery than she ever had been except in the moment of
actual war, or than she ever would be again.

The whole southern part of the city was deserted.
The Palatine was a mass of grass-grown débris. The
Forum was a pasture under whose sod were hidden dismantled foundations and quarries of broken blocks and
mutilated columns and statues. Hills were rounded and
valleys filled. In the middle of the century, the western
half of the great shell of the Coliseum had come crashing to the ground, and a mountain of travertine blocks
lay at the base of the gigantic remains. Column, façade,
and wall throughout the city were pitted and scarred by
the tools of the searcher after the coveted clamps of
metal hidden in their joints. On the crumbling foundations of concrete, stripped of their marble and useless
now, shrubbery and grass were growing, and ivy mantled the great walls of bath and circus, and the marble
pillars that still stood; while here and there from amid
the desolate ruins of the civilization whose origin and
character were an enigma to the generation that walked
among its remnants, rose convent, monastery, and
church, with bell-towers of brick and marble and colored
stones, and rugged feudal strongholds dotting the crests
and slopes of the hills. There were waste areas even in
the more densely peopled quarters, and vacant, tumble-
down dwellings with staring windows stood side by side

with the habitations of the noble. Eleven of the four hundred and twenty-four churches were in ruins, forty-four were without clergy, and the rest but poorly provided. The gable of the Lateran had fallen in an earthquake, and the upper half of the Torre delle Milizie. The church of the Twelve Apostles was overthrown, Saint Paul's lay a heap of ruins, Saint Peter's stood abandoned. The Black Death had visited the city in 1348; in Florence, three out of five had fallen its prey. The population may have been as low as seventeen thousand, or as high as fifty thousand, but it was only a handful in the capacious area girdled by the eleven miles of turret-crowned walls.

Upon the once great capital had been stretched out the line of confusion, and the stones of emptiness. It was as if the words of an Isaiah were upon her, and she was to lie waste from generation to generation. An English chronicler wrote: "O God, how pitiable is Rome! Once she was filled with great nobles and palaces, now with huts, thieves, wolves, and vermin, with waste places, and the Romans themselves tear each other to pieces."

Let Petrarch, with the eloquence of sorrow, picture the desolation of the beloved city: "The houses are overthrown, the walls come to the ground, the temples fall, the sanctuaries perish, the laws are trodden underfoot. The Lateran lies on the ground, and the Mother of all the churches stands without a roof and exposed to wind and rain. The holy dwellings of Saint Peter and Saint Paul totter, and what was lately the temple of the Apostles is a shapeless heap of ruins to excite pity in hearts of stone."

Or, let the author of the *Life of Cola di Rienzo* depict the sufferings of the people to whom the tribune's

THE TORRE DELLE MILIZIE

ERECTED ABOUT 1200 A.D.

heart was burning to restore the proud heritage of Roman citizenship: "The city of Rome was sunk in the deepest distress. There was no one to govern. Fighting was of daily occurrence; robbery was rife. Nuns, even children, were outraged, wives were torn from their husbands' beds. Laborers on their way to work were robbed at the very gates of the city. Pilgrims were plundered and strangled; the priests were evil-doers; every sin was unbridled. There was only one law,—the law of the sword. There was no other remedy than self-defence in combination with relatives and friends. Armed men assembled together every day."

It is not to be wondered at that the scriptural simile of the city as a widow was already worn when Petrarch used it in 1351: "How doth the city sit solitary that was full of people! how is she become as a widow!" Dante, half a century before, had seen her in the same guise:

Vieni a veder la tua Roma che piagne,
Vedova, sola, e dì e notte chiama,
Cesare mio, perchè non m'accompagne?
[*Purgatorio*, VI: 112-114]

Come, see thy Rome that weeping still doth bide,
Widowed, alone, and calling night and day,
Cæsar, my son, why hast thou left my side?

ROMA CAPUT MUNDI

THE history and description of the city in which the
mediæval Roman dwelt are in themselves an eloquent commentary upon his character. It remains to
give the commentary an ampler meaning by comparing
him with other men of the times.

To look upon any single generation or individual as
a type of the whole would betray scant appreciation of
the length and content of an era whose duration was
more than twice the time elapsed since the New World
was discovered, and which was itself made up of periods
almost as distinct from each other as the whole is from
either the age which preceded it or the age which followed. And yet, just as there are certain traits belonging to the whole Dark Age, so are there certain ones
which mark the Roman of the period. For the most part,
they are not peculiar to him. The distinction between
the Roman and the rest of the world of his time lies
not so much in exclusive traits as in the exaggerated
strength or weakness with which traits common to
mediæval men appear in him. In the ebb and flow of
this exaggeration, too, and not in the appearance of
aught that was new, are to be sought the differences
that mark his character in the different epochs of the
age.

It is true of the Roman more than of other mediæval
men that he was a composite of the Christian and the
pagan. He was the fulfilment in one person of the
promises of both paganism and Christianity, the incar-

nation of the compromise already in the fourth century far on in the process of formation. He neither sank, however, to the utter perdition of which decadent paganism had seemed to be the prophecy, nor reached the sublime heights to which the nascent Church had given promise of rising. His Christian inheritance kept him from the one, the burden of his pagan legacy from the other.

The Roman of the Dark Age was a duality. All men of his age were, and all Christians of all ages have been. From the very nature of his religion, the Christian is at constant war with himself. There were, however, reasons why the Roman was especially divided against himself. He was the descendant of classical civilization, he was an Italian, and he was a Roman. Nations just emerging from the darkness of barbarism could receive the Christian faith and be transformed by it; but for classic Italy, already ancient and of a culture highly expert, such rebirth was hardly possible. It was the difference between the conversion of childhood and of old age. Barbarism believed, experienced the inner change, and began gradually to grow into new being. Classic civilization, although it accepted Christianity, asserting its regeneration and really believing in its own belief, could not so easily put off the old man. What the humble and secluded early Church could do, comprising the merest handful of the city's population, was no longer possible when it became coextensive with Roman society and found itself infinitely entangled in the meshes of pagan tradition.

It should not be forgotten that the Christian culture was at once nascent and decadent. Just as Christianity possessed itself of pagan art and infused into it a new

purpose without arresting its decline into the art of
barbarism, so did it seize upon the whole body of pagan
society in the fourth century and change its attitude
without arresting its decay. The principle of life was
planted; but a gradual death of the old and the painful
birth of the new were necessary before the seed could
come to fruition.

As far as view of life was concerned, the Roman of
the Dark Age differed greatly from his ancestor of
Augustan times. The ancient Roman, whose ideas of
righteousness had been concerned with conduct rather
than attitude; who conceived of the spring of action as
lying in himself alone, and who was his own last resort;
who looked upon good fortune as his own to win and
enjoy, and upon ill fortune and death as his own to
meet and endure; to whom earth was reality, and future existence a pale and shadowy imitation of earthly
things; who, in a word, was self-controlled and self-
reliant,—had by the sixth century evolved into the
mediæval Roman, who had learned that there was a
power not himself which made for righteousness, and
without which his own efforts were in vain; to whom
heaven and hell were realities, and this world but an
uncertain tarrying-place; whose sorrows were lightened
by divine consolation, and whose joys were the gift of
the grace of God; whose ideas of virtue were based upon
attitude rather than conduct. The thorough impression
of this manner of thought upon the minds of men was
the Church's great achievement.

Under the right conditions, such a theory of life results in chastened conduct. The earliest Roman Christians had proved it. It is broadly true, however, that it
was in theory alone that the Roman of later time dif-

fered from the pagan Roman, and that his actual conduct remained in most particulars the same. Christianity had possessed itself of the fabric of paganism, but was itself possessed in the process. The decline of literature, art, and intelligence in general, the weakening of the state's resources, the loss of vigor, the decay of civic responsibility, and the universal disintegration of forces went on uninterrupted.

That the ruin of character also, if farther ruin was possible, was involved in the general downfall of the ancient civilization at Rome, or at least that the progress of regeneration was imperceptible, is the conclusion forced upon the reader of the city's history during the Dark Ages. If morals and the Church were still inseparably associated, as they had been in the time of Paul and the martyrs, it was more in theory than in practice. The story of Rome during the Dark Ages is in large part the narrative of worldly ambition. Up to the time of Charlemagne, the Church had striven for supremacy over the churches of the western world; from that time, its ambition was to make itself temporal as well as spiritual ruler over the empire. In the endless series of embroilments and wars, foreign and domestic, which followed the one the other without intermission, there were few in which the pope was not actively concerned, and of most he was the actual cause. If he differed from other temporal rulers in his use of political and military means, the difference is not apparent without the closest examination. The conscious employment of the donation of Constantine and the Isidorian decretals, the decree of the senate against the sale of the papacy in the early sixth century, and the declaration of Leo the Ninth's Council in 1049, that if he should carry out his measures of reform the Roman churches would be left entirely without priests, suggest the strength of ecclesiastical and personal selfishness in the vicar of Christ and his servants. The excesses of a John the Twelfth or a John the Twenty-second, or of a Benedict the Ninth, made pope at the age of twelve, and described as "more boyish than Caligula, more criminal than Heliogabalus," indicate the depths to which the holy office could plunge. The exhumation, trial, and throwing of Formosus into the Tiber in 897 to satisfy the hatred of Stephen the Sixth, the cruelty of Stephen the Third and his party, 766-772, who imprisoned and blinded opposing cardinals and bishops and cut out their tongues, and inflicted upon the pope's fallen rival the unspeakable mutilation, the pollution of the altars of Saint Peter's itself by theft, lust, and murder,—such things as these could come to pass in the spiritual capital of the western world.

During the two hundred years between 872 and 1073 there were forty-nine popes, and the scenes recorded of the times are worse than the scenes of ancient Rome. The riots of democrats and aristocrats and blues and greens of the olden time were continued in the factional fights of rivals for the papal throne. The bread and games with which the emperors had purchased the good will of the pagan populace were succeeded by the dole dispensed by the pope to a mob of ravenous Christians ready to turn and rend him at the first sign of denying them their desires. The Roman accepted without question the Christian doctrine, and recognized as a matter of course the authority of the Church; but the weakness of his decadent character made the pleasing of God by self-restraint so difficult that he lapsed into the old

method of establishing himself in the right relation with
God through formal acts. He believed what he was told
to believe, rendered what he was told to render, observed
the forms required by the discipline of the Church, and
went on with the life according to this world.

It would be far from true to say that the Christian
faith was inoperative, and it would be less truthful to
say that there were no popes of lofty purpose and upright lives, or that there was nothing in the circumstances of the age to excuse the means at times adopted
by those whose greatest fault was ambition for the
Church; but it must be said that the disparity between
the Christian ideal and the practice of men was greater
in the Christianized capital of paganism than elsewhere.
Rome was so barren of spirituality and so fertile in disorder and crime that she outraged even the blunt mediæval sense. Visitors from outside Italy were shocked by
what they saw in the city which from childhood they
had been taught to love and venerate as the seat of
spiritual empire.

"Rome," declared Arnulf of Orleans in the tenth century, "is the seat of every iniquity. While learning and
piety are being cultivated in all the nations of the north,
Rome is sunk in ignorance and sin." Gaufried, a Norman monk of Hildebrand's time, may exaggerate, but
his words are not surprising to the reader of history:
"Rome, thou decayest in thy despicable cunning; no
one fears thee; thou offerest thy neck to every scourge.
Thy weapons are blunted, thy laws are falsified. Thou
art full of lies, of trickery and avarice. No faith, no
chastity, nothing but simoniacal pestilence is found
within thee. With thee all is venal. Instead of one pope,
thou must have two. Does one give? thou drivest the

other away; does one cease to give? thou callest the other back. Thou threatenest one with the other and so thou fillest thy wallet. Once the source of all virtues, now the pit of all disgrace. No noble customs dwell longer in thee, but with unabashed forehead thou prosecutest the vile arts of gain."

Crusaders, piously halting in the capital of the great head of the Church at whose behest they were on the way to slay the enemies of the Christian faith in the east, were sometimes struck with wonder at sights which were not the least item in the experience among men which fell to the lot of the soldier of the Cross. Besides finding themselves called upon to fight out the quarrels of rival claimants to the papacy, they were not left unmolested in Saint Peter's itself. "As we entered the basilica," says one of them, "we found the people of the imbecile pope Wibert with swords in their hands; they seized the votive offerings which we had placed on the altars, they climbed on the beams of the church and threw stones down on us; when we knelt in prayer they desired to murder everyone who appeared to them as the follower of Urban."

Rome herself, the inspirer of the Crusades, took no part worth mention in their execution. The light of chivalry does not relieve her dark centuries; her fighting and robbery were not in the least romantic. It may not have been political prejudice alone that prompted a French monk, the partisan of Avignon, to preach on his return from Rome on the text, "A certain man went down from Jerusalem to Jericho and fell among thieves"; and to charge the Romans with cowardice, greed, and degradation deeper than he could have believed had he not seen it with his own eyes. "The scepter

of Rome and her lofty palaces," says an epigram of the
time, "are prostrate in the mire; the towering home of
Cæsar is now the mean hovel of the pauper. Rome is
nothing now; there is nothing left of her but a trace;
Cæsar in his own city beholds nothing worthy of Cæsar."

Again and again was the Church's influence saved
from the ruin with which worldly and unscrupulous
leadership threatened it. Hardly was the Christian
world free from persecution before monasticism arose
to make possible for those who believed in the ways of
the primitive Church the life which their consciences
demanded. From the Benedictines of Monte Cassino
in the sixth century, from their brethren of Cluny in
the eleventh, from the mendicant order of Francis and
the missionaries of Dominic in the twelfth, came the
infusions of moral and spiritual lifeblood which set
Church and papacy again on the road to health; but
Rome herself was so far from being the immediate
source of reform that her atmosphere endangered the
ideals of every reformer who sat on the throne of Peter.
During the two hundred and fifty years following the
acquisition of the temporal power at the hands of Pepin,
the period of lowest ebb in Roman morality, forty-five
of the forty-seven popes were either from Rome or from
the states of the Church. When reform on the papal
throne did come, it was with the northern and Cluniac
popes, while its effect, always less at Rome than elsewhere, soon gave way to renewed decline.

And it was not only in these respects that the Roman
of the Dark Ages was worse than others of his time.
Nowhere else did ignorance seem so great as in the
presence of the classical monuments. In 683 a man who
knew both Greek and Latin was a phenomenon. The

only women remarkable for learning from 476 to 800 were Amalasuntha and Adalberga, both of northern blood. What knowledge had been saved from the ruins of the ancient world was in the hands of the Church, but Rome was not its seat. The monasteries whose inmates fanned the sacred embers were elsewhere. Gregory the Great, Roman-born and prefect of the city, nuncio to Constantinople, knew no Greek, prohibited the reading of the pagan authors by the clergy, and was hostile to humane learning. Not a single Roman name conspicuous for talent of any kind appears in the history of the tenth century. The priest's education was finished when he was able to read the service. The common people spoke a barbarous corruption of the ancient Roman tongue which did not begin to be Italian as distinguished from Latin until at least the latter part of the ninth century. Gregory of Tours in the sixth probably reflects the cultural deficiencies of the clergy when he confesses difficulties with syntax and betrays an ignorance of the ancient authors. At the end of the thirteenth, the idiom of the capital was still so graceless that Dante called it "the melancholy language of the Romans."

Men forgot not only the tongue of their ancestors, but its literature was no longer intelligible to them. In the lack of both ambition and ability to read the little that had not been lost, they became possessed of the strangest ideas regarding the great men and events of ancient times. It was the age of legend-making. The myths of Isis and Mithras and the tales of astrologer and magician lived on in the wonder-tales of relics and sainted martyrs. The religion of the present and the history of the past, as well as the life to come, were seen in the light of the magic and supernatural. Virgil was

THE ROUND TEMPLE NEAR THE TIBER

ERECTED IN THE FIRST CENTURY AFTER CHRIST;
IN THE TWELFTH CENTURY IT WAS CALLED SANTO STEFANO,
IN THE SIXTEENTH SANTA MARIA DEL SOLE

a necromancer who escaped from prison in Rome and was borne by ship through the air to Apulia. His poems were valuable chiefly for the casting of lots. The wonderlands in which adventurous Moor and Frank and Crusader and Saracen roved came into being in minds prepared and willing. The remnants of the greatness of ancient Rome that lay on every hand were interpreted in the same fantastic manner as the memories of Virgil and the relics that reposed in every church. Greek, Roman, and Biblical heroes were ludicrously mingled in the stories that went from mouth to mouth and from generation to generation in an age which did not read and write, and classical times were dressed in mediæval garments. What the men of the dark centuries thought, if indeed they ever thought, as they looked upon the remnants of the dead city, may be suggested by the statistics and tales which represent the guide-book and travel knowledge of the times.

"Rome," quaintly begins Benjamin of Tudela in Spain, a Hebrew visitor to the city about the latter part of the twelfth century,—"Rome is divided into two parts by the river of Tiber, the one part being on one side, the other part on the other. In the first is a right great temple, that is called Saint Peter's of Rome, and there also is the palace of the great Julius Cæsar; and there, moreover, are full many buildings and works, the like whereunto are not in the world. And around the part of Rome wherein men dwell, are spread out twenty and four miles of ruins. And there be found therein eighty Palaces of full mighty kings, that be all called emperors from Tarquin's reign unto the reign of Pepin son of Charles, who first conquered Spain, when it was holden of the Ishmaelites. The Palace of Titus is without Rome, who was not received by the three hundred Senators, because he had not fulfilled their commandment, and had not taken Jerusalem until the third year, whereas they had set him to do it in two years. Moreover there is the Palace of Vespasian, after the manner of a castle, a right great building and a strong. There also is the Palace of King Malgalbinus, in whose palace there be three hundred and three score houses, after the number of days in the year, the compass whereof reacheth unto three miles. And whereas upon a time war arose among them, more than an hundred thousand men were slain in this palace, whose bones are hung there unto this day; and the Emperor set forth in carved work all that had happened in that war, how faction was set against faction, host against host, men and horses with their armour, all in marble, for to show unto them that came after how great a war had once been. Moreover is found there a cave under ground, where the Emperor and the Empress his wife sit on thrones, and an hundred barons of his realm stand around, all embalmed with drugs unto this day.

"And there be there, in Saint John's church at the Latin Gate, at the altar, two brazen pillars of the works of King Solomon, to whom be peace; and in each of them is cut the inscription, Solomon Son of David; and it was told unto me by Jews abiding in Rome, that every year on the ninth day of the month Abib, a sweat like unto water droppeth from those pillars. And there is a crypt, or privy chamber, wherein Titus, son of Vespasian, did hide the holy vessels taken from Jerusalem.

"There is also another crypt, in a hill by the shore of the river Tiber, wherein be buried the ten righteous men of blessed memory, who were slain. . . .

"Moreover, before the basilica of the Lateran is Samson carved in stone, holding a globe in his hand. Then there is Absalom, son of David, and the Emperor Constantine, who built the city that is called after his name Constantinople; whose image with his horse is of gilded bronze. There be moreover other buildings and works in Rome, the number whereof no man can tell."

The legends appearing in the *Mirabilia,* an anonymous document of the same period, and in the *Graphia,* a recension of it at a not much later date, are no less characteristic.

"There is at the Lateran a certain brazen horse, that is called Constantine's horse," says the author of the former, in the attempt to account for the equestrian statue, it may be, of Marcus Aurelius; "but it is not so, for whosoever will know the truth thereof, let him read it here.

"In the time of the Consuls and Senators, a certain full mighty king from the parts of the East came to Italy, and besieged Rome on the side of the Lateran, and with much slaughter and war afflicted the Roman people. Then a certain squire of great beauty and virtue, bold and subtle, arose and said to the Consuls and Senators: If there were one that should deliver you from this tribulation, what would he deserve from the Senate? and they answered and said: What thing soever he shall ask, he shall presently obtain it. Give me, said he, thirty thousand sesterces, and ye shall make me a memorial of the victory, when the fight is done, and a horse of gilded bronze of the best. And they promised to do all that he asked. Then said he, Arise at midnight and arm you all, and stand at watch within the walls, and whatsoever I shall say to you, that shall ye do. And they forthwith did that he bade them. Then he mounted an horse without a saddle, and took a sickle. For he had seen of many nights the king come to the foot of a certain tree for his bodily need, at whose coming an owlet, that sat in the tree, always hooted. The squire therefore went forth of the city and made forage, which he carried before him tied up in a truss, after the fashion of a groom. And as soon as he heard the hooting of the owlet, he drew near, and perceived that the king was come to the tree. He went therefore straightway towards him. The lords that were with the king, thought he was one of their own people and began to cry, that he should take himself out of the way from before the king. But he, not leaving his purpose for their shouting, whiles he feigned to go from the place, bore down upon the king; and such was his hardihood that in spite of them all he seized the king by force, and carried him away. Anon, when he was come to the walls of the city, he began to cry, Go forth and slay all the king's army, for lo! I have taken him captive. And they, going forth, slew some and put the others to flight; and the Romans had from that field an untold weight of gold and silver. So they returned glorious to the city; and all that they had promised to the aforesaid squire they paid and performed, to wit, thirty thousand sesterces, and an horse of gilded brass without a saddle for a memorial of him, with the man himself riding thereon, having his right hand stretched forth, that he took the king withal, and on the horse's head a memorial of the owlet, upon whose hooting he had won the victory. The king, which was of little stature, with his hands bound behind him, as he had been taken, was also figured, by way of remembrance, under the hoof of the horse."

Another legend begins: "In the times of the Consuls and Senators, the prefect Agrippa, with four legions of soldiers, subjugated to the Roman Senate the Suevians, Saxons, and other western nations. Upon whose return the bell of the image of the kingdom of the Persians, that was in the Capitol, rang. For in the temple of Jupiter and Moneta in the Capitol was an image of every kingdom of the world, with a bell about his neck, and as soon as the bell sounded, they knew that the country was rebellious. The priest therefore that was on watch in his week, hearing the sound of the bell, shewed the same to the Senators."

Again, the founding of Rome is recorded in the *Graphia:* "After the sons of Noah built the Tower of Confusion, Noah with his sons entered into a ship, as Hescodius writeth, and came unto Italy. And not far from the place where now is Rome, he founded a city of his own name; wherein he brought his travail and his life to an end. Then his son Janus, with Janus his son, Japhet his grandson, and Camese a man of the country, building a city, Janiculum, in the Palatine mountain, succeeded to the kingdom; and when Camese had gone the way of all flesh, the kingdom passed to Janus alone. The same, with the aforesaid Camese, did build him a palace in Transtiberim, that he called Janiculum, to wit, in that place where the church of Saint John at Janiculum now standeth. But he had the seat of his kingdom in the palace that he had builded in the mountain Palatine; wherein all the Emperors and Cæsars of after times did gloriously dwell. . . . Now when the four hundred and thirty-third year was fulfilled after the destruction of the town of Troy, Romulus was born of the blood of Priam, king of the Trojans. And in the twenty-second year of his age, in the fifteenth day of the Calends of May, he encompassed all the said cities with a wall, and called the same Rome after his own name. And in her Etrurians, Sabines, Albans, Tusculans, Politanes, Tellenes, Ficanians, Janiculans, Camerians, Capenates, Faliscans, Lucanians, Italians, and, as one may say, all the noble folk of the whole earth, with their wives and children, came together for to dwell."

So run these mediæval efforts to edify the pilgrim in the city or the curious of distant lands regarding the ruins among which sat the Cæsars of the Church. With the exception of here and there a reverend father in some secluded cloister which still possessed and valued the books of Latin times, this is the manner in which the Romans and the friends of Rome thought of the ancient city in which they dwelt or travelled. One may well believe Petrarch when he says that "Rome was known nowhere less than at Rome."

Not only was the city of the popes more ignorant than other cities of the darkest centuries, but more dead to the impulse of the new learning and art of the eleventh and twelfth centuries. Paris and Bologna had been great centers of study for more than a century when a Frenchman, Charles of Anjou, appointed senator of the Romans, announced his purpose of founding a university at Rome, and it was not until 1303 that the famous Sapienza was actually created. By this time Padua had been celebrated for eighty-one years and Naples for seventy-nine, and Bologna had become the world's center for the study of law. It was the English chroniclers of the twelfth century, and not the Roman, that wrote the history of Rome. And while in the cities of France and England the wonders of vault and tower and spire were being reared to heaven in the most impressive architecture of all time, the spiritual capital of Europe was miserably propping and patching its collapsing sanctuaries with marbles quarried from the ruins of classic Rome; while mediæval sculpture was reaching the zenith in Paris and Chartres and Amiens and Rheims, and Pisa, Siena, and Pistoia were carving their beautiful pulpits, and Giotto in Assisi and Florence was bringing to life the painter's art, Rome's only distinction in art was in marble work and mosaic.

To bring properly into relief the essential traits of an age so long and so varied as the mediæval centuries of Rome is impossible without the risk of falsifying. Not every year of the Dark Age found the city a prey to anarchy. In all but the times of actual warfare, there existed a manner of government. In the midst of the deepest ignorance education did not wholly die. From 1198 to 1303, however small the contribution of Rome to intellectual progress, the greater number of the eighteen popes and their cardinals, at least in the law, were men of learning. The makeshift art of her poverty has a beauty and fascination of its own. The bearing of her best citizens no doubt partook to some degree of the general refinement of Italian manners which was often the subject of comment on the part of the rougher men from the north.

And yet, even could it be supposed that the degradation of Rome was no deeper than that of other cities of the time, it must seem the deeper against the luminous background of the Christian ideal; and before the minds of her own sons and of the pilgrim throngs that came to tread her streets, in the darkest times there hovered continually in addition the vision of a past the more glorious because vague and indistinct. "The history of the city in the Middle Ages," writes its historian, "was frequently nothing more than a continued funeral oration over the splendor of the ancient city." The most degraded never forgot entirely that Rome had once ruled the world by the power of her arms, and their leaders in the Church never lost the consciousness that Cæsar's authority had perished only to give place to the authority of God. When at last the idea of the material empire built by pagan Rome had begun unwillingly to die, the conception of spiritual empire was not only already formed, but well on the way to realization. Men revered her not only as the historic seat of the greatest power and magnificence the world had ever seen, but also as the divinely appointed abiding-place of the successors to the Apostle into whose hands had been given the holy keys, as the Mother of the Church, the tomb of the martyrs, the goal of pilgrimage, the instrument of God in the spiritualization of the world. Her destiny was more sublime than ever.

Not only was the mediæval city thus venerated for her past, but the prophecy of the future made her a living fountain of hope. The deepest night of the Dark Ages was not without its flashes of the old splendor, and again and again there seemed to be the promise of a new day. The ancient pagan idea of worldly dominion never wholly died out. With the rise of the Church and the creation of a papal state, it came to life again, sprang into prominence, and lived on for a thousand years, to be the source of wretchedness as well as honor to the strife-torn city. Fifty years after Romulus Augustulus, when in reality for over a hundred years Gothic armies had ruled Italy from their camps, Boethius could still

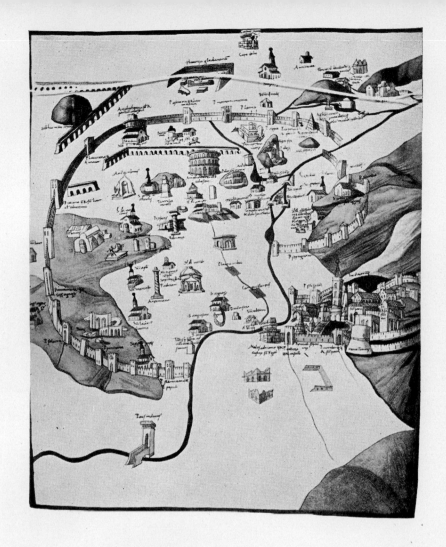

PLAN OF ROME IN THE FIFTEENTH CENTURY

THIS SUGGESTS THE CHARACTER OF THE CITY BEFORE THE RENAISSANCE

REPRODUCED FROM DE ROSSI'S PIANTE ICONOGRAFICHE E
PROSPETTICHE DI ROMA ANTERIORI AL SECOLO XVI

dream of the restoration of the empire. Two hundred
and fifty years later, when Pepin and Charlemagne con-
jured up the ghost of the western empire, in the minds
of men it was as if Rome had again become the mistress
of the world. Two hundred years after Charlemagne,
when the city had faded to the shadow of its former self,
the enthusiastic Otto the Third called himself Emperor
of the Romans, and had his crown inscribed, "Rome,
Capital of the World, Queen of all the Globe," and on
the installation of his judiciary used the formula,
"Judge Rome and the Leonine city and the whole world
according to this book." The book was the code of
Justinian. The envoys of the Roman republic who came
forth from their ruined and powerless city to meet the
great Barbarossa addressed the emperor with all the
dignity of the times when the senate was an assembly
of kings: "We, ambassadors of the city, not insignificant
men of Rome, are sent to thine Excellency by the senate
and people. Benevolently hear what the illustrious mistress of the world, whose sovereign, with God's help,
thou soon shalt be, doth offer thee. Dost thou come in
peace, I rejoice. Thou desirest the empire of the world,
and I gladly rise to hasten forward with the crown. . . .
May the splendor of ancient times, the freedom of the
illustrious city, return. May Rome, under such an emperor, again seize the reins of supremacy over a rebellious world, and may her ruler with the name unite
also the glory of Augustus." In the rebellion of 1234,
the citizens demanded of the pope that they should be
exempt from excommunication and other ecclesiastical
punishments, as their ancient ancestors had been exempt
from scourging. A senator in the same century glorified
the city as "the eyebrow of the world, the tribunal of

justice, the seat of holiness, the throne of glory." John the Twenty-second, as he sat in Avignon and thought of the deserted hills of the sacred city, cried out, "*Velimus nolimus enim rerum caput Roma erit,*—For, will we or no, Rome will be the capital of the world."

Such language and such pretensions as these would have been ridiculous uttered regarding any other spot in the world than Rome. A monk on the throne of Peter could seriously claim the sovereignty of the world, and almost attain it. The fantastic visions of a Cola di Rienzo were almost realized before his astonished opponents had ceased to be amused by his arrogance. The son of a poor tavern-keeper, a dreamer devoid of common sense, to say nothing of statesmanship, could revolutionize the government of the city, organize its armies, make war on the Latin cities, summon prince and pope to yield to the rightful mistress of the world, and not be universally laughed at. Rome is one of history's greatest examples of the persistence of an idea.

But if the idea of military and political sovereignty over the world was never again to be realized, the dominion of Rome over the hearts of men continued and increased. In theory, Rome strove for temporal control over the world in order that she might exercise a control of the spirit; in actual fact, it was a spiritual and sentimental dominion already exercised that made the world willing to pause and attend. However degraded by ignorance, ruin, and lawlessness, she still remained Eternal Rome, at frequent intervals the center of politics, always the center of sentiment. Philip the Arab, in the midst of a century of convulsions, had celebrated in the Coliseum in 247 the thousandth anniversary of the city's founding. Constantius, whose capital was on the

Bosporus, and Honorius, who ruled from Ravenna and Milan, had chosen the ancient city as the scene of their triumphs. Alaric and his wild soldiery, like the Gauls eight centuries before them, had withheld their hands in awe for a moment before profaning the venerable seat of civilization. Theodoric had poured out money in her embellishment, Justinian had sought to regain control of her, Constans the Second in 663, arrived by the Appian Way, went straightway to lay his gifts with prayers on the altar of Peter. Belisarius, one hundred and seventeen years before, by an appeal to reason and sentiment, had stayed the hand of Totila, who had already torn down part of the walls and now threatened to turn the entire city into a pasture for cattle. "Beyond all cities upon earth," he writes the victor from Ostia, "Rome is the greatest and most wonderful. . . . She remains a monument of the virtues of the world to all posterity, and a trespass against her greatness would justly be regarded as an outrage against all time." The Gothic king had celebrated the races in the olden fashion, and Narses after him reproduced the triumph of the Cæsars' times. The leaders and tyrants of civic Rome adopted such titles as "Prince and Senator of all the Romans," "Tribune of Freedom, of Peace and Justice, and Illustrious Redeemer of the Holy Roman Republic," "Candidate of the Holy Spirit," "Deliverer of the City," "Zealot for Italy," "Friend of the World," "Tribune of Augustus." The rulers of vast realms beyond Italy styled themselves "Emperors of the Romans," and confessed their dependence upon the City of God on the Tiber banks. By her kings reigned, and princes decreed justice, and to her, for the healing of their souls, all nations flowed.

The city had always been the goal of travel; but by the seventh century the formal pilgrimage had begun to be an established custom. From every quarter of Europe came penitents to gaze upon the relics of the saints, to offer prayers and gifts, to receive baptism and blessing from the vicar of Christ. Among them came the great of the earth. Cadwalla, king of the West Saxons, died in Rome on a pilgrimage in 689. A score of years later, Conrad of Mercia and Offa of Essex were there to take the cowl. Charlemagne, on his first visit in April, 774, ascended to Saint Peter's on his knees, kissing each step as he went; and twenty-six years later the somber nave and aisles of the ancient basilica of the Apostle resounded with enthusiastic cries from the brilliant trains of monarch and pope as the great Frank was divinely invested with authority over the world by the successor of the Fisherman. In 1027, with wallet and staff, came Canute the Dane, to be horrified at the scenes he witnessed, but to go his way with heart none the less softened to repentance and swelling with reverence. In 1050 came Macbeth of Scotland, free-handed with the poor of Rome. Into and out of the gates flowed an unceasing stream of pilgrims from nations far and near, swelled alike by the saintly who hungered and thirsted after righteousness and by the criminal compelled by conscience or confessor.

The external features of the city whose thoroughfares the pilgrims actually trod, as well as the character of its inhabitants, were far from reproducing the Rome of their dreams. It was a motley city that met their eyes. Mounted barons in armor rode in from the Campagna with their bands of retainers bristling with halberd and lance. Visitors wandered among ruins or marched in solemn silence to the goal of their pilgrimage in half-ruined basilicas. There were swarms of squalid beggars with outstretched hands. A funeral conducted by a confraternity in masks progressed over pavement uneven and neglected. Grimy artisan and indolent tradesman looked on from the thresholds of miserable shops, and tattered vendors cried their wares. The sunny places in winter and the shady in summer were populous with chattering idlers. The streets were in movement with nuns and barefoot monks, with magnificent cardinals and their trains, with guides and traffickers in dubious relics, with painted courtesans and aimless idlers. The niche in the wall, with painted or sculptured image and burning lamp, and the bells of church and cloister, were the ceaseless reminder of the claims of another world. Rough outside stairways and forbidding archways led to dwellings and courts that were dark and unsanitary. The air was heavy with the odors of an ill-kept city. The people drank of the turbid Tiber or from wells at the foot of the hills. Their sewerage, if they had it, was the poor service rendered by the decayed and choked-up remains of the ancient system. The princely themselves were none too cleanly, the populace unkempt and dirty. There was swindling, quarrelling, thievery, and riot. Layman and ecclesiastic alike looked on the stranger with the eye of greed.

Yet not all this could rob the city of its charm, and it never ceased to cast its mystic spell. Men came and saw, and were shocked at the sights their eyes beheld; but in their day, as in better days that have followed, the mean reality was submerged in love for the holy capital. At the last prayerful salutation of the venerable city as they climbed the height of Monte Mario and looked the final farewell, their hearts were no less filled with reverence than when suddenly from its brow they had first caught the vision of the holy place and fallen upon their knees in fulness of heart at the realization of their vows.

In the century which saw the departure of the papacy and the culmination of Roman wretchedness, nothing was more remarkable than this hold which the city retained upon the love and the fears of men. She was more than ever the Queen and Mother of the world. The jubilee of 1300 drew an unparalleled concourse of pilgrims. The amount of money poured into the papal treasury was enormous. Thirty thousand persons, said one chronicler, went into and out of the city every day, and two hundred thousand might have been counted within the walls at any time.

"Of bread, wine, meat, fish, and oats," says another, "there was plenty to be had in the market, and cheap. The hay was very dear, and the inns exceedingly expensive. It cost me for my lodging and the stabling of my horse, over and above the hay and oats, a Tornese groat (a third of a franc). As I went out of Rome on Christmas Eve, I saw leaving the city a throng so great that no one could count the number, and the talk among the Romans was that there had been more than two millions of men and women. Several times I saw men as well as women trodden under foot, and more than once I escaped the same danger myself."

In 1334 came the Flagellants, as they had come in 1260, and as they were to come once more in 1400, the sign of the spirit of repentance abroad in the world. Men, women, and children, monks, priests, and hermits, the innocent and the guilty alike, caught up by the spirit of the time, set out by tens, and hundreds, and thousands, from all parts of Italy and from beyond the Alps, treading the rough ways with bare feet and scourging their unprotected shoulders, preaching repentance and crying, "Peace and Mercy,"—driven by common impulse to the one city whose sovereignty over the souls of men was undisputed, and to which they looked for salvation in spite of its sordidness and ruin, and in spite of its shameless inhabitants, who laughed in the face of the Dominican leader of the Penitents, Fra Venturino, when he declared that only the dead were holy at Rome, the living godless.

Incredible numbers were again in the city during the jubilee of 1350. Five thousand pilgrims daily entered and left the gates, and one reckless estimate placed the number during Lent at a million two hundred thousand. The highways of Italy were channels through which flowed streams of pilgrims, the vacant spaces of the city were their camping-places, the city itself a huge inn. Nine years before the jubilee, there had occurred the crowning of Petrarch on the Capitol, followed on the next day by the poet's capture by brigands almost at the gates of the city. Three years before, in 1347, the momentary success of Cola di Rienzo's fantastic ideas had cast its glamour over the city. In August of that year it was filled by envoys from abroad, its palaces and streets bright with banquets and processions, the populace in a frenzy of delight as the horse of Marcus Aurelius spouted wine and water from its nostrils. In November the old-time Roman valor had once more demonstrated itself in the great victory at the gate of San Lorenzo, where fell eighty nobles, the flower of the princely families of Rome, victims of the sentimental might of the Eternal City. Meanwhile the Romans in deepest misery bewailed the absence of the papal court.

It was indeed a motley city, a city of violent contrasts. It was a city of beauty and desolation, of ill-kept and odorous streets under skies of azure and gold, streets today empty and tomorrow filled with endless trains of chanting pilgrims, a city of deserted and grass-grown regions ghastly with crumbling ruins, through which moved gorgeous retinues of cardinal, prince, and pope. It was a city of self-contradiction, a city of weakness and of strength, of penitential processions and of bloody riot, of devotion to the Church and of rebellion against its head, of saintly reputation and of satanic conduct, of spirituality in theory and of brutal worldliness in practice; of solemn crownings of emperors in gloomy and decaying churches by those who styled themselves Servants of the Servants of God.

X.

THE RENAISSANCE

Urbe Roma in pristinam formam rinascente,—

The city of Rome rising again into its ancient form.

LAURENTIUS MANLIUS, Inscription on his house, Via del Pianto (1468)

Visebamus sæpe deserta urbis Antonius Luscus vir clarissimus egoque, admirantes animo tum ob veterum collapsorum ædificiorum magnitudinem et vastas urbis antiquæ ruinas, tum ob tanti imperii ingentem stragem stupendam profecto ac deplorandam fortunæ varietatem. . . . Cæteros urbis collis perlustra; omnia vacua ædificiis ruinis vineis oppleta conspicies,—

We used often to visit the deserted places of the city, Antonius Luscus the senator and I, marvelling now at the magnitude of the fallen edifices of antiquity and the vast ruins of the ancient city, and now at the stupendous and deplorable change of fortune to be seen in the great downfall of so mighty an empire. . . . Cast the eye over the other hills of the city; you will see them all empty of buildings and filled with ruins and vineyards.

POGGIO BRACCIOLINI, De Varietate Fortunæ

AUGUSTANS RETURNED

THE papal absence was the darkest hour in the night of mediæval Rome. The attempt of Cola di Rienzo to revive the liberties of the Roman people and to unite Italy under the dominion of the ancient city was an empty dream of what was to prove possible only after five centuries more had rolled by, and the utterances of Petrarch were heavy with the despair of Rome's time of deepest degradation. Yet with both came the first streaks that heralded the day of the rebirth. The fantastic tribune who dreamed among the fallen columns and scattered inscriptions of the ancient city and declaimed in Latin on her lost glories, and the devoted poet who received the crown of laurel on the Capitol, were chief contributors to the impulse that started into wakefulness the arts of the ancient civilization.

Little more than a score of years after the death of Cola di Rienzo, and but three years after Petrarch's life had ended, the papacy returned to the long-deserted city. On January 17, 1377, preceded by dancing buffoons and accompanied by two thousand men-at-arms, Gregory the Eleventh entered the city by the Ostian gate and made his way through its desolate southern portion, past the Aventine and Capitoline, through the Campus Martius, and across the Tiber to Saint Peter's, treading on flowers strewn in the streets by the rejoicing Romans.

The seemingly interminable widowhood of three score years and ten was at an end. In their enthusiasm at the return of the fountain of what little prosperity and well-being had been theirs in the dark centuries preceding, the citizens momentarily forgot the repeated failures which had attended their efforts to found an independent commonwealth, and looked to the future with new confidence.

The return of the papacy, however, brought in its train no immediate cessation of the woes from which the city had suffered. Strife and bloodshed continued without abatement. With the death of Gregory and the armed conflict between the rival claimants of the tiara, Urban the Sixth and Robert of Geneva, the anti-pope Clement the Seventh, came the beginning of the Great Schism. For forty years both Avignon and Rome were the seats of papal courts whose quarrels were reflected in the Church and empire at large and in the ancient capital.

Nor were the contests which sprang from the rivalry of pope and anti-pope the only sources of disorder in Rome. The ancient quarrels of the city still raged. Pope and people still struggled for control. Popes were expelled, and foreign armies intervened. The broils of the Colonna, who under their relative Martin the Fifth became masters of the greater part of Latium, with the Orsini, who were powerful in Tuscany and the Sabines, were as fierce as ever. The terrors of brigandage in the Campagna were unabated. A population whose passions were without restraint and whose conscience knew no scruple continued in the barbarous satisfaction of private enmities.

The city was really in a state of intermittent anarchy. The streets were as unsafe as ever, and the citizens as incapable as ever of maintaining the dignity of which

they knew their city to be worthy. Twice in 1417, the
year of Martin the Fifth's accession and the end of the
schism, was the Rome which had been for a thousand
years the spiritual head of the world, and which had in
her time been the mistress of civilized mankind, entered
and ruled by mere *condottieri*. Ignorance continued to
prevail no less than disorder. The University had fallen
into decay, not to be permanently restored until 1431.
The destruction of the ancient monuments went on. It
was almost as if Petrarch and Cola di Rienzo had not
lived, and the day had not already broken elsewhere.

Not even with the reign of Martin the Fifth did the
city permanently afford the atmosphere of safety and
stability necessary for the encouragement of the new
learning and art. Firm and vigorous though "The Happiness of his Times," as his tomb in the Lateran describes him, proved himself, after his death and the
accession of Eugenius the Fourth the city and Campagna again became the prey to papal and feudal
quarrels. "Owing to the absence of the pope," says
Vespasiano in his *Life of Eugenius,* who had been the
victim of an uprising, "the city had become like a village of cowherds; sheep and cattle wandered through
the streets, to the very spot now occupied by the merchants' stalls."

The Campagna and other lands of the Church suffered especially. "Seldom has the rule of any other
pope," says the humanist Poggio Bracciolini, "produced
equal devastation in the provinces of the Roman Church.
The country scourged by war, the depopulated and
ruined towns, the devastated fields, the roads infested
by robbers, more than fifty places partly destroyed,
partly sacked by soldiery, have suffered from every

species of revenge. After the destruction of their cities, many citizens have been sold as slaves; many have died in prison."

Martin and Eugenius had nevertheless been favorably disposed toward learning and the arts. Not even the turbulence of Eugenius' times wholly checked the rapidly increasing momentum of the intellectual movement. The famous Bessarion was cardinal under him; Poggio and Biondo were among his secretaries; the University was rehabilitated, and became a center to which even foreigners resorted.

But neither Martin nor Eugenius was a scholar. It was in the person of Nicholas the Fifth, imbued with the spirit of Florence, the great intellectual and æsthetic center of the time, that the first humanist sat on the papal throne. It was now that the jocund day of the Renaissance stood tiptoe on the misty mountain-top, and flooded with brightness and warmth the heap of ruins and wretched hovels which constituted Rome at the end of the Dark Age. The seed which had long been in the soil and had recently put forth the first shoots now started into vigorous life. A new spirit sprang into being, in Rome as elsewhere in Italy, as mysterious in its rise as it was powerful in its influence. The authority of mediævalism went out, and the individualism of modern times came in. A new culture and new ideas arose and possessed themselves of Italian society. The gloom of ignorance was dispelled by the brilliance of a revived paganism. The love of learning, beauty, and elegance became as great in reality as the contempt for the world and the flesh had been in theory. A great impulse to worldliness possessed itself of the Church at Rome, and the papacy entered upon the secular career which was to culminate in a martial Julius the Second and a diplomatic and splendor-loving Leo the Tenth.

Rome found herself for the third time and in a third capacity the capital of the world. She had been its political and military capital under the Empire, its spiritual capital during the Dark Age. She now became its æsthetic and intellectual capital. Barren though she herself was of talent of any kind, she was the inspiration and means by which it rose, and her popes afforded the center about which it gathered. Florence indeed was the great fountain of genius for the age, and many of the less famed cities of Italy received the light earlier; but from the accession of Nicholas the Fifth in 1447 to the sack of 1527 the papal court was the magnet which drew and encouraged the talent of the world, and Rome was the Alma Mater from whom it drank in vigor.

Few were the years when a Mæcenas or an Augustus did not sit upon the throne. Those popes who were least in sympathy with art and learning were nevertheless caught up by the spirit of the times and inspired by a love of beauty and splendor which caused them to foster the work of genius for the sake of display if not for its own sake; while the activities of those whose love of culture was genuine and whose patriotism embraced even the great past knew no bounds save the limits imposed by mortality and the exhaustion of means.

The ruling passion of Nicholas the Fifth, 1447-1455, to whom "what was unknown lay outside the sphere of human knowledge," was the collection of books and the founding of a great Vatican library. Calixtus the Third of Valencia, the first Borgia, 1455-1458, though less a humanist, was the first jurist of his age. Pius the Second, Æneas Sylvius Piccolomini, 1458-1464, was de-

voted to the muses of poetry and history, and left as a
witness his *Commentarii*. Paul the Second, Pietro Barbo
of Venice, 1464-1471, founded a museum of antiquities,
of which he was a learned and enthusiastic lover. Sixtus
the Fourth, Francesco Rovere, 1471-1484, the great
builder, was a willing victim to the same passion. Innocent the Eighth, Cibo, 1484-1492, built the Belvedere.
Alexander the Sixth, Rodrigo Borgia, 1492-1503,
brought to Rome Pinturicchio, Perugino, and Michelangelo. Julius the Second, nephew of Sixtus the Fourth,
1503-1513, founded the Vatican museum, and employed
both the great sculptor and Raphael. The tenth Leo,
Giovanni Medici of Florence, 1513-1521, was the greatest of all papal patrons of the revived culture. With few
exceptions, the popes of the entire period invited to
Rome and supported every form of talent which could
give pleasure to the court or confer glory on the city
and the Church.

There was hardly a humanist of reputation who was
not at some time in the service of the popes and resident
at Rome. Poggio Bracciolini of Arezzo, the great discoverer of ancient manuscripts, was fifty years in the
employ of eight of them; Filelfo of Tolentino was the
secretary of Nicholas; Valla, in spite of his exposure of
the false donation of Constantine, was a friend of the
same pope; Eugenius the Fourth was the patron of
Cyriac of Ancona. The revival of Greek was actively
encouraged; Chrysoloras, George of Trebizond, with
Bessarion and the circle of learned Greek scholars whom
he befriended, all owed their privileges at Rome to the
papal court. Flavio Biondo, author of *Roma Instaurata,
Roma Triumphans,* and *Italia Illustrata,* lived on the
Via Flaminia near Montecitorio, was secretary to

PLAN OF ROME IN 1551

BY LEONARDO BUFALINI,
INDICATING THE LIMITS OF THE CITY
IN THE HIGH RENAISSANCE

REPRODUCED FROM ROCCHI, PIANTE DI ROMA

Eugenius the Fourth, and enjoyed the patronage of
Nicholas the Fifth, Calixtus the Third, and Pius the
Second. Andrea Fulvio, his emulator, composed his
Antichità di Roma at the suggestion of Leo the Tenth.
Paul the Second patronized the German printers Pan-
nartz and Schweinheim, who first brought the art to
Rome. Pomponius Lætus, pupil of Valla, Professor of
Eloquence in the University and head of the Roman
Academy, lived on the Quirinal. Platina was custodian
of the Vatican library and historian of the popes. Sigis-
mondo dei Conti and Paolo Giovio, historians of the
times, were protégés of Julius the Second and Leo the
Tenth.

No less brilliant was the galaxy of poets. The age was
as fertile in poetry as in rhetoric, the humanistic art *par
excellence*. Vegio, who added a thirteenth book to the
Æneid; Valla, translator of Hesiod and Homer; San-
nazzaro, author of *Eclogues* and *De Partu Virginis;*
Vida, who wrote a *Christiad* modelled on Virgil; Fracastoro, noted for his poem, *Syphilis;* with scores of
others whose works, famous in their own day, have
found places on dusty shelves whence they never descend save at the bidding of the delver, all enjoyed high
favor at the ecclesiastical court. The Italian poets were
encouraged equally with the neo-Latin. Vittoria Colonna, Berni, Ariosto, and Trissino were among their
leaders; while the Vatican swarmed with a thousand
sonneteers and rhymesters. It was the age of all ages
when a Horace might have uttered the famous *Scribi-
mus indocti doctique poemata passim,*—"All of us,
clever and stupid alike, are writing poetry helter-
skelter."

If, however, the literature of the period was destined

in great part to fail of immortality, it was not so with the other arts. Hardly a painter of note, from Fra Angelico to Raphael, is missing from the list of those who left masterpieces on the walls of Roman palace and church. Masaccio under Martin the Fifth executed frescoes in San Clemente, and Gentile da Fabriano in the Lateran. Giovanni da Fiesole, the famous friar, was already at work under Eugenius. Benozzo Gozzoli and Piero della Francesca and Bramantino came to Rome under Nicholas. The Sistine chapel and other chambers of the Vatican illustrate the painters' art from the time of Sixtus the Fourth to the end of the Renaissance. Melozzo, Cosimo Roselli, Botticelli, Ghirlandaio, Mantegna, Lippi, Perugino, Pinturicchio, Signorelli, Michelangelo, and Raphael, besides numerous pupils and imitators, all pass in review before the visitor to the seat of the popes.

Of sculpture the same was true. There was hardly a sculptor of note from Eugenius to the noonday of the Renaissance under Leo the Tenth whose work is not illustrated in Rome. Chief among them were Donatello, Mino, the Pollaiuoli, Verrocchio, Rossellino, and Michelangelo.

The architects of the day above all were in demand. Martin and Eugenius themselves displayed no slight activity in restoring and building; but Nicholas, with more enthusiasm for the task than realization of its magnitude, cherished the design of a mighty restoration that should change the whole city. The great wall was repaired, the Capitol refortified, the Mulvian and Nomentan bridges equipped with military defences; the forty station churches were restored, the palace of the Conservatori rebuilt. The people were to be en-

couraged to occupy the deserted quarters. The Leonine
city, first walled by Leo the Fourth, 845-857, after the
Saracen invasion, was to be reconstructed, and its im-
pregnable new walls were to surround a great papal
city containing a magnificent new Vatican palace and a
gigantic new cathedral of Saint Peter. The whole was
to be an eighth wonder of the world. The talents of
Rossellino and Leon Battista Alberti were employed,
and the pope urged on the execution of his plans with
feverish haste. All Rome was aglow with the work, and
the failure to press the great scheme to its realization
was due only to its author's death.

Calixtus was less active, Pius built for the most part
in Siena and Pienza, and Paul reared the Palazzo San
Marco, later called Venezia. The greatest builder of
all was Sixtus the Fourth. It was under him that modern Rome first began to take form. The hospital of
Santo Spirito was rebuilt by him, Santa Maria Maggiore restored, the Ponte Sisto and the Sistine chapel
built. The churches of Santa Maria del Popolo, Santa
Maria della Pace, and Sant' Agostino owe their present
form to him and his cardinals, as well as San Pietro in
Vincoli and the Santi Apostoli. Many palaces also were
erected, and such was the activity of Sixtus in the laying
out of new streets and the improvement of old ones that
he was said to have "found Rome mud and left it tile."

The successors of this pope carried the work forward
in worthy manner. Innocent the Eighth built the Villa
Belvedere in the gardens of the Vatican. Under Alexander the Sixth the church of Trinità dei Monti was
founded, Sant' Angelo was converted into a fortress
with walls and battlements, the street called Borgo
Nuovo laid out, the Vatican building enterprises of

Nicholas magnificently completed, and the Cancelleria reared. From the time of Alexander to the sack of 1527, the names of Bramante, Peruzzi, Raphael, Sangallo, and Michelangelo figure prominently in the architectural history of the city,—Bramante in connection with Saint Peter's, founded April 18, 1506, but not to be dedicated until November 18, 1626; Peruzzi in connection with the famous Farnesina; Raphael for his plan of the city and his employment on Saint Peter's and the Vatican; Sangallo and Michelangelo for their work on the Palazzo Farnese. All these were the greater activities only.

Never had Rome assembled within her walls in the period of a hundred years so many men of culture and genius. Never had she shone with so great a luster. Not only the arts of sculpture and painting, of rhetoric and literature, entered upon a career unequalled for enthusiasm and brilliance, but the city was splendid with luxurious appointments, elegant manners, gorgeous festivals, elaborate ceremonials, and material display of every kind. In brilliance if not in depth and breadth, in alertness of mind if not in political stability, in achievement of individuals if not in the sway of masses of mankind, in the creation of modern art if not in the rivalling of ancient art, the age went far toward justifying its enthusiasts in comparing it with the age of Augustus himself.

In all the glowing activity of the time, no motive was more prominent or more fruitful of results than the imitation of antiquity. The period deserved its name; it was first of all a rebirth. The ancient culture revived and renewed was the great foundation on which rested all its achievement. For the cities of Italy it was as if the long period of the Dark Age, with its ignorance and gloom, had been only a dream, and classical culture had again awakened to its own. The ancient Roman language was the language of the rebirth, and the ancient love of rhetoric, which never fails the Latin races, the chief motive which prompted its use. Ancient architecture afforded inspiration for the edifices which began to be reared from the remains of ancient material. The ancient love of form underlay not only the literary art, but the arts of painting and sculpture. The figures of Michelangelo, whether chiselled or painted, were only nude classical sculpture in a new guise, and beauty of person is much more apparent in the creations of Raphael than saintliness. If exquisite religious sentiment breathes a benediction from the canvas of Renaissance painting, that its source in a great number of instances lay rather in the powerful artistic imagination of the painter than in real religious emotion must be the conclusion of every person familiar with the spirit of that most easy-minded and irresponsible century in the history of Christian Rome.

It was, to be sure, natural enough that the art which arose from the ruins of the ancient civilization should partake of its character. The extent to which Renaissance culture did partake of the ancient culture, however, was in excess of what was merely natural. Imitation of antiquity became conscious to exaggeration. The quickened knowledge of his glorious past stirred the vanity as well as the pride of the Renaissance Roman. He revived the literary tongue and the manners of his predecessor of over a thousand years before, seriously looked on him as his direct ancestor, and was finally so carried away by the result of the effort as to fancy that he rivalled him. The poet of the time of Leo the Tenth who compares the bards of his own day with those of the age of Virgil and Horace, and is really perplexed as to which are more deserving of the laurel, reflects the thought of many men of his time.

In his enthusiasm for antiquity lies the most notable trait of the Roman of the Renaissance. The imitation of it was extended to every possible detail, and amounted to little less than a cult. Cola di Rienzo, Tribune of the People, saw in himself the restorer of the ancient republic. Petrarch, crowned on the Capitol, was reviving an ancient ceremony of the time of Domitian. A Nicholas, a Pius, a Julius, or a Leo, saw in himself an Augustus or a Mæcenas. The swarms of speechmakers, scholars, poets, and historians, great and small, who buzzed about the Vatican, masquerading under Latin names, imagined themselves Livys, Virgils, Quintilians, Varros, and Ciceros. Petty plotters against authority saw tyrants on every throne and felt the blood of Brutus surging in their veins. Triumphal processions were modelled on the great parades of the ancient emperors. Splendid ceremonials were performed in the spirit of the ancient pagan church. Pomponius Lætus, wholly absorbed in the contemplation of antiquity, a belated pagan, organized the Roman Academy at his home on the Quirinal, where its members, adopting ancient names,—Callimachus Experiens, Glaucus, Petreius, Asclepiades, and the like,—gathered to hold discussions, read papers, present Latin comedy, and in other ways to glorify the past. The anniversary celebration of the founding of Rome, the festival of the ancient Palilia revived, was observed by them on April 20, 1483, for the first time in over a thousand years, and is still an event of each recurring April 21.

The collection of antiquities became a passion. Artificial ruins were the vogue, and indispensable to every garden. Not only was the language of the ancient Romans regarded as the most dignified vehicle of expression, but the nomenclature of Greek and Latin antiquity was adopted in the most affected manner. Men christened their children by such names as Agamemnon, Minerva, and Apelles with a facility as great as that of late nineteenth century parents choosing names from the most recent popular novel. The pope was Pontifex Maximus, the saints were Divi, nuns became Virgines Vestales, Heaven was Olympus, and its ruler once more Jupiter or Zeus. The senators again became Patres Conscripti, the Carnival the Lupercalia. Even courtesans took to themselves the beautiful and honored names of antiquity, and Rome afforded the novel spectacle of profligate women masquerading under the names of Cassandra, Penthesilea, Portia, Virginia, and even Lucretia.

Not content with such superficial ties, the society of the time looked seriously upon itself as really Roman. Individuals prided themselves on direct descent from the ancient Roman families, doing violence to every probability of history and etymology in the effort to prove a connection. The Massimi with at least a show of reason looked on their house as descended from Fabius Maximus Cunctator of Hannibalic fame; but Paul the Second, a Barbo of Venice, perhaps of barbarian ancestry, regarded himself as the son of the ancient Ahenobarbi.

Cities, as well as individuals, felt it a great distinction if Roman origin could be proved. To partake of the character of ancient Rome and her civilization in every aspect became the fashion. Pagan philosophy and religion made dangerous inroads on the fidelity of churchmen high in authority. Men could openly deny the existence of a Paradise and cast doubt on the doctrine of the immortality of the soul. Leo the Tenth himself was said to have been so under the charm of Greek philosophy as almost to adopt it. Skepticism was a characteristic of the age, and if it did not get the dark house and the whip as it did later, the reason why it was not so punished and cured was that the lunacy was so ordinary that the whippers were skeptical too.

The natural consequence of all this enthusiasm was that the times were full of the unreal and the superficial, and guilty of errors in taste and judgment. In their blind admiration for everything ancient, scholars and men of letters were almost without discrimination, and valued alike every monument or literary remnant of ancient times. No less infatuated with their own facile powers, they fancied themselves rivals of Virgil and Cicero and Horace. The Sabine Farms and other rewards of the learned brow were showered on the clever declaimer, the skilful improvisator, and the deft imitator of the ancient masterpieces as well as on the contributor to the genuine in poetry and knowledge. Learned and unlearned were writing, making speeches, acting parts, everywhere, all the time. The language in which they clothed their scant thought was often such as the ancients themselves would have laughed at, and the whole tremendous output scarcely outlived its authors.

Yet the age deserves none the less the praises of its

most enthusiastic eulogizers. It was the age in which
the Italians rediscovered learning, the world about them,
and, greatest of all, themselves and humanity. If the
achievements of the time in Latin literature, in which
its representatives probably thought its greatest claim
to immortality lay, were in reality its least permanent
contribution to culture, it was different with native
Italian literature, with sculpture, with architecture, and,
above all, with painting. "The Italian was the first-born
among the sons of modern Europe." The impulse given
by Italy to the appreciation and love of the beautiful
and all that concerned the intellectual life and human
personality was such that it has not yet lost its momentum. Forth from her inspired cities in valley and
plain and from her little towns aloft on crag and hill
came the life and vigor of modern culture, and to her
the generations of today may trace whatever in their
life is due to the awakening of the love for the gracious
and the beautiful; for we are still only in the afterglow
of that incomparably brilliant day.

2.

GOD AND MAMMON

BRILLIANT as was the Renaissance, and great as was its ultimate service to both the intellectual and the moral advance of the world, it was the rebirth not of morals and religion, but only of intellect and art. No sun rose upon the Dark Age of morals at Rome. No century in the history of culture, certainly not in the history of Italy, has left behind it a more shameful record morally than the Renaissance in the Eternal City. If Rome herself was no worse than other cities of the time, the fact of her being the religious capital of the world made her at least seem so, and warrants the severity of the judgment which history has passed upon her.

Just as the papal court affords an index of the intellectual and art activities of the Renaissance, its life presents also evidence quite as eloquent of the morals of the age. It was during the Renaissance that the secularization of the papacy became for the moment practically complete. The development of the ecclesiastical state through diplomacy and war, the encouragement of building and the fine arts for the aggrandizement of the Church and the pleasures of the court, were the activities to which the wearer of the tiara now looked, rather than the duties of the chief priest of Christendom. The pope was a monarch, distinguished from the many monarchs of petty Italian states of the time only by his dignity as head of the Church Universal, and protected only by that dignity from the fate which most of them sooner or later met.

Not that worldliness then for the first time possessed the leadership of the Church. The Dark Ages, and even the later Roman empire, had seen popes and bishops with secular aspirations. The greatest popes of the Dark Ages, however, had been at the same time the greatest priests. The greatest popes of the Renaissance, on the contrary, were the greatest monarchs who sat on the papal throne. There is a great difference between a Gregory the Seventh and a Julius the Second. At the turn of the sixteenth century for the first time occurred an extended period in which the priestly function of the head of Christendom became secondary, and almost disappeared.

It is still possible to see in Nicholas the Fifth, scholar, builder, and enthusiast, and in Pius the Second, æsthete, diplomat, and would-be crusader, a semblance of the priest. It is a matter of much greater difficulty in the case of the vain Paul the Second, the ambitious Sixtus the Fourth, and the sordid Innocent the Eighth. When the imagination is called on to regard as the keeper of the holy office a cunning and pitiless Alexander the Sixth, a military Julius the Second, or a voluptuous Leo the Tenth, it shrinks. Julius, the Pontiff Terrible, invading rebellious provinces at the head of armies, active even in the trenches, bestirring himself in the formation of great military leagues, is to be classed, not with priests, but with statesmen and soldiers; and Leo, patron of the arts, in the midst of a brilliant court resounding with music and laughter, saying to his brother, Julian Medici, "Let us enjoy the papacy, for God hath given it to us," is surely in the category of merry

monarchs. Even the one distinction between the papacy
and ordinary monarchies, which lay in the lack of heredi-
tary succession, bade fair to be removed by the abuses
of nepotism. The famous jest of Erasmus, who was
astonished at what he saw in Italy and Rome in the early
sixteenth century, could not have fallen on an age when
the priesthood was more deserving of it: *Vocantur
patres,—et sæpe sunt.*

Had the secularization of the papacy and priesthood
been all, the times would deserve less condemnation;
but many vices were added to it. For popes to scheme
for the advancement of nephews, even when the term
covertly meant sons, was mild in comparison with other
abuses. The holy office was openly and unblushingly
bought by the candidate, who afterward, with equal
frankness and shamelessness, sold to the most profitable
customer the dignities in his hand. "There is now no
difference between the papacy and the sultanship," said
the Venetian ambassador at Rome after the election of
Julius the Second; "the dignity falls to the highest
bidder." Nor was the evil recent. Fifty years before,
Æneas Sylvius, not yet elevated to the throne, had declared: "There is nothing to be obtained from the Roman Curia without money. For even ordination and
the gifts of the Holy Ghost are sold."

Not only offices were bought, but freedom from all
ecclesiastical interference. The traffic in indulgences was
enormous, and carried on the world over. Even false
bulls were issued by impostors in the court. "Forgiveness of sins can be obtained only by purchase," said
Æneas Sylvius, and after his election declared that God
had appointed him pope to rescue the Church from her
affliction. The vice-chamberlain of Innocent the Eighth

THE ANCIENT CHURCH OF SAINT PETER

THE PREDECESSOR OF THE PRESENT CHURCH, AND DATING FROM CONSTANTINE

could humorously declare, "God wills not the death of a sinner, but that he should live and pay." The circumstances attending the death of the unsuccessful Flemish pope, Hadrian the Sixth, 1522-1523, student, ascetic, priest, and reformer, illustrate the spirit and manners left as a legacy to the papal court and the Roman people by the six papal administrations of the Church's most secular period. Brutal cardinals surrounded his bed demanding to be told where his money was; the youth of the city inscribed the door of his physician with the words, "To the Liberator of the Country, the Senate and the People of Rome"; and the scholar Valeriano, favorite of Leo the Tenth, afterward wrote, "Had this bitter enemy of the muses of eloquence and the beautiful lived longer, the times of Gothic barbarism must have been revived."

The immorality of greed, however, was not all. Sensuality, open and undisguised, invaded the life of the court. Cardinals and courtesans banqueted together. Popes were as ambitious for their children as other potentates, and almost as careless of appearances. The disease that followed the French expedition into Italy in 1494 was not confined to soldiers and civilians. Crimes of actual bloodshed and poisoning were frequent among the high officials of the Church and their followers, and were not unsuspected in the popes themselves. Sixtus the Fourth may have been innocent of contemplating the death of the Medici in the Pazzi conspiracy, but his wrathful excommunication of the Florentines for their punishment of the murderers did not indicate the deepest horror at the deed. Of Alexander the Sixth, Panvinio declared, "He would have put all the other rich cardinals out of the way, to get their property, had he not, in the midst of his great plans for his son (Cæsar Borgia), been struck down by death." In him and his sons were summed up the passions and abuses of a passionate and corrupt age.

The papacy was a scandal to all the world. Visitors to Rome from the northern countries, and even from the cities of Italy, were inexpressibly shocked to find the actual life of the Church at the capital worse than rumor had pictured it. It was not only a scandal to the world, but a source of corruption. All Christendom was tainted by the evils of simony and the sale of indulgences, if not by the viler examples of immorality, and if the effect of example could extend beyond the borders of Italy, its working in the peninsula and in the city of the popes may be imagined. Cruelty and corruption found sanction in the conduct of the highest spiritual authority in the world, and was restrained by little except the financial sense of ecclesiastical monitors who saw a connection between the Church's reputation and the contributions of her admirers. The blackness of Roman immorality was made blacker than that of other cities of Italy by the shining background of the ideal.

Especially in the last part of the fifteenth century and the beginning of the sixteenth did the society of Rome present a fearful spectacle of license and crime. The white light of intellectual intensity was accompanied by the white heat of passion. The brilliant age of the revived learning was also an age of terrible vendetta, when men washed their faces in the blood of murdered enemies, when spirits

> Ranging for revenge,
> With Ate by their side, come hot from hell,

filled the streets of the city and the ways of the Campagna with carrion men groaning for burial.

It was an age notorious no less for deliberate murder done for selfish ends,—an age of slow poisons, bravi, secret daggers, and assassinations in church. "Every night," said the Venetian ambassador in 1500, during the last part of the Borgia's reign, "four or five murdered men are discovered,—bishops, prelates, and others,—so that all Rome is trembling for fear of being destroyed by the duke (Cæsar Borgia)." The charcoal-seller who had seen the duke of Gandia's body thrown into the Tiber at the Ripetta excused himself for not having reported the fact by saying that in his time he had seen probably a hundred corpses thrown into the river by night and no one had ever troubled about them.

Egidius of Viterbo leaves the following picture of the city as he knew it under Alexander the Sixth: "Everything was hidden in darkness and stormy night; of the things that were done in the family and the Thyestean tragedies, I will keep silence; never were more terrible revolts in the cities of the ecclesiastical state, more sacks and more bloody deaths. Never were robberies committed with such impunity in the streets; never was Rome so full of criminals; never was the multitude of robbers and informers so audacious. People could neither leave the gates of the city nor dwell within it. To own money or valuable property was equivalent to being guilty of high treason. There was no protection either in house, sleeping-room, or tower. Justice was effaced. Money, power, and lust governed everything. Hitherto, since Italy had emancipated herself from foreign tyranny, she had remained exempt from the rule of the stranger, for, although King Alfonso was an Aragonese, in neither culture, liberality, nor magnanimity was he inferior to any Italian. Now, however, slavery followed freedom, now the Italians sank from independence into darkest servitude to the foreigner."

Nor is it only the reign of Alexander, culmination though it was of all the disorders which characterized the age, which affords such pictures. The intensity of passion which was the special mark of the time is to be seen as well before him in the reigns of Innocent and Sixtus, nor did it die out under the firmer hand of Julius. No one unacquainted with the ways of Rome would have dreamed that the fortified palaces, loopholed and artilleried, which met his eye in the thoroughfares of the city, were the homes of cardinals, or that the warlike chief with retinue armed to the teeth, guardedly advancing in the middle of the street, was the spiritual father of the human kind.

Social immorality was no less widely diffused than crime and disorder. From the licentious tales of Boccaccio, from the indecent *Facetiæ* of Poggio, from the *Hermaphroditus* of Beccadelli, a collection of obscene epigrams that won its author the laurel at Siena and a place in the literary court of Alfonso of Naples, the spirit of the earlier Renaissance may be judged. Its later phase may be suspected from the estimate that under Innocent the Eighth there were said to be five thousand public prostitutes in the city. Perhaps there were not so many as six thousand in 1490, as Infessura records, about one for every ten of the population, not including those kept in the homes of their patrons; but the accuracy of the number is not important. In 1494 the corruption was deepened by the army of Charles the Eighth of France, in the wake of which came what is called the *malattia francese* by Italians and by the French the *mal napolitain,* spreading over all Italy, and numbering among its victims at Rome Cæsar Borgia and Pope Julius.

Nor, even if crimes of disorder and bloodshed underwent some diminution after the Borgia, was the same true of social immorality. It went on unchecked to the gay noonday of the Renaissance under Leo the Tenth. Noble women could not properly mingle in the society of the papal court at any period as they did in other Italian courts; but in the later Renaissance the fear they felt of compromising the dignity of the Church was a less restraining influence than regard for their own reputations. It may not have been without reason that Vittoria Colonna while at Rome resided most of the time in a convent. The place of ladies at court and in the society of the city at large was in no small part usurped by accomplished courtesans, whom the antiquity-loving age dignified with the ancient Greek name of *hetairai.* The most attractive of them lived lives of elegance and luxury in homes of their own or their admirers in Ponte, near the bridge of Sant' Angelo, while the common sort were massed together in Ripa, the southernmost rione. It was in the exquisite home of the accomplished and dazzling Imperia, of the time of Julius the Second, that "the noble Spanish ambassador one day spat in the face of a servant, because he could find no other place suitable for the purpose." Beccadelli had propounded the theory that courtesans were more useful members of society than nuns; the age of Leo the Tenth at Rome went far toward putting it into practice.

Indecent letters flourished. The promise of Boccaccio and Poggio bore abundant fruitage in an unexampled harvest of foul literature, whose mere production would have been a sufficient index of the time had not the reception which it met been enthusiastic. To say nothing of the obscene stories of Bandello, a Dominican monk afterward made bishop, or of the foul wit of Pietro Aretino, who wrote the Virgin's life as well as celebrated in his compositions the orgies of lust and was made a Knight of Saint Peter by the pope, it is enough to mention the fact that one of the most admired poems of the age was the *Syphilis* of Fracastoro, dedicated to Cardinal Bembo and declared a "divine poem" by Julius Cæsar Scaliger. The revived pagan love of form in literature made the times as blind to its content as the revived love of personal beauty and indulgence of the senses made them indifferent to personal character. The same poet could write of religion and the lusts of the flesh; and artists painted or modelled many a Virgin and saint from not at all saintly models.

Thus had the Eternal City emerged from the Dark Ages to become at the same time the center of all that was most brilliant in a brilliant new era, and the vortex into which was gathered all that was depraved. The papacy had been irresistibly drawn back to her from Avignon, and she had been the inspiration and the promoter of the new culture, though, like the Rome of the Empire, barren herself, she had wrought with the hands of sons by adoption and assimilation. That the Reformation was late in coming and its effect less revolutionary is one more evidence of her great power over men.

For men still revered the historic city, still felt the spiritual refreshment of contact with soil once trodden

by the feet of the saints and enriched by the blood of
the martyrs, still coveted the blessing of the visible head
of the Church. Their hearts and their reason alike told
them that the glitter and the scandal of worldliness and
carelessness were only accidents, and that behind them
were the realities of Eternal Rome. Each recurrence of
the jubilee, which had been held three times in the fourteenth century, again in 1400 and 1450, and was fixed
by Paul the Second for every twenty-five years, saw
multitudes filling the ways of Europe to stream through
the gates of Rome. The jubilee of Nicholas, in 1450,
attracted a throng so dense that on one occasion two
hundred people were trampled down or plunged into
the Tiber at the Ponte Sant' Angelo, and witnesses
compared the crowds to ants, exaggerating the daily
multitude of visitors to three millions. The papal
treasury was filled to overflowing. On Easter Sunday,
1500, two hundred thousand persons knelt before Saint
Peter's to receive the benediction from Alexander the
Sixth. Luther, at his first sight of Rome, in 1510, had
prostrated himself and cried, "Hail to thee, thou sacred
Rome: yea, truly sacred by thy holy Martyrs and their
blood that was shed within thee!" It was seven years
after he had entered the gates, to find the Holy City
built upon hell, that the reformer was at last driven to
loose the ties that bound his soul to it. Erasmus was so
under its spell as to declare that it would take a Lethe
to make him forget it.

There were indeed attractions in the society of the
people who made up the Rome of the time, to say nothing of the sentiment roused by the ruins of ancient
empire and the sanctuaries of fifteen hundred years.
What Erasmus saw during his visit, could it be seen

through his eyes by the modern moralist under whose condemnation the city of the Renaissance lies, would go far toward lessening the harshness of that condemnation.

"Rome as the theatre of the world and its culture fascinated the greatest scholar of the time," says Gregorovius, reproducing the social Rome in which the great Dutchman found himself. "Monuments, art and collections, libraries, the wealth of learning and intellect, the grandiose style of life, all filled him with admiration. As a satirist it seemed to him a great European carnival, where worldly vanity went masked in spiritual attire, where were represented all lusts and desires, all intrigues and crimes, their magnet the Vatican, and thirst for gold, honors and power the forces that moved them. Sailing on this tumultuous sea he seemed to behold Sebastian Brand's overcrowded Ship of Fools; and, in fact, soon after his arrival in London in 1509, he wrote his celebrated *Praise of Folly* in the house of Thomas More.

"As a Christian he was astonished at the bold and glaring colouring borrowed from paganism by the Roman religion, of which nothing remained that was not false, and whose formerly revered temple had been transformed by the ambition and rapacity of the priesthood into a European banking house and a retail market for diplomas of favors, indulgences, and objects of superstition. As a man of the world, however, Erasmus could not feel otherwise than at ease in the courts of cardinals, and above all he had to acknowledge that in this corrupt Rome were found the most liberal form of intercourse and the most exquisite courtesy. In the age when in his *Cortegiano* Castiglione drew the ideal courtier, ancient urbanity was revived, and even if only the mask of inward corruption, it must have enchanted every northerner.

"The papacy, learning, antiquity, art, all linked Roman society in correspondence with the world. In Rome the most important matters of the time were discussed, or actively taken in hand; cosmopolitan politics, cosmopolitan literature, for in the Renaissance of Latinism we may speak of such a thing, the arts, poetry, the rising drama,—above all, science. The wealth of intellectual life flourished here in the morass of vice. It is, moreover, only just to admit that alongside of sensuality and avarice, pride and self-importance, hypocrisy and falsehood, conspicuous virtues were seen; generosity, friendship and benevolence, respect paid to talent, and love of all that was beautiful. In nobler natures even unchastity was accompanied by a liberal humanity, which was the true flower of the culture of the Italians. No other city could show a society so universally educated as that of the wholly corrupt city of Rome. Florence had emigrated to Rome, or the city of Lorenzo Medici had become a stepping stone to the Academy of the world. Valerianus might justly say that Rome at this period did more for intellectual culture than the whole of the rest of Italy. With equal justice Cardinal Riario called Rome the common fatherland of all scholars."

3.

THE CITY OF RAPHAEL

BEFORE the savagery of sack and carnage descends to wreck the iridescent fabric of the Renaissance at Rome, let us re-present to the imagination the city in which the fabric has been reared.

It was a rapidly growing and changing city of some fifty thousand inhabitants in which Leo the Tenth and Clement the Seventh reigned before the great catastrophe. The transformation which at the present day is so complete that of mediæval Rome, with the exception of the older churches, a few ruined tower-strongholds of the barons, the so-called house of Crescentius, and here or there the remnants of portal, wall, or window imbedded in recent masonry, nothing is longer visible, had its beginnings under Eugenius the Fourth. Among his successors, the greatest architectural renovators were Nicholas, Paul, Sixtus, Alexander, and Julius. The recital of the more important activities of their times is the story of magnificent change. Among their palaces and villas were the Conservatori, the San Marco, later the Venezia, the Borgia, later the Sforza-Cesarini, the original Colonna, the Cancelleria, the Adriano Castelli, later the Giraud-Torlonia, the original Madama, the Farnesina, the Belvedere, and the new Vatican, with the Sistine chapel. Among churches built, restored, or embellished were Santa Maria del Popolo, San Pietro in Montorio, Sant' Agostino, Santa Maria della Pace, Trinità dei Monti, San Pietro in Vincoli, the Santi Apostoli, the Lateran, and the earliest part of the new Saint Peter's. The Ponte Sisto was built, streets were straightened and paved, new avenues were laid out. The Corso took more definite form; the Via Alessandrina, later Borgo Nuovo, the Via Giulia, the Lungara, and the Lungaretta became what at that time were great thoroughfares.

To think of the Rome of Leo and Clement, however, as bearing a closer resemblance to the city of our own times than to that of the age preceding would be far from truth. The Rome of the Dark Ages was beginning to disappear, and modern Rome was taking form, but the new was only a small proportion of the whole. The palaces, churches, and other creations of the Renaissance stood out among the ancient and mediæval surroundings like a scattering of purple patches.

The identity of the Fourteen Regions of Augustus had long since been lost, with both the ancient numbers and names. They had been succeeded in the early Dark Ages by ten regions, later increased to twelve on the left bank, with the Trastevere as a thirteenth on the right. Already known by name and number during the Avignon period, at the end of the century they appear officially in the order which they have since preserved. I. Regio Montium, Italian Rione Monti, was so named from the hills in the northeastern part of the city; II. Regio Trivii, Italian Trevi, contained the famous fountain; III. Columnæ, or Colonna, had its name from the column of Marcus Aurelius; IV. Campimartis, or Campo Marzo, from the great Campus; V. Pontis, or Ponte, from the bridge of Sant' Angelo; VI. Parionis, or Parione, from the walls remaining from the stadium of Domitian or the theater of Pompey; VII. Arenulæ, or Regola, from the sand of the Tiber bank; VIII.

Sancti Eustachii, or Sant' Eustachio, from the church of the Saint; IX. Pineæ, or Pigna, from the pine-cone, a relic of antiquity probably forming a fountain; X. Campitelli, from the Capitol, or from the capitals of ancient columns; XI. Sancti Angeli, or Sant' Angelo, from the church in the ruined portico of Octavia; XII. Ripæ, or Ripa, from the bank of the Tiber from the island to below the Aventine; XIII. Transtiberim, or Trastevere, from its position across the river under the brow of the Janiculum. The Borgo, containing Saint Peter's, the Vatican, and the Castello Sant' Angelo, was the property of the popes as heads of the Church, not within the bounds of the municipal jurisdiction until the reign of Sixtus the Fifth, 1585-1590, who made it Rione XIV.

Of these regiones, or rioni, or districts, or wards, Borgo was the seat of the papal court and the goal of the great concourse of pilgrims. There were in it a great many inns, most of them kept by Swiss and Germans. The latter nationality alone in Eugenius' time had more than sixty hostelries and wine-shops in this region. The many vacant spaces still to be seen in it, in which rose here and there the palaces of cardinals and courtiers, were usually lone and quiet, but thronged with life on every jubilee. The great pile of the Vatican, always in some part in process of construction, and the beginnings of the new Saint Peter's, rising from 1506, contributed to the roughness and irregularity natural to the Borgo as to other parts of the city. From the castle of Sant' Angelo and the Ponte Sisto, a private covered way and the Via Alessandrina led to the Vatican and Saint Peter's. The old basilica, with its broad flight of steps, great court and campanile, and interior of five

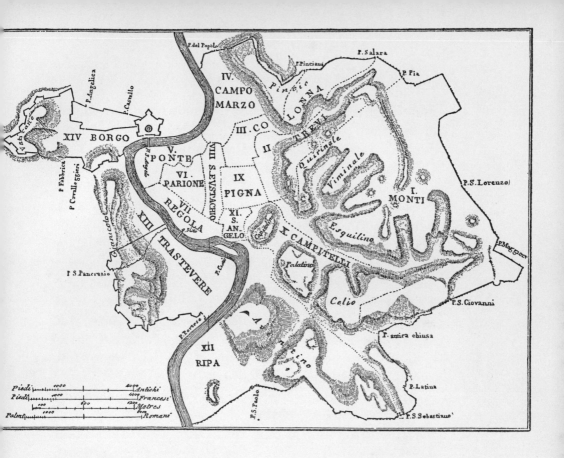

THE REGIONS OF RENAISSANCE ROME

A PLAN OF THE CITY IN THE FIFTEENTH CENTURY

REPRODUCED BY PERMISSION OF THE HERDERSCHE VERLAGSHANDLUNG FROM
L. VON PASTOR'S DIE STADT ROM ZU ENDE DER RENAISSANCE

long aisles rich with the monuments and memories of more than a thousand years, had not yet disappeared.

Trastevere, south of the Borgo, was thickly inhabited by a humble and sturdy population of boatmen, porters, gardeners, millers, and wine-sellers, who lived in the lower part near the Tiber. Always a comparatively isolated region, it was strongly marked by mediæval features. It contained many strong-built palaces and churches of ancient appearance. Towers frowned down upon its tortuous streets, and vineyards, gardens, and deserted fields occupied the slopes and summit of the Janiculum which rose above them. A bridge led from the rione to the city on the left bank by way of the island, on which were three churches and a convent, one of them the church of Saint Bartholomew, lodged in the ancient temple of Æsculapius.

Rione Sant' Angelo lay opposite the island, and contained the crowded quarter of the Jews, the fish-market in the ruins of the portico of Octavia, the theater of Marcellus with smoke-blackened shops in the grottoes formed by its arcades and the palace of the Savelli imbedded in its mass, and the Circus Flaminius, also with palace, house, and shop built into and about its remains. Sant' Angelo was a maze of narrow, obscure streets befouled by heaps of ruins and rubbish, and somber with turreted strongholds still rising amid the confusion of common houses and shops.

Regola, a long, narrow area extending from Sant' Angelo northward to Ponte, also contained many towers and palaces, the residences of powerful families like the Cenci, between which and the Tiber lay a long stretch of gardens. It abounded in petty tradesmen and artisans, and its southern part was filled with Jews,

the piazza before the Cenci palace being already called
La Giudecca. Cola di Rienzo's home had been in this
rione. The Spada and the Farnese had not yet risen.

Ponte, north of Regola and opposite the mausoleum
of Hadrian, was traversed by the chief avenues of approach to the Borgo and Trastevere, and was the busiest rione in the city. Near the bridge was the quarter of
the great bankers, which is still marked by the Via dei
Banchi Vecchi and the Via del Banco di Santo Spirito.
There were great numbers of merchants in the same
neighborhood. Ponte was the favorite residence of the
most noted courtesans. Palace and dwelling still displayed the mediæval round-arched portal and window,
the corbelled cornice, the massive wall, and the pillared
portico. The Orsini quarter and palace on Monte Giordano was still fortified in 1500, and lay in the midst of
unpaved streets and muddy lanes. Among its inns was
the Orso, existing today with altered exterior; among
its palaces, the present Sforza-Cesarini and Cicciaporci,
with many lesser ones in the neighborhood of the Via
dei Coronari of today, which received its name from a
prosperous trade in rosaries and other sacred articles.
The rione as a whole was irregular, containing fields and
gardens, crooked streets, and obscure dwellings. Under
Julius the Second and Leo the Tenth it was filling with
Florentines, whose church of San Giovanni had begun
to rise in 1488, and the neighborhood was undergoing
rapid change.

The life of Parione, which lay in the broad angle
between Ponte and Regola, had its center about the
Campo dei Fiori and the Piazza Navona, then the most
important squares of the city. The former, in a space
near where the theater of Pompey had once risen and

still survived in remnants below the ground, was from Sixtus the Fourth onward the center of civil life,—the forum of Renaissance Rome. It was the scene of many popular gatherings, the horse-market, the place of execution, the location of the larger inns, and in it the papal bulls were published. The special Wednesday fairs of today were already in vogue. At its north rose the Cancelleria, and the early palaces of the Massimi and Orsini were in the vicinity. Near the Orsini stood Pasquino, the instrument in the single year 1509 of three thousand of the celebrated pasquinades. Piazza Navona, the space where formerly had stood the stadium of Domitian, had received the market on its transfer from the Capitol in 1477, and was already the heart of merriment in Carnival season. It was still surrounded by gardens as well as buildings. Traders and artisans formed the greater portion of the population of Parione, though where it bordered Ponte it sheltered many of the clerkly caste. Under Nicholas the Fifth it had been the center of the copyists.

Sant' Eustachio, east of Parione, and with Regola and Ponte forming the triangle which enclosed it, was long, narrow, and closely built. The church of the name, the University, the palace of Cardinal Giovanni dei Medici, later Pope Leo, which afterward received the name of Madama and was rebuilt in 1642, and the Collegio Capranica, now the oldest in Rome, were among its many important buildings, and the Caffarelli, the Cesarini, and the Della Valle among the great families who dwelt in it. Johannes Burckard of Strassburg, master of ceremonies under Alexander the Sixth, had a palace there whose tower, inscribed "Argentina," in reminiscence of Strassburg's ancient Roman name, Ar-

gentoratum, gave the name to the present street and
theater.

Pigna, nearly square, and east of Sant' Eustachio,
contained the Pantheon, then lower than the surrounding earth and obscured by mean buildings of the earlier
time. Its arcaded Romanesque tower of 1270 still rose
above the gable of the portico, and in front of it were
two basalt lions later placed in the Vatican. The Dominican church of Santa Maria Sopra Minerva was
there, with the tomb of Catherine of Siena, canonized
under Pius the Second. The papal and imperial processions after coronation or on other occasions were
wont to pass the Pantheon and Santa Maria on the way
from Saint Peter's to the Lateran. The Palazzo San
Marco, with its basilica of the same name, was at the
southeast corner of Pigna, and the Corso formed its
eastern bound. The church of the Gesù and the Collegio
Romano were not yet in existence, for it was not until
later that Pigna became the great Jesuit quarter.

The rioni of the east bank of the Tiber thus briefly
characterized, with the Borgo and Trastevere on the
west bank, contained by far the greater part of the city's
buildings and population. The most striking differences
between them and the corresponding areas of Rome
today, not to mention the absence of many churches,
palaces, and wide streets of a later date, consisted in a
somewhat greater abundance of conspicuous ruins, in
decaying tenements, walls, and towers of the mediæval
centuries, in foul and unpaved streets, and in the presence of deserted areas, gardens, and fields.

Besides these there were but two rioni which bore
more than a remote resemblance to the districts of the
same name today. These were Ripa and Campitelli.

Ripa, the southernmost of all, extending from the Capitol and Sant' Angelo south along the Tiber bank to where the wall of Aurelian left the river to skirt the Aventine, was densely inhabited then, as now, only in the extreme northern portion, from Santa Maria in Cosmedin to the Tiber island. The greater part of the five or six thousand courtesans ascribed to Renaissance Rome lived here. In the street leading to Santa Maria was the scaffold to which the brotherhood of the Misericordia of San Giovanni Decollato accompanied the doomed wretches to whose last needs they ministered. Near the river was the eleventh century building, still surviving in part, called the house of Pilate, Cola di Rienzo, or Crescentius. The greater part of the rione was a vast and almost uninhabited area. The Aventine was occupied by a few lonely ancient churches and the ruined fortress of the Savelli. The marmorata, or marble wharf, at its foot by the Tiber was buried and its content almost unsuspected. The Circus Maximus had fallen into ruin, been plundered of material, and survived only in the great fragments of its concrete substructures; its obelisks were deep in rubbish and vegetation, and its race-course covered by vegetable-gardens. The immense ruins of the baths of Caracalla rose mightily from the midst of lone fields and cultivated areas.

Campitelli, where had been the heart of ancient Rome, was north of Ripa, and included the Capitol, Forum, Palatine, and part of the Cælian. It was even more deserted than now. Active life had left the Capitol, which had so long been the center of the ancient and mediæval city. The palace of the Senator, restored by Sixtus the Fourth but still of mediæval aspect, and the palace of

the Conservators, erected by Nicholas the Fifth and
already visited for the Wolf, the Thorn-extractor, and
other statues, stood alone in the piazza, which was
graced by a few antiquities; and the church of the
Aracœli rose on the site of the arx and the temple of
Juno, with the famous stairway of ancient marble built
in 1348. The rest of the arx, and all of the ancient Capitolium, were covered with vineyards and gardens in
whose midst lay ruined foundations in heaps. The statue
of Marcus Aurelius was still at the Lateran. The famous
hill was now known as Monte Caprino, perhaps from
the goats that browsed over the ruins of the temple of
Jupiter Optimus Maximus. At its southern base where
began the life that circled the hill to the south and west
lay the church of Santa Maria della Consolazione. The
Forum, with a wretched hovel here and there on its
borders and against its ruins, was buried beneath the
débris of centuries, and served as a cattle-market, or as
mere pasture, from which it long kept the name of
Campo Vaccino. The column of Phocas and the shafts
of Castor and Pollux rose above the deep and unex-
cavated political center of the ancient capital, and on
either side of the arch of Severus, half buried and surmounted by a tower, rose the church of Saints Sergius
and Bacchus and the church of Saint Hadrian. The
arch of Titus was built into a fortress-tower. The Palatine was a maze of romantic ruins in the midst of olives,
vines, and shrubbery, with San Teodoro and Santa
Anastasia at its western and southern base. The Coliseum was a vast ruin overgrown by shrubbery and with
half its former self lying in mountainous heaps at its
base, a gigantic quarry of travertine for the builders
of the time. Beside it stood the arch of Constantine,

built against until scarcely visible, and beyond them both lay the Cælian, a wide expanse of deserted fields with a few lonely churches rising in their midst, and with the great Lateran group at their southeastern limit.

At the north border of the more populous district next the Tiber lay the rioni of Campo Marzo, Colonna, and Trevi, all of them in large part wild and abandoned. The southern portion only of Campo Marzo, which lay along the Tiber, was thickly populated. The northern part, between the river and the Pincio and the Porta Salaria, was an expanse of vineyards, gardens, and groves. In and about the fortress-ruins of the mausoleum of Augustus, soon to contain the Soderini gardens, cattle were pasturing. The obelisk lay in four pieces in the street by the river called Ripetta. The area now occupied by the Piazza di Spagna, and that by the Piazza del Popolo, which was fronted by the important and solitary church of Santa Maria del Popolo, were covered by vacant fields, and the Pincio was overgrown with trees and shrubs. The Via del Babuino and the Corso, like the Ripetta, in their northern parts were unbordered by houses. A path shaded by trees led from the populous parts near the Tiber to the just erected Trinità dei Monti, whose background was an almost uninhabited wilderness.

Colonna, next to Campo Marzo, reached far to the northeast, including the gardens of Sallust, which, with the area of the present Piazza Barberini, were deserted and wild. Montecitorio was covered by gardens and dwellings, and the column of Marcus Aurelius rose in a narrow and irregular piazza, its base half buried. The buildings of the city to its north were rare; the name of the Via Capo le Case survives as a witness to the fact.

Trevi was thickly inhabited only in the vicinity of the Santi Apostoli. No palace of great importance had been built in it until the beginning of the sixteenth century, and its upper parts on the Quirinal were still occupied by vineyards, villas, and groves, out of which rose the remnants of Constantine's baths and the temples of Serapis and the Sun. The Colonna gardens were near San Silvestro, and the villas of Platina and Pomponius Lætus were also on the Quirinal. The Horse-tamers gave their neighborhood the name of Monte Cavallo. The fountain of Trevi, thus known from the meeting of three roads, was still in the modest form in which it had been built by Nicholas the Fifth and Sixtus the Fourth.

Of all the rioni, Monti was the most desolate and perhaps the most impressive. A broad wedge whose north-eastern base was formed by a wide stretch of the wall of Aurelian and whose point reached to the Corso, it was the largest of all, and contained the greater portion of the Quirinal, the Viminal, and the Esquiline, and a part of the Cælian. The old Lateran, in the midst of ruined towers and the arches of the Claudian aqueduct, Santa Maria Maggiore, San Clemente, San Martino, and San Pietro in Vincoli, were the centers of its life, and the enormous ruins of the baths of Diocletian, the Prætorian camp, the Sette Sale, the baths of Constantine, and the fora of Augustus, Nerva, and Trajan were its most prominent remains of antiquity. The population of the Subura district was considerable, but all the rest of the rione was lived in only here and there. It was a wilderness of orchards and gardens intersected

THE FORUM AND PALATINE IN THE SIXTEENTH CENTURY

A DRAWING OF ÉTIENNE DU PÉRAC,
WHO INTERPRETED THE RUINS WITH GREAT FREEDOM

REPRODUCED BY PERMISSION OF THE HERDERSCHE VERLAGSHANDLUNG FROM
L. VON PASTOR'S DIE STADT ROM ZU ENDE DER RENAISSANCE

by irregular lanes and country roads, with giant spectral ruins rising from the midst of neglected solitudes. Had it not been for the wall of Aurelian, which enclosed it and marked the limit of the ancient city, Monti would have seemed more like a great area of straggling suburban fields than an integral part of Rome.

The whole city of the earliest sixteenth century was thus only the pitiful ghost of imperial Rome. The Borgo alone contained buildings and life to be compared with the life and monuments of the ancient empire, and Trastevere was the only one of the regions of Augustus which approximated the ancient density of habitation. Of the other thirteen ancient regions, the ninth alone, Campus Martius, was now thickly populated, and was enough in itself to contain the great majority of the people on the left bank. The remaining twelve, to the north and east and south, save for churches and towers, with scattered little clusters of houses, some the modest forerunners of the great villas of later years, were a wide expanse of vast and rolling fields, picturesque with vineyards and verdure-covered ruins, and made one with the rest of the city only by being within the great wall. Even the denser parts had their vacant and deserted areas, and presented a motley aspect. Here and there only, out of squalid surroundings, crowded and obscure, or from the midst of solitary unpaved areas, rose in striking contrast the palaces of the great, centers of refinement and magnificence. In spite of its fame and wealth and rapid growth, it was a thing of shreds and patches, a city ragged and picturesque with ruin and dirt and splendid with luxury and pomp, a resurrected body awake from long slumber and still enveloped in the clinging remnants of its ancient mortality.

The visitor who ascends the Janiculum today and looks forth upon the incomparable panorama of Rome, the Tiber, the Campagna, and the distant mountains, may easily picture to himself the scene as it appeared to the eye of the famous constable of Bourbon when, on May 5, 1527, serving Emperor Charles the Fifth in his quarrel with Pope Clement the Seventh, he established his headquarters in the convent of Sant' Onofrio and prepared to storm the city. Occupying the merest niche in the great space once covered by the Eternal Rome of the ancient emperors, turbulent with passion and marred by immorality, it was nevertheless the seat of an intensely brilliant culture, filled not only with treasures of art and learning, but with material wealth such as few cities of the age possessed.

XI.

THE ROME OF THE POPES

And I say also unto thee, That thou art Peter, and upon this rock I will build my church; and the gates of hell shall not prevail against it.

And I will give unto thee the keys of the kingdom of heaven: and whatsoever thou shalt bind on earth shall be bound in heaven: and whatsoever thou shalt loose on earth shall be loosed in heaven.

MATTHEW XVI: 18, 19

1.

THE REVELS ENDED

AT dawn on the morning of May 6, 1527, the forty thousand German, Spanish, and Italian soldiers of the constable of Bourbon stormed the walls of the Leonine city, bearing with them their mortally wounded and already dying leader. Pope Clement took refuge in the Castello Sant' Angelo. By nightfall the feeble resistance offered by the Romans in the Trastevere and at the Ponte Sisto had been overcome; the Germans were in the Campo dei Fiori, the Spaniards in the Piazza Navona, the Italians near the bridge, and all Rome was at the mercy of an army composed of adventurers, the only safeguard against whose brutality and greed had been removed by the death of their captain. By midnight, the weak-hearted defenders of the degenerate city not having dared to molest them, they realized that Rome was theirs to be treated according to the practices of war.

Then began the horrors of a sack worse than the sacks of Goth and Vandal. Before dawn the city was lurid with the smoke and flame of burning houses and resonant with the shrieks of wounded men and violated women. When Clement looked from Sant' Angelo at break of day, it was upon a waste of blackened ruins.

For eight days no form of suffering such as is wont at the worst to befall cities taken by storm failed to be visited on the wretched population. The city was pillaged from attic to cellar; the search was continued even in the sewers, suspected of being the repository of treasure. Every visible object of value was seized, every citizen taken was held for ransom. Neither high nor low escaped. Many paid for freedom only to be retaken and compelled a second time to purchase liberty. Torture of every description was applied. Thousands fled, thousands were slain, and corpses filled the streets.

And yet the passion of avarice was not the most terrible. Noble ladies, nuns, and little girls fell a prey to the fierceness of a soldiery knowing no mercy. Churches were profaned in the most revolting manner. The whole city was a turmoil of rapine, pillage, drunkenness, debauchery, lewdness, murder, sacrilege, and disease, and its population despoiled of every earthly possession. The actual pillage brought to an end through exhaustion of plunder, pestilence added terrors of its own. For the month before Clement's surrender, for the six months that followed before his flight northward in December, and for the ten months of the papal absence, disease, death, and despair inhabited the city. If violence was less employed, it was only that the incentives to its use were no longer there.

When finally, on the sixth of October, 1528, seventeen months after the terrible experience, the pope could return, four-fifths of the city of Rome was empty. Pestilence, famine, and the hand of the enemy had caused the death of thirty thousand persons, and hardly fewer had disappeared by flight. The eighty-five thousand of the city of Leo the Tenth had been reduced to thirty-two. Hospitals were crowded with the wounded and the sick, and beggars filled the streets; rubbish and the ruins of thousands of burned buildings choked the thoroughfares. The deluge of rain which descended upon the scant papal party was hardly more violent than the torrent of tears that poured from the eyes of the unfortunate Clement as he made his sorrowful progress through the city to throw himself in anguish and despair before the desecrated altar of Saint Peter's.

More had been lost from the city, however, than mere population and buildings. The sack of 1527 marked an epoch in the history of Roman and Italian culture. The brightness of the Renaissance was indeed darkened throughout the length and breadth of Italy by the clouds of war which swept over the peninsula; but at Rome, where the storm burst with greatest fury, its light for the time was extinguished utterly, and never did it regain its former brilliance. The revels of the court of Leo were ended; their actors, in so far as they had to do with art, learning, and manners, were scattered, together with many of the incomparable treasures with which they had enriched the city, to the four corners of the world; and the bright-hued life of culture and display which had filled its gorgeous palaces, and even its solemn temples, like an insubstantial pageant faded, left scarce a rack behind.

The travail of the city was not all in vain. Once more had Rome lost her life to save it. As in the latter days of the ancient empire she had gradually yielded up her life to communicate to the barbarian world the life of civilization, now again she perished, this time to give to the modern world her art and learning. Dispersed over the face of Europe, her sons carried with them the fame and culture of the city and peninsula, and gave an impulse to culture in every clime.

Yet Eternal Rome itself did not perish utterly, though it never again recovered the worldly glamour of the golden days of Julius and Leo. The fugitive popula-

tion began in time to straggle back, and the city rose
once more from its ashes. If its sufferings had been
greater than in the times of Alaric and Genseric, its
recovery also was more rapid. This time it entered upon
no long process of decay and decline.

The shifty and unfortunate Clement the Seventh was
succeeded by the vigorous and princely Paul the Third,
Alexander Farnese, 1534-1549, who appointed Michelangelo as chief architect, painter, and sculptor, continued the work on Saint Peter's and the Vatican,
planned and partially executed the bastion at Santo
Spirito to strengthen the decaying walls of the Leonine
city, and for the greater safety of the capital on the
left bank reared the huge bastions on the Aventine and
in the wall of Aurelian between the Ostian and Appian
gates. With an eye to the beauty and dignity of the
city as well as its safety, he added the staircase to the
Palazzo del Senatore on the Capitol, laid out the broad
approach to the piazza on which it fronted, removed
the statue of Marcus Aurelius from the Lateran square
to its present position, and connected the bridge of Sant'
Angelo with the Via Giulia by the Via Paola. His reign
saw the first steps in the conversion of the Palatine from
a wilderness into the Farnese gardens, and the rise of
the great Farnese palace, with the Caffarelli on the
Capitol, the Spada near the Campo dei Fiori, the Villa
Ricci, later Medici, on the Pincian, and the church of
Santa Caterina dei Funari in the ruins of the Circus
Flaminius.

The reigns of the succeeding popes also to the end
of the sixteenth century were marked by the rise of
many edifices and monuments which still give character to Rome. Julius the Third, Giovanni del Monte,

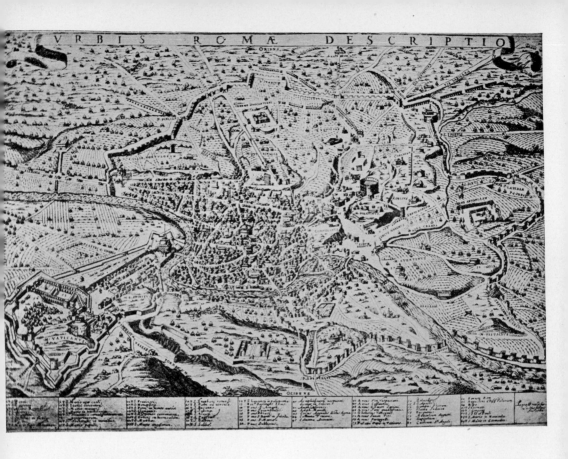

PLAN OF ROME IN 1584

BY JACOBO FRANCO,
SHOWING THE GROWTH OF THE CITY

REPRODUCED FROM ROCCHI, PIANTE DI ROMA

1550-1555, built the Villa di Papa Giulio outside the Porta del Popolo. Paul the Fourth, Pietro Carafa, 1555-1559, built the gate of Sant' Angelo. Pius the Fourth, Gian Angelo dei Medici of Milan, 1559-1565, erected the Porta Angelica, to the north of Saint Peter's, completed the defences of the Leonine city, repaired the wall of Aurelian, and entrusted to Michelangelo the erection of Santa Maria degli Angeli and the Carthusian cloisters in the ruins of Diocletian's baths, where they now form the Museo Nazionale, and the building of the Porta Pia, not to be completed until the nineteenth century under Pius the Ninth. It was under Pius the Fourth that the Palazzo Mattei, to receive its final form a half-century later, was erected from the ruins of the Circus Flaminius. Pius the Fifth, Michele Ghislieri, 1566-1572, began the church of the Gesù.

Under Gregory the Thirteenth, Ugo Boncompagni, 1572-1585, the fountains in the Piazza Navona were erected and the first great impulse thus given to the development of one of the most beautiful features of Rome today. The Palatine bridge was rebuilt, in the great flood of twenty-three years later to become the Ponte Rotto, the broad Via Merulana was laid out between the villas and gardens that covered the area between Santa Maria Maggiore and the Lateran, the Via di Monte Tarpeio was built on the northeast slope of the Capitol, the Porta San Giovanni took the place of the old Porta Asinaria. The abandoned and ruinous region between the forum of Augustus and the Quirinal began to fill with dwellings, the tower on the Capitol was rebuilt, the façade of the Conservatori was begun, the Palazzo Salviati was erected on the Lungara across the Tiber, the Rucellai, later the Ruspoli, rose on the Corso,

and the beautiful grounds of the Villa Mattei on the
Cælian were laid out.

In blunt and energetic Sixtus the Fifth, Felice
Peretti, 1585-1590, arose the greatest builder of the century. He pushed to completion the great dome, employing eight hundred men, at times even by night, from
July 15, 1588, to May 14, 1590. He brought from
twenty-two miles along the course of the ancient con-
duits the second great aqueduct of modern Rome, the
Acqua Felice, with twenty-seven fountains that discharge more than twenty thousand cubic meters of
water in twenty-four hours. He erected the four obelisks now standing before Saint Peter's and the Lateran,
in the Piazza dell' Esquilino, and in the Piazza del
Popolo, and set the statues of Peter and Paul on the
columns of Trajan and Marcus Aurelius. He built the
residence portion and library wing of the Vatican, the
new Lateran palace, the Scala Santa, and a hospital
for the poor at the Ponte Sisto, and laid out the Via
Sistina and other thoroughfares radiating from Santa
Maria Maggiore, where finally he was laid to rest.

With Clement the Eighth, Ippolito Aldobrandini,
1592-1605, who began the church of Sant' Andrea della
Valle, the sixteenth century closed. Its popes in the
main had followed the example of Sixtus the Fourth and
freely thrown opportunity before their relatives. The
papal favoritism, however, had undergone a change.
The ambition of popes to aggrandize their families by
the creation of dukedoms and principalities outside of
Rome was now for the most part replaced by the more
easily accomplished purpose of adding to their standing
and wealth within the city. With the Aldobrandini pope
began the line of seventeenth and eighteenth century

pontiffs whose administrations left in their train the enriched nephews and brothers whose families still form in great part what is left of the higher aristocracy of Rome, and whose palaces, villas, and public monuments constitute much of the city's adornment as it appears today. Above a million scudi went to the kinsmen of Clement the Eighth in the course of his thirteen years in the holy seat.

From the reign of Paul the Fifth, Camillo Borghese, 1605-1621, who made his nephew Scipio cardinal and chief adviser, date the Acqua Paola and its magnificent fountains across the Tiber, the Borghese and Rospigliosi palaces, the latter built out of the baths of Constantine, the Villa Borghese, the completion of Saint Peter's, the erection of the column from the basilica of Constantine before Santa Maria Maggiore, and the restoration and building of many churches. Ludovico, the cardinal-nephew of Gregory the Fifteenth, Alessandro Ludovisi, 1621-1623, reared the church of Sant' Ignazio, and transformed the northern area of ancient Rome by the laying out of the Villa Ludovisi.

Urban the Eighth, Maffeo Barberini of Florence, 1623-1644, constructed the square bastions enclosing the Castello Sant' Angelo, strengthened the fortress with a hundred guns made from the bronze of the Pantheon, repaired the wall of Aurelian, and reared the huge defences extending from the Porta Cavalleggeri to the summit and along the slopes of the Janiculum down to the Tiber at the Porta Portese, a fortification destined to prove its usefulness in the siege of 1849. The same pontiff built also the Palazzo Barberini, the fountain of the Triton, and the famous baldacchino in Saint Peter's, and enclosed the papal gardens on the Quirinal between the Rospigliosi and Colonna grounds with a high wall whose material came from Aurelian's ruined temple of the Sun.

Innocent the Tenth, Giovanni Battista Pamfili, 1644-1655, erected the Palazzo Pamfili and the church of Sant' Agnese at the Piazza Navona, and the Villa Pamfili outside the Porta San Pancrazio. Alexander the Seventh, Fabio Chigi, 1655-1667, nephew of Paul the Fifth, transformed the Piazza Colonna by the building of the Palazzo Chigi and the enlargement of the square, set up the obelisk before Santa Maria Sopra Minerva, and built the gigantic colonnade about the Piazza di San Pietro, with one of the magnificent fountains.

Under Clement the Tenth, Emilio Altieri, 1670-1676, the other fountain rose, the ten statues of Carrara marble were placed on the Ponte Sant' Angelo, and the Palazzo Altieri, opposite the Gesù, was built by the pope's adoptive cardinal-nephew and administrator. The name of Innocent the Eleventh, Benedetto Odescalchi, 1676-1689, is preserved in the Palazzo Odescalchi, on the Corso. The neighboring Palazzo Doria Pamfili, which had stood since the time of Julius the Second, received its present façade about the same time. The work of the century, for good and ill, was dominated by the masterful genius of Bernini.

From the beginning of the eighteenth century, the building of monumental edifices diminished very greatly, and the city underwent little change in character. Among the restricted activities of the period were the rebuilding of the façade of Santi Apostoli by Clement the Eleventh, Giovanni Francesco Albani, 1700-1721; the Spanish stairs, by Benedict the Thirteenth, Vincenzo Orsini, 1724-1730; the transformation of the

SCENE IN THE VILLA BORGHESE

THE NAME HAS BEEN CHANGED TO VILLA UMBERTO

Palazzo Riario into the Corsini on the Lungara, the embellishment of the fountain of Trevi, the restoration of the arch of Constantine, and the enlargement of the Capitoline museum, by Clement the Twelfth, Lorenzo Corsini, 1730-1740; the building of the façade of Santa Maria Maggiore, by Benedict the Fourteenth, Prospero Lambertini, 1740-1758; the beginning of the Vatican museum, by Clement the Thirteenth, Carlo Rezzonico, 1758-1769; its continuation, and the building of the sacristy of Saint Peter's and the Palazzo Braschi, by Pius the Sixth, Angelo Braschi, 1775-1799; the Museo Chiaramonti and the Braccio Nuovo in the Vatican, and the restoration of the arch of Titus, by Pius the Seventh, Gregorio Chiaramonti, 1800-1823; the restoration of the Porta Maggiore and the rebuilding, by Gregory the Sixteenth, Mauro Capellari, 1831-1846, of Saint Paul's Outside the Walls, burned in 1823 while Pius the Seventh lay dying; and the works of Pius the Ninth.

The modification of the city's aspect for better or worse by these changes, however, was but slight as compared with the changes of the two centuries preceding. By the opening of the eighteenth century, the architectural character of Rome for the one hundred and seventy years that were to intervene from that time to the fall of the temporal power was fixed, and such modification as took place consisted for the most part in mere growth.

Of the architectural aspect of the city at the end of the papal sovereignty, both the best and the worst that may be said is that it was characterized by uniformity and substantiality and by a lack of distinction. The rapid increase of Rome from the thirty-two thousand of the pope's return after the sack of 1527 to the one

hundred thousand of less than a century later, to the
one hundred and sixty-six thousand of 1776, and to
the two hundred and twenty-five thousand of 1870, filling the Campus Martius, climbing the adjacent slopes,
more or less sparsely covering the nearer reaches of
Quirinal and Viminal, and enveloping the older city in
a monotonous stuccoed rectangularity, produced a uniformity of its own which palace and church, however
numerous and however pretentious, did not possess
sufficient distinction to enliven. There were three palaces
of the first order from the high Renaissance,—the Farnese, the Cancelleria, and the San Marco, later called
Venezia. Ranking with these, there was the fine ensem-
ble of the Piazza del Campidoglio. Of the remainder,
with the doubtful exception of the Barberini, the Borghese, the Sciarra, and the Salviati, it may be said that,
though they were often rich in some single detail, as
the Sapienza in its court, the Spada in its decoration by
relief, or the Mattei in its ornament of ancient sculptural fragments, their claim to distinction lay rather
in bigness and in the spaciousness of court, staircase,
and hall than in material, proportion, or external impressiveness. On the multitudinous churches that had
risen during the seventeenth century or been restored
into conformity with the prevailing architectural taste,
the same judgment may be pronounced. There was the
gigantic Gesù, dating from 1568, with heavy exterior
and luxurious nave and chapels, the great baroque
exemplar whose erection determined the architectural
ambition of seventeenth and eighteenth century ecclesiastical Rome, and filled it with clumsy scrolled and over-
ornamented façades, and overloaded, overcolored, over-
gilded interiors whose only claim to fitness is more often

PLAN OF ROME IN 1650

BY JACOPO DE ROSSI;
THE LEFT OF THE PLAN IS NORTH

REPRODUCED FROM ROCCHI, PIANTE DI ROMA

than not the poor one that they impress the beholder with the power and splendor of the Church. The domes which at the same time arose in more or less humble imitation of the great dome, and came to characterize the architectural landscape of the capital, blended well with the mass of roofs and the city's irregular lines, though no one of them by itself could claim great beauty. That Rome under the last pope-kings was, and that it still is, after all, a beautiful city and an impressive one is due not to the architecture of the Renaissance and the post-Renaissance, but to a certain unity of material and line, to a variety within the unity which results from the piquancy of the Romanesque campanile and basilica appearing unexpectedly here and there, to the richness of the massive monuments of the ancient empire, to the generous sweeping of her outlines over hill and valley, and to the historical, cultural, and spiritual interests that cast a glamour on every block and brick and tile.

The growth of the cultural, historical, and spiritual interest of Rome during the two hundred years that followed the sack of 1527 was hardly less pronounced than the amplification of its bounds and the multiplication of its churches and palaces. It was a period marvellous for enrichment. In spite of the passing of the high noon of the Renaissance, in spite of the dispersion of artists and scholars to the far ends of Italy and Europe, it was a period which saw a long procession of talented men whose presence not only left greater the material charm of the city, but added to the opportunities it afforded the world for intellectual profit and enjoyment. Among architects, it saw the great Renaissance figures of Michelangelo, Sangallo, and Peruzzi, and the lesser figures of Fontana, Della Porta, Maderna, and Borro-

mini. Among its sculptors, besides Michelangelo, were
Benvenuto Cellini, Bernini, and Canova. Its painters
included Taddeo Zuccaro, the young decorator of the
Villa di Papa Giulio, Sebastiano del Piombo, Guido
Reni, Sassoferrato, Domenichino, Guercino, and the
Caracci, the French Poussin and Claude Lorrain, and
the German Raphael Mengs. The celebrated name of
Piranesi is among its engravers and proudest orna-
ments. Among its poets were Tasso, Tassoni, Chiabrera,
Metastasio, Monti, Prati, and Belli, the Romanesco
sonneteer. Palestrina in the sixteenth century, and
Verdi in the nineteenth, alone would make it famous in
the annals of music.

If it be remarked that these names represent on the
whole the decline of artistic and intellectual genius in
both frequency and brilliance, and the substitution for it
in ever-increasing degree of mere imitative talent, and
that the eighteenth and nineteenth centuries are not
conspicuous even for men of talent, the observation
nevertheless does not signify the decay of Rome's contribution to culture. In the appraisal of her service in
this regard, account must be taken of the products of
intellectual effort as distinguished from the creations of
genius. Roughly speaking, it is true of European culture that the fifteenth century and the first half of the
sixteenth were the period of curiosity, inspiration, and
creation, the later sixteenth and the seventeenth the
period of imitative talent, artificiality, and decadence,
and the eighteenth and nineteenth the period of criticism, research, and facilitation of cultural means.

It was in the eighteenth and nineteenth centuries that
most of the great libraries, galleries, and museums of
Rome were formed or attained to their modern propor-

tions. Of these the Vatican is the great example. The
Vatican library, little more than projected by Nicholas
the Fifth and Sixtus the Fourth, was increased under
Clement the Eighth at the beginning of the seventeenth
century by the addition of the Orsini collection, under
Paul the Fifth by the acquisition of the Bobbio manuscripts, under Gregory the Fifteenth and Urban the
Eighth by the Heidelberg collection, under Alexander
the Seventh by the library of the dukes of Urbino, under
Alexander the Eighth by the collection of Queen Christina of Sweden, and finally, after various other acquisi-
tions, under Pius the Ninth by the library of Angelo
Mai. The gallery and museum of the Vatican grew in
the same manner to be parallel great influences in the
world of sculpture and painting. The lesser museums
of the Capitol, the Lateran, the Villa Borghese, and the
Kircherian collection, are also creations of this period.
Most of the collections of size were formed by the aggre-
gation of smaller private ones. The original number and
richness of these latter may be inferred from the fact
that Aldovrandi in his guide of 1550 mentions over one
hundred houses where were to be seen statues, busts,
and reliefs of note.

In nothing was the activity of the period more remarkable, however, than in the development of the
study and care of the ancient Roman monuments. The
origin and growth of the scientific interest in classical
archæology goes back into the Dark Ages. Cola di
Rienzo, deciphering inscriptions and identifying monuments, Nicholas Signorili, secretary to the senate under
Martin the Fifth, appending a description of the city
to a compilation of its laws, and Cyriac of Ancona,
enthusiastic traveller, draughtsman, recorder, and col-

lector, visiting Rome in 1424, the humanist Poggio, cataloguer of ruins, and Flavio Biondo, author of *Rome Restored* and *Rome Triumphant*, were its apostles and founders. By the time their line had been continued into the nineteenth century by such scholars as Francesco Bianchini, excavator of the Flavian palace on the Palatine in 1720-1726, by Canina, Winckelmann, Visconti, Fea, Nibby, and De Rossi, it was no longer possible for curio-hunters or speculators to lay hands unhindered on the relics of the ancient city, or for either pope or prince to entertain the notions of a Sixtus the Fifth, who destroyed the Septizonium, and, when reproved for violence to the monuments, promised henceforth to respect only what was not ugly, or of Paul the Fifth, who despoiled the forum of Nerva, or of Urban the Eighth, who stripped the Pantheon roof of four hundred and fifty thousand pounds of bronze to make the hundred guns of the Castello Sant' Angelo, and would have destroyed the tomb of Cecilia Metella to use its material for the fountain of Trevi, or of the various cardinal builders responsible for the disappearance of Constantine's baths and Aurelian's temple of the Sun on the Quirinal.

The Rome of the pope-kings was rich not only in the æsthetic and intellectual opportunity afforded by her palaces and monuments, by her galleries and museums, and by her libraries and academies; it was rich also in splendors. It was the old, aristocratic Rome of luxurious apparel and gorgeous retinues, of velvet jackets and knee breeches and buckles and capes and swords and ruffles and long hair and two-pointed hats, of silks and satins and lace and gold and jewels, of dinners and balls and elaborate etiquette, of private theaters and gambling and liaisons, of nobles who were almost kings with their gilded coaches and innumerable servants and mounted followers on fancy horses. A great part of the Campagna was the property of patrician families. The Borghese in 1770 held thirty-six estates. When Maria Carolina of Austria passed through in 1768, on her way to be queen of Ferdinand the Fourth of Naples, the men-at-arms of the Colonna's twenty-seven estates were gathered by their masters to do honor to her as guest at Marino.

The city was richer still in another way. Its palaces were the resort not only of a brilliant Roman society which included the great among princes, prelates, artists, and intellectuals, but of distinguished visitors from all parts of Europe, and even of other continents. Rabelais, Montaigne, Cardinal du Bellay, and his nephew Joachim had been among those who trod its streets in the earlier time, and Charles de Brosses, Goethe, Alfieri, Thorwaldsen, Gibbon, Keats, Shelley, Wordsworth, Hawthorne, Bayard Taylor, and Longfellow were among those who came later. The diplomatic corps alone, with visiting monarchs, statesmen, and princes of the Church, were themselves the world in small. There were those who made Rome a more permanent residence, like Winckelmann, Zoega, Raphael Mengs, Angelica Kaufmann, and the legion of scholars, painters, and sculptors of every nation who came for longer or shorter periods. Not least, there were the numerous royal personages who came as suppliants for the freely granted refuge from the storms of revolution or in search of spiritual repose. Christina of Sweden, the abdicating daughter of Gustavus Adolphus, after embracing the Catholic faith made the city her home from 1668 to her death in

1689 at the age of sixty-three, occupying the Palazzo
Riario, later Corsini. In 1719, Clement the Eleventh received James Stuart the Pretender, whose son Charles
Edward, the Chevalier St. George, was born in the city
the next year, where, in Saint Peter's, are to be seen the
tombs of all the last of the Stuarts. Their presence
brought also the Pretender's wife, the countess of Al-
bany and friend of Alfieri; the Pretender's brother, the
cardinal duke of York; and their mother, Maria Clemen-
tina Sobieski. The Bonapartes, Lucien, Louis, Pauline,
the brothers and sister of Napoleon, the last the wife
of Camillo Borghese, lived there in the early part of
the nineteenth century, and Charles Emmanuel of Savoy, after abdicating in 1802, died there in 1819, a
member of the Society of Jesus. In the last days of the
papal sovereignty, the Bourbon house made Rome their
residence on being driven from Naples.

A paragraph from President de Brosses, written in
1739-1740, is as true for all the period as for his own
time. "All in all," he wrote, "I know in all Europe no
city which is more agreeable and more convenient and
where I would rather live, not even Paris excepted.
Everybody knows everybody here, and all are continually meeting. Everyone is acquainted with everyone else's affairs, and everything is, to a certain extent,
the common property of gossip, and yet absolute freedom of action reigns. The rest may talk: they let you
do as you please."

Rich, however, as was the intellectual and social life
of Rome during these three hundred years, its most
abundant and its most characteristic wealth was in the
life of the Church. In no respect had the downfall of
the city at the hands of Charles the Fifth been followed

by a greater change and a better change than in the attitude of pope and people toward religion.

The relation was hardly that of mere cause and effect. The protest of Martin Luther had been uttered ten years before the great disaster befell the city and the papal court; the Reformation had already come, and the counter-Reformation would have come as surely, if not as suddenly, had there been no sack. The world of the Church was ripe for change. The shock produced by the remorseless overthrow of the papal power and the city's dignity only made easier the path of reform.

It was a different Rome whose streets Pope Clement trod after the return from Viterbo. The spirit of Leo the Tenth had forever departed from it. The city of pagan brightness and festivity was soon succeeded by the city of Loyola and the Jesuits, the Index Expurgatorius, and the Inquisition. Coming as they did but little after the heyday of license at Rome, the humiliation and prostration of the papacy were so timely as to seem a manifestation of the wrath of God. The life of the court now no longer blazed with scandal. Orthodoxy and conduct came suddenly into their right. Before a half-century had passed, the world was surprised at the spectacle of a pope not only refusing to favor relatives, but even forestalling criticism by their removal from privilege. Hardly less novel was the combination once more, in the person of Pius the Fifth, of pope and ascetic, with an austerity of conduct one day to be rewarded by canonization. In 1576, the Venetian ambassador Paolo Tiepolo could write: "It has contributed infinitely to the advantage of the Church that several popes in succession have been men of irreproachable lives; hence all others are become better, or have at

least assumed the appearance of being so. Cardinals
and prelates attend mass punctually; their households
are studious to avoid anything that can give scandal; the
whole city has put off its old recklessness, and is become
much more Christian-like in life and manners than formerly. It may be affirmed that Rome, in matters of religion, is not far from that degree of perfection which
human nature can attain to."

The long period from the Renaissance to the read-
justments of the nineteenth century may appropriately
be called the period of the pope-kings. It was not indeed
the beginning of the double authority exercised by the
ruler of the Church, for the exercise of temporal as well
as spiritual power had begun far back in the early ages
of the Church, and the temporal sway had probably
reached its maximum extent before the Reformation;
but it was the longest period during which the power
of the Church over the territory to which it had laid
claim since the time of Pepin seemed most firmly established and was least often questioned, and it was a period
during which the ecclesiastical state enjoyed more of
the peace and order of organized government than had
hitherto been its fortune. Something of the severe spirit
of mediævalism, without the worse features of its life,
had fallen again upon the city. Brigandage tormented
its neighborhood from time to time, and violence was
still all too well known in its streets; but feudalism no
longer ruled, and drawn battles between the great families of Rome and the Campagna belonged to the past.
The old ambition to rule the political destinies of Europe had been shattered by the blow of the emperor
Charles; in its place remained the less impossible and
the more fit ambition to be influential in the keeping of

PLAN OF ROME IN EARLY EIGHTEENTH CENTURY

SHOWING THE SPREAD OF THE CITY TOWARD THE HILLS
TO NORTH AND EAST

REPRODUCED FROM ROCCHI, PIANTE DI ROMA

peace and in the legitimate, or at least the pacific, advancement of the Church and its friends. However busily concerned in the councils of European monarchs, the papal court had never for so long a time taken so little visible part in their activities. Italy was no longer independent; Spaniard, Frenchman, and Teuton were at various times and in varying degree her masters. Rome and the central territories were quiet under papal rule, which was fostered and kept secure by the Powers, and were no longer in danger of invasion and overthrow. The temporal government had never been so free, though its freedom consisted only in being left to itself so long as it did not offend its protectors. Both the virtues and the vices of the holy seat were less loudly heralded to the world. Its abuses were those of peace rather than war, of administration rather than personal conduct, of provincial import rather than national, of incapacity and error rather than evil intent.

2.

THE POPE-KINGS

TO understand the evolution by which in the course of the long centuries the head of the Christian community of Rome came to be at the same time the spiritual sovereign of the world, the lord of Rome, and the monarch of the states of the Church, will be the better to appreciate both the significance of the spiritual change that came over city and papacy after the sack of 1527 and the importance of the movement which later resulted in the abolition of the temporal power. To arrive at this understanding, and to enter into the spirit of the Rome of the pope-kings, there could be no better means than to cast a glance in review over the history of the anomalous and self-contradictory, yet wholly human and natural, condition whose forcible termination in the nineteenth century was the occasion of so much agitation, and left in its train such deep and intense feeling.

Whether we accept, with Gregorovius and controversial Protestants in general, the view that "history knows nothing of Saint Peter's presence at Rome," or, with Lanciani and controversial Catholics, the view that "for the archæologist the presence and execution of Saints Peter and Paul in Rome are facts established beyond a shadow of doubt by purely monumental evidence," there is at any rate no doubt that, at least from 354, and perhaps from 170 or even 100, Peter was believed by the heads of the Church to have been at Rome, and that his presence as founder of the Church was the basis of the Roman bishop's claim to authority over other ecclesiastical heads. Likewise, whether we assent or not to the Roman Catholic interpretation of the words, "Thou art Peter, and upon this rock I will build my church," or to that of Beet, who asserts that the passage "makes excellent sense without in the least implying that Saint Peter was created by the Savior His sole Vicegerent upon earth, the one visible Head of the Church, and a spiritual monarch among his brethren," and that "there is also ample evidence which goes to show that the leading expositors of the Early Church never read it in the sense that the papal theory requires to be put upon it in violent contradiction to the whole tenor of the New Testament," in any case we must recognize that there was scriptural warrant for believing Peter the divinely ordained founder of the Church, that in the minds of all his successors from a very early time it was at Rome that the founder had his seat, and that the real or supposed fact of his presence at Rome had inestimable weight in the building of Rome's authority. The bishop of Rome was able to claim the descent of his primacy not only from an apostle, but from the only apostolic founder in the western Church, and from the chosen apostle of Christ.

This claim, nevertheless, however strong in later years, was not in the early years of the Church the chief cause of the growth in power of the bishop of Rome. The chief cause was Rome itself. Rome was the greatest city in the west and the capital of the world; it was natural that the Christian community of Rome should soon reflect the importance of its seat. Less than forty years after the apostle's death, Bishop Clement's letter to the Corinthians regarding certain disorders in their community is written in a manner which clearly indicates, if it does not actually assert, the authority of Rome. In the second century, Rome has become beyond a doubt the center of the Christian movement. At its close, in 195, Bishop Victor makes the unsuccessful but significant attempt to compel obedience in doctrinal matters by the excommunication of individuals and of entire churches,—the first employment in the grand manner of the weapon later wielded with such frequency and effect.

Calixtus, not long afterward, by disregard of certain marriage laws of the state which wrought injustice to Christian ladies, seems to show again the growing strength of the Church and its head. The same is to be said of his claim that the bishops, even though guilty of mortal sin, should be immune from deposition. That the assumption of authority on the part of the bishop of Rome, however, did not find the Christian world everywhere submissive, is evident from the indignation of Cyprian of Carthage and his friends, excommunicated by Stephen the First for maintaining that rebaptism must be performed in the case of repentant heretics. The African bishop nevertheless contributed directly to the upbuilding of episcopal power, and indirectly to the supremacy of Rome, by strict insistence on the duties of obedience and respect to bishops on the part of the laity; the layman, for example, must rise to his feet on the entrance of the priest. The original democracy of the Church was fast becoming a hierarchy. To this there contributed in no small part the increasing frequency of deliberation and legislation by council, which developed the authority of the bishop in the province, of the metropolitan in the wider territory, and of the greater metropolitans in the universal Church. As the Roman bishop was the only metropolitan in the broad area of Africa, Italy, Spain, and Gaul who claimed the apostolic tradition, he had naturally soon become the most prominent and authoritative in the west.

The prominence thus encouraged could only have been greatly magnified when Constantine, together with his approval of Christianity, presented the bishop of Rome with the Lateran palace. Yet this prestige had by no means yet become absolute authority over all the west, to say nothing of the east, where a number of metropolitans, notably at Alexandria, Antioch, Jerusalem, and Constantinople, were each more or less independent of the others, and all independent of Rome, and where there never came into being the intense concentration later developed in the west. The great council of Nicæa in 325 was called, not by Pope Sylvester, but by Emperor Constantine; Sylvester was not even present, but was represented by Vito and Vicentius of Rome.

The authority of Rome grew none the less steadily. During the progress of the Arian quarrel in 340, the western bishop, called to be mediator and judge between Athanasius and Eusebius, favored the views of the former, from that time called orthodox. Three years later, the council of Sardica, in Dacia, acknowledged certain rights of Rome which in after time developed into its bishop's "perpetual prerogative of summoning at will all cases to be heard before himself in Rome." The Roman bishop was thus evolving into a sort of supreme judge, and not so much by divine warrant as by the action of an ecclesiastical organization desirous of the convenience of ultimate appeal. The growing strength of the bishop's position in the Church is farther indicated

by the continual courting of Liberius' approval by both
parties to the Arian dispute; in the Roman empire it is
shown by the same bishop's defiance of Constantius in
355, when commanded to condemn Athanasius, a defiance which ended in forcible abduction. The esteem in
which Liberius and his office were held in Rome caused
a rising of the people in the effort to protect him, followed later by a petition to the emperor for his return.
Not long afterward, the prestige of the city and its
bishop is again increased when Damasus becomes the
patron of Jerome in the publication of the Vulgate.

Ammianus Marcellinus, the pagan officer of Constantius who visited Rome in 356, was struck by the
power of the clergy, and especially by the worldly
splendor of the bishop, who passed through the streets
in his chariot like a consul riding in triumph. Jerome
addresses him after the fashion of the time as "Your
Greatness," "Your Blessedness," and, more familiar to
modern ears, "Your Holiness." In 378, the emperor
Gratian, who refuses the time-honored title of pontifex
maximus, rules at the request of a Roman council that
henceforth deposed bishops who will not submit must
be sent by the imperial prefects or vice-prefects to
Rome. In 390, after the massacre at Thessalonica, the
emperor Theodosius is refused entrance into the church
at Milan by Bishop Ambrose, who readmits him to the
sacrament only after eight months of penitence. If
Ambrose was for a time another head of the Church in
the west and in authority rivalled the bishop of Rome,
such was the power over both Church and state which
he had developed and revealed to the world that it could
not but contribute to the authority of his colleague in
the more venerable city.

Leo the Great, subjugator of heresies and called the founder of the dogmatic supremacy of the apostolic chair, advanced the Roman bishopric still farther on the road to both prestige and substantial power. Envoy of Rome to Attila in 452, he succeeded, together with his colleague from the senate, in dissuading the "Scourge of God" from his march against the city, and saved it from the horrors of murder, sack, and fire. Three years later, in a similar manner and with perhaps equal good fortune, he won the promise of Genseric to respect the lives of the Romans and to remain content with only the pillage of the city. In 445, he had already secured from Valentinian the Third a rescript recognizing the rights of the bishop of Rome over all the provinces of Italy, and did not hesitate to assert supremacy over Illyria and Gaul, and to dispute the claims of Constantinople to equal authority with Rome.

The spiritual primacy thus established over the west and claimed over the east was fostered in the west by the growing dependence of the sinking empire upon episcopal aid in the maintenance of order and authority. From the time of Constantine's approval of the Christian religion and the departure of government from Rome to Constantinople, Ravenna, and Milan, in measure as the imperial authority in Rome and Italy grew weaker and the disorders of barbarian aggression increased, and in measure as the east concerned itself less with the ancient capital, the power of the Church through its bishops, and the power of the bishops of Rome themselves, became greater and greater. Justinian bestowed upon bishops in general the right of supervision not only over clergy, but over imperial agents, and even over provincial judges. Both the prefect of

Italy and the Roman prefect were to be appointed only on recommendation by the bishop of Rome.

At exactly what date the process of spiritual centralization was complete, and the bishop of Rome, who from the fourth and fifth centuries had been known, with some other bishops, under the title of papa, became known as *the* papa, or pope, is as impossible to determine as the critical date in any other evolutionary process. It was never complete in the east, which from the fifth to the tenth centuries, in a progressive development marked by its anger at Leo's claim to supremacy in 451, the iconoclastic controversy in the eighth century, led by Gregory the Second in Rome and Leo the Isaurian in Constantinople, the doctrinal dispute over the phrases *filioque* and *et filio,* and the crusaders' abuse of the eastern capital, became more and more widely separated from the west until it broke away entirely. In Italy and the west, if it was not an accomplished fact by the time of Leo the Great, it was practically complete a hundred and fifty years later under Gregory the Great, the first of the name. It reached its sublimest result under Gregory the Seventh, five hundred years later, when a pope with the single weapon of excommunication compelled an emperor to submission.

Thus far of the growth of the spiritual power of Rome. But it was not only dogmatic and spiritual sovereignty that resulted from the drifting of the ancient civilization into the decline that ended in the Dark Ages. Given the conditions, it is wholly natural that the Roman episcopate should have laid also the foundations of a temporal sovereignty. Entirely to separate the two would be impossible. To assert that either grew out of the other, or that either at any time was independent

THE CASTLE OF CANOSSA, NEAR REGGIO EMILIA

THE SCENE OF GREGORY THE SEVENTH'S
HUMILIATION OF HENRY THE FOURTH

of the other, would be failure to appreciate their mutual relationship, and would be to presume overmuch upon the possibility of defining precisely the nature of the spiritual and the temporal. Was the pope's exercise of civil power, with the prestige it conferred upon his priestly office, a wholly temporal power, or was it partly spiritual? Was his possession of property, with the freedom it conveyed in the advancement of the Church, a temporal power, or a spiritual? Was the power of excommunication, by which he compelled the obedience of monarchs, a spiritual sovereignty, or a temporal?

The rise of the temporal power of the popes over Rome and its adjacent territory was a growth as easily understood, and, within limits, as legitimate, as the acquisition of spiritual supremacy. Its beginning is to be sought in the desire of the Roman faithful, especially the well-to-do, to add to the comfort and effectiveness of their bishop and Church at the same time that they obeyed their own impulses of gratitude and love toward the shepherd of their souls. Even before the emperor Constantine made legacy or donation to the Church a legal act, and by his own gift of the Lateran palace made it also a popular act, both Church and bishop were the possessors of a certain amount of property. The landed estates under private control of the Roman emperor in the Campagna, in Italy, and in the provinces, partly personal and partly held for the state, and known as the *patrimonium Cæsaris,* including such holdings near Rome as the villa of Hadrian not far from Tivoli and the villa-camp of Severus at Albano, came soon after the removal of the ban by Constantine to be paralleled by the *patrimonium pontificium* and the *patrimonium ecclesiasticum,* also outside of the city and including estates in Italy and the provinces. The patrimony of the Church is first mentioned in the sixth century by Pelagius the First. From the seventh century on, exemptions of the Church from taxation, with other favors, so aided agriculture in the Roman neighborhood that a more generous treatment of tenants became possible, and the population of the Campagna increased. The districts of the patrimonium were divided into many small dioceses, and supported many churches. Between the fifth and sixth milestones of the Via Labicana, for example, there were twelve churches. There were other parts of the patrimony on the Via Appia and the Via Tiburtina, and a fourth was called the *patrimonium Tusciæ*. Besides the estates of the Campagna, the gifts and bequests of houses and gardens within the city, and of sums of money, the patrimony was swelled also by the transfer of pagan temple property, and by lands and other possessions in more distant parts of the empire. By the time of Gregory the Great, 590-604, the bishop of Rome was the largest and richest landholder in Italy and the west.

It is not difficult to understand that the mere administration of the four parts of the patrimony in the Roman Campagna, of the property within the city, and of extensive possessions in Liguria, the Cottian Alps, Campania, southern Italy, Sicily, Dalmatia, Illyria, Gaul, Sardinia, and Corsica, accomplished through the deacons and sub-deacons who constituted the rectors of the patrimony, officials patterned after the imperial procurators, could of itself place the pope in the light of a temporal prince. When it is remembered that, in addition to this, Gregory himself was a noble and ex-prefect of Rome whose good offices were often sought, that his

recommendation in the appointment of civil officials
both in Italy and in Rome was both solicited by the
appointee and regarded by the emperor as a favor and
a duty, it is easy to believe with Gregorovius that, in
spite of his authority being generally restricted to the
Church, the great pope, "as possessing the faculties
suited to the circumstances of the time, was brought into
a position which made him the tacitly recognized head of
Rome, and with perfect right he is looked upon as the
founder of the temporal dominion of the papacy."

The pope thus enjoyed extensive temporal powers
even before the foundation of the political ecclesiastical
state. This latter was accomplished in 754, when Pepin,
king of the Franks and patrician of the Romans, at the
despairing entreaties of Stephen the Second, rescued
Rome from the Lombards, restored to the Church the
patrimonies it had lost, and by deed made over to it
both these and certain other territories of which he dispossessed both the Lombards and the Byzantines. The
act of Pepin was later confirmed by Charlemagne. Paul
the First, 757-767, is the first pope who may be called
formally a territorial prince. The precise limits of the
lands thus coming under control of the Church are unknown, but they included the exarchate of Ravenna, the
Adriatic cities of Ancona, Sinigaglia, Fano, Pesaro,
and Rimini, collectively called the Pentapolis, and in
general the not very clearly defined provinces extending
across central Italy to seventy-five miles south of Rome
at Terracina; roughly speaking, the area which, after
many vicissitudes, formed the states of the Church until
the temporal power was overwhelmed by the rising flood
of Italian nationalism. When Pius the Ninth came to
the throne in 1846, the states formed an irregular band

about four hundred miles long and one hundred and twenty-five wide, reaching from Terracina to Ferrara and from the Esino to the coast of the Maremma, and containing eighteen provinces.

If it is impossible to set definite boundaries to the new papal territory of the eighth century, it would be no less impossible to define the limits of papal authority over city and country. The acts of Pepin and Charles were probably in the main but the confirmation of conditions already in existence when Lombard aggression became too harsh to be endured. The relations between the pope and the people of the city and its adjacent territories which the decline of imperial Rome, the necessity of supplementing decayed authority, the distance and impotence of the Byzantine government, and the never-forgotten model of Cæsarism, had all contributed to bring about in essence, were now made formal and substantial. Those relations, however, had never been perfectly definite, and did not now become so. For nearly three hundred years the status of Rome had been prejudiced by the contentions of Goth, Lombard, and Byzantine with the pope and the Roman people; from now on it was to be kept in uncertainty and disorder by the never-ending and always conflicting claims of the imperial authority founded by Charlemagne, the papal authority confirmed by the same hand but not made wholly independent of the emperor, and the municipal ambitions that came into being on the city's acquisition of freedom from the interference of Lombard and Byzantine and its passage practically into the pope's control.

At first governed, so far as the emperor was concerned, only by the *missi,* who were little more than inspectors, the papal dominions soon lost the sense of imperial control. It was not long before the Romans, having thus had experience of liberty, became resentful of the more substantial and more directly applied authority of the pope. The consequence was that on the death of Charlemagne they rose against Leo the Third. Their independence was not long sustained. Fifty years later the energetic Nicholas the First, 858-867, is found ruling with firmness and vigor a realm from Terracina to Ravenna, restoring two aqueducts in the city, repairing the defences of Ostia, building lavishly, patronizing the liberal arts of a generation sunk in ignorance, relieving the poverty of the multitude in the grand style of a Cæsar, and successfully maintaining both his rights against the emperor and his authority over disobedient bishops. In him is to be seen the first papal ruler conscious of worldly kingship, the first pope-king.

The pope-kings, however, were not destined to exercise undisputed sway, at least over the city of Rome. The municipal party, which had attained to self-consciousness but not to power during the reign of Charlemagne, had risen against Leo the Third, and had been held in check by the strong hand of Nicholas, now rapidly grew in strength, and under the leadership of the nobility began again to dispute the sovereignty of the pope. In the popular uprising of 932 against the rule of Hugo and Marozia, the temporal power of the pope, and the authority of the emperor, the papal dominions were seized by the citizens led by the second Alberic, who for twenty years ruled as *Princeps atque omnium Romanorum Senator,* and made the city and its territories an independent kingdom like other Italian principalities. But the change was not for long. Octavian, the son of Alberic, having become John the Twelfth, incidentally founding the papal custom of changing the name on accession, united the offices of prince and pope, and Rome and the ecclesiastical state came once more under papal authority.

In spite of the troubles between pope and nobles, pope and emperor, and emperor and people which characterized the middle centuries at Rome, and in spite of the fact that the head of the world-Church, the king of an extensive realm, and the creator of emperors was frequently unable to rule his own Romans, the normal and usual state of the city up to the year 1143 was obedience to the papal authority. Its principal officials were the prefect, a survival of the ancient *præfectus urbis,* who received his office from both emperor and pope, but in reality from the latter, and exercised civil and criminal jurisdiction over the city and adjacent territory within the limit of a hundred miles; the consuls or dukes of the Romans, *consules* or *duces Romanorum,* pontifical functionaries chosen from among the nobles, with duties concerning prosecutions and executions of judgment; and a varying number of clerical judges whose duties ranged from the purely and simply judicial to financial and other administrative functions in the papal palace, then still the Lateran, which was not abandoned for the Vatican as permanent seat of the popes until 1377.

In 1143, however, stimulated by the example of the northern Italian cities, which had erected themselves into independent communes, the Roman people rose in revolution, overthrew the papal and aristocratic régime of prefect and judges, and installed a popular senate or common council on the Capitol. The change was not so sweeping as might seem. Eugenius the Third, compelled two years afterward to recognize the new order, retained the appointment of the prefect and the right to approve the senators. In 1188, a renewed compact gave the pope again his revenues, with militia to defend his patrimony. The direct exercise of legislative and executive authority, which was still withheld, was no doubt more or less replaced by the power inherent in the administration of the patrimony; it is significant that the pope paid the salaries of senators and other functionaries. On the whole, however, there was a distinct tendency in this century and the next toward the absorption by the commune of the former civil powers of the pope. The prefect's authority was taken over by it, and the power of coinage, which had been restored to the pope but not exercised, remained in its hands.

The senate of the twelfth century, consisting of senators ordinary and senators counsellor, was theoretically supreme in the affairs of Rome. It was not, however, an oligarchy. Its measures were executed only after being prepared by a council chosen from the leading citizens, a council which met in the Aracœli and at one time consisted of eighty-four men, and after approval on the Capitol by a convocation of the total citizenship of Rome. The senatorial elections were annual, by parliament of all the citizens. The number of senators varied. At first there were twenty-five; in 1152, two thousand citizens decreed the election of a senate of one hundred; a usual number was fifty-six, representing each region by four. As time passed, the tendency was strongly toward reduction to a very few; by the thirteenth century, the rule was one. At times the pope was commissioned to nominate a council of middle-men, *mediani.*

who elected the incumbent, a service which he probably performed after in some manner taking counsel with the people. In proportion as the number of senators decreased, the number of functionaries at their service was multiplied. In the thirteenth century, there are to be heard of two *vestararii,* or guards of the treasury, six *assectatores,* or ushers, twenty-eight *iustitiarii* for the execution of sentences, *mandatarii* to give to interested parties the notices of senatorial decrees, a *præco,* or herald, a seneschal, a palatine judge, appointed for not more than three months, and five *scriniarii palatini,* or senatorial secretaries.

In 1198, during a momentary collapse of the emperor's authority in Rome, Innocent the Third, the imperious pope who exterminated the Albigenses and revived the ambition for world-domination which had decayed with the death of Gregory the Seventh, regained control of both prefect and senate, and in a measure recovered the one-time papal supremacy over the dominions which had fallen into the hands of the nobles. Rome continued to be independent, but was subject to the will of the pope. Gregory the Ninth, another strong will and zealous persecutor of unbelief, acquired such authority over the senator as to make him the official instrument of the seizure and execution of heretics. The representative of the city was obliged to pronounce the ban against all who should be guilty, to seize those listed by the Inquisition, and within eight days of the sentence, which was read by the inquisitor on the Capitol, to put them to death. The place of trial and execution was in front of Santa Maria Maggiore. The Romans, themselves carried along in the current of the times, became through religious zeal the more or less willing contributors to their own subjugation to the temporal power.

From the beginning of the thirteenth century it had been the custom of Rome as well as other Italian communes to elect as their annual senator or *podestà* a distinguished citizen of a sister city. With a cabinet of five notaries and six judges, and an advisory council of Capitoline judges, the senator was entrusted with full power except as he was subject to the desires of the civic assembly. Brancaleone of Bologna, who held the office from 1252 to 1255, supported the people against the nobles, who were at this time in the main subservient to the pope. In 1261, King Manfred was elected senator, an example of Ghibelline reaction, and in 1263 the Guelfs in turn elected Charles of Anjou, brother of Saint Louis of France. In 1278, Nicholas the Third, an Orsini of secular ambition whose first purpose was to establish the states of the Church on a basis of law, having won from the emperor the recognition of the papal sovereignty over the Romagna, including Bologna, as well as over the widest boundaries of the ancient ecclesiastical claims, compelled the resignation of Charles, and issued a constitution providing that henceforth the senatorial and other important offices should never be held by any emperor or king, prince, margrave, duke, count, baron, or any person of noble standing who was kinsman to them, but excepting citizens of Rome. The result of the exception was the encouragement of Roman patricians to aim at the senatorial power, and their acquisition of a new importance. Nicholas the Third himself, though he did not make official use of the title, was a senator for life, and his successors were for a long time chosen to the dignity. That they were made senators as individuals rather than as popes could hardly have affected the degree of influence they exercised. They were at once the heads of the Church and the chief officials of the Roman commonwealth.

Another significant moment in the history of Roman independence occurred in the fourteenth century during the absence of the papacy at Avignon. When Cola di Rienzo in 1347 overthrew the barons, proclaimed the Roman republic, and invited the cities of Italy to form themselves into a federation under the leadership of Rome and to make common cause of "the whole of sacred Italy," he was entertaining, though more dimly, the idea and the hope that five centuries later were to send men to martyrdom and sweep the invader from the length and breadth of the land.

The times, however, were not ripe. In spite of the absence and comparative unconcern of the papacy, the weakness of the imperial authority, and the spell of the name of Rome, the Festival of the Unity of Italy only demonstrated the impossibility of animating with a single purpose the scattered and diverse communes and principalities that went to make up the Italian race. The seven exalted but vain months of Cola's rule were soon over, the old round of anarchy, conspiracy, insurrection, and violence began once more, with now the papal party, now the nobles, now the people, now the emperors, as the principal figures in the tragic succession of events, until Gregory the Eleventh in 1377 returned to a still conspiring and distracted capital, and farther until 1398, when Boniface the Ninth adroitly made the papacy again supreme, and the efforts of the two hundred and fifty years since the revolution of 1143 to establish an independent civil state at Rome were practically at an end. Eugenius the Fourth was compelled in 1434 to renounce the temporal power, but two years later was reinstated by armed force. The failure of Stephen Porcaro's attempt at revolution in 1453 may be called the last protest of Rome against the temporal power until the middle of the nineteenth century. Under Nicholas the Fifth, the same pope who hanged Stephen Porcaro in a tower of Hadrian's mausoleum, began the splendid secularization which continued under Paul the Second, Sixtus the Fourth, and Alexander the Sixth, and culminated in the times of Julius the Second and Leo the Tenth.

3.

THE HOLY CITY

"FROM the time of Charles the Fifth's coronation (1530) until the end of the eighteenth century," writes Gregorovius, "the popes ruled Rome in such perfect tranquillity, that during this period of the political extinction of Italy, as well as of the torpor of the papacy, they enjoyed their happiest but most inglorious term of government."

This is hardly giving the times or the popes the credit they deserve. If the popes are to be judged wholly as kings and politicians, we may accept the verdict. If we judge them as men and priests as well as monarchs, and measure their importance by the more purely ecclesiastical and spiritual effort put forth by them, they will be found a memorable line, and their times worthy of comparison with any period of the same length in the history of the holy office.

Whatever their errors as pontiffs and their defects as men, the popes from Paul the Third to the end of the temporal power were distinguished as a whole by earnestness of purpose and uprightness of character. Paul the Third, magnificent and easy in secular matters, was exceedingly strict in what concerned the duties of religion. Paul the Fourth was ascetic and reformer, and Pius the Fifth was rigidly severe with himself as well as others. Gregory the Thirteenth was austere, Clement the Eighth self-denying, Clement the Ninth and Clement the Tenth gentle and charitable, Clement the Eleventh abstemious and the foe of abuse. Benedict

the Thirteenth allowed sixpence a day for his table and
opened the Vatican doors to the poor, whom he called
his relatives. Benedict the Fourteenth, independent
and impartial, diminishing the number of useless holidays and discouraging superstition, brought upon himself the name of "the Protestant Pope," the thirteenth
and fourteenth Clements and the last four Piuses were
men of cultivated tastes whose conduct was above reproach, and even Leo the Twelfth and Gregory the
Sixteenth, whatever their lack of vision, were actuated
by serious purpose. Gregory the Sixteenth performed
at least one great liberal act, the abolition of the anti-
quated and barbarous penal code, with its trials in
secret, its tortures, floggings, interrogations, and abuses
of asylum and pardon.

The same praise may be awarded to the character of
the papal administrations in general. Many of them
initiated, or, if the initiation was rather of the times
than of pope or cabinet, at least witnessed and fostered
the initiation of great movements. The council of Trent
was in session for the forty years from Paul the Third
to Pius the Fourth, and Paul's reign saw also the formation of Filippo Neri's brotherhood of the Oratory
at Rome, and the rise of Loyola and the Society of
Jesus, at first by no means the offensive order it later
came to be, but a great teaching brotherhood whose
contribution to lay intelligence and the spirit of loyalty
was sorely needed. The movement of the times toward
greater strictness in the discipline of the Church, of
which the Index was the sign, was continued by vigorous
measures against heresy, which, however exaggerated
or mistaken, were sprung of a seriousness regarding
sacred matters to which the curia had been too long a

stranger. To Gregory the Thirteenth's zeal for Catholic instruction was due the foundation of twenty or more colleges in Rome and Italy. Sixtus the Fifth's appointment of more churchmen to responsible positions in the government was due to moral as well as ecclesiastical purpose. Clement the Eighth was an active disciplinarian. Gregory the Fifteenth's reign was marked by world-wide missionary enterprise; it was he who founded and endowed for the supervision of foreign missions the congregation of cardinals called the Propaganda, canonized Francis Xavier, the apostle to the Indies, and built the cathedral at Los Angeles in California. By this time there were in South America five archbishops, twenty-seven bishops, four hundred monasteries, and parish churches without number. Innocent the Eleventh enacted sumptuary laws, legislated against immodesty in dress, closed the gaming-houses, and insisted on the greater fitness of candidates for the office of bishop. Innocent the Twelfth legislated against nepotism, refusing his nephew permission even to reside in the Vatican. Clement the Eleventh was the enemy of abuses, and actively fostered missions. Benedict the Fourteenth founded four academies for the study of history and canon law, and opposed the Jesuits in their excesses among the Indians. The reign of Clement the Fourteenth saw the dissolution of the Jesuit society. If from the days of Clement to the end of the temporal power no great constructive movements took place, sufficient reason is to be found in the troubled nature of Napoleonic and Risorgimento times. Throughout the period, however, not only the popes personally, but their administrations, were characterized by great attention to charities, and by open-handedness in general.

It would be a distortion of the truth to assume that either all of the popes or all of their administrations were free from fault. Nepotism was long in dying, or rather in being throttled; yet from the time of Paul the Third, the last to practice it in the grand style, it could not be practiced at all without universal reproach. But nepotism even in its days of least restraint was not without excuse, if indeed excuse was demanded in an age when its practice was so largely taken for granted. Given the circumstances of a pope who was aged, lonely, and in need of younger and stronger men for counsellors, it was natural enough for the capable relatives of the ruler to be summoned to his aid. Not all nephews were elevated because of mere family ambition, nor did all of them make selfish use of their power. It needs but a glance over the line of cardinal-nephews of the sixteenth and seventeenth centuries to realize the indebtedness of Roman building and Roman culture to their presence, to say nothing of Roman general welfare. If they sometimes proved unworthy, they were more often both competent and public-spirited. An Alessandro or a Ranuccio Farnese or a Scipione Borghese was more frequent than a Carlo Caraffa or a Pietro Aldobrandini. These facts considered, it is no mean tribute to the dignity and moral earnestness of the times that even the least objectionable kind of nepotism came to be condemned, and that the offence was frowned out of existence.

The excesses of nepotism, however, were not the worst. There were abuses of incapacity in the administration of both city and state. It was a standing charge that bandits infested the country, and violence the streets of the city. In vain did Sixtus the Fifth hang

four men for possessing firearms, and a boy in the
Trastevere for resisting officers, and erect twelve gallows between Anagni and Frosinone for the execution
and display of marauders, and adorn the Ponte Sant'
Angelo with heads until they were "more numerous
than melons in the Via dei Banchi." In spite of six thousand five hundred commitments and many executions
by Gregory the Thirteenth in 1582, and in spite of the
deaths of five thousand men on both sides in the wars
with outlaws between 1590 and 1595, the insecurity of
the papal dominions continued, and came to an end only
with the advent of the Italian monarchy. Clement the
Thirteenth's reign of less than eleven years, 1758-1769,
saw ten thousand murders in the states of the Church,
four thousand of them in Rome, a city of one hundred
and sixty thousand. There were three hundred and
thirty-nine executions under Leo the Twelfth, 1823-
1829. Windows were ordered closed at eight in the evening during the interval between deaths and elections,
and lamps set in them, for the sake of the public safety.
It was not infrequent for bishop or abbot to lay aside
sword and pistols and to perform the holy office booted
and spurred. The knife-duel was the commonest occurrence. Contraband went hand in hand with brigandage
as both result and cause, and was the normal condition.
In the city, periods of incapable policing alternated
with periods of ferocious severity when men were condemned to death for trifling infringement of unwise
laws. As is likely to be the case with feeble governments,
weakness went hand in hand with cruelty. Mere theft
was sometimes punished by death. For blasphemy, libel,
defacement of doors and walls, possession of arms, entrance into a nunnery, there were public flogging and

the galleys, "with death at the pleasure of His Eminence"; and death might be by strangulation, walling up, hanging, burning, or beheading. The horrors of the mediæval code lasted on until 1833. In the time of Pius the Fifth, in 1566, an edict to expel the courtesans from the city disclosed the fact that twenty thousand of the fifty thousand inhabitants were estimated to belong to that class, and roused a protest which the pope was compelled to heed. The prison near the Porta Portese, in which political offenders were kept from 1849 to 1870, had long been a place of detention for dissolute women.

There was not only incapacity, but neglect and immorality. The example of the holy seat was not always followed by its ministers of secular affairs. Judges under Alexander the Seventh took four months' vacation, accepted rich Christmas gifts from interested parties, yielded to pressure, and were dilatory and arbitrary in decisions. Innocent the Tenth was ruled by an unscrupulous sister-in-law, and Benedict the Thirteenth chose unwisely in his favorite, Nicholas Coscia. In the sixteenth and seventeenth centuries at least, wealth and birth were privileged in the selection of bishops and cardinals, and success depended often upon the favor of the pope's kinsmen. The cardinal-nephews received not only legitimate compensation, but suddenly accumulated vast fortunes; the Borghese and Aldobrandini families in the short periods of their ascendency received a total of at least a million scudi. The financing of the papal administration was uncertain and shifty, depending much upon the ingenious loan establishments of the monti, the sale of offices, and the influx of voluntary contributions from abroad. In 1471 there were already six hundred and fifty salable offices, and by the time of

Pius the Fourth the number had grown to three thou-sand five hundred. "Give him pencil and paper, and he will create money out of nothing," said an enthusiastic admirer of one pope's financial genius.

It was to be expected that the foibles of the popes and their administrators, to say nothing of the more serious offences, would rouse the spirit of satire that has always belonged to the Romans. With the return of letters in the Renaissance, and with the return of a measure of intellectual independence and individuality, what criticism had hitherto been rare and privately murmured began to be vocal. Its most eloquent and pungent expression was through Pasquino, the muti-lated statue of obscure origin still standing today at the angle of the Palazzo Braschi. Pasquino began his career in about 1500, and for three hundred and seventy years, with the occasional aid of Marforio, another ancient relic, supplied the place of the modern satirical sheet and the opposition newspaper. His origin and end coin-cide with the rise and fall of the pope-kings.

In July, 1497, for example, Alexander Borgia is having the Tiber dragged in the search for the murdered duke of Gandia, his son, and in the morning a slip of paper is found attached to Pasquino's person. "Lest we think thee no Fisher of Men, O Sextus," it says, "thou art casting the net for thy son,—"

Piscatorem hominum ne te non, Sexte, putemus
Piscaris natum retibus ecce tuum.

Or, Urban the Eighth, the princely Barberini, is dead. In his good fortune he did not forget his family, which is symbolized on the Barberini coat-of-arms by the bees. Pasquino appears with an epigram, as usual, in Latin:

Pauca hæc Urbani sint verba incisa sepulchro:
Quam bene pavit Apes tam male pavit Oves,—

Let these few words be cut on Urban's tomb:
He fed his Lambs as badly as he fed his Bees well.

Again, Pius the Sixth has been too frugal to meet Roman expectations in time of famine. Pasquino calls to his aid the art of design, and displays to Rome one morning the figure of a single tiny roll of bread, with the legend so often seen on the pope's public monuments:

Munificentia Pii Sexti,—

Through the Munificence of Pius the Sixth.

Sometimes Pasquino is moved to homelier expression, and then the pasquinade is in his native tongue. Clement the Eleventh has been free-handed with his relatives at Urbino, and Pasquino does not relish the sight of Roman money departing in such quantity for the little provincial town. He and Marforio pass the word as they meet:

Che fai, Pasquino?
Eh, guardo Roma, che non vada ad Urbino,—

What art doing, Pasquino?
Oh, I am keeping an eye on Rome, to see that it
doesn't leave for Urbino.

And one morning in the reign of Sixtus the Fifth, whose sister, said once to have been a washerwoman, has married a duke, Pasquino is found in a soiled shirt.

His friends are surprised and curious. He explains to them:

Eh, adesso che la mia lavandaia è stata fatta duchessa, ha tutt' altro da fare che curarmi la biancheria,—

Oh, since my washerwoman has got to be a duchess, she has quite other things to do than look after my linen.

The bluff pope receives the stinging shaft, but pretends to admire its neatness, and skilfully baits a hook for the unknown author, who greedily takes it, pockets the promised reward, and has his right hand chopped off. "I didn't promise not to cut his hand off," says the keen Sixtus.

When the angered old man in the Vatican has forbidden farther words, Pasquino refrains from specific utterance, but manages to relieve himself without exposure to penalty. He is constrained to ease his feelings more than once:

Crepo per non poter parlare,—
I am bursting for want of a chance to speak.

Son crepato per avermi troppo chiuso la bocca,—
I've burst from having kept my mouth shut too long.

Amo meglio crepare che tacere,—
I'd rather burst than not speak out.

But if the natural preference of brothers and nephews, the futilities of incapable men and measures, and the petty immoralities of the public service are to be considered in the light of abuses and weaknesses rather than more serious offence, the same may hardly be said of other excesses, also grounded in nature but less innocent in their consequences. The desire to save

souls and to advance the glory of the Church cannot
excuse the lengths to which the Index went in the suppression of freedom of thought and speech. It cannot
excuse the horrible and futile cruelties of the Inquisition, or the petty and exasperating tyrannies of espio-
nage. Pius the Fifth approving the Spanish burning
of heretics and lighting the fires in Rome, Gregory the
Thirteenth ordering a Te Deum and striking a medal
after the massacre of Saint Bartholomew, the burning
of Giordano Bruno at the stake under Clement the
Eighth, Urban the Eighth and his treatment of Galileo,
Pius the Seventh as late as the beginning of the nineteenth century reviving the severities of persecution and
suppression, Leo the Twelfth with his spies, Gregory
the Sixteenth forbidding the Bible in the vulgar tongues
and condemning the liberty of the press, Pius the Ninth
with his approval of Christianization by kidnapping,
are examples of zeal which hardly find place in the
category of the virtues.

These instances of papal frailty, it is true, cover a
wide space of time; but, with others like them, they have
afforded later generations the grounds for their appraisal of the papal state during the two hundred and
fifty years before its fall. It will be seen that its sins
were due in part to mistaken zeal, in part to the occupation of office, from the time of Sixtus the Fifth, almost
exclusively by clericals, in part to provincialism, in
part to the natural resistance to progress of the most
stable and slow-moving of the world's institutions, in
part to the neglect and arrogance which are the sure
accompaniments of security, in part to the universal
character of the times, and in part, but only in small
part, to actual viciousness. That they existed may

modify our notion as to the possibility of uniting spiritual and temporal powers to the advantage of the spiritual, but it should not hinder the conclusion that the popes in the great majority were men of a high order, that in the main the measures of the Church were directed toward lofty ends, and that, compared with the secular states and their rulers of the same period, the papal state and its princes do not appear at serious disadvantage.

If the authority of living witness be desired, no more interesting expression can be found regarding the Rome of the pope-kings than that of the learned and witty Charles de Brosses, president of the parliament of Burgundy, who visited Rome in 1740 under Clement the Twelfth. In *Lettres familières écrites d'Italie,* he comments in the genial mood of the amused spectator on the weaknesses of papal rule and the charm of the city:

"The rulers who, since Sixtus the Fifth, have done endless things for the beautification of the city, have done nothing toward the cultivation of the Campagna, where one sees, literally, not a single house or shrub. The government is as bad as could be imagined were one to draw on the fancy at pleasure. Machiavelli and More amused themselves in the constructing of a Utopia; here one finds in the reality the exact opposite. Imagine the state of things, with a population one-third priests, one-third people who do next to nothing, and one-third who do nothing at all; where there is neither agriculture nor commerce nor manufacturing, though the city is in the midst of a fertile country and on a navigable river; where the prince, always old, with few years to sit on the throne, and often incapable of taking any action

THE CHURCH OF SAINT PETER IN FEBRUARY, 1922

THE CROWD IS EXPECTING THE ANNOUNCEMENT
OF THE POPE'S ELECTION

of his own will, is surrounded by relatives possessed by
no other idea than that of promptly laying hands on
what they can get while they have the opportunity, and
where, at each change of administration, one sees new
plunderers arrive to take the place of those who no
longer have need to plunder; where impunity is assured to anyone who cares to disturb his environment,
provided only he has acquaintance among the great or
is within reach of an asylum; where all the money required for the necessities of life has its only source in
other lands, a contribution constantly growing less; and
where, in a word, the system which we have seen in
France is established forever, though indeed not practiced with the same fury. Note, however, that, since
the paper money has no circulation outside of Rome, all
the necessaries of life, because they must be purchased
elsewhere, must be paid for in silver, and that the place
produces nothing, a fact which in the course of time
has so reduced the quantity of coin that today it is almost impossible longer to obtain it. . . .

"But this is a great deal of fault that I am finding with
a place which, after all I have said, is very agreeable to
strangers not only for motives of curiosity, but because
of the extreme liberty which reigns there, and because
of the courteousness of its inhabitants, who in general
are characterized, if not by cordiality, at least by at-
tentiveness, and who are obliging and easy of access to
a much greater degree than the people of any other part
of Italy. It is also very easy for strangers here to gain
admission to society and to find a welcome everywhere,
and the Romans are beginning to live with each other
on familiar terms, and to dine together, as in France.

"You would of course like to have a word about the

vineyards of Rome and Frascati. I will say as to this only that the Italians esteem them too much and the French too little. Although we are as much superior to them in gardens as they surpass us in buildings, it is always a great pleasure to see, what I find in no other place, trees in the wintertime all green and leafy, and in summer the most beautiful and the clearest waters one could know. The views here are also very much praised, but they hardly give me pleasure, for what is there in the view of a plain far extended but barren and deserted? I might say as much of the houses; they are covered with reliefs, from ground to roof, but they have no bedrooms."

To this vivacious witness may be added the picturesque summary of the late eighteenth and early nineteenth centuries by Silvagni, drawn largely from the diary of the Abbé Benedetti, who died in 1837 at over eighty, and who remembered the popes and the city from Clement the Thirteenth to Gregory the Sixteenth:

"The streets were without signs and had no lamps, there were no sidewalks, the houses were without numbers, the roofs without gutters, and the shop windows without glass. There were no names over the tradespeople's premises. Iron and wooden signboards, typical of the business carried on within, were substituted for names. Thus a cardinal's red hat or a priest's black beretta could be seen swinging before a hatter's; a huge pair of red or black hands pointed out a glover's; a snake hung over a chemist's; cocks, eagles, hawks, suns, and bears marked the inns, on whose doors were often nailed falcons; a bush indicated a wine-shop; a foot or arm with blood issuing from it, a bloodletter; a copper basin, a barber's; one of the Swiss guard, a dealer in lace and trimmings; a pair of scissors, a tailor's; a Turk with a pipe, a tobacconist; a horn, the post-horses; a piece of blue woolen goods, a cloth merchant; etc.

"Most of the Roman tradespeople carried on the greater part of their business in the street. There, too, people did money transactions, cooked potatoes, or egg-plant, or chestnuts. At San Carlo al Corso they fried fish, and sold tripe, chickens, and slaughtered meats. There were open sewers full of filth in the middle of most of the streets, including the Corso. Sales of all kinds were strictly regulated by officials called *calmieri,* and many articles were monopolies of the great families, who had at some time or other bought the exclusive privilege of selling wax, arms, cosmetics, balsam, tap-estry, gunpowder, leather, and even pins. The Albani princes, for example, possessed the right to make pins at Urbino, and whoever ventured to import them from elsewhere was punished with fines and flogging. The emasculation of boys was almost a monopoly, and be-longed to a barber in the Via Papali, who had the fol-lowing announcement above his door:

Qui si castrono li cantori delle cappelle papali

. . . The Via del Babuino was mean and squalid. . . . From the Piazza Colonna to the Porta del Popolo there were only small and wretched houses. . . .

"Locomotion indeed was difficult during the day in Rome, because of the vendors' stalls and heaps of stones and dust and refuse of every kind encumbering the streets. It was in vain that placards were issued pro-hibiting the accumulation of filth and rubbish in public places; that stones were set up at the sides of the Via

Borgognona and other streets, some of which may still be seen, with inscriptions to the effect that anyone found committing an offence would be punished with fines, imprisonment, *ed altre pene ad arbitrio di Sua Eccellenza*. All the streets and chance nooks were filled with every sort of refuse and waste. Occasionally some culprit was caught by the *sbirri* and publicly punished, either in the Campo dei Fiori, at the corner of the Via della Corda, or in the Corso at the street of the same name, or he was flogged at the head of the Via del Babuino. . . . But the evil was without remedy because it was always done at night, and at night the whole city was enveloped in darkness. Indeed the only light in the streets came from some little lamp burning before the shrine of a Madonna, or from some flickering torch at the corner of a palace. In most of the streets, therefore, it was perfectly dark, and the few passers-by either carried lanterns themselves, or had well-armed servants with them for the purpose.

"Now and then loud cries and desperate screams for help rent the air. Now it was those whose shop or house doors were being broken in by thieves, and now women who had been compelled to venture out and were being carried off or violated. The patrol frequently came to blows with the evildoers, and with the hired assassins of princes, ambassadors, and cardinals.

"Morning often brought strange disclosures of crimes done in the hours of darkness, and it was no uncommon sight to see a culprit taken past on a mule, exposed in the pillory, and then subjected to the Cavalletto,—an infamous spectacle which Antonelli had the glory of reviving in 1856, with the applause of the Catholic world,—or to watch another poor wretch dangling from the gallows in the Piazza del Popolo, without process, without form of trial, and without defence."

Yet, whatever the defects of the papal administration, and whatever its fluctuations in morals and capacity, there was one respect in which it did not change, and there was one remedy which it consistently refused to consider. The claim to both spiritual and temporal sovereignty had long ago taken on canonical form. Dogmatically, it rested on the divinely appointed headship of Peter which descended to all his successors on the throne; historically, on the patrimonium, on the deed of Pepin and its confirmation by Charlemagne, and on the transfer of Byzantine authority under the same kings from the east to Rome. More or less quiescent from the return of Clement the Seventh until the end of the eighteenth century because rarely questioned, the idea of temporal sovereignty was roused to greater assertiveness by the Napoleonic aggressions and the rise of modern Italian ambitions; but it was never at any time forgotten, and never laid aside. The popes in their own eyes were kings as well as priests. There were those in whom, like Sixtus the Fifth, Paul the Fifth, and Urban the Eighth, the consciousness of regal authority almost equalled, if it did not exceed, that of the priestly office. If there were the less princely and imperious, like the eighth and ninth Clements, Gregory the Fifteenth, and Benedict the Thirteenth, whose thoughts were fixed more on the matters of the other world than of this, their cardinal-nephews and favored counsellors saw to it that the pomp and circumstance of kingship, together with the retainer's privileges, were not abated. If there were many who personally did not value the powers and the splendors of monarchy, and some who persisted in the

Franciscan or Dominican humility and self-denial to which they had been bred in their earlier days of service, there were probably none who did not firmly believe that the temporal power was necessary to the freedom of the Church and its capacity for good. To suppose that a Paul the Third, with his princely magnificence, or a Julius the Third, fond of ease and retirement, or a Pius the Fourth and an Urban the Eighth, with their erection of elaborate military defences, or a Sixtus the Fifth, insisting on the papal right to dethrone the kings of Europe, or a Paul the Fifth, zealous for the extension of papal authority, or a Pius the Sixth, refusing to surrender the temporal power and dying in exile and captivity, or a Pius the Ninth, refusing to recognize the state whose rise had finally deprived the Church of her domains,—to suppose that all or any of these were not actuated principally by the conviction that they were advancing the interests of the Church and faithfully discharging the obligation they had assumed at the beginning of their careers, would be to wrong magnanimous men.

It was but rarely that the pope conceived the idea of enlarging his territory by actual conquest. The army of Sixtus the Fifth, outside of the thirty thousand militia scattered through the states of the Church and not kept up, consisted of two hundred watchmen and one hundred infantry in Rome, sixty-three infantry in Perugia, forty-three in Ancona, and twenty-five each in Orvieto and Civitavecchia. He had a navy of six ships. The papal armament rose and fell according to circumstance, but in time of need, which meant in time of the defence of the temporal right, the military force of the Church consisted usually of troops from friendly monarchs abroad. The frequent remark of Paul the Third that in case the potentates did him an evil turn he would have to use words in defence, rather than action, in order not to disclose how weak he was, might have been made by the pope at any time up to the twentieth of September, 1870, when Pius the Ninth instructed his army to make no farther resistance than would serve as a protest.

It is thus to be seen that in the theory of government and in the administration of the states of the Church, no less than in the architectural character of the city, there was always a mingling of the religious and the secular. The same alliance of the eternal and the temporal was also visible in the great spectacles in the churches and streets of Rome. The splendid ceremonial, the parade, and the triumphal procession of the ancient empire retained their place in the affections of the people and their rulers in the altered form of the papal coronation, the funerals of pope and cardinal, and the gorgeous ceremonies and processions of the great Church festivals. Their presence through the ages was not only a manifestation of the unchanging nature of papal theory and practice, but one of the characteristic features of the city as long as its destinies were ruled by the papacy, or as long as the pope continued freely to go and come in its thoroughfares.

Already in the fourth century the court of the bishop of Rome had begun to imitate the ways of the imperial court. It was probably after witnessing the episcopal procession on some great holy day that Ammianus noted satirically the resemblance of the bishop's progress to that of a Roman emperor in his triumph. The more or less direct influence of the Roman court,

not excluding that of the imperial religious functions
so inseparable from it, had soon acted upon the simple
ceremonial of the early Church, already affected con-
siderably by the comparative elaboration and splendor of the Jewish ritual. The character thus formed
was later again enriched, as Rome and Constantinople
touched each other through Ravenna and the eastern
supervision of Italy, by the influence of the Byzantine
court and the eastern Church. It was from these sources,
especially the Jewish and Byzantine, that there came
into the Church the golden, beaten, chased, inlaid,
enamelled, and begemmed crucifixes, vessels, and candle-
sticks of the service, and the splendid vestments, altar-
cloths, and tapestries, blazing with color or stiff with
gold and precious stones, which never ceased, and never
cease today, as the Church well knows, to fascinate the
eye and captivate the imagination.

It was from the same sources, and especially from the
Byzantine and Roman, that the great processions also
received their character. Let us witness one of them. We
may well take leave of the Rome of the pope-kings by
letting the eye rest for a moment on some of the color
and picturesqueness which lent it charm throughout
the ages.

On February 22, 1198, Innocent the Third, after consecration by the bishops of Ostia, Albano, and Porto
in the already ancient and historic basilica of Saint
Peter's, appears with glittering retinue on the broad
platform before it and solemnly seats himself on the
papal throne. As the bishop's miter is removed from his
head and its place is taken by the golden and jewelled
crown, the archdeacon who sets it there in the presence
of the Roman multitude drawn from the thirty-five

thousand or so inhabitants, swelled by the crowd of strangers from every quarter of the world who never cease to stream to Rome, pronounces the impressive words: "Receive the tiara, that thou mayst know thyself the father of princes and kings, the ruler of the world, the vicar on earth of our Savior, Jesus Christ, to whom is honor and glory through the ages of the ages." The coronation done, the pope, gorgeous in rich apparel, resplendent with jewels and gold, and wearing the crown, mounts a horse in scarlet trappings, the stirrup and bridle of which, as he proceeds, are held for a few moments by an emperor or king, or, in their absence, by a senator or noble of Rome. After this preliminary, the great cavalcade begins its progress. It is headed by one of the pope's splendid and richly caparisoned horses. After it come the mounted cross-bearers and twelve mounted standard-bearers with red banners, and two horsemen with lances supporting golden cherubim; then prefects of the marine, advocates, clerks, judges in black gowns, all mounted; the singers, deacons, and subdeacons, foreign abbots, bishops and archbishops, the twenty abbots of the Roman abbeys, the patriarchs, cardinal-bishops, cardinal-presbyters, cardinal-deacons, many of them white-haired and venerable, on horseback like all the rest; then the pope, on a white horse, with senators or nobles leading and sub-deacons and city prefect at his side, and the college of judges; then the civic guilds, the militia, and the knights and nobles in glittering arms, each with the arms and colors of his house.

For the space of an hour, along streets wreathed and garlanded, under lofty triumphal arches, through the lanes of densely packed and staring people, to the solemn chant of priests and the ringing of all the city's bells, the splendid procession passes. It passes to the bridge across the Tiber and through the still standing arch of Gratian, Theodosius, and Valentinian; halts in Parione, where, according to the custom of newly crowned pope-kings, the pope receives the humble submission of the Jews to their Christian lord; proceeds through the Campus Martius, through the forums of Trajan and Cæsar, across the Great Forum under the arches of Severus and Titus, and past the Coliseum and San Clemente to the piazza of the Lateran, where the clergy welcome their new head with the solemn chant, conduct him to the arcade, and seat him on the symbolic *sella stercoraria,* the seat of abasement, whence he soon rises to scatter among the people from the lap of a chamberlain three handfuls of gold, silver, and copper, repeating as he throws it, "Gold and silver have I none, but what I have that I give thee," after which he enters the Lateran church to offer prayer, and receives the homage of the chapter.

Issuing from the church, the pope next enters and takes possession of the Lateran palace, where he receives the pastoral staff, the keys of the church and palace, and is seated on a porphyry chair, clad in a girdle of red silk from which is suspended a purple purse containing musk and twelve seals of precious stones, the symbols of the apostolic power and the Christian virtues. The palace retinue is admitted to kiss the papal foot, and the cardinals and prelates kneel before their lord to receive the usual donation. At the banquet in the palace which follows the oath of homage by the senate and concludes the ceremonies of the day, the pope sits apart at a table with costly service, churchmen

THE ATRIUM OF SAN CLEMENTE

COLUMNS AND PAVEMENT ARE OF ANCIENT MATERIAL;
BELOW AN UPPER AND A LOWER CHURCH ARE A GROT OF MITHRAS
AND REMNANTS FROM THE REPUBLIC

and nobles are placed at another, and senators, prefects, and judges at a third. If kings were present, they would carry to the pope the first dishes, afterward seating themselves beside the cardinals, while the most distinguished of the nobility would serve him for the remainder of the banquet.

If some of the mediæval features of the coronation parade and other spectacles disappeared or were transformed at the coming of the Renaissance, their spirit and effect never ceased to be the same. The great annual parade of the Chinea on June 28 was hardly less splendid than the coronation procession. The Chinea lasted up to 1787, when, after twelve years of contention as to whether the seven thousand ducats sent by the king of Naples was tribute or a voluntary gift, the money was simply deposited and the parade discontinued. The procession began at the Palazzo Colonna and ended at the Vatican. At its head moved the Drummers of the Faithful from the Capitol in red and yellow stripes, and trumpeters with the Colonna standard flying from their instruments. Then came the pope's lancers, officers, cuirassiers, the captain of the Swiss Guard with drummers, the Neapolitan ambassador on horseback, the Swiss Guard, twelve pages, footmen, attendants, and the white mule or horse bearing the seven thousand ducats, followed by more of the Swiss Guard, prelates and cardinals from Naples, four gilt coaches, drawn by six horses and with postillions in red, and many other carriages. It was all concluded by a great reception in the Palazzo Colonna.

And what is true of the material splendors of the coronation and the Chinea is as true of the spiritual splendors of the more deeply religious events that called

to the streets the faithful and the curious from at home
and abroad. From the fourteenth century, on the evening of Holy Friday a great procession of the brothers
of the Gonfalone across the city to the Coliseum took
place. In the jubilee of 1550, fifteen hundred men were
in the procession, three hundred and thirty-five of them
bearing great crosses. In the same year the brothers of
the Cross to the number of twelve hundred wound in
solemn procession from San Marcello, many scourging
themselves as they walked.

In 1581, Montaigne, adopted as a citizen by the city
which, "as it stands now, deserveth to be loved, being
the only common and universal city," witnessed the
exposition of the napkin of Veronica, and afterward
wrote: "All the people were on their knees, crying
misericordia, most of them with tears in their eyes. . . .
There were infinite numbers present. Not only the
church was filled with people; in the Piazza, from as far
as one could see the pulpit and the relic, surged the
press of men and women. Almost all men of considera-
tion belong to brotherhoods, of which there are more
than a hundred, with some especially for strangers.
These brotherhoods perform their offices especially in
Lent, but on this day they march by troupes through
the streets enveloped in mantles, each troupe after its
fashion, in white, red, green, blue, or black, and for the
most part with covered faces. I have never seen anything so noble and so magnificent as the incredible
throng of persons throughout the city at the ceremonies
of the day, and especially these companies. For, besides the great number of others whom we had seen in the
daylight and who had come to Saint Peter's, when the
night fell, with all the brotherhoods marching in order

toward the church, every one with a blazing torch in his hand, almost all of white wax, it seemed as if the whole city had burst into flame. I believe that at least twelve thousand torches passed me where I stood; from eight until midnight the street was continually filled by the procession, which moved with such orderliness and measure that, though the numerous brotherhoods had to assemble from various localities, there were to be seen no gaps or breaks in the line. Every section had its choir, and all were singing as they went. Between the lines went a line of penitents scourging themselves; I counted at least five hundred with pitiably raw and bleeding backs. It is an enigma which I do not yet well understand; they were all cruelly bruised and lacerated, and beat and tormented themselves incessantly. From their countenances, the assurance of their step, the firmness of their speech, for I heard some of them speak and the faces of a number of them were uncovered, one could not detect that they were suffering pain; though there were among them boys of twelve and thirteen. As an attractive-looking and very young man was on his way past me, a young woman among the bystanders expressed pity to see him thus lacerated. He turned to us and said to her, with a smile, 'Do not pity me; not for my own sins am I doing this, but to atone for yours.' . . . Arrived in Saint Peter's, they merely filed past and were shown the Holy Face, and then left the church to give place to others. Women on this day enjoy great freedom. Far into the night the streets are filled with them, nearly all of them on foot; but all play of eyes and coquettish expression are at an end."

Such was the city of the pope-kings. It was first of all the Holy City. Rome was the capital now, not merely

of Europe and the Mediterranean fringes of Africa and
Asia, but of an empire that had crossed the seas and
lodged in strange islands and far-distant continents.
Whatever the mordant comment of Pasquino and the
sharp-tongued people when in moments of irritation
or malice their vision penetrated the envelope of pomp
and pretence and surprised poor humanity in its natural
stature and lineaments, whatever the little tempests of
ecclesiastical and mundane politics that obscured the
vision of pope and prelate, whatever the contempt that
was bred of familiarity in a population reared in the
shadow of the Vatican, the fact of the Church's greatness and of her identity with Rome was seldom long
forgotten by the Romans themselves, and never by the
stranger within the gates. The local was forgotten or
forgiven in the universal. It was not the sceptered sway
of kings that made the city great in the eyes of men and
gave her power over their hearts, but a spiritual authority that had its warrant in the long ages of her own
and her Church's existence, and in the infinite spaces
over which she had diffused the faith.

XII.

ROME AND THE RISORGIMENTO

Ora, o signori, in Roma concorrono tutte le circostanze storiche, intellettuali, morali, che devono determinare le condizioni della capitale di un grande stato. Roma è la sola città d' Italia che non abbia memorie esclusivamente municipali; tutta la storia di Roma, dal tempo dei Cesari al tempo d' oggi, è la storia di una città la cui importanza si estende infinitamente al di là del suo territorio, di una città cioè destinata ad essere la capitale di un grande stato,—

Now, gentlemen, we find meeting in Rome all the circumstances historical, intellectual, and moral which should determine the capital of a great state. Rome is the only city of Italy which has memories not exclusively municipal; the entire history of Rome, from the time of the Cæsars to our own of today, is the history of a city whose importance has extended infinitely beyond its own territory, of a city, that is to say, destined to be the capital of a great state.

Cavour in Parliament, March 25, 1861

necessary, if not indeed imposed, to the Church's essential power.

1.

THE RISE OF MODERN ITALY

THE process by which the Roman Christian Church
came gradually to supplant the Roman pagan
Church was in the way of nature. The process by which
the bishop of Rome came to be the head of the Christian
communities of Italy and the west, and the claimant to
authority over all the Christian world, was quite as
much in the way of nature. In the same manner, it was
natural for the Church, which was the only authority to
survive intact the ruin of the ancient civilization, and
which was frequently invited by circumstance to assume
the control of a world where earthly government had
gone by default, to become in time the sovereign not
only of souls but of material possessions, and in the confusion of temporal and spiritual rights to become entangled in politics and war, thus to lose the directness
of vision and singleness of purpose that characterized
the primitive communities in Christ. And, finally, it
was again natural that, having acquired this double
power, and through use having grown accustomed to
the employment of the temporal to promote the spiritual, and of the spiritual to justify the temporal, the
Church should resist all attempt to deprive her of the
temporal power as an infringement upon her rights, her
dignity, and her usefulness.

If, however, the long course of the papacy's development of the temporal claim did not lack the warrant of
nature, the same is to be said of another process destined
at last to destroy the ecclesiastical claim. The political

unification of Italy and the denial of the Church's right
to hinder it by the exercise of a claim which was un-
necessary, if not indeed opposed, to the Church's essential purpose, was also wholly natural.

And yet, to say that the unification of Italy was
wholly natural is not strictly the truth, however true it
is that the denial of the Church's right to stand in the
way was natural. The presence of the papal state was
not the only obstruction in the path of nationalism.
Nature herself has been an obstruction as well as a
facilitation. A disproportionate length and narrowness,
with altitudes that range from marsh to mountain-top,
have been the causes of great variety in climate, product,
language, and temperament. Again, the barriers of sea
and mountain have always encouraged the separation
of territorial unit from unit, and exaggerated the in-
dividualization of customs and character. Finally, with
these causes is to be counted a racial diversity; the Mediterranean stock and the Indo-European, the Etruscan,
the Greek, the Arab, the Teuton, and the Celt, and the
medley of modern European nations, have all played
parts in sundering community from community and
man from man in a country which for all time has been
noted for the turmoil of cross purposes.

The forces of unification, however, are more powerful than those of separation. The sea on three sides and
the wall of the Alps on the fourth shut Italy off from
easy and rapid communication with the world. Her
language, after all, has been since the beginning of
Roman times a single tongue. Whatever her differences
of altitude, they have not in themselves been sufficient
to cause total divisions of interest; the life of the whole

MAP OF ITALY IN RISORGIMENTO TIMES

SHOWING THE PROCESS OF UNIFICATION

REPRODUCED BY PERMISSION OF CHARLES SCRIBNER'S SONS FROM
PAGE'S ITALY AND THE WORLD WAR

peninsula derives from the soil. Whatever her diversity of race, it is not enough to rob the designation "Italian" of a well-defined content as to complexion, temperament, and bearing.

"Isolated within her natural limits," Napoleon is said to have declared, "she is destined to form a great and powerful nation. Italy is one nation; unity of customs, language, and literature must in a period more or less distant unite her inhabitants under one sole government, and Rome will without the slightest doubt be chosen by the Italians as their capital." "I will make of the scattered peoples of Italy a single nation," he said at Elba in 1814 to the committee of patriot-conspirators who offered him the time-honored title of Emperor of the Romans and King of Italy; "I will give them the unity of customs which they lack, and it will be the most difficult task yet undertaken by me. I will open roads and canals and multiply communications. . . . I will make of Rome a seaport. In twenty years Italy will have a population of thirty millions and will be the most powerful nation in Europe. . . . The foreigner will cease to tread the Capitol, and will never again return."

It is to be added, too, that from the time of the earliest Roman conquests Italy has been a unit in religion. It is still true, after fifty years of freedom from compulsion, that the population of the peninsula is practically of one spiritual mode.

It is frequently said that in 1870 for the first time since Theodoric Italy became a unit. This is true only if it means that then first she was again under the sway of one will. The unity of the later nineteenth century, however, was different from that of Roman times. In

1870 Italy not only became once more the willing subject to a single authority, but for the first time in all
history existed as a unit by herself. The ancient Roman
state was never coterminous with Italy. Before the Roman republic had reduced or persuaded all the peninsula
to obedience, it had come to include Africa, Spain, the
Gauls, and Macedonia, and was in reality an empire.
By Augustan times, the short interval during which, if
at any time, Italy rather than Rome could have claimed
to be the mistress of the world, had passed, and the
peninsula was hardly more than a division among other
divisions of the great empire. When Theodoric's beneficent hand had relaxed in death, and the discords of the
Goths began the long history of disunion which lasted
fourteen hundred years, it was the province rather than
the state of Italy which ceased to exist as a unit.

Nor was the spiritual unity of that Italy which
emerged from the chaos of barbarian invasion and native
decadence a unity of the national sort, but of the universal. Not the bounds of Italy, but the bounds of the
world, were the limits of the spiritual empire. And when
in the earliest dawn of the Renaissance the idea of Italy
as a political unit came into being, it was hardly the conception of Italy as a self-sufficing, national entity. The
call of Rienzo to the cities of Italy in 1347 to unite in
federation under the presidency of Rome was not
sprung of nationalism, but of the desire to revive the
glories of ancient Rome. It was Rome that was to be
glorified, not Italy. Petrarch's appeal to the tribune,
like the tribune's call, was the result of regret for the
past rather than of vision into the future.

The cry of Pope Julius the Second, *Fuori i barbari!*—
"Out with the barbarians!" was again not the cry of

patriotism later to make itself heard in the impassioned
"Forth from Italy, O stranger!" of Garibaldi's hymn,—

> *Va fuora d' Italia, va fuora ch' è l' ora,*
> *Va fuora d' Italia, va fuora, o stranier!*

The warrior-pope voiced the passion of a strong man
irritated by opposition and of a people wearied by war
and taxation, but hardly as yet the patriotism of a nation. It was the cry of an Italian, but not of an Italian
whose first longing was the unity of Italy; it was the
cry of an ecclesiastic who would have welcomed the
liberation of Italy only on condition of its subjugation
to his own will. It was not far from Julius' own prime
that Machiavelli laid at the door of the papacy the impossibility of making Italy into a single state; basing
his imputation, as others have based their approval of
it, upon the reading of a history which reveals the
papacy taking thought rather of its own estate than of
the welfare of Italy as an entity, and again and again
inviting the foreigner in to crush Italians who set themselves in opposition to the papal will. From the times
when Pepin and Charlemagne, called to the aid of the
Church by Stephen the Second and Hadrian the First,
made the papacy a territorially interested partner in the
affairs of monarchs, to the days of Napoleon the Third
and Pius the Ninth, the invaders of Italy were drawn
by the solicitations of the pope in straits, or were provoked by his interference, or were otherwise concerned
in the ambitions of the Church.

Had Italy at any time before the modern era been
really capable of unification, there was one juncture of
circumstances when the papacy, stripped of temporal
possessions and crushed as a political power, could have

offered no opposition. When Charles the Fifth's army under the constable of Bourbon had taken the city of the popes and destroyed its friends so far as they were his own enemies, his will could have organized the peninsula into a state. But the time was not ripe for an Italian state. The age had hardly passed yet in which the imperial ideal was unquestioned; the age of national consciousness, later to create a new map of Europe, had hardly begun. The state was still the prince, the empire the emperor. Three centuries more were to elapse before men in the mass began to be united in common aspiration for national independence.

When the new movement began, the French revolution was at the same time its effect and cause. Accomplished by a great wave of popular indignation against the presumption of aristocratic government, maintained at first by resistance to and then by aggression against the enemies who sought the annihilation of its purpose, the French revolution spread through Europe the ideas which made the nineteenth century the most significant in the history of the western races. Whatever its failures, its great achievement was to discredit the past, and to clear the way.

With the opening of the century, the spirit of change which affected the life of all Europe elsewhere touched Italy also as with a flame. The times were filled with significant events,—the Italian campaign of Napoleon in 1796, the formation of the Cisalpine republic, the invasion of the Legations and the seizure of Bologna and the Romagna in 1797, the Roman republic of 1798, with the overthrow of the papacy, and the captivity, exile, and death of Pius the Sixth, the incorporation of the papal dominions into the French empire in 1804, the transformation of the Cisalpine republic into the kingdom of Italy in 1805, the declaration of the end of the temporal power in 1809 and the captivity of Pius the Seventh, and the subjection of Italy to the will of the militant champion of human rights. All these were acts of violence which roused both enthusiasms and hatreds, but their great effect over and above this was the quickening of thought and feeling throughout the peninsula. It mattered little that at the downfall of Napoleon the congress of Vienna reëstablished as far as possible the status of Europe before the war, and that Italy especially, divided into Piedmont and Savoy under Victor Emmanuel the First, Lombardy and Venetia under Francis of Austria, Modena and Reggio under the Austrian archduke Francis of Este, Parma and Piacenza under Maria Louisa, daughter of the emperor of Austria and wife of Napoleon, Lucca under Maria Louisa of Spain, Tuscany under the archduke Ferdinand of Austria, Naples and Sicily under Ferdinand the Fourth, and the papal states, was again in the usual condition of dismemberment. If there was not outward and visible union, there was an inner union one day to bring it about. The Italians had caught glimpses of the possibility of unification, progressive ideas had followed in the wake of the French army and the French régime, and dead matter had been galvanized into life. Henceforth Italy was in a ferment which increased yearly and hourly until she developed the ideal and realized the rights of a national life. The story of Italy's rise is one of the most stirring in the annals of the struggle of mankind for liberty.

To fix a date on which the movement for the liberation of Italy was begun would hardly be more possible than to name the person who first conceived it as an ideal to be aspired to. The rise of the secret society of the Carbonari, who first became distinctly influential in 1808, was not far from the active beginning of the struggle. By his treatment of the two Piuses and his creation, if only for the moment, of a united Italy, Napoleon had shown both that the papacy was not divinely immune and that an Italy was possible. Alfieri had lived and died protesting against his country's tyrants, and Foscolo was giving noble utterance to the aspiration for liberty. Of the three hundred and sixty thousand Italian soldiers who campaigned in Napoleon's armies between 1796 and 1814, enough had already mingled thoughts one with another and with the outside world to diminish provincialism and to encourage the national idea. The spirit of discontent with a dismembered and shackled Italy, already active under the tyrannous régime of the French revolution in the peninsula, needed only the change from this tyranny to that of the returned reactionary despots in 1815 to convert it into the consuming zeal of martyrdom.

The Carbonari movement spread like fire before the wind. Other societies of like import sprang into being. There were the American Hunters at Ravenna, of which Byron was a member, the Savages of the university of Padua, the Sons of Mars in the Romagna, and more. An unsuccessful attempt at revolution in Macerata and Bologna took place in 1817. In 1820, following on the Spanish constitution forced by Riego, occurred the first of the explosions that from now on mark the progress of Italy toward freedom and unity. Tumultuous uprisings took place in Naples and Palermo, and a constitution was wrung from Ferdinand. In March, 1821, a rising in Piedmont caused the abdication of Victor Emmanuel the First, and the willing young Charles Albert granted a constitution on the model of the Spanish. It was immediately disavowed by Charles Felix, who degraded the prince and routed the constitutionalists not long after the Austrians had defeated Guglielmo Pepe and the reformers of Naples and reinstated Ferdinand. For nearly ten years the patriotic movement was without visible manifestation, and absolutism seemed firmly restored.

Meanwhile, however, Leopardi had inspired a burning sense of shame in the hearts of his countrymen, Manzoni had made them feel the need of moral regeneration as the great condition of patriotism, and Pellico was soon to rouse them to furious anger by the recital of his wrongs and those of his compatriots in the prisons of Austria. Repression and violence served only to intensify the heat of the flame. Rebellion against despotism, whether that of the Austrian, the Piedmontese, or the holy seat at Rome, became a passion that amounted to religion. What the ancient Christian had suffered for the Christian commonwealth, the Italian patriot now suffered for the cause of freedom.

The hatred in the provinces under Austrian dominion was twofold; there was the hatred of tyranny, and the hatred of the foreigner. The desire of the patriot was above all to drive the stranger from the throne and from the land. Beyond that, he hardly reasoned, farther than to take for granted that the blessings of liberty would follow of themselves, and all be well with Italy. It was a process of years before the blind passion for freedom was purified and refined and sanctified into the reasoned and unswerving purpose of national unification.

In July, 1830, the success of the Paris revolution inspired fresh hope in Italy. In 1831, the repressed energies of Italian patriotism burst their bounds a second time. Tumults in Palermo, the arrest of Menotti in Modena, and the uprisings in the papal states,—at Bologna, Imola, Faenza, and elsewhere,—which at every turn confronted the newly crowned Gregory the Sixteenth, caused all Italy to glow with patriotic feeling. It was during this year that Young Italy was organized, the creation of Mazzini, and from now on there were few years not marked by some venture for liberty. It was only through Austrian intervention that Gregory was able to retain authority over the papal dominions. In February, 1832, not to yield first place in the defence of the Church to Austria, France occupied the port of Ancona, where, from 1832 to 1838, she retained the office of protector while Austria assumed a similar duty in the provinces known as the Legations because of their administration by papal legates.

Meanwhile Mazzini continued to plot. Garibaldi, who had met him at Marseilles, had been exiled after the attempt upon Piedmont in 1834, and, with heart in Italy, was fighting the battles of freedom in South America. In 1841, there were one hundred and fifty arrests in Aquila. In 1842, a movement to revolt in the papal states and Naples resulted in nothing, but the spirit that roused it lost nothing of its power. The Italian Legion sprang into being as a parallel to Young Italy. In 1843, a hundred suspects were arrested in the province of Salerno. Gioberti's *Moral and Civil Primacy of the Italian People* was published, to be followed in 1844 by Cesare Balbo's *Hopes of Italy,* and together with Balbo's book to take the place of a throttled press as the means of spreading the patriotic idea. In the same year, the arrest of conspirators in Calabria, and the shooting of the brothers Bandiera, aroused feeling more intense than ever. In 1845, a revolt in Rimini brought various places in the papal states under martial law.

In 1848 and 1849 occurred the third of the great explosions, more violent than its predecessors. Partly owing to the universal spirit of revolution in Europe, partly to the culmination of local feeling, encouraged by the liberalism of Pius the Ninth, and partly owing to the example of France, risings took place throughout the peninsula. On New Year's day, and on February 8 and 10, there were movements at Rome whose suppression necessitated the use of arms. In March, Charles Albert granted the famous constitution in Piedmont. The pope in his turn proclaimed a constitution at Rome. The famous Five Days in March at Milan were followed by the five months' campaign of Charles Albert which ended in his defeat and the reëstablishment of Austrian power. The republic of Venice was declared. The pope revealed himself as opposed to the war, and in November was finally compelled to leave his capital. In 1849, the army of Charles Albert was again driven back. The Roman republic was proclaimed, to be terminated after a brief existence by the expedition from France under Oudinot. The soldiers of Catholic Europe restored the papal sway, and Venice fell once more under Austrian rule.

Meanwhile Cavour was becoming a power. His influence increased the prestige of Piedmont, intensified the idea of nationality, and widened the breach between the ecclesiastical state and Piedmont, now the recognized champion of the Italian state. The Siccardi laws in 1850 abolished ecclesiastical courts and immunities, diminished useless holidays, and suppressed the giving of legacy without the consent of the state. In April, Pius the Ninth returned, and the reactionary cardinal Antonelli became his prime minister. In 1851, the sensational letters of Gladstone, revealing the horrors of Neapolitan rule, were published. Absolutists in Italy took fresh courage at the news of Louis Napoleon's extinction of the French republic. In 1852, the Mantuan conspirators whose arrest, trial, and torture had occupied two years, were condemned and executed. The bill for Civil Marriage, argued with intense heat by the nationalists and furiously opposed by clericals, was withdrawn. In 1853, an attempt at revolution in Rome was thwarted. In 1854 and 1855, Piedmont won the good will of the Powers by participation in the Crimean war. The Rattazzi bill was passed, abolishing three hundred and thirty-four religious houses involving five thousand five hundred and six monks and nuns, but leaving still untouched two hundred and seventy-four houses belonging to twenty-one orders and involving four thousand and fifty persons. In 1858, the gradual increase of cordiality between Napoleon and Cavour, grounded in general good will toward Italy, culminated in the understanding of Plombières. "Have confidence in me, as I have confidence in you," the emperor said as they parted.

In 1859 and 1860 occurred the fourth outburst. The seven weeks' campaign of Piedmont and France against Austria, with its victories of Montebello, Palestro, Magenta, Melegnano, and Solferino, accompanied by risings in the papal cities and active sympathy everywhere, was concluded by the sudden peace of Villafranca, the cession of Lombardy, the disappointing retention of

Venetia, and the speechless indignation of the friends of Italy at the to them at the time incomprehensible act of Napoleon, who foresaw Prussian interference, in treating at the moment when their utmost hopes were seemingly assured.

But the march of freedom was not halted. By the plebiscite of March 11 and 12, 1860, Tuscany and the Emilia united themselves to Piedmont. The distrust of those who suspected selfish motives in Piedmont, the unwillingness of Piedmontese statesmen to risk the provocation of France by declaring a united Italy to be their ultimate purpose, now vanished entirely. On the sixth of May, the Thousand embarked for Sicily, and by October 9 the revolution of Sicily and Naples was accomplished, and Garibaldi at the Volturno saluted Victor Emmanuel the Second, whose army had invaded and annexed the papal states up to Rome and the immediate patrimony, as king of Italy. In 1861, the first Italian parliament met at Turin.

There still remained outside the national communion the province of Venetia, the Trieste region, the Trentino, and the city of Rome and its environs. The Venetian question was settled in 1866, when Italy as the ally of Prussia in the swift defeat of Austria received Venetia as her reward. The Roman question was less easy of solution. Garibaldi's expedition, ending with his wound and arrest at Aspromonte in 1862, was but one sign of the inevitable result. The pope's encyclical of 1864, maintaining rigidly every ecclesiastical claim to sovereignty over the papal state, was a contrary sign of the same result. The Catholic party was influential with Napoleon, who would not consent to farther reduction of the papal sovereignty; by the convention of 1864, the

Italian government was to protect the papal frontier, to allow the papal state a reasonable army, and to remove the capital to Florence, while France in two years was to recall her soldiers.

But the establishment of the capital at Florence did not realize the emperor's plan of insuring Rome against farther encroachment. In 1867, the second attempt of Garibaldi against the papal capital, ending with the failure at Mentana, preceded by the death of the brothers Cairoli at Villa Glori, was a failure which only manifested a determination that would not accept defeat.

The dogma of Infallibility, in July, 1870, was by many looked upon as the discharge of a last vain weapon. When in August, 1870, the French troops sailed from Civitavecchia to the aid of Napoleon, soon at Sedan to bid farewell to all his greatness, the last material defence of the papal state was removed. The breach in the wall of Aurelian at the Porta Pia on the twentieth of September, and the plebiscite of October 2, made Rome the capital of the United Kingdom of Italy and Sicily. On December 5 there took place at Florence the first parliament of Italy entire, and on the second of July, 1871, occurred the formal transfer of the capital to Rome, marked by Victor Emmanuel's occupation of the Quirinal, the establishment of the chamber of deputies in the Palazzo Chigi, in the Piazza di Montecitorio, and of the senate in the Madama. The pope, refusing to recognize the law of Guarantees, except in so far as its provisions confirmed him in the possession of the Vatican and its grounds, declared himself a prisoner, and adopted the policy of ignoring the Italian state.

THE CAIROLI TREE AT VILLA GLORI

THE SCENE OF ENRICO CAIROLI'S DEATH IN 1867;
CESARE PASCARELLA CELEBRATES THE CAIROLI ADVENTURE
IN HIS ROMANESCO POEM VILLA GLORI

2.

THE NATIONAL MOVEMENT
AND ROME

THUS had Italy arisen to take her place among the
free nations of Europe. Trieste and Trent alone,
with their adjacent territories reaching up to where
nature herself has drawn the boundary line along the
mountain ridges, were left to be redeemed at a future
day. Eternal Rome had again become the capital of a
united and willing people.

What was the part played by Rome the city in this
drama of nearly a hundred years?

It can hardly be said that nineteenth century Rome
pursued the ideal of Italian freedom and unity with the
same intensity of passion and the same singleness of
purpose as many a sister city. Before she is charged with
indifference or neglect, however, account should be
taken of certain special circumstances.

In the first place, Rome was already in her own right
the capital of an Italian state in which the ruler, whatever his abuse of power, was always Italian, and always
the venerated head of a state whose limits far tran-
scended the bounds of the papal provinces, and of Europe itself. To desire the expulsion of such a ruler, or
to consent to his forced, or even voluntary, withdrawal,
was for a long time far from the thought of all but a
few extremists. The Rome of modern times without the
popes would have gone far toward becoming a desert,
as the Rome of the Dark Ages, without the accident of
their lodgment in her, would have remained a desert.

What those who came to be disaffected wished was never the absence of the pope, but his renunciation of the temporal power in favor of the Italian state.

In the second place, not even in the wish for this renunciation was there a perfect unanimity. There never ceased to be a party, nor has it yet disappeared, which believed not only in the Church but in the papal claim to sovereignty over Rome and the ecclesiastical state. There were those who believed in it sincerely on dogmatic and historic grounds, and there were those who believed in it on practical grounds. Both were convinced that the good of religion required that the Church at Rome should be apparelled in the splendors of a court and that her head should move with the monarchs of Europe.

There were those who stood for the papal right for reasons less ideal. There were the more thoughtful who would have considered it a misfortune for the city to lose the social and material benefits of papal munificence; there was the populace who enjoyed the spectacles and profited by the bounties of the Church as bestowed in the form of employment, charity, or largess; and there was the bureaucratic class, a multitude of dignitaries and petty office-holders, clerical and secular, in city and province, with the army of those who directly or indirectly depended upon their will, and whose unanimous desire was for the preservation of things as they were.

And there was still another force besides sincere conviction and material self-interest to retard the rise of nationalism in Rome. There was also a spiritual self-interest. Its disappearance required education and time. The natural deference to worldly authority was rein-

forced by the dread of disapproval by pope and Church.
Not even the most enlightened and independent found
pleasure in the prospect of running counter to the power
that had their souls in keeping and by the pronounce-
ment of solemn words could open a gulf between themselves and the great communion. The ignorant and
superstitious, who lacked the support of reason, would
hardly risk the damnation kept before their minds by
a clergy who could be astute when not sincere. The
yellow badge of excommunication, worn pinned on the
hat, with all the distress of mind and body it brought to
those thus set apart from the fellowship of heaven and
earth, was still in vogue as late as the coming of the
French, who hastened its disappearance. The Romanesco poet Belli, whose sonnets up to 1847 are filled with
satire on the papal government, became in later days
the prey to spiritual fears and knew no limit in his
penitence.

In a word, Rome was still papal Rome, still governed
by a power which, if it could have separated distinctly
between purely spiritual and purely civic authority,
would have found it on many occasions inconvenient to
do so. It was in this respect not unlike other cities of
the papal dominions except in degree; but the degree
was great. It was very much unlike cities like Bologna,
beyond the Apennines, or Milan and Venice, outside the
papal state, where the immediate and sweeping expulsion of the stranger and the establishment of Italian
sovereignty were remedies opposed by none but the
timid and the time-serving few.

It is customary to think of the patriotic movement as
being obstructed by two powers: one, the despotism of
Austria, Naples, and the petty Italian states, and the

other, the papal state. These two forces, however, were not wholly distinct one from the other. They were in reality homogeneous. The papacy was an obstruction, not in its character as a religious entity, but because it was an absolutism precisely like other despotisms of Italy. Pius the Seventh, reverting to repressive methods, Leo the Twelfth, fiercely reactionary, Pius the Eighth, fulminating against secret societies, Gregory the Sixteenth and Pius the Ninth, ruling by the aid of foreign bayonets, and all of them resorting to imprisonment and exile as remedies for disaffection, are to be classed, in so far as their contact with the nationalists is concerned, not as heads of the Church, but as despotical monarchs. The nationalists did not forsake the religion of their fathers nor disbelieve in the Church's authority so far as it was exercised over the conscience; it was against the pope as a political obstacle that their opposition was directed. If their acts at times took on the color of hostility to the holy seat, it was because the pope's misuse of religion as a weapon of political coercion provoked rebellion. It was the double character of the papal resistance that placed the popes as the enemies of Italian freedom in a class apart from other despots.

Such considerations as these will make clear why Rome in general from the beginning of the French revolution to the rise of Piedmont as the declared champion of Italian statehood in 1848 retained a conservative character. Her manifestations of impatience were neither frequent nor pronounced, and were more often the result of local dissatisfactions than of patriotic purpose. It was not until the middle of the nineteenth century that she had become educated to the high conception that animated the great souls of Italy.

The outbreak of the French revolution and the proclamation of the republic resulted in the immediate suspension of diplomatic relations between France and Rome. A French banker resident in the city, however, and performing the duties of consul, hoisted over his habitation the arms of the new state. Opposed in this act by the cardinal secretary of state of Pius the Sixth, he was supported by the French minister at Naples, who in the name of the republic ordered the raising of the insignia again within twenty-four hours. To make sure of the execution of the order, and to cultivate such sympathizers with France as might be at Rome, he despatched to the city Hugo Basseville, secretary of the French legation, and with him a naval officer. On the thirteenth of January, 1793, the display of the insignia at his order over the door of the Palazzo Salviati, then the seat of the French Academy, raised so fierce a storm of anger that Basseville, driving down the Corso with his wife and son and several compatriots, all wearing the cockade, which he had caused widely to be distributed, was stoned the length of the street, and finally, after the infuriation of the mob by the discharge of a pistol in the hands of one of the party, was killed on the steps of his residence for the time, the Palazzo Palombara, in the Via dell' Impresa. The event caused a frenzy of joy. A chorus of poets great and small celebrated it in sonnets, and the populace after its own manner of expression.

To the Roman of 1793, every Frenchman was the enemy of Rome, of the pope, and of God. "Holy Father," runs one of the versified utterances of the time, which represents the savage spirit of them all, "give us leave to kill the Frenchmen every one; and then grant us indulgence, and we will go into their country and annihilate the breed. So will thrones remain undisturbed." Two *stornelli* are no less bloodthirsty:

> *Me so' fatto un cortello genovese,*
> *Che ce sbucio le porte delle case;*
> *Figurete una pancia de francese,—*

> I've made me a Genoese knife
> That I could rip open a house-door with;
> Say nothing of a Frenchman's belly!

> *Fiore de rapa:*
> *Magna l' alio, francese, schiatta, crepa,*
> *Ma qui se more pe' difenne er Papa,—*

> Flower of the turnip:
> Eat your garlic, Frenchman, split, burst,
> But here we defend the Pope to the death!

The murderers of Basseville went unpunished; but the killing of General Duphot, attendant on Joseph Bonaparte, ambassador of the republic, in a riot before the official quarters in the Palazzo Corsini on December 28, 1797, did not find the way of revenge so difficult. The Directorate immediately ordered Napoleon to occupy Rome, which General Berthier's army found no difficulty in doing on February 13, 1798, having first allowed three hundred Romans to declare their freedom from the papacy in the Campo Vaccino, as the Forum was still called, and to invite him in. The Roman republic was proclaimed, and Pius the Sixth was given forty-eight hours to make ready for departure from the Quirinal and the city. "You can die in any place," was the answer to the dignified eighty-years-old pope's prayer to be allowed to end his days in Rome.

The republic received some support from patricians

and middle class, but was met by the fiercest opposition on the part of the lower order. On the twenty-fifth, five days after the venerable and infirm pontiff had left the city by the Porta Angelica for Valence and captivity, the people rose against Berthier, rushed from the Trastevere across the Ponte Sisto to the Piazza Navona, the Piazza di Spagna, and other centers, killed a number of French sympathizers, and then, having turned inconsequentially, after the manner of mobs in Rome, to sack the Ghetto, were scattered by the soldiery. Two hundred prisoners were taken and tried, and twenty-two were convicted and shot.

The levies of the French in 1797, together with their character as revolutionists and enemies of the Church, had been the cause of the riots that ended in Duphot's death. They had taken within four months over thirty-two million francs, and the art treasures confiscated by them required a million francs for transportation. The plundering and extortion continued in 1798. Private citizens were the objects of special assessment; the princes Borghese and Piombino were obliged each to pay one hundred and thirty thousand scudi, the princes Colonna and Doria eighty thousand each.

Pasquino and Marforio were not unobservant. On a festal day when two statues were seen, a larger one representing the French republic and inscribed *Magnæ Matri,* To the Great Mother, and a smaller one representing the Roman republic and inscribed *Filia Grata,* Her Grateful Daughter, Marforio, who had small Latin, demanded: "Pasquino, what does it say?" "Simple enough," answered Pasquino, in his native Romanesco; *"la madre magna, e la figlia,—si gratta:* the mother eats, and the daughter—scratches!" Another

day Marforio greets his friend with, *"Pasquino, è vero
che i francesi sono tutti ladri,*—Pasquino, is it true that
the French are all robbers?" *"Tutti no,"* replies Pasquino, *"ma buona parte,*—not all, but a good part
(Bonaparte)."

Pius the Sixth died at Valence on the Rhone the
twenty-ninth of August, 1799. The part played by Pius
the Seventh was hardly so dignified. After the concordat
with Napoleon in 1801, by which four hundred million
francs' worth of church property was given over, the
pope was persuaded on December 2, 1804, to crown his
tyrant emperor at Paris. Pasquino, somewhat less than
charitable to the unfortunate pope, who acted in honest
effort to make the emperor a friend of religion and the
Church, contrasted him with his predecessor in a stinging epigram:

> *Pio Sesto, per conservar la fede,*
> *Perdè la sede;*
> *Pio Settimo, per conservar la sede,*
> *Perdè la fede,*—
>
> Pius the Sixth, his faith not to forsake,
> Gave up his throne;
> Pius the Seventh, his throne more sure to make,
> Gave up his faith.

Yet, whether we call the pope's action subservience
to the imperial greatness, or dignify it as diplomatic
wisdom, it did not suffice to protect the holy seat. The
papal state was made part of the French empire and of
the kingdom of Italy; and in 1808, having dared in a
last desperate act of defiance to excommunicate the
spoilers of the Church, the pope on July 5 was taken
by force from the Quirinal palace and conducted to

France over the same route as that traversed by his predecessor, to find himself at last an exile in the château at Fontainebleau. In 1809, the temporal power was declared at an end.

The return of Pius the Seventh on May 24, 1814, marked the sudden termination at Rome of the revolutionary period with its uncertainties and disorders, and the equally sudden coming of reaction. The excesses of the French and the revolutionary partisans, and especially the wrongs and absence of the pope, had prepared the city for the return of absolutism in exaggerated form. True to its character as an eternal city and the capital of the Church, it had not allowed itself to become unduly excited by the later eighteenth century movements in letters and philosophy. A few of its intellectuals had considered the new ideas curiously, contemplatively, and academically, but the city had never been really touched by them. The Inquisition and the Index, suspended under Clement the Fourteenth, were again set in motion, though the Inquisition never with its old-time violence, and the Jesuit order was reinstated. The arbitrary and repressive measures of Pius the Seventh, who in other circumstances would have been a ruler of much more liberal spirit, were increased in number and aggravated in character by his successors, Leo the Twelfth, Pius the Eighth, and Gregory the Sixteenth, to such an extent that from almost unanimous support of the popes against not only the French but every liberal tendency, the population of Rome and the papal states gradually passed to the spirit of rebellion against the exercise of civil authority by the holy seat, and became enthusiastic for independence. The character of the popes and their government is indicated, if by nothing else, by the fact that the common people of Rome and the rank and file of the provincials, who were their most fanatical defenders while the French were in power, soon after the reaction came to be the source of movements against them. One of the most wicked of the pasquinades went the rounds after the death of Leo the Twelfth by an operation:

> *Al chirurgo s' appone*
> *La morte di Leone;*
> *Roma però sostiene*
> *Che egli ha operato bene,—*

> The death of Pope Leo
> People lay to the doctor;
> But a different result
> Rome says would have shocked her.

When Gregory the Sixteenth came to the throne, the papal states were ablaze with sedition and overt rebellion, and the period of forty years had begun during which the throne was kept from falling only by the support of foreign diplomacy and foreign soldiery. The Carbonari and Young Italy and the Italian Legion now found Rome as well as places remoter from the holy seat a good recruiting-ground. The names of Mazzini and Garibaldi began to employ Roman lips also.

The immense relief of the Romans at the death of Gregory the Sixteenth in 1846 was followed by the boundless popularity of Pius the Ninth. The government was actively reformed in the direction of liberalism, and for two years its head was the idol of Rome and the hope of Italian patriots. These were the days when the genial Angelo Brunetti, called Ciceruacchio, was "the

Pope's Angel," and gathered the common people about the carriage of the handsome and benign pontiff to form his escort while they shouted enthusiastic *vivas*. Nor were the aristocracy behind in their support; all classes vied with each other in the demonstration of loyalty.

Both pope and people, however, were soon to be disillusioned. The people were unanimously loyal only so long as they believed in the pope's friendliness toward liberalism and the movement for the rescue of Italy from the Austrian. The methods of Gregory the Sixteenth and his Teutonic patrons, which provoked the memorandum of the Powers in 1831, had by this time kindled a spirit not to be quenched. Even before the granting of the Tuscan constitution or the news of the French revolution of 1848, the Romans had helped to initiate the series of risings which were to occupy the next two years. On New Year's day of 1848, while the Milanese were inaugurating their famous non-smoking campaign, their brethren in Rome engaged in demonstrations which had to be suppressed by the papal troops. Other disturbances on February 8 and 10 were quieted by the promise of an increase in the proportion of lay ministers. On March 14, ten days after the constitution of Charles Albert in Piedmont, Pius the Ninth felt obliged to promulgate the Roman constitution. Four days after this, the fury of Milan burst its bounds, and Austria suddenly found herself driven from Lombardy and Venice. However great the enthusiasm of the Romans for Pius the Ninth, their enthusiasm for the Italian cause rose far above it. Angelo Brunetti was its symbol in the flesh, and headed the popular demonstrations. Twelve thousand volunteers soon left Rome for the front.

But in the midst of the Italian army's successful

sweep across Lombardy came the startling news of the pope's allocution, in which for the first time he made it clear that the liberal program was not suited to the interests of the papacy: he could not allow himself to be a partner in the humiliation of Austria, the friend of the Church. The immediate resignation of his ministry, with a two days' threat of revolution in Rome, showed unmistakably the length to which the patriotic movement had gone, and made clear the relative strength of the temporal power and the nationalist cause.

The Romans had never suffered greater disappointment. In vain did the pope create a new ministry on the fourth of May, with the liberal Mamiani at its head. From April 29, the date of the allocution, began the swift descent of the temporal power; on that date for the first time the temporal subjects of the pope were in a majority for Italy and against the temporal claim.

The disastrous end of the Italian campaign at Custozza on July 25 did not improve the temper of Roman patriots. The pope attempted to strengthen his position by the appointment on September 16 of Pellegrino Rossi as prime minister; but the combination of popular ill humor and ministerial firmness provoked the murder of the able diplomat on November 15 on the steps of the Cancelleria. By the twenty-fifth of November, conditions were so ominous that the pope took to flight and sought refuge as the guest of King Ferdinand at Gaeta.

On December 29, the triumvirate into whose hands the guidance of Rome had been placed soon after the flight of Pius the Ninth announced a constituent assembly for February 5. On February 9, the one hundred and forty-four members of this assembly who had been elected on January 21 proclaimed from the Capitol the

Roman republic. At first under the triumvirs, Mazzini, Armellini, and Saffi, later under two consuls, twelve tribunes, and assembly, the object of papal enmity and the outraged feeling of Catholics abroad, and from the beginning doomed to failure, the Roman republic of 1849 in its five months' existence was nevertheless one of the most inspiring episodes in the life of Eternal Rome.

On March 23, when the republic was six weeks old, the brief and inglorious campaign of Charles Albert had already come to an end with Novara and the abdication of the king. On April 6, the French expedition to reinstate the pope was determined on, and on the twentieth it sailed, the day on which Pius the Ninth removed any remaining vestige of doubt by disowning every liberal act. The republicans of Rome, however, were not shaken in their determination. Mazzini had reached the city soon after the republic was proclaimed. Garibaldi, who had left his command in the northern part of the states of the Church in December for a flying visit to Rome, and had gone again in February as member of the assembly from Macerata, rode into the city a last time on April 27 with his Italian legion, thirteen hundred intelligent, enthusiastic, adventure-loving spirits, largely from the commercial and artisan classes, who were ready for anything in the cause of reform.

"He has come!" the cry travelled down the Corso as they rode to quarters in San Silvestro. The Eternal City had never seen such troopers. They were sunburned, dusty, shaggy, and gaunt, with conical hats and black, waving plumes, and their leader on his white horse in the midst of them was a wonderful figure. Among the legionaries were forty-two lancers under Angelo Ma-

sina, the wealthy young Bolognese who had forsaken a
life of ease and pleasure to devote his all to the struggle
for Italian freedom. On the twenty-ninth came the gallant young Milanese noble, Luciano Manara, with his
troop of six hundred Lombard bersaglieri. The defenders of the Roman republic numbered in all some
nine thousand men.

On the thirtieth of April, the army of Oudinot advanced from Civitavecchia to the western corner of the
Leonine city walls. Surprised to find no longer in existence the Porta Pertusa, which in the event of need they
had intended to force, surprised also at being received
with cannon-shots from the Romans, who were expected
to be neither numerous nor courageous enough to offer
actual resistance, the French columns proceeded east-
ward along the walls to the Porta Cavalleggeri, where,
again meeting opposition, they turned about and made
the circuit of the Leonine fortification to the Porta Angelica on the north, equally to no purpose.

Meanwhile Garibaldi, at the Porta San Pancrazio,
ordered out of the Villa Pamfili a body of youthful
defenders stationed there and despatched them toward
the Leonine city to take the enemy on the flank. As they
left the villa and were crossing the deep Via Aurelia
Antica, they were surprised by a French column which
had been detached by Oudinot, in passing, for the very
purpose of cutting off any such movement. The spirited
fight that followed left the Romans finally in possession
of the Pamfili and its surroundings, which, by reason of
their elevation, dominated the Porta San Pancrazio and
the neighboring bastions in the wall of Urban the
Eighth, and were necessary to the holding of the Janiculum, there at its highest point. It also left the French

THE GARIBALDI MONUMENT IN ROME

IT OVERLOOKS THE CITY FROM THE JANICULUM
NEAR THE GARIBALDI HEADQUARTERS OF 1849

commander convinced that for the present he was not
strong enough to enter the city. Withdrawing on the
road to Civitavecchia, for the next four weeks he saw
to the reinforcement of his army, securing time for the
safe prosecution of this purpose by conspiring with his
government to send the innocent young Ferdinand de
Lesseps to treat with the Romans on conditions sure to
be refused. Garibaldi spent the month in confounding
the Neapolitan armies at Palestrina and Velletri.

At three o'clock on the morning of June 3, while the
Romans were resting secure in the understanding that
Oudinot had promised not to attack before the fourth,
the French blew in the roadside wall near the chapel of
San Pancrazio, penetrated the extensive grounds of the
Villa Pamfili and the Villa Corsini, and drove the Romans out. Garibaldi and his men, quartered in and near
the convent of San Silvestro, now the post office of
Rome, were roused by messengers. The chief rushed his
men to the piazza of Saint Peter's, and thence by the
Via di San Pancrazio, just north of the Acqua Paola
and San Pietro in Montorio, to the scene of action, while
the bells of all the city rang the alarm. Manara and the
bersaglieri, through misunderstanding, were held in the
Roman Forum, and did not arrive until eight.

From dawn until dark of the memorable day, Garibaldi from just outside the Porta San Pancrazio directed the fight, calling for additional men as he needed
them from the troopers assembled and awaiting orders
in the vacant fields inside the gate where now stands the
American Academy. The Villa Corsini, at the head of
the slope two-thirds of a mile from the gate, and ap-
proachable only through the long and narrow pass
formed by the high walls of the road, continued by the

avenue that led to its broad flights of stairs, was the sole
objective of the Garibaldian attack. Again and again
the troopers took the word from their commander at
the gate and dashed down the road and up the avenue
under the murderous fire, leaving the way lined and
the villa terraces and stairs covered with their dead.
Again and again the French, well sheltered and with
abundant reserves, repulsed them, or at most yielded
a momentary possession until reinforced from the Pamfili behind them. Angelo Masina fell early in the day,
and his body lay under fire on the steps of the Corsini
for that and the succeeding days. With him fell Enrico
Dandolo, one of Luciano Manara's captains, the elder
of two spirited and lovable brothers of twenty-one and
nineteen, and Daverio, Garibaldi's chief of staff. Nino
Bixio, later of the Thousand, was wounded. In the last
furious charge, at dusk, when the Corsini and the chapel
of San Pancrazio were once more taken but found impossible to hold, the beloved Goffredo Mameli, then
twenty-one years old, and at nineteen the author of
Fratelli d' Italia, received the wound that one month
later caused his death. The desperate day ended at last
with the French in sure possession of the Pamfili and the
Corsini, and the Garibaldians and Manara in the Vascello, just at the villa entrance.

From the fourth of June until the second, of July,
Rome was in a state of siege. The Garibaldians held the
Vascello and the Casa Giacometti, now Scarpone's, both
across the road from the Corsini and less than a fourth
of a mile apart, and the lofty Villa Savorelli, just inside
the Porta San Pancrazio where now stands the Villa
Aurelia, built into and almost entirely composed of its
scarred remains, besides the bastions of Urban's wall to

the south of the gate. There could be only one conclusion to the matter, and there was none who did not know it well; yet the divine instinct of patriotism kept the defenders of one mind until the very end, and in defeat made perfect an example which was of greater effect than many victories. The Giacometti, the Vascello, and Garibaldi's headquarters in the Savorelli were slowly battered into ruin, the French line of trenches advanced yard by yard, until in the darkness of early morning on June 21 the Central and Barberini bastions were breached and taken, the Casa Giacometti was abandoned, and only the Vascello, captained by Giacomo Medici with what was left of the Medici Legion, held out. The French were at last within the walls of Rome.

The Romans now made a new line behind the remnants of Aurelian's wall where it ran across the open spaces and down the hill, with a battery under the pines where now is the garden next San Pietro in Montorio. From now on, the Garibaldian headquarters were in the adjoining Villa Spada, today Nobilia. In this house, for over a week the crumbling target of the French artillery, Luciano Manara, at twenty-four the veteran of many gallant fights, rendered up his life in the final assault by the enemy which brought all hope to an end. "What! Are you always the one to be struck? Am I to take nothing away from Rome?" he had said a few moments before to Emilio Dandolo, his comrade of nineteen, just wounded in the arm.

On the second of July, in the great space before Saint Peter's, occurred the never-to-be-forgotten review. Arrived at last with great difficulty at the obelisk, in the midst of the thousands and tens of thousands that pressed about him, Garibaldi "stopped his horse and turned, and when his staff had joined him, gave a sign with his hand to stop the cheers. After they had been repeated with double force, there was a dead calm on the square." Then, from the serene figure in the midst of the sea of faces upturned to him in the greatest emotion of their lives, came the memorable call: "Fortune, who betrays us today, will smile on us tomorrow. I am going out from Rome. Let those who wish to continue the war against the stranger, come with me. I offer neither pay, nor quarters, nor provisions; I offer hunger, thirst, forced marches, battles, and death. Let him who loves his country in his heart and not with his lips only, follow me."

At eight on the evening of the same day, with four thousand men, and with his wife Anita at his side, the chieftain left the city by the Lateran gate for Tivoli, to begin the retreat in whose sixty days and five hundred miles, by inspired strategy and through divinely sent friends, he eluded the thirty thousand French, the fifteen thousand Austrians, the twelve thousand Neapolitans, the six thousand Spaniards, the two thousand Tuscans, and the innumerable Catholic faithful along the route, the sole object of all of whom for the time being was the capture of the bandit enemy of the Holy Church. On the next day, the Roman assembly, having agreed upon surrender, awaited in dignified body on the Capitol the arrival of Oudinot and his men. On July 14, at a moment when Garibaldi was between Todi and Orvieto and the puzzled and anxious enemy could form no idea of his whereabouts, the temporal power was declared once more restored. On August 28, twenty-four days after the death of Anita in the marshes of Ravenna by the Adriatic, when he was now nearing the coast of the

GARIBALDI HUT IN THE MARSHES NEAR RAVENNA

HERE GARIBALDI FOUND REFUGE ON THE NIGHT OF AUGUST 6, 1849,
TWO DAYS AFTER ANITA'S DEATH

Tuscan Maremma and safety, the one hundred and twenty-six days of the siege of Venice were ended by her surrender, and Italian hopes were again ended,— for the time.

At four in the afternoon on April 12, 1850, Pius the Ninth again saw the streets of his capital, having several days before taken leave of Ferdinand the Second between Fondi and Terracina, whither his host of the preceding seven months had escorted him. Met far out on the road that led from Albano to Rome, saluted with the booming of guns, he entered at the Porta San Giovanni, to find the giant square thronged and the steps of the church covered by the brilliantly robed and uniformed ecclesiastics and diplomats who had gathered to confer distinction on his welcome. Advancing between the lanes of French and papal troops, and preceded by a squadron of French cavalry, to the cry of *Viva il Papa!* and the ringing of all the bells of Rome, the pope traversed the piazza and halted at the steps of the basilica, where he alighted from his carriage to receive from kneeling commissioners the keys of the city, and from the diplomatic corps their salutations. Then, having entered the church to receive the benediction at the hand of Cardinal Barberini, its archpriest, he took his place in the pontifical carriage and resumed his progress, escorted by the French General Baraguay on the right and on the left by Prince Altieri of the Noble Guards, between lines of soldiers and the cheering multitudes across the city to Saint Peter's, where, after receiving the benediction from Cardinal Mattei, he kissed the toe of the saint and, eager for rest, retired to the Vatican, while the Romans entered upon a night of festivity in the brightly illuminated city.

On the morning of the fifteenth, the pope received in solemn audience the diplomatic corps, whose sentiments were formally expressed by the Spanish ambassador. In the afternoon, first visiting Santa Maria Maggiore, he went to the French military hospital at Sant' Andrea on the Quirinal, where to their great emotion he distributed crosses and medals to the sick and wounded. On the sixteenth he had pass in review before him in the Piazza San Pietro fourteen thousand of the men to whom he owed the rescue of his authority, and on whom he bestowed the apostolic benediction. On the twenty-ninth he visited in detail the scenes of the battles and siege of the year before.

On the morning of the next day, the anniversary of the first battle at the Villa Pamfili, on the doors of several churches and on the walls of several palaces appeared in glaring red the words:

"Priests, the blood of the martyrs cries aloud for vengeance!"

3.

THE CITY OF PIUS THE NINTH

WITH the return of the pope, the Red Triumvirate of the cardinals Vannicelli, Altieri, and
Della Genga, who had governed from the Quirinal
since the restoration of the temporal power the year before, and by their reactionary policy had made themselves obnoxious to all classes but their own, came to
an end. Their ministry had consisted of five depart-
ments: War; Justice; Finance; Interior and Police;
Agriculture, Commerce, Industry, and Public Works
and Arts. But the laicization of the ministry was no
easy undertaking; the clerics were jealous of their
authority, and the fear was prevalent that the policy
was a sure step toward the loss of the temporal power.
By 1854, even the minister of war was a prelate.

In the city, the form of autonomy was preserved, but
the form only. By edict of the secretary of state on
January 25, 1851, the senate was again established in
its seat, though its members were not named until the
twelfth of March. It consisted of forty-eight councillors,
evenly divided between nobles and borghesi, eight conservators, and one senator, the senator to be chosen from
one of the Roman families most conspicuous for nobility
and wealth. The senator's office was for six years, and
half of his colleagues in the council were either chosen
or confirmed every three years, the appointment being
made by the pope from a list including the actual councillors and two other candidates acceptable to each of
the fourteen rioni. This is the SPQR whose initials,

together with the papal insignia, appear on the marble tablets let into the wall of Urban where they were repaired after the breaches of 1849. How far it was from being the equivalent of the *sindaco, assessori,* and *consiglieri* who later constituted the SPQR, may be realized by remembering that it was the creation of the pope, that few public works were due to purely municipal means or initiative, that education and charities were almost entirely ecclesiastical, and that a civic consciousness hardly existed; in a word, that the city was not bred to self-dependence.

The difficulties of government did not cease with the restoration. From now on, besides the confusion of temporal and spiritual authority, there was the complication caused by the continual presence of the French soldiery. The fierce rancors that had sprung up in the hearts of the common people fifty years before during the Napoleonic occupation had changed rather than died out. The rabble that had hated the foreigner as an enemy of thrones and the papacy, and had been devoted to the pope, now hated both foreigner and pope as the enemies of Italian unity and the freedom of Rome. There were many Roman families of note, as well as the nameless, whose sons and brothers had shed their blood in the cause whose opponents now ruled the city. There were petty riots, and murderous deeds in the dark. The French commandant was driven to forbid the carrying of weapons, and followed his prohibition by the public shooting of culprits in the Piazza del Popolo and at the Bocca della Verità.

Apart from the disorders of passion, there were those of incapacity and selfishness. Brigandage continued to torment the Campagna and provinces. In 1851, the famous Passatore, long sought by both Austrian and papal gendarmes, was finally slain and his band destroyed; but not even then did the evil cease to be a reproach to the government. The running of contraband, more or less closely allied with brigandage, was more notorious still. The papal states bordered on Naples, Tuscany, Modena, and the Romagna, to say nothing of the two seas; the imposts were high, the morality of collectors and population low, the temptation great, the love of adventure not without its part, and in spite of all attempts at suppression the practice continued. The elaboration of customs laws as a means of prevention was effective chiefly in establishing the transgression as a lucrative occupation for the principal violators, and a convenient means on the part of the border population for adding to their livelihood in a way that did not lack the element of pleasure. The duties brought little to the state, and their evasion came to an end only when they disappeared with the border itself in the territorial changes of 1860.

Nor were those branches of the public service which were less provocative of temptation free from reproach. The larger abuses of the princely period were succeeded by the peculation and petty theft of minor functionaries. The inauguration of the postage stamp in 1852, for example, was soon followed by its covert sale at half price by postal employees, or by the sale of stamps purposely left uncancelled, and detached from their envelopes.

In the city, the most prominent abuses of the sort not grounded in actual disorder were idleness, dirt, and beggary. The Campagna had declined in productiveness and healthfulness in the seventeenth century, and the fact no doubt had its influence in the multiplication of idlers and the poor. The lottery had been established by Clement the Twelfth over a hundred years before, and was now a passion of the people, especially of the lower order, who resorted to dreams and signs and the prophetic confidences of priests in their choice of numbers. The drawings were held at first in the loggia of Montecitorio, then at the Madama, and afterward on the Ripetta; an orphan boy in white drew from an urn of silver, and the numbers were cried by a herald at the sound of a trumpet.

There were not only the idle poor, but the idle rich. The patriciate, living from the rents of estates of whose management they knew little, entertained as great a scorn for actual work as they did for alliance with the social rank below them; "to enrabble oneself," *incanagliarsi,* was their description of marriage with an inferior. The idle poor were innumerable. The city administration really amounted to an institution of charity spending under the pope's direction something like one-third of its annual moneys. There were three thousand two hundred and eighty-one families permanently on the list of those receiving daily aid, and there were, besides, innumerable special expenditures for the welfare of the poor. But this direct material aid was as nothing compared with the broader activities of the more regular institutions of charity. There were hospitals, refuges, loan offices, infant homes, orphan asylums, retreats, monasteries, chapters, and congregations of all kinds to an extent probably unequalled in any other city of the world.

How wise this wholesale administration of charity is to be judged, and in what degree to be condemned as

palliative rather than remedial, are questions not easy
to answer; but from the time of the Gracchi to the
present there is no doubt of the continual necessity of
some sort of aid to the population of a city whose attractions have always been great, whose industries have
always been few, whose environment has been unhealthy,
and whose poor have been bred to the idea of relying
on subsidy. By the census of 1871, which yielded figures
in general confirmatory of the census of 1857, the fact
was revealed that, of a population of about two hundred
thousand, there were one hundred and twelve thousand
of both sexes, including children, who declared no occupation, representing about seventy thousand adults
unemployed and subsisting in part on some form of
charity. That there were abuses on the part of both
giver and recipient need hardly be said; that calculation
as well as love sometimes prompted the giving, and that
gratitude was not always in the heart of the recipient,
is equally probable.

The general laxity was reflected nowhere more than
in the care of the streets. Until 1853, they were lighted
by oil lamps, far apart, somewhat aided by the flames
burning before the numerous wayside images. The new
gaslights were at first confined to certain principal
thoroughfares. In spite of legislation for cleanliness such
as the imposition of a fine of five scudi for the throwing of refuse from the windows, in itself a comment,
Rome had the reputation of being the filthiest city in
Italy except Naples. It had open sewers that went un-
challenged, it swarmed with dogs, and its alleys and
streets were in certain respects the annexes of the houses,
and even of palaces. Cholera had swept it in 1836 and
1837, and came again in 1867, when Maria Theresa,

widow of Ferdinand the Second, died of it at Albano.
For all its being the capital of the world and the goal
of travel for the enlightened of all parts of the old hemi-
sphere and the new, for all its incomparably rich and
beautiful palaces and wonderful villa-gardens, the city
was in many ways hardly more than an overgrown and
neglected village.

If we seek a cause for this condition outside of the
more or less natural laxity of a southern people, we are
most likely to find it in the simple fact that the city was
not its own mistress and had not been bred to civic pride.
The pope was the state, and the pope was the city of
Rome. The powers of the senate were merely rhetorical.
The pope, it is true, repaired and constructed, and to
him were owing many an improvement and many a
beautification which the municipality unaided would
have either considered impossible or refused to execute.
The repair of the breaches in Urban's wall, the rebuilding of the Porta San Pancrazio, the great tobacco manu-
factory in the Piazza Mastai, the Acqua Marcia, the
completion of the Porta Pia, the erection of the column
of the Immaculate Conception, the laying of the railway
lines from Rome to Frascati in 1856, from Rome to
Civitavecchia in 1859, from Rome to Ancona and
Bologna in 1861, and from Rome to Ceprano in 1862,
with their four inconvenient stations at the Porta Maggiore, the Porta Portese, the Porta Angelica, and the
Termini, and many less imposing buildings and monuments which his fondness for epigraphical ornamenta-
tion has marked for the gaze of posterity, were the work
of his reign. But the assumption of authority and consequently of responsibility on the part of the popes had
long since confirmed the Romans in carelessness and

indolence. In major matters, they were obliged to submit; as a natural consequence, when the ruler was negligent in minor matters, or sought their coöperation in details that called for municipal pride and individual public spirit, they lacked the concern of a city accustomed to do its own thinking and to pay its own bills.

There were, however, compensations. Outside of the circle of necessary restriction, there was a large liberty. If Rome was an overgrown village, it also gave the freedom of the village. If it was careless of sanitation and public appearances, its private intercourse also had something of the comfort of unstarched and not too tidy garments. If there was not perfect freedom of initiative, there was also not the tyranny of responsibility. The pope concerned himself for the proper living of his subjects; he was answerable, too, for their proper dying.

Foreigners especially continued to find the life of the city unconstrained and congenial. The hotels and houses of Rome were filled with visitors, and then as now the entertainment of the stranger was the city's chief industry. The scholars and writers and artists resided in modest quarters about the Piazza di Spagna. Gregorovius entered the city by the Porta del Popolo at half-past four on the afternoon of October 2, 1852, and on the fourth moved into his "little room under the roof of the dwelling of Vincenzo the sculptor," to begin his Roman literary career of twenty-two years, living later in the Via Gregoriana. On October 3, 1854, he records that he "must undertake something great, something that will lend a purpose to my life." It is to write the history of the city of Rome in the Middle Ages, the thought of which he suddenly conceives, "struck by the view of the city as seen from the bridge leading to the island of Saint Bartholomew." Dr. Braun, secretary to the Archæological Institute, listens attentively to the plan, and then says, "It is an attempt in which anyone must fail."

The journal of Gregorovius sparkles with the names of interesting sojourners in Rome. He meets a young, uncouth poet, Buchanan Read, with "a fair little wife who looks like a sacrificial lamb." He meets Ampère, "one of the most brilliant Frenchmen, good-natured, kind, versatile, and, what is rare among Frenchmen, devoid of vanity, who invariably carries paper and pencil, and instead of smoking always chews a cigar." He knows Alfred von Reumont, diplomat and writer, the first volume of whose *History of the City of Rome,* appearing in 1867, displays lack of "the higher æsthetic sense, and the power for putting his knowledge into shape." In April, 1860, while Garibaldi and King Victor Emmanuel are threatening the papal state from both sides, he goes to call on Theodore Parker, who is ill and soon to die in Florence. Mr. Parker says, with great energy, "The pope is a fool, pure and simple." He makes the acquaintance of Browning, "the celebrated English poet, who with his delicate wife, a gifted poetess, has lived for years in Florence." He meets Mommsen, whose appearance is "a curious mixture of youthfulness and pedagogic conscientiousness," which "in great part explains his work, distinguished by critical, destructive acumen and erudition, but rather a pamphlet than history."

In 1864, Guizot and Villemain are the orators at Ampère's funeral. The next year, Gregorovius meets "the talented Englishman, Bryce, author of *The Holy Roman Empire,*" and hears Liszt in the Palazzo Bar-

THEODORE PARKER'S TOMB IN FLORENCE

HE HAD COME TO ITALY IN THE HOPE OF RECOVERING HEALTH

berini in the concert which is his farewell to the profane world, with no one suspecting that he has "the abbé's stockings in his pocket,"—"the end of the gifted virtuoso, a truly sovereign personality," at one with his instrument, "as it were, a piano centaur." Gounod, who was in the French Academy in the Villa Medici in 1869, he does not mention. Ranke, the historian of the popes, who "sees in history no factor but diplomacy, does not recognize the people," and "goes through history as he would go through a picture gallery, writing acute notes," he finally meets in Germany, and after returning to Rome records that he has added so much to his information by research during his absence, "especially concerning the sack of Rome, as will rejoice the heart of Ranke, who told me in Munich that there was no longer anything fresh to add, he having already explored every source." In 1868, he has seen Professors Adams and Curtis, from America; "also Bayard Taylor, a celebrated author, a serious, energetic, and almost heroic-looking man." The following year, he meets Longfellow at Princess Wittgenstein's: "he has a fine head; striking features, liberal and open; white hair and a white beard,—is entering on old age in full possession of his energies . . . on Tuesday was with him at Mrs. Terry's, the widow of Crawford, the American sculptor." He makes friends with Ferdinand Keller, the discoverer of the lake-dwellings, and goes to the funeral of Overbeck in the church of San Bernardo alle Terme, incidentally seeing "the entire company of dethroned royalties driving with smiles from the railway station." He knows Döllinger, the rebel against the dogma of papal infallibility.

The social life of the aristocratic circles was in the

grand style, and brilliant with the participation of
diplomatic representatives and other notable foreigners,
to say nothing of great churchmen. On March 3, 1853,
at the ball of Alessandro Torlonia and his wife Teresa
Colonna in their great palace in the Borgo, thirteen
hundred guests were invited, among them ministers,
ambassadors, cardinals, generals, and foreigners of distinction; and the dance, beginning with the withdrawal
of the cardinals at midnight, except Antonelli and
Ugolini, continued until seven in the morning. In the
Golden Book of 1746, the aristocracy had numbered
one hundred and eighty-seven families. By the decree
of Pius the Ninth on May 2, 1853, the qualifications of
Nobilis Romanus were defined as personal or ancestral
participation in the municipal government in the capacity of either conservator or head of a rione; accretions were to take place, when advisable, through a
heraldic commission. It was in 1853 that society life on
a grand scale was first resumed after the pope's absence, and the Torlonia ball, though eclipsing the others,
was only one of many. In 1859, Prince Borghese entertained two hundred persons at dinner. Such was the
frequency of balls that at one time the Portuguese
ambassador went begging for a date on which to invite
his guests, and Hooker, the American banker, unable
to find an evening free, in desperation gave a ball by
day. The Carnival was at its height, and every Monday
and Thursday saw gatherings in the Campagna for the
chase. The great religious functions vied in brilliance
with the social.

There were, to be sure, a few active tyrannies in this
easy-going society. There was the tyranny of rank; each
class was at ease within its limits, but any mingling not

purely formal of the aristocracy with the middle class
was still impossible. There were religious tyrannies
which were more serious because not self-imposed. Con-
fessors exercised great influence on the individual conscience, and were not always the safe depository of confidences. To be known as a liberal was to be under
suspicion, and perhaps to have one's means of livelihood
endangered. There was one newspaper, the *Giornale di
Roma,* and its news was confined to official and religious
notices and events. "Let them publish papal news and
the news of the Chinese insurrections," said Cardinal
Antonelli, the bitter enemy of liberty of the press. The
Jews, except in special cases, were not allowed outside
the Ghetto, and the time was hardly past when they
were compelled to attend mass in Sant' Angelo in Pes-
cheria, with an officer and whip to insure attention. The
theaters were more or less under surveillance. During
concerts in the Corea, as the mausoleum of Augustus
was then called, the ringing of church bells near at hand
was allowed to annoy the auditors, as is still the case
both there and in many another hall in Rome; and conscientious listeners to music and the drama were mad-
dened then, as they are today, by the atrocious manners
of gabbling neighbors. The security of officialdom in
general was an irritation to such as had to deal with it.
The Legations were abandoned to the whims of cardinal-
governors. Sacerdotal zeal for the welfare of soul and
Church might go too far, as seems to have been the case
in the Mortara affair, when it was charged, whether
rightly or wrongly, that a Jewish boy had been secretly
baptized and forcibly taken from his parents to be bred
for the priesthood, or in the affair of the Mudai, converts to Protestantism who, because they interpreted

the Bible to neighbors and solicited their conversion, were imprisoned for four years. No Protestant church was allowed within the walls of Rome. The English Protestants had their place of worship outside of the Porta del Popolo in a granary, watched by the papal police to prevent the entrance of Catholics. The first Presbyterian church was built near by in 1868-1869. Services were conducted by the denomination within the gates from 1862 until forbidden in 1866. Its minister from 1864 to as late as 1872 warned his congregation to "avoid openly carrying their Bibles when assembling, and to dismiss . . . dropping out by twos and threes"; and "no psalms were sung lest praising God with a loud voice should betray us to the police." The Protestant embassies were obliged to confine religious services to private chapels in their official apartments. Rufus King, the American envoy, used a room in the Palazzo Salviati, much to the scandal of the owner of the house, who on his departure had the chamber cleansed of the stain. On March 28, 1870, Gregorovius is refused by the Jesuit in charge the use of certain manuscript in the Vatican library: "Seeing his malicious smile, I recognized that my hour had struck. Have gone to the library apparently for the last time; but I too can smile, for my work is almost finished." On March 1, 1874, he hears that *The History of the City of Rome in the Middle Ages* has been placed on the Index. At Saint Peter's, he reads the decree "posted up on the first marble column of the outer entrance. The honored cathedral suddenly acquired a personal relation to myself. . . . Everyone congratulates me on the merited honor."

For all these tyrannies, however, and for the harsher

THE CHURCH OF SAINT PETER IN 1913

THE ORIGINAL PLAN OF THE CHURCH
IN THE FORM OF A GREEK CROSS
WOULD HAVE ALLOWED THE DOME GREATER PROMINENCE

crimes against liberty in whose perpetration the papacy shared with other despotisms of the time,—for exile and imprisonment without statement of cause or limit, for delays of the law, for shameful punishments without due trial, for the exclusion of seven thousand five hundred and twenty-six persons from the amnesty of 1850, for the abandonment of the merely suspected to the discretion of the police,—for all these, the spirit of modern enlightenment was preparing an end in the papal state as in other states it had already prepared an end. From the restoration in 1850 until 1870, the holy seat was never quite free from the shadow of the great threat. The Siccardi laws, the rise of Cavour and his open challenge of the Church's civil authority, the Gladstone letters, the civil marriage agitation, the Rattazzi bill, the growing friendship between Piedmont and Napoleon the Third, the campaign of 1859, causing transports of joy in the city, were the constant reminders of insecurity. Since the days of Mazzini and Garibaldi and Masina and Dandolo and Mameli and Morosini and Manara and the victorious defeat on the Janiculum, the sentiment of Rome was no longer to be counted on. An abortive movement in 1853 resulted in the capital sentence for five men, heavy punishments for a score of others, and lighter ones for many more; and the reduction of all the sentences was quite as significant as the movement itself. The time was passing when the spirit of revolt was confined to a few and could be repressed by a heavy penalty or two. Five thousand Romans volunteered for the national cause in 1859; the population divided itself into clerical and national partisans; and Napoleon's sudden termination of the campaign struck Rome as well as other cities dumb with surprise and wrath. On January 27, 1860, one hundred and thirty-four Roman nobles thought it worth while to sign and present an address of loyalty to the pope. It had been preceded on the twenty-second, and perhaps caused, by a popular nationalistic demonstration. The Romans began to imitate the Milanese by refusing to smoke. The students and young intellectuals in general were for Piedmont. The Comitato Nazionale Romano had reached a membership of six thousand. Gregorovius notes that "the pope asked Torlonia for a loan, but the banker referred him to the Roman princes and especially to Antonelli, who has placed two millions in the English Bank." By June 27, "there is nothing but prayers and processions, and Garibaldi's name is in every mouth." In 1861, Rome is in angry passivity, but on March 17 there is a great demonstration from the Forum to the Lateran. On May 21, ten thousand signatures are forwarded inviting Victor Emmanuel to Rome. The cession of Venetia in 1866 and the removal of Austria from direct contact with the papal territory, the steady pressure of the growing Italian state, the gallant adventure of the Cairoli and their devoted band at Villa Glori, and above all the terrible Garibaldi, unsuccessful at Aspromonte but never ceasing to breathe out threatenings and slaughter, while disorders in the city made clear on which side sympathy lay,—all these were the signs of a progress whose inevitable end could be seen by everybody but those who feared it and felt it coming, and would not see it.

The proof that it was feared and felt to be coming had long been manifest. The syllabus of 1864, in which every ecclesiastical claim was reaffirmed, was Pius the Ninth's confession of it. The convention of September, stipulating that the capital was to be fixed at Florence and the Italian government was to allow the papal state a reasonable army and to protect the papal frontiers, was Napoleon's. A farther confession was seen by the on-looking world in the Infallibility council of 1869 and 1870. If its purpose was political as well as spiritual, even this was no new plan. Gregory the Sixteenth, thirty years before in the midst of unmanageable re-bellions against the temporal power, had conceived the idea of buttressing the Church's territorial structure by conferring upon its head a divine and unchallenge-able authority. The authority of Catholic arms, how-ever, was made to serve instead, until it came to be seen that even bayonets and cannon were a weak and ephem-eral resort.

On the twenty-ninth of June, 1868, from a pulpit on the terrace in front of Saint Peter's, with eight Swiss Guards and four of the Faithful of the Senate as an escort, one of a company of notaries read aloud to the world the bull which summoned the council of December 8, 1869. The bull itself was then affixed to the doors of the great church, and to the doors of Saint John in Lateran, Santa Maria Maggiore, and the Cancelleria, and in the Campo dei Fiori. By October 10, 1869, the preparations for the great assembly, the successor, after three hundred years, of Trent, were almost complete. In the church of Saint Peter, a horseshoe of wooden seats had been erected, with a chapel at either side. The places for cardinals were covered with red, for the bishops, with green. There were tribunes for royalty, for the diplomatic corps, for the Roman nobility. In the middle stood an altar, with a speaker's tribune be-hind it and facing the papal throne. Antonelli thought that the council might last for years, but in seven months the long series of discussions, debates, intrigues, briberies, and coercion by which the original opposition had been worn down from over one hundred adherents to two, was ended. The two whose courage proved indomitable were Luigi Riccio, a Neapolitan and bishop of Caiazzo, and Edward Fitzgerald, bishop of Little Rock, Arkansas.

On the sixteenth of June, 1870, a month before the council's findings were given to the world, occurred the usual procession of Corpus Domini. Of all the processions descended through the ages, it was the greatest and the most picturesque, and on this occasion, by reason of the participation of seven hundred bishops who were in attendance on the council, it was the greatest and most spectacular of all its line. Issuing from the Sistine chapel, it descended the Scala Regia, passed through the bronze portals, filed into the curved length of the colossal colonnade of Bernini, and entered the spacious farther square which fronts the great piazza itself. Attended by the Guardie Nobili and their captains in full uniform, with the standard-bearers and the great gonfaloni of the Church, the papal train advanced, Pope Pius himself under the great baldacchino and bearing the sacrament. Traversing the space between, which was resplendent with a great display of bright-colored flowers and hangings of every hue, the procession re-entered the colonnade on the other side by the statue of Charlemagne, and made its deliberate and majestic way between the mighty columns to the church again, which it reached two hours after its setting forth.

This was the last procession and the last solemn pontifical mass of Pius the Ninth before the world. One

month afterward, on the eighteenth of July, 1870, the
decree of the dogma of Papal Infallibility went forth,
which, at least so charged the patriotic party, was meant
to stem the tide of Italian nationalism as well as to accomplish its more spiritual purpose. There were even
those, including friends of the Church and delegates to
the council, who were apprehensive of a movement in
the direction of a dogma of the Temporal Power, or
of some equivalent, which would have endangered still
more the peace of Europe. Another month, and the
French army, whose presence in Rome had kept the
pope on his throne since the days of 1849, had been re-
called to fight the calamitous battles of its emperor of
clay. The pope was left alone with the single weapon of
dogma. On the twentieth of September, the soldiers of
Victor Emmanuel burst through the walls of Rome, and
the edifice of the Temporal Sovereignty, so near to its
completion and yet so far from the possibility, fell to the
ground in ruin.

XIII.

ETERNAL ROME

But its importance in universal history it can
never lose. For into it all the life of the ancient
world was gathered: out of it all the life of the
modern world arose.

BRYCE, The Holy Roman Empire, chapter 21

1.

THE NEW CAPITAL

WITH the breach at the Porta Pia on the twentieth of September, 1870; with the plebiscite of October 2, in which one hundred and thirty-three thousand six hundred and eighty-one votes were for union with Italy and one thousand five hundred and seven against, and in which the Leonine city itself insisted on having a part; with the meeting of the first Italian parliament at Florence on December 5; and with the transfer of the government from the Arno to the Tiber on July 2, 1871,—Eternal Rome took her place among the national capitals of the world.

The part she was now called upon to play was a new one. She had been the capital of the ecclesiastical despotism, she had been the capital of the Holy Roman empire and of the ancient Roman empire, she had been the capital of an oligarchical republic whose victorious arms rapidly swept it on to absolutism. Now she was the constitutional capital of an independent Italy, the minister rather than the tyrant of her realms, the subject rather than the ruler of her peoples. Nor did she forfeit her place as capital of the more universal realm of the spirit. The fall of the temporal power was not the defeat of religion. It was with only a seeming violence that the beneficent spirit of progress had struck a mighty shackle from both the Church and Italy. What Cardinal Pacca had said when the temporal power was lost in Pius the Seventh's time could be said again: "Providence has taken away the temporary power from the Holy See.

. . . The popes, relieved from the burden of the temporal power, which obliged them to devote a great part of their time to secular affairs, may now turn all their attention, and all their care, to the spiritual government of the Church; and when the Roman Church lacks the pomp and magnificence which temporal sovereignty has given her, there will be numbered among her clergy only those who *bonum opus desiderant.*" The Church at Rome was set free from selfish distractions that wasted its time, scattered its energies, and corroded its character. The state was free from the embarrassing presence of a hostile power in its midst, and from the interference of arms from abroad. The *chiesa libera in stato libero* of Cavour was at last a fact.

Yet neither the Church nor the Italian state, though each was free from the other, was wholly free. The Church, indeed, by refusing the advances of the state as expressed in the law of Guarantees, which made large concessions in civil, legal, financial, residential, and diplomatic directions, renounced the freedom it might have enjoyed through coöperation with a willing government and people. The Church was not yet emancipated from the bonds of pride and worldly desire. The Church was not out of bondage to itself.

As for the state, it had but set foot in the path of freedom. "Italy is free and united," the king had said at the opening of parliament in Florence on December 5; "it depends on us to make her great and happy." To drive the Austrian from her borders by the wars, conspiracies, and martyrdoms of fifty years, to defend her own rights against a militant French Catholicism, to remove the obstacle of the temporal sovereignty without the embroilment of Europe, were all enterprises that had called for infinite patience, time, and suffering; but they were enterprises whose conclusion could be clearly seen by the smaller company of the intensely patriotic all the time, and in the periods of outburst could be seen by all the people at once. It was the genuine and irresistible stirring of nature that drove the people of Italy into the paths and along the great highways of action which led to the gates of Rome.

The highways of Italy, however, lead not only to the capital, but from it. It was after the permanence of Rome as the capital had been confirmed beyond question by the self-sacrificing surrender of their claims by rival Italian cities, by Victor Emmanuel's words on entrance into the city, *A Roma ci siamo, e ci resteremo,*—"In Rome we are, and in Rome we remain,"—and by the approval of a world which would not respond to the papal appeal for a forcible reinstatement, that Italy and Rome were face to face with their real task.

"Falling in love and winning love," writes Stevenson, "are often difficult tasks to overbearing and rebellious spirits; but to keep in love is also a business of some importance, to which both man and wife must bring kindness and good-will. The true love-story commences at the altar, when there lies before the married pair a most beautiful contest of wisdom and generosity." Italy was united; the task from now on was to keep united. The enthusiastic Italians who had hitherto faced toward Rome and territorial unification now had to turn and face toward every part of Italy and civic unification. The forces of territorial union which had been active so long as there were enemies to vanquish and obstacles to overcome, when once their object had been realized, soon slackened in their vigor. Now that there was no foreigner to hate and fear, now that there was no longer a dispute as to the claims of Rome to leadership, the forces that had always wrought to keep Italy in disunion revived with all their ancient potency. The armed opposition of the Church and its partisans had ceased, but the hatreds and rancors of the Roman question persisted. The differences in race, productivity, and commercial aptitude were felt now in their full magnitude. The smaller cities as well as the large found it hard to forget their separateness in dialect, in situation, and interest. The south charged the busy, capable, and self-reliant north with selfishness. The north charged the indigent and indolent south with idleness and disaffection. Government was found to be expensive; to be heavily assessed for the benefit of communities far removed and unknown was an irritation. The sacrifices of peace were harder than the sacrifices of martyrdom and war.

The Italian character while in the mood of exaltation achieves the supremest heroisms. The individual in the heat of passion unflinchingly faces the martyr's end; collectively, too, when dominated by enthusiasm, the Italian is stopped by nothing. In the moment of incandescence he gladly gives up life; in the mild warmth and light of common day, for the common good, like other human beings, he finds difficult the sacrifice of the least advantage or the slightest personal inclination. The era of patriotism passed into the era of politics. A liberal king and a liberal people had freed the land from the absolutist, but with the purpose achieved the hitherto unanimous nation became the victim of divided desire. The antagonism of right and left, which before 1870 had centered in the Roman question, after the taking of

Rome lapsed into the conventional opposition between conservative and liberal. The scattered and somewhat purposeless elements of the left had attained by 1876 enough coherency and strength to succeed to the government. The legislative energies, however, continued to scatter. The increase of the population from twenty-eight and a half millions in 1882, or two hundred and fifty-seven to the square mile, to the thirty-six millions of 1921, or three hundred and twenty-five to the square mile, was felt in an ever-increasing pressure of the masses. Socialism developed a party and became articulate, and the franchise was more than once extended, until it was all but universal. From 1876 on, there were no longer two distinct parties, but an ever-growing number of groups from whose shifting and shifty leadership was drawn the material for brief-lived ministries. To the original conservatives and liberals were soon added not only the socialists, and the republicans, who could not forget Mazzini, but the democrats, and the social-democrats, and the nationalists, and the clericals, allowed at last by the Church to participate in politics and finally by combination transformed into the Italian People's party, and, most recent of all, the fascisti, first organized as groups from among the ex-soldiers of the World War and without interference in politics, but finally, in 1921, provoked by the long-continued disorders and threats of communism into formal declaration of themselves as the party pledged to strong government under the monarchy. The purchase of support from faction or district by the distribution of local favors, a marked form of abuse in earlier years, was followed in later years by the practice of conciliating, through bestowal of ministerial posts, the various groups necessary to a majority. The ministry in the years succeeding the World War no longer represented a definite party or principle, but an equilibrium of forces. Its formation was for the most part a matter of slate and pencil. By 1922, so numerous were the groups, and so inflexible in selfish purpose, that legislation became impossible. Italian politics were chaos. There were no great ideals, no great measures, no great men, and no great common purpose. The rising temper of the fascisti, the increasing frequency of their forcible appropriation of the government in disaffected cities, their appearance at last with Benito Mussolini sixty thousand strong in the streets of Rome, and their practical seizure of the government, were not unwelcome even to those who had felt alarm at their excesses.

Yet, in spite of a legislative system by reason of its liability to change but ill adapted to an excitable race, in spite of an infinite diversity of interests, in spite of the lack of natural resources in coal and iron, in spite of the assaults of communism, the harassings of clericalism, and the disaffection of republicanism, in spite of the abuses of bureaucracy and personal interest and favoritism, the Italy of a half century after the taking of Rome looks back upon a progress which in its total is reassuring. She has made the best of the exceedingly difficult Roman question; the papal court is still intransigent, but the Church at large exists in easy and almost cordial relation with the state. She has wonderfully reduced the numbers of the illiterate even in parts where nature delights in throwing the obstacles of poverty and custom in the way of education. She has set in order her countless museums and national monuments for the delight of the world and the profit of her

FASCISTI IN THE VIALE DEL RE

THEY ARE ASSEMBLING FOR THE FUNERAL OF
AVANGUARDISTA DUILIO GUARDABASSI,
KILLED BY A COMMUNIST SYMPATHIZER

citizenry. Through education directly, and indirectly through the mingling of men in army service, she has decreased the intensity of provincialism and established the sentiment of nationalism. She has met with patience and generosity the political demands of her needy and nameless, and notably increased the means of health, enjoyment, and livelihood. She has remembered her sons in the lands left unredeemed in 1866, and rescued them by a war initiated and carried through with intense popular enthusiasm. She has remained faithful to the memory of the Victor Emmanuel who fought her battles against the Austrian, and loves with a like devotion the Victor Emmanuel of today and his queen, who in quite as dangerous and trying times have proved their greatness by the Platonic virtues of wisdom, courage, and temperance. She has weathered the storms of communism and of attempted revolution, and weathered also the storms of the fascista contra-revolution that reduced to impotence both the anarchy of communism and the anarchy of decrepit government. Whatever regret may be entertained that violence was inevitable in the achievement of a stabilized Italy, it is a fact that the year since Mussolini and the fascisti assumed absolute control has been a year of promises kept, of growth in enlightenment on the part of governors and in faith on the part of the governed, of work taking the place of words, of patriotism translated into action. The suns of 1924 shine on an Italy well out of the great ordeal of the war and the greater ordeal of the years of disillusion after the war, and treading with firm and spirited step in the paths of recovery. Whatever the difficulties still to be met, the unity of Italy will not be readily called into question. The passion for nationality has proved itself in the course of a hundred years in many a trial by fire. The reflecting reader who has learned to think of Eternal Rome and Italy by ages rather than by scores of years may cautiously hesitate to call it a fundamental and permanent trait of Italian character, but will see in it none the less clearly a steadfast and long-enduring trait.

The achievement of Italy at large has been shared by its capital, and is reflected in her character. In the interval between the sack of 1527 and the fall of the temporal power in 1870, the circuit of the city had gradually widened until many a deserted garden and field was covered, and the still vast emptiness of Aurelian's city was partially filled. A century after the sack, the population of Rome had risen to over one hundred thousand. At the end of the eighteenth century, it had reached one hundred and fifty thousand. Reduced in the period of Napoleonic troubles to one hundred and seventeen thousand, it soon increased again, and entered upon a still more rapid growth. In 1870, Rome contained over two hundred and twenty-five thousand inhabitants.

It was in the period after the erection of the capital at Rome, however, that the most rapid and marvellous increase took place. To what was left of the army of clericals that had been supported by the old régime was now added the larger army of those employed by the Italian government, and in the wake of peace and railway extension came transient multitudes of tourists and pilgrims, with all the permanent population necessary for their maintenance. Vast building enterprises were inaugurated to supply the needs of the inflowing numbers, and great changes in topography occurred.

Large areas in Monti and the northern rioni, and in the field of Nero's house, were built over. Regular streets, broad and well-paved, supplanted the country paths and lanes of the Renaissance and the papal city, and many a beautiful private garden and orchard gave way to blocks of monotonous modern buildings. The picturesque gardens of Sallust, since Gregory the Fifteenth known as the Villa Ludovisi, with their groves and charming irregularities, were levelled and transformed into monumental squares of dwelling houses. The broad Via Nazionale, now almost the heart of the city, was the result of a similar change. The Via Cavour ran its spacious course from railway station to Forum. The Corso Vittorio Emanuele was made to furnish a convenient channel for traffic between the Piazza Venezia and the Castello Sant' Angelo. A great tunnel was inoffensively driven under the Quirinal to facilitate communication between the northeastern quarters and the Campus Martius. The Palazzo di Giustizia, the Monumento Vittorio Emanuele, the Termini station, the great government buildings, and the masses of monumental apartment houses have given the city a modern air. Suburban building has filled with teeming life the hitherto quiet fields outside Aurelian's great wall. Over the north and northeastern portions, and in the more adaptable areas beyond the walls in every direction, has been reared the new Rome, with a population which has increased from the two hundred and twenty-five thousand of 1870 to the five hundred thousand of the first years of the twentieth century, and to the seven hundred and sixty-two thousand three hundred and sixty-four of 1922.

The changes apparent in twentieth century Rome,

however, are not merely those of numbers and area. The change in the character of the city's life has been no less pronounced. The present Rome of three-fourths of a million differs from the papal Rome of fifty years ago hardly less than the city of that period differed from the Rome of the Renaissance.

How great has been the transformation can be appreciated only by those who have seen the city in both of these recent phases. It had already begun to change in the papal days, but with nothing like the present rapidity. Rome has suddenly become a great modern city, —modern in spirit as well as in appearance. The advent of the railway and the presence of the government have changed it from a provincial into a cosmopolitan city. Instead of leisurely approaching Rome in a coach or diligence from Civitavecchia or Viterbo, the visitor of today is whirled into a modern station filled with the smoke of monster locomotives. The rattle of carriages over the streets has been largely replaced by the whir of the automobile and the clang of electric cars that penetrate to every part of the city. A dozen daily newspapers are cried in the streets, a dozen other sheets are published, and modern methods of advertising have been adopted. Disorder has disappeared from the city and its environs, and the brigands that of old haunted the papal territories have taken their places in legend. Rome is among well-kept cities, with a death rate as low as that of the average modern capital.

Welcome as have been many of the changes, however, they have been accompanied by less desirable transformations. In the minds of those who, whether through experience or investigation, are acquainted with the Rome of papal days, there is lodged a sense of regret,

MODERN ROME

SCALE OF METRES

0 100 200 300 400 500   1000

REPRODUCED BY PERMISSION OF ALLYN & BACON FROM PLATNER'S TOPOGRAPHY AND MONUMENTS OF ANCIENT ROME

MAP OF MODERN ROME

for together with modern improvement has come the disappearance of much that gave the city distinctive character. Gregorovius felt the change on his return from the north not six weeks after the Italian army's entry, and his soul was filled with regret. He did not believe in the temporal authority, but he rebelled against seeing Rome made like other cities. "Rome should not be cosmopolitanized," he wrote. "She will sink into becoming the capital of the Italians." He would have had the city set apart, no longer possessed by the popes, yet not profaned by politics.

The dread of the historian and his kind has been realized. The secluded, almost monastic life of the old city of the popes, with its flavor of mediævalism, has made way for the matter-of-fact uniformity of the modern capital. The gilded coach no longer parades the streets with its burden of pontifex or cardinal; only sequestered within the precincts of the Vatican may be seen, if seen at all, the gorgeous relics of the old-time splendor. In place of the princely equipage with its retinue of brilliant liveries now rolls the monotonous cab or automobile. In place of the papal troops now march the drab soldiers of the Italian army. The tourist comes rushing in by train, encompassed by crowds of other tourists. Instead of leisurely dreaming in romantic solitude among ivy-covered ruins, like Shelley a hundred years ago, he hurriedly sees the sights of the city and dashes on. The native costumes of street and Campagna have become things of the past, to be seen only on models in the artist's studio. The Carnival at the outbreak of the World War was the mere ghost of its old self, and for the present at least, now that the public masque is not allowed, has altogether disappeared.

Pasquino and Marforio were dumb from the day the streets of the city were profaned by the soldiers of the king and the press began to speak for the people in the language of liberty. The Ghetto and its life are gone. Not even the picturesqueness of dirt and neglect has escaped the sacrifice; the dirt of modern Rome is not the dirt of a holy city. Not only has color faded from the street, but has grown less vivid in the countenances of the people. The machine of modern life runs at full speed. Everywhere are the dust and business and din so much disliked by the genial poet of the Sabine farm. The twentieth century spirit of method has extended even to the care of the ancient remains, and the Rome of seventy years ago, with grassy ruins clad in trailing clouds of ivy, has changed to a Rome of monuments whose environment indeed is graced by the replanted flora of the Cæsars' times, but in the crannies of whose naked walls not a blade is allowed to root.

2.

THE CITY OF THE SOUL

Y ET those who remember or by study try to recall the old régime are few, and rapidly becoming fewer. Newer generations, with no sense of the transformation which has taken place, and with no regret, are as much under the spell of the city as have been all other generations. The monuments of ancient Rome still rise in solitary and solemn grandeur throughout the southern part of the city, still line the ways that lead to mountain and sea. A century of scientific excavation and preservation has made of Rome the greatest archæological center of the world. The student, his understanding illumined and fertilized by the vision of so much in her streets and museums that concerns the past of all nations; the traveller, overwhelmed and humbled by the wealth of historic association on every hand; the pilgrim, awed and inspired by the magnificence and the antiquity of the religion he loves,—all depart with veneration and regret, and if a kindly fortune grants them the longed-for return it is with a great wave of affection sweeping over the soul that they are borne past grey Soracte into the brown reaches of the Campagna and see once more the Great Dome swing into sight. Venice they may remember for moonlit lagoons, lapping waters, and *dolce far niente,* Florence for the warm hues and gracious shapes of the Renaissance, Naples for picturesqueness and gaiety; but the feeling for Rome which sways their hearts is different. It is not her beauty which wins them, though she is beautiful; nor her quiet and calm, though she sets the spirit free in a peace which passeth understanding; nor the fascination of her art, though in that least of all is she lacking. The charm which Rome exercises upon the senses is indeed great, but it is not first of all the senses that she takes captive. Rome's dominion is of the spirit. She is ever "the city of the soul." There resides in her atmosphere an intense spiritual quality that gives her a sovereignty unlike that of any other city. There is no other spot on the globe so rich with experience, so fraught with memories.

There is no other spot where the soul is so wrought upon by the sense of that which is old. This is true because nowhere else is there so great an abundance of important ruins of an important age. Of all the periods of the city's history into whose life the imagination is stimulated to enter, the most Roman, the most fascinating, and the most absorbing, is that of antiquity. The Rome of the popes is indeed everywhere visible in palace and monument, but its resemblance to and its blending with the modern city are such that it may fail to charm the imagination. Rome of the Renaissance is bodied forth by its architecture, painting, and sculpture, but its monuments are not, like those of Florence, the genuine, unforced, and exuberant witness of native genius, and lack somewhat its vividness and warmth. Rome of the Dark Ages, existing only in ruined towers, in the older churches, and in musty papal documents which never see the light, is so obscured by distant and endless dead historical detail that few can conjure it to life again. Early Christian Rome lives mainly in monuments of the dead. But the Rome of the Empire is everywhere strikingly visible. Great areas in the southern part of the city,—the Forum, the Palatine, the Aventine, the Cælian,—are only the *regiones* of antiquity, still vacant of the life of which the Dark Ages despoiled them, and containing little beyond the ruins of their times. The wide fields of Monti itself are not yet entirely covered by the modern city; and in the newest and most recent districts, where at first sight nothing seems visible older than the present, a few steps may bring to the eye the ruins of two thousand years ago.

Not even the casual visitor escapes entirely the spell of the ancient city. Confused and overwhelmed though he is by the multitude of monuments which call up in his mind only dim and shadowy imaginations of the past, he departs none the less with a reverent sense of the age and authority of the city and her institutions. The sojourner of a longer time enters into communion with ancient Rome, and lives her life again. Daily his eye is met by a thousand things that make him a citizen of the past.

It may be a few blocks of the Servian wall that confront him, imbedded and preserved in the masonry of ten years ago, or ivy-covered in some garden; or an imperial arch in the midst of habitations on the Esquiline; or a tomb of the Republic, once part of the wall in a narrow thoroughfare, now left alone by itself in the midst of public improvement; or a battered column, standing deep in the ground by the side of the street; or an altar, rising from the pavement of an obscure corner in the Campus Martius; or in some alley the arch of a portico, buried almost to its spring; or, towering about him in a leafy garden-restaurant remote from the sights and sounds of the outside world, the giant curving walls of Trajan's forum. Or, he may attend a service in the

Pantheon, and look up through the apex of the vast
dome into the same sky whose scintillating golden-blue
depths met the worshipper's gaze in Agrippa's or Hadrian's time; or sit in patient study of the wreck of the
Forum; or walk in contemplative mood apart from men
some sunlit morning among the more picturesque ruins
of the Palatine, finally losing all consciousness of self
and the present as he sits in silent solitude upon what
is left of the palace of Severus and lets his vision range
over the reposeful fields of the Campagna to the slopes
and summit of the Alban Mount. Or, it may be the
sight of still yellow Father Tiber that provokes the
inner eye until he is in mystic communion with the far-
off time; or of white little Tivoli, supine on its hillside;
or of cool Præneste far away in the gap toward the
Volscian country; or of Monte Cavo, dark with the
Alban herbage of springtime; or of Soracte, white and
gleaming with the deep snows of winter.

But it is not only the physical and literary remains
of antiquity that cause him to dream dreams and see
visions. The life of modern Rome itself is full of traditions that illuminate the life of the ancient day. The
wine-carts of the Alban vineyards still make their way
to and from the city. Flocks and herds still roam the
grassy pastures, and the simple folk of the Latin hamlet
still make of seedtime, harvest, or vintage, as in the
olden time, a festal season. The same beautiful white
cattle, wide-eyed, black-muzzled, grey-flanked, with long
and sweeping horns, draw the plough and the wagon
of the Campagna, as perfect an offering to the gods as
when in the time of Horace and Propertius they waited
at the altar, garlanded with flowers and holy with sacrificial fillet. The high priest of the Church of Rome still

CATTLE OF THE ROMAN CAMPAGNA

THE BACKGROUND IS AN ARCH OF THE ACQUA CLAUDIA

calls himself pontifex maximus. The Vestal and the
holy ones of Isis are perpetuated in the nun, the sodality
member in the monk, the tunic in the aube, the pænula
in the chasuble. In place of the thousands of shrines to
pagan deities which stood in the ancient streets are wayside shrines innumerable to Madonna and saints, by
whom men blaspheme now instead of by Bacchus and
Castor and Hercules. The spirit of ancient ceremonial,
with many of its details, survives in the ritual of the
modern Church, many of whose temples are the one-
time abodes of the gods of ancient times. Pulcinella and
the Dottore are the lineal descendants of the ancient
farce. The SPQR of ancient days still greets the eye
on official notices, and the *regio* survives in the rione.
The modern house, like the ancient, is rectangular, and
encloses a court, its life looking only less within than
before the age of many windows. Like the house of
Augustus and Trajan, its height is limited by law, and
not far from the same dimension. The doves still frequent the roofs and eaves as in Juvenal's time, tenements grow weary of their burdens and collapse as in
Strabo's day, and the endless procession of carts is still
seen at its work of building Eternal Rome from the
tufa and pozzolana of the Campagna pits and quarries.
The corridors of the house, until the coming of the
electric bulb a score of years ago, were often lighted by
bronze or terra cotta lamps in the ancient style, filled
with oil the same as that used by the remotest forefathers
of the present generation. On the table of the Roman
of today is the same clear, cold mountain water that his
ancestors drank, brought in from the same sources, over
the same routes, and sometimes in the identical channels
employed by the Romans of Frontinus' time. His heart

is made strong and glad by bread and wine from the same fields and vineyards that the citizen-soldier tilled before Cato's time, and his face made to shine by oil from the same olive slopes. The very language he speaks, the best beloved and most beautiful child of the ancient tongue, daughter more beautiful than beautiful mother, has hardly ceased to be Latin.

Nor are these externals the only survivals of the Rome of long ago. It is indeed vain to look to the Rome of today for one drop of blood transmitted from the ancient city of Rome. The populations of capital cities are ever fluid and changing. Even today the Roman praisers of the good old times look back to the men of 1849 and lament that Roman blood has been replaced by provincial in three score years and ten. Yet Nature is constant and eternal. The Tiber, the Hills, the Campagna, the skies, the mountains remain, and with them, in spite of the vicissitudes of time and fortune, their product, the Italian people. In the remote seclusion of the unchanging country, and not in the great cities, are to be sought the human remnants of ancient Italy. The Roman of even today possesses some traits of the men of two thousand years ago; for the forces of nature are still at work, and the life of Rome is still compounded of the life of Italy.

The same lively temperament that characterized the Roman of Livy's pictured page, the same vivacity of feeling, whether in anger, mirth, grief, or compassion, is present still in his modern descendant in city and country. The ancient delight in the spectacle is as strong as ever in him. A parade, a saint's procession, a great funeral, is still the occasion of as much climbing up to towers, windows, and chimney-tops to sit in patient ex-

pectation as when great Pompey passed the streets of
Rome. The passion for the stage is as great as when
there were three great theaters and their thirty thousand
seats in ancient Rome. The riotousness of Roman audiences is as great as when in Cicero's time unpopular
politicians on taking their seats were hissed by the multitude. The Camera dei Diputati, with its tumultuous
displays of excitability, makes the passionate popular
assemblies of Clodius and Cæsar live again. The street
riots of optimate and democrat, of senatorial and Cæsarian, are still to be seen in the frays of communist
and fascista. The funerals of slain partisans are still
as much the opportunity for demonstration as in Grac-
chan times. The same tendency to sudden passion and
unpremeditated violence, to instant pacification and
reconciliation, to extremes of hopefulness and despair,
is still to be reckoned with, in both individual and mob.
The same strange, contradictory blend of independence
and pride with servility and meanness still exists that
marked the populace of imperial times. The servant,
the janitor, the waiter, the barber, the petty public
servant of every sort, who for six months have done their
duties with arrogant ill will, at Christmas and Easter
hold out their hands with no more thought of degradation than did the ancient clients receiving the dole from
the patrons against whom they wagged an evil tongue.
The ancient mobs that fawned on their master and then
dragged his dishonored corpse through the streets, survived in the mediæval mob that rejoiced in the death of
the popes who had given them less than their expectation, and lived once more in the general strikers of pre-
fascista times, who, to avenge the real or fancied slight

put upon their class, would turn and rend the city that
gave them livelihood.

But the same ever-varying and mutable nature in
the people at large is also tempered by something of the
same seriousness that was at the root of representative
Roman character in its sternest days, and that gave
Virgil's lay its charm of sober and stately dignity. Not
to be described or analyzed, it may be appreciated by
one who comes from the gay and explosive communities
of lower Italy to the comparatively monumental calm
and repose of the Roman atmosphere. The old-time
simplicity and frugality survive among the masses of
the people, even in the city's rapidly changing life. The
modern Roman loves as well as Horace the unbought
enjoyments of life,—the genial pleasures of the holiday,
the sunny gardens of the Pincio or the Janiculum, the
open-air concert in park or piazza, the October excur-
sion outside the gates, the simple repast under the dense
arbor of some unpretentious osteria. Underneath all the
apparent lightness and instability of the Italian character,—and the Rome of today depends upon all Italy
for life and character, as did the Rome of ancient days,
—there lies a certain austerity, the quality which lay at
the foundation of the heroism of the Punic wars, which
inspired the martyrdoms of the Church, and which in
the nineteenth century made possible the freeing of
Italy. The dignity of the Italian senate, with its grave
and distinguished membership, goes far toward recall-
ing the time when the Roman senate seemed like an
assembly of kings. The call of the nation in the great
crises of modern times has found response in deeds of
valor and consecration worthy to stand beside those of
the Decii and Regulus.

Yet, impressive as are the remains of the ancient empire, Rome is far from being a city of a single interest or of a single period. Her appeal is as broad and as deep as humanity itself.

This is not the rhetorical claim of enthusiasm. It is the sincere and eloquent witness of generations of men on whom the spell of Rome has been cast. It is true that there are those who do not bear this witness; Rome does not yield her secrets in an hour. The shallow, the indolent, and the hurried may tread her streets and pass untouched by the sacred flame; but it is not so with the serious, the philosophic, and the sensitive of soul. To them, Rome is not a mere Italian city on the main travelled road from the Alps to the southern sea, nor yet only the scene of sometime grandeur which custom constrains them to visit; but a city which is still the capital of the most widespread empire in existence, the goal of profane as well as pious pilgrimage, within whose walls are spoken the languages of the world; the Inn of the Universe as truly now as in the days of the emperors.

But Rome is not cosmopolitan merely in the ordinary sense. The culture and the religion of the modern day are not all she represents. She stands as well for all the past. She represents the sum of human experience in the western world. From the beginnings of history in Italy to the present day, she has passed through and participated in all the vicissitudes of ancient and modern times. Rising as older civilizations fell, Roman civilization continued and perpetuated what was best in them. Gradually expanding until her realm included all Latium, all Italy, all that was possible in her times

of Europe, Africa, and Asia, besides the near-by islands
of the sea, Rome of the Empire came to include within
her borders all the known world and all the life of west-
ward-marching civilization. Whatever had evolved from
the experience of mankind in the most diverse and
widely distant climes,—from the experience of Egypt,
ancient of days, of the gorgeous east, of intellectual and
scientific Greece, of Palestine that walked with God, of
enterprising Carthage, of the rugged and unspoiled nations of northern and western Europe,—passed into the
keeping of the city which ruled them from the banks of
the Tiber. She was the heir of all the ages. The words of
the eloquent historian of the Holy Roman empire may
be used of the city of the ancient as well as of the mediæval empire: "Into her all the life of the ancient world
was gathered."

And she not only became possessed of what the world
could give; she set upon it her seal. With unequalled
genius for converting into actual life whatever was
capable of service, she selected from the store that became hers all that could be of use in the constitution of
the new culture. The art, literature, science, inventions,
philosophy, religions, and institutions of her subject
states she took to herself, so far as appropriation was
possible, set upon them the seal of practical value, conserved them, and sent them forth for the healing of the
nations of modern times.

Rome was not only the conserver of what was worth
while in ancient days, but the dispenser of what has
entered into modern life. She gathered together the
precious metal of ancient civilization, fused and coined
it anew, and put it once more into circulation. She was
the lens which received, condensed, and transmitted the

rays of human experience. She was the bridge to which all the ways of the old pagan times converged, and from which diverged all the ways of Christian times. She was the channel into which the streams of ancient civilization flowed together to mingle their waters before being swept on to divide and subdivide into the currents of modern civilization. The legacy of preceding ages, administered and increased by her, became the inheritance of ages succeeding. "Into her all the life of the ancient world was gathered, out of her all the life of the modern world arose." Whatever in the culture of our own day is held dear,—in art, literature, learning, in juristic or religious institutions,—is traceable first to Italy of the Renaissance, and then to ancient Rome, where it either came into being or was adapted to the needs of practical experience. The generations of today are still subjects of the empire of Rome. Her line has gone out through all the earth, and her words to the end of the world,—to Africa, to Gaul, to Spain, to northern and eastern Europe, to the British isles, to the Americas, to Japan and the Philippines, to Asia. The Roman empire has girdled the earth.

And not only has Rome been the channel through which has flowed the current of occidental civilization, but her waters have never ceased to flow. She has never lost her hold upon the life of the world. Memphis and Thebes, Babylon and Nineveh, representing great civilizations, perished before Rome had come into her inheritance, and have lain dead through all the ages under an ever-deepening mantle of dust. Athens disappeared for centuries from the world's visible activities, a hamlet of Turkish hovels. But Rome has been unlike all these. It was not idle fancy, but the intuition of the prophet, that bestowed upon her the name of URBS ÆTERNA: THE ETERNAL CITY. Repeatedly conquered and put to the sack, phœnix-like she has ever risen again and resumed her part in the drama of life. Apart from the times when her population has temporarily fled from the horrors of murder and rapine, she has never ceased to be dwelt in, has never ceased to be intimately concerned in the world's life. She has always been a capital. With few of the physical, commercial, or strategic advantages of great cities, she became the military and political capital of the ancient world; when that supremacy had passed, she became the spiritual head of the mediæval and modern world; and when Italy had finally freed herself from the bond of the stranger and was ready to become for the first time in history a national unit, it was Rome, despite the opposition of papal sympathizers, despite the superior practical claims of other great cities of Italy, for which the citizens of the peninsula and the onlookers of the whole world clamored as the capital of the new state.

Thus it is that Eternal Rome is the one place in all the world where the student may be stimulated to pass in review the whole course of western history. Nor is it the stimulation of a mere abstraction. The "lone mother of dead empires" has preserved more than merely site and name in common with the city of the past. Of all the long ages through which she has played her prominent part, from the Palatine settlement to the present day, there is no period of which she does not present some visible sign in the monuments within or near her walls. The prehistoric past is to be read in the earliest

THE CHURCH OF SAINT PETER, FEBRUARY 12, 1922

PIUS THE ELEVENTH HAS JUST BEEN CROWNED,
AND IS ABOUT TO APPEAR IN THE BALCONY
TO IMPART HIS BENEDICTION

REPRODUCED FROM A COMMERCIAL PHOTOGRAPH

cemeteries of Forum and Esquiline and on the museum shelves they have served to fill; the life of the cave has not disappeared from the tufa rocks of Parioli; the hillocks and ravines of the Campagna tell the tale of the geologic age. Of all the various lands whose culture she utilized in the fabric of her own civilization, of all the widely separated climes upon whose life she has reacted, from Egypt and Greece to the states of modern Europe, there is none of which she does not afford concrete representation somewhere in her streets, museums, galleries, and libraries. There are obelisk and tomb and statue from Egypt; there are hoards of coins from the England of Alfred's time; there are the busts of emperors from Spain and Africa and Thrace; there are gods from the Orient; there is all the life of the German on the upper Rhine and the Dacian on the lower Danube to be read on the imperial columns; the history of the Middle Age and of the nations of modern times is recorded in her manuscripts and on her monuments. Of all the phases of the religious experience through which mankind in Europe and the west has passed, her Church has retained the essential. It is ready to minister to every obedient soul, whatever its position in the scale of rank or intellect; it serves the poor and the rich, the nameless and the known, the humble and the proud, the ignorant and the enlightened, the superstitious and the rational, the democrat and the aristocrat, the young and the old, the white and the black and the yellow and the brown, the simple and the splendid. It is as comprehensive and as contradictory and as human as mankind itself. The study of the monuments and life of Rome is the study of human culture and its sources, and their appreciation is the appreciation of western history. Rome is the epitome of occidental civilization.

The flame of Rome's destiny burns serenely and clear. The greatness of her past has made her future forever sure. That she will ever again possess the supreme political and military importance once hers can hardly be conceived,—unless indeed the failure of coal and oil and iron shall humble the proud and restore the parity of ancient times. With the conquest, amalgamation, and civilization of the world, and with the preservation through her Church of its cultural unity during the Dark Ages, she fulfilled her mission in that field. In the world of the arts and learning, too, it may be that she has performed the task assigned to her by Providence in the encouragement, conservation, and dissemination, through the same instrumentality, of the intellectual achievements of Greek, Roman, and Renaissance times. Of her mission in the realm of religion, it may here be said only that imagination will not conceive of her ceasing to be the capital of the great masses of Christendom.

But whatever her political, intellectual, or ecclesiastical part in the affairs of the future, Rome will never lose her importance in the history of human culture. In the domain of the spirit, she will indeed be the Eternal City. So long as the civilization of Italy, Europe, and the western world shall be conscious of its origin and of its progress from age to age, she will continue to be the one point on the surface of the earth where the white man may best pause to contemplate the cycles of experience through which his race has passed, and best meditate on the frailty of human nature, the mutability of fortune, the woeful pageants of "this wide and universal theater," the remoteness and yet the nearness of antiquity, the continuity of history, and the divine strain in the affairs of men.

THE END

CHRONOLOGY

Chapter I.

B.C. 1100 Approximate date of Dorian invasion of Greece.

1000 Approximate date of northern invaders' arrival in Latium.

800 Approximate date of Etruscan arrival in Italy.

Chapter II.

753 Traditional date of the founding of Rome.

510-509 Expulsion of the kings and beginning of the Republic.

Chapter III.

494 Beginning of tribunate of the people.

493 Rome at the head of the Latin league.

480 Defeat of Carthaginians by Sicilian Greeks at the Himera.

474 Defeat of Carthaginians and Etruscans by Greeks at Cumæ.

449 The Twelve Tables.

445 Plebeians win right to intermarriage with patricians.

443 Censorship established.

431 Roman supremacy from Fidenæ to Tarracina.

400-200 Planting of Roman colonies in Italy.

396 Fall of Veii.

390 Approximate date of taking of Rome by Gauls.

367 Licinian laws; first plebeian consul.

351 First plebeian censor.

338 Final defeat of Latin allies.

337 First plebeian prætor.

290 Samnite wars end with submission to Rome.

272 Fall of Tarentum and control of southern Italy.

265-241 First Punic war.

252 First plebeian pontifex maximus.

238-149 Cato.

218-202 Second Punic war.

197 Defeat of Macedonians at Cynoscephalæ and liberation of Greece.

190 The Romans in Asia.

185 Death of Scipio Africanus.

168 Pydna and the subjugation of Macedon.

149 Death of Cato.

Chapter IV.

149-146 Third Punic war.

146 Destruction of Carthage and Corinth.

140 War in Lusitania.

153-133 War in Spain; the fall of Numantia.

133 Death of Tiberius Gracchus.

121 Death of Gaius Gracchus.

102-101 Victories of Marius and Catulus over Cimbri and Teutons.

102-88 Marian influence.

90-89 Social war; the Italians win rights from Rome.

88-78 Sullan régime.

86 Death of Marius.

70-66 Rise of Pompey.

63 Cicero's consulship and the conspiracy of Catiline.

62 Death of Catiline.

58-49 Cæsar's conquest of Gaul.

48-44 Cæsarian régime.

43 Death of Cicero.

42-28 Establishment of the Augustan régime.

27-14 A.D. Reign of Augustus.

Chapter V.

B.C. 1000 The earliest Greeks in Italy at Cumæ.

735 Beginning of active colonial movement to Italy and Sicily.

600 Approximate date of the founding of Marseilles.

583 First statue of a deity at Rome.

578-534 Traditional date of Servian reform.

431 Temple to Apollo vowed.

293 The worship of Æsculapius brought to Rome.

272 Conquest of Magna Græcia and beginning of active Greek influence.

240 First Græco-Roman poems and plays.

217 All the principal Greek deities now established at Rome.

212 Capture of Syracuse with Greek spoils.

197 Flamininus and the liberation of the Greek cities from Macedon.

168 Paullus' defeat of Perseus and tour of Greek centers.

173 Dismissal of Epicurean teachers from Rome.

161 Banishment of Greek philosophers and rhetors.

155 Dismissal of Greek philosopher-envoys from Rome.

150 The stone theater ordered down.

146 Sack of Corinth.

106-43 Cicero.

96-55 Lucretius.

70-19 Virgil.

65-8 Horace.

63-14 A.D. Augustus.

Chapter VI.

A.D.　14-37 Tiberius.

37 Caligula.

41 Claudius; expedition to Britain.

54 Nero.

68-69 Galba, Otho, Vitellius.

69 Vespasian.

79 Titus; Jerusalem.

81 Domitian.

96 Nerva.

98 Trajan; Dacia and the east.

117 Hadrian.

138 Antoninus Pius.

161 Marcus Aurelius; the north.

180 Commodus.

Chapter VII.

Chapter VIII.

58 Paul's Epistle to the Romans.
64 Nero's persecution.
84-96 Domitian.
111-113 Pliny and the Christians in Bithynia.
124 *circa* Hadrian's rescript.
160 *circa* Birth of Tertullian.
164 and 167 *circa* Persecutions of Marcus Aurelius.
210 *circa* Persecution of Severus.
217 Calixtus I.
235-238 Maximin.
249-251 Decius.
251-252 Gallus.
257-258 Valerian's persecution.
269-270 Persecutions of Claudius and Aurelian.
303-305 Diocletian's persecution.
313 Edict of Constantine.
341 Prohibition of sacrifices.
348-420 Jerome.
354-430 Augustine.
361-363 Julian's attempt to revive paganism.
366-384 Damasus; rioting Christians.
379-395 Reign of Theodosius. Prohibition of pagan worship
and confiscation of temples.
374-397 Ambrose bishop of Milan.
387 Augustine baptized at Milan.
394 Momentary revival of paganism under Eugenius.

Chapter IX.

404 Visit of Honorius to Rome.
410 Alaric takes the city.
440-461 Leo I.
455 Genseric sacks Rome.
472 Siege of Rome and death of Anthemius.
476 Odoacer succeeds Romulus Augustulus.
489-526 Theodoric the Ostrogoth.

536-567 Goth and Byzantine: Vitiges and Belisarius; Totila and Narses.

568-774 The Lombard supremacy.

590-604 Gregory I.

754, 756 Pepin in Italy.

800-888 Charlemagne and the Carolingians.

845-857 Leo IV; Saracen invasion; building of Leonine walls.

888-962 Varied control of Rome: Marozia, Theodora, Hugo, Alberic.

962-1024 Otto I and the Saxon line.

1024-1125 The Franconians.

1073-1085 Gregory VII.

1077 Gregory VII and Henry IV at Canossa.

1084 Robert Guiscard's sack of Rome.

1096-1291 The crusades.

1125-1254 The Hohenstaufen.

1182-1226 Saint Francis of Assisi.

1190 Death of Barbarossa.

1198-1216 Innocent III.

1250 Death of Frederick II.

1265 Charles of Anjou senator of Rome.

1265-1321 Dante.

1267-1337 Giotto.

1304-1374 Petrarch.

1305-1377 The papacy at Avignon.

1347 Cola di Rienzo tribune of Rome.

Chapter X.

1377 Return of the papacy under Gregory XI.

1417 Martin V, Colonna, and the end of the forty years' schism.

1431 Eugenius IV, Condolmieri.

1444-1510 Botticelli.

1444-1514 Bramante.

1446-1524 Perugino.

1447 Nicholas V, Parentucelli.

1452-1519 Leonardo da Vinci.

1455 Calixtus III, Borgia.

1458 Pius II, Piccolomini.
1464 Paul II, Barbo.
1471 Sixtus IV, Rovere.
1475-1564 Michelangelo.
1481-1537 Peruzzi.
1483-1520 Raphael.
1484 Innocent VIII, Cibo.
1485-1546 Sangallo the younger.
1492 Alexander VI, Borgia.
1503 Julius II, Rovere.
1507-1573 Vignola.
1513 Leo X, Medici.
1522 Hadrian VI, Dedel.
1523 Clement VII, Medici.

Chapter XI.

1525 Defeat of Francis I, ally of Clement VII, at Pavia.
1527 Sack of Rome by the constable of Bourbon, general of
         Charles V.
1534 Paul III, Farnese, and the counter-Reformation.
1541-1604 Della Porta.
1550 Julius III, Del Monte.
1555 Paul IV, Caraffa.
1556-1629 Maderna.
1559 Pius IV, Medici.
1566 Pius V, Ghislieri.
1572 Gregory XIII, Boncompagni.
1585 Sixtus V, Peretti.
1590 Urban VII, Castagna.
1591 Innocent IX, Facchinetti.
1592 Clement VIII, Aldobrandini.
1598-1680 Bernini.
1599-1667 Borromini.
1605 Paul V, Borghese.
1621 Gregory XV, Ludovisi.
1623 Urban VIII, Barberini.
1644 Innocent X, Pamfili.
1655 Alexander VII, Chigi.

1667 Clement IX, Rospigliosi.
1670 Clement X, Altieri.
1676 Innocent XI, Odescalchi.
1689 Alexander VIII, Ottobuoni.
1691 Innocent XII, Pignatelli.
1700 Clement XI, Albani.
1721 Innocent XIII, De Conti.
1724 Benedict XIII, Orsini.
1730 Clement XII, Corsini.
1740 Benedict XIV, Lambertini.
1758 Clement XIII, Rezzonico.
1769 Clement XIV, Ganganelli.
1775 Pius VI, Braschi.

Chapter XII.

1749-1803 Alfieri.
1785-1873 Manzoni.
1789-1854 Pellico.
1789-1815 French revolution and Napoleon.
1796 Cisalpine republic.
1798 Roman republic.
1798-1837 Leopardi.
1799 Death of Pius VI in exile.
1800-1823 Pius VII, Chiaramonti.
1804 French empire absorbs Rome.
1805 End of Holy Roman empire; kingdom of Italy.
1805-1872 Mazzini.
1807-1882 Garibaldi.
1808 Rise of the Carbonari.
1809 Captivity of Pius VII.
1810-1861 Cavour.
1814 Return of Pius VII.
1815 Return of the despots.
1820-1821 Risings in Naples and Piedmont.
1820-1878 Victor Emmanuel.
1823 Leo XII, Della Genga.
1829 Pius VIII, Castiglione.
1830 Paris revolution.

1831 Gregory XVI, Capellari; risings; Young Italy.

1834 Garibaldi's attempt on Piedmont, and flight.

1834-1848 Garibaldi in South America.

1846 Pius IX, Mastai.

1848-1849 Constitution of Charles Albert; flight of Pius IX;
Roman republic.

1850 Return of Pius IX.

1851 Napoleon III.

1859 French and Italians defeat the Austrians; cession of
Lombardy.

1860 Garibaldi and the Thousand.

1860 Annexation of Emilia, Tuscany, and the papal states.

1861 First Italian parliament at Turin; death of Cavour.

1866 War with Austria and cession of Venetia.

1867 Garibaldi's defeat at Mentana.

1870 The Italian army enters Rome.

Chapter XIII.

1871 The government transferred to Rome.

1876 The liberals in control.

1878 Deaths of Victor Emmanuel and Pius IX.

1878 Humbert; Leo XIII, Pecci.

1882 Triple Alliance; death of Garibaldi.

1896 Marriage of Victor Emmanuel and Helen of Montenegro.

1900 Victor Emmanuel III.

1903 Pius X, Sarto.

1911-1913 War with Turkey; annexation of Tripoli.

1914 Benedict XV, Della Chiesa.

1915-1918 The World War; annexation of Trieste and the
Trentino.

1922 Pius XI, Ratti; the fascisti assume the government.

1922-1924 Mussolini with full powers.

NOTES

The plan and the scope of ETERNAL ROME will have made clear the reason for such omissions as may disappoint the reader in search of special detail. It is not meant for the specialist, except as it may help him to the sense of proportion and continuity. It is written chiefly for those who feel the need of large vision, and who will be thankful for such vision of the city which has been continuously dwelt in for upwards of thirty centuries, for twenty centuries has played a leading part on the stage of occidental life, and is still more than any other spot the capital city of the world. Its origin was in the inspiration of residence as student and lecturer in the American Academy in Rome.

The notes which follow, and especially the bibliography comprised by them, are not intended to be exhaustive, or even extensive, but only to indicate main currents of information, which will themselves conduct those who desire it back to more devious tributaries; and no pretence is made to conclusive discussion in matters of controversy which from the nature of the case will never cease to be such.

CHAPTER I

Page

3. The submerged area extended to the Apennines at Lucca and Pistoia, and was marked in the north by many islands; but our interest will be confined to the portion lying south of Soracte and the lake of Bracciano and including the Alban mountains. These are roughly the limits of the Roman Campagna. The term Latium will denote the wider area including also the borders of the Apennines.

3-7. For the geology of Latium: Brocchi, *Dello stato fisico del suolo di Roma*, 1820; Paolo Mantovani, in *Monografie della città di Roma*, 1879; Plattner, Bunsen, et al., *Beschreibung der Stadt Rom*, I, p. 45.

For the geology of Rome: A. Verri, *Carta geografica di Roma*, Novara, 1915. Verri distinguishes the following geologic planes: 1, sediment of the open sea; 2, coast and marsh deposits; 3, lower tufa, dark or yellowish grey; 4, lower pozzolana or ash, blackish or ruddy-brown; 5, upper pozzolana, ruddy or violet-brown, largely converted by the action of water into the tufa of the Roman builders; 6, fluvio-lacustrine deposits; 7, lacustrine deposits and alluvium with ruins and débris. Many of these planes are easily detected, but it must not be supposed that they are all to be read in any single place. Volcanic upheaval and rushing water confused and sometimes even obliterated them.

8. There were plenty of Chelléen and Moustérien men in central Italy not far from Latium, as well as in other parts of the peninsula; to deny all significance to the isolated palæolithic finds in the gravel of the Tiber and Anio and elsewhere, and to say that no men of the old stone age saw Latium, is austere treatment of evidence.

8-16. For early Italian race-character and movement: Peet, *The Stone and Bronze Ages in Italy and Sicily*, Oxford, 1909. See also Sergi, *The Mediterranean Race*, English edition, 1901; and, for greater detail, Pigorini, *Le più antiche civiltà dell' Italia*, in *Bullettino di paletnologia italiana*, vol. xxix, and Helbig, *Die Italiker in der Poebene*, Leipzig, 1879, and Leopold, *Mededeelingen van het Neederlandsch Historisch Instituut te Rome*, 1922.

9. The custom of painting the bones was known also in the Balkans.
    Sergi has the Mediterranean race originate in northeastern Africa and cross to Europe through Crete and Asia Minor (Pelasgians), Spain (Iberians), and Sicily. Peet thinks that it entered Italy through both Sicily

(Proto-Sicilians) and Spain and France (Ligurians). The African branch is called Libyan.

Wace, *Literary Supplement of the London Times*, Oct. 13, 1921, p. 660, attributes the building of Mycenæan walls in Greece to the Achæans.

Pigorini sees the successive inhabitants of Italy as follows: 1, palæolithic cave-men; 2, neolithic Ibero-Ligurians, bringing hut-building but also inhabiting the palæolithic caves; 3, new race, Aryan, over the central Alps, eneolithic, lake-dwellers, bringing cremation; 4, second invasion, over eastern Alps, full bronze, lake-dwellers and *terramara* men; 5, partial emigration to Etruria and Latium, where the Villanova culture is developed.

Brizio, *Epoca preistorica*, p. xlii ff., differs from Pigorini: 1 and 2, the same; 3, the lake-dwellers and *terramara* men are not a new race, but the Ibero-Ligurians developed; 4, the *terramare* are a development of the hut-villages, which are a transition to them from the earlier hut-habitations of the Ibero-Ligurians; 5, same as Pigorini; 6, conquest by the Etruscans, in the fifth century, of the *terramara* civilization in Umbria and the Emilia.

Peet, p. 510, concludes with Pigorini that lake-dwellers and *terramara* men came from central Europe.

Helbig's view that it was the Etruscans who crossed the Alps and crowded the *terramara* people out of the Po valley receives little support.

A cemetery near Castel Gandolfo, on the rim of the Alban lake, was found in 1817 resting in a stratum of 50 inches of yellow volcanic ash covered, first, by a thin stratum of vegetable soil, second, by 36 inches of peperino, and, third, by a stratum of soil 14 inches deep: Lanciani, *Ancient Rome*, II.

10, §2. The picture is Helbig's.

CHAPTER II

21-23. Platner, *Topography and Monuments of Rome*, revised, Boston, 1911, IV.

24-31. *Æneid*, VII, 25-36, VIII, 26-65, 102-370; Tibullus, II, 5, 23-38; Ovid, *Fasti*, I, 243-248, VI, 401-414; Cicero, *De Republica*, II; Livy, I. Translations are by the author unless otherwise stated.

32-42. Platner, *Early Legends and Recent Discoveries, Classical Journal*, I, 3, 78-83, suggests the general relation of the monuments of early Rome to the ancient traditional accounts.

34. For the earliest burial-places, in the Forum and on the Esquiline: Platner, 188, 445.

35. For commercial movement in Latin Italy for the period covered by this chapter: Louise E. W. Adams, *A Study in the Commerce of Latium*, Northampton, Mass., 1921; Tenney Frank, *An Economic History of Rome*, Baltimore, 1920, 1-35.
In the matter of the stages through which the early city passed, what may be called the canonical account is here adopted. Its clearest statement is in Platner, IV. In spite of objections, it remains the most satisfactory and best attested account of the rise of historic Rome.

37. Livy, V, 54, 4.

38. Cicero, *De Republica*, II, 6, 11.

39. On the Etruscans and Rome: Frank, II; Adams, V.

46. On primitive Roman religion: Warde Fowler, *The Religious Experience of the Roman People*, London, 1911, VI and VII; Carter, *The Religion of Numa*, 1906, 1-61; Wissowa, *Religion und Kultus der Römer*, Munich, ed. of 1912, 18-38.

49, §3. Not the Servian wall, which in its final form could not have been built in the time of the kings; but the preceding circuit of defence, either on or near the line of the Servian wall, which we must assume to have enclosed the city of the later kings.

CHAPTER III

61. Tables of these colonies may be found in Heitland, *The Roman Republic*, Cambridge, 1909, I, 172, 222.

67. These figures are from Livy and the *periochæ*.

67-70. For individual monuments: Platner; Carter-Huelsen, *The Roman Forum*.

70. The naval yards: Livy, XLII, 27, 1.

70, §3. The legendary events commemorated by these ætiological monuments are narrated in Livy, I, 4, 26, 36, 45; II, 10.

71. Livy, XXXIV, 4, 4; XL, 5, 7; Cicero, *De Lege Agraria*, II, 96.

72-74. Livy, XXIV, 47, 16; XXXV, 40, 7; XXXIV, 44, 7; XXXV, 21, 5; XXXVIII, 28, 4; XLI, 21, 6; XLII, 10, 6.

74, §2. Livy, XLI, 8, 6-7; XXXIX, 3, 4.

74, §3. Frank, 51 ff.

77. *Æneid*, IX, 601-612; Ennius, *Annales*, XV, 401-409 (Vahlen).

78. Livy, XLII, 34.

80. XXIII, 12.

80-81. Warde Fowler, *The Roman Festivals of the Republic;* Tomassetti, *La Campagna romana*, I, 98.

81, l. 15. Livy, III, 26, 7-12.

81-82. Cicero, *De Senec.*, 56; Cato, *De Agri Cultura, Præfatio;* Varro, *Rer. Rust.*, II, 1, 1; Horace, *Odes*, III, 6.

82. Frank, VII, on industry and commerce.

83, l. 1. Livy, XXI, 63, 3.

83, §1. Frank, VI.

84. Livy, XXIII, 14, 1 ; IV, 45, 2.

85. Cicero, *Brutus*, 25, 95-96.

86. Lucilius (Marx), 1326-1338.

87. Quintilian, I, 6, 40 ; Horace, *Epistles*, II, 1, 86.

87-88. Wissowa, 504 ff. ; Fowler, 34-35.

88, ll. 21-28. Livy, XXXII, 1, 9 ; XXXIX, 7, 8 ; II, 36 ; *Periocha* XIX ; Cicero, *De Div.*, I, 16, 29.

89. Livy, XLIII, 13, 1-2.

90. Wissowa, pp. 47 ff. ; Showerman, *The Great Mother of the Gods*, Madison, Wisconsin, 1901.

90. Cato, *Orig.*, V, 1 ; Livy, XXI, 1.

91. XXII, 7, 6-14.

91-93. Livy, XXII, 32, 9 ; 36, 9 ; 37, 1-12 ; 38, 1-5 ; XXII, 49, 15-17 ; 55, 6-8 ; 58, 6-9 ; 57, 9-10 ; 61, 1-4, 11-15.

93, §2. XXXIV, 6, 11-14.

93. XXVI, 10, 3 ; 11, 5-7.

94. XLII, 62, 11 and 13.

94-99. For individual characters, see index of Livy.

96-97. Decius: Cicero, *De Finibus*, II, 61 ; *Tusc. Disp.*, I, 89 (*cf.* Pauly-Wissowa, *Real. Encyc.*, 2284).

97, §2. Livy, IX, 16, 12 ; *Periochæ*, XI-XIV, Valerius Maximus, IV, 3, 5, Cicero, *De Senec.*, 43 and 55 ; *De Senec.*, 16 ; Plutarch, *Pyrrhus*, 20 ; Cicero, *De Senec.*, 15 ; Aulus Gellius, III, 8 ; Horace, *Odes*, III, 5 ; Cicero, *De Senec.*, 44 ; Livy, XXI, 46 ; XXVI, 50 ; XXXII, 51.

97, §3. Horace, *Odes*, I, 12 ; Cicero, *De Senec.*, 10-12.

100-102. Plutarch, *Cato*, tr. by Perrin (Loeb Library) ; Livy, XXXIV, 18 ; XXXIX, 40 ; Cicero, *De Senec.*

103. Livy, V, 21, 9.

103, §2. Livy, XXIV, 39 ; XXXI, 46, 16 ; XXXVI, 24, 7 ; XL, 38.

104. *Curculio*, 466-484.

105. Ennius, *Scenica*, 319-323.
Cicero, *De Or.*, II, 276.

105, §3. Plutarch, *Cato*.

106. Livy, IX, 17, 14; Plutarch, *Pyrrhus*, 19.
107. Livy, V, 21, 9.

CHAPTER IV

111-122. For the period from Cato's death to the end of the
    Augustan age: Heitland, *The Roman Republic;* Firth,
    Augustus. For the expansion of Rome in general: Frank,
    Roman Imperialism.
117. Livy, *Præfatio*, 4.
119. Strabo, III, 3, 5, tr. Hamilton; Velleius Paterculus, II,
    90, 4.

123. Platner, 57-64.
124, §2. Strabo, V, 3, 5.
126. Horace, *Odes*, II, 15, 12-20; Cicero, *Ad Att.*, I, 6, 8, 9,
    10; Pliny, *N. H.*, XXXVI, 7 and 114; Strabo, V, 3, 7.
127. *Res Gestæ Divi Augusti*, Mommsen, Berlin (1883).
128. Suetonius, *Augustus*, 29, tr. Rolfe (Loeb Library).
129. Strabo, V, 3, 7: "Such is the Roman rampart, which
    seems to stand in need of other ramparts itself."
130. Strabo, V, 3, 8, tr. Hamilton.
133. Horace, *Sat.*, I, 9, *Odes*, III, 30; Propertius, II, 31;
    Horace, *Carmen Sæc.* For Altar of Peace, see Platner.
134. Ovid, *Amores*, III, 2.
135. Polybius, VI, 53, 6; Servius, *Ad Aen.*, VI, 861; Suetonius,
    Aug., 100.

137. Frank, *An Economic History of Rome*, X.
139. *De Petit. Cons.*, 54.
141. Livy, XXXIV, 1; XXXIX, 6, 7-9.
144. Suetonius, *Aug.*, 99.
145. Livy, *Præf.*, IV, 6, 12; Horace, *Odes*, III, 6, 45-48.

CHAPTER V

156. Adams, III; Wissowa, I, 3, pp. 60-75.

159. Duff, *Literary History of Rome*, II.

176. Cicero, *De Or.*, I, 158-159; Showerman, *Cicero's Appreciation of Art*, in *Am. Jour. Phil.*, XXV, 306-314.

178. Showerman, *Horace and His Influence*, 23-43, Boston, 1922.

180. Livy, XL, 29.

181. Athenodorus, XII, 547; Plutarch, *Cato*, XXII.

182. *Pro Flac.*, IV, 9, 12, 16.

183. *De Rep.*, II, 4, 8; Livy, XXXI, 44, 9. In general: Mahaffy, *The Greek World Under Roman Sway*, London, 1890.

CHAPTER VI

191. Cumont, *Comment la Belgique fut romanisée*, second ed., Brussels, 1919, pp. 11, 105; Haverfield, *The Romanization of Roman Britain*, third ed., Oxford, 1914, p. 31; Cumont, 6; Plut., 32, in Mahaffy, 303.

192. Cumont, 95, 96.

193. Gibbon, ch. 3.

194. Pliny, III, 66-67.

195. Strabo, V, 3, 7-8.
     For the fires: Jordan, *Topographie der Stadt Rom im Alterthum* (Huelsen), Berlin, 1906, I, 1, 482; Friedlaender, *Sittengeschichte Roms*, ninth ed., Leipzig, 1919, I, 23.

198-200. Platner, index.

200. Pliny, XXXVI, 123; Fowler, *Social Life at Rome in the Time of Cicero*, London, 1908, 39-42.

203. Frank, 153; Dill, *Social Life in Rome from Nero to Marcus Aurelius*, London, 1905, 69.

205. Frank, 159-162.

209 ff. For the morals of the Empire: Dill, I and II; Friedlaender, II, IV, and V.

216. Juvenal, VIII, 20; X, 363; XIV, 47; Tacitus, IV, 62-63.

217. Tacitus, XV, 63.

220. Frank, 136, 137.

222-223. Dill, 76, on women.

223. Tacitus, XI, 21: Curtius Rufus videtur mihi ex se natus; Plutarch, *De Is.*, 66, 79.

CHAPTER VII

234. Dill, *Roman Society in the Last Century of the Western Empire*, London, 1899, book III

242. Claudian, *De Bello Gild.*, 70; 17-27.

243. Symmachus, *Relationes*, III (*Epist.*, X, 54, 9); Prudentius, *Contra Sym.*, II, 635-648.

245 ff. Platner, index.

247. *Curiosum* and *Notitia*, in Urlichs, *Codex Urbis Topographicus;* or in Richter, *Topographie der Stadt Rom*, 371-391.

249. Claudian, *De Sexto Cons. Hon.*, 35-52.

250. Ammianus Marcellinus, XIV, 6.

252. XVI, 10.

256. XIV, 6; XXVIII, 4; the substance of the two passages is here woven together.

For appreciations of Ammianus, Claudian, Symmachus, Julian, Macrobius, Ausonius, and other representative characters of the fourth century: Glover, *Life and Letters in the Fourth Century*, Cambridge, 1901.

264. Dill, 149.

267. On military decadence: Dill, 235; Gibbon, ch. 7.

269. Dill, 210.

270. Claudian, *De Cons. Stil.*, III, 136-160; *De Bello Goth.*, 54.

271. Symmachus, *Orationes*, III, 9.

CHAPTER VIII

276. On the catacombs: Lowrie, *Monuments of the Early Church*, New York, 1901, II; Marucchi, *Éléments d'archéologie chrétienne*, Rome, 1899, I, *livre deuxième*.

282. Marucchi, *livre premier*; Firth, *Constantine*, New York, 1905, II; *Acts*, XXVIII.

283. Tacitus, *Ab Exc. Div. Aug.*, XV, 44.
     Firth, *Augustus*, 287.

285. Pliny, *Ad Traianum*, 96, 97.

289. Tertullian, *Apol.*, 40; 37; Renan, *Marc Aurèle*, Paris, 447.

290. Lowrie, 39; Renan, 451; Burckhardt, *Die Zeit Constantins des Grossen*, Leipzig, 1880, 137; Firth, *Constantine*, 23.

293. *Cf.* above, pages 46-48.

294. Apuleius, *Metam.*, XI, 5.

295-297. Cumont, *Les religions orientales dans le paganisme romain*, Paris, 1907, VII.

298. Cicero, *Somn. Scip.*; *De Senec.*, 72-85.

304. Pliny, *Ad Traianum*, 96.

305. Firth, *Constantine*, 15.

306. Tertullian, *De Spectaculis*, 3.

307. Firth, 19; Spence-Jones, *The Early Christians in Rome*, London, 1910, 193-205.

309. Minucius Felix, *Octavius*, 8-13.

321. Jerome, *Epist.*, XXII, 30. On the influence of Cicero on the Church: Zielinski, *Cicero im Wandel der Jahrhunderte*, Leipzig, 1908, pp. 106-145.

322. For a survey of the arts: Lowrie.

323. For the underground basilica, see Curtis, *Art and Archæology*, June, 1920; Cumont, *Revue Archéologique*, 1918, VIII, 52.

324-325. Cumont: *Les Mystères de Mithra*, IV, 1896-1899; *The After Life in Paganism*, Boston, 1922, VIII.

326. The shows in Rome: Rutil. Namat., I, 201-205.

327. De Broglie, *L'église et l'empire romain au quatrième siècle*, L'avertissement, iv.

327. Christians reproved by Jerome: *Epist.* 107, *ad Lætam;* 22, *ad Eustachium; cf.* Ammianus, XXVII, 3.

328. The agape: Lowrie, 51.

328. Renan, 629; *Codex Theodos.*

329. Ammianus, XXII, 5, 4; XXVII, 3.

CHAPTER IX

336. Jerome, *Epist.*, LX, 16.

337. CXXVII, 12.

338. Dill, *Society in Rome in the Last Century of the Western Empire*, 309-312; Rutil. Namat., I.

339. Bury, *History of the Later Roman Empire*, I, 31 ff.

340, §2. Gregorovius, *History of Rome during the Middle Ages*, tr. by Annie Hamilton, London, 1900, I, 493 n. Much of the detail of this chapter is taken from Gregorovius.

341. *Homily I on the Gospels*, in Gregorovius, II, 36.

345. For the theory of the mediæval empire: Bryce, *The Holy Roman Empire*, VII.
Patrimonium: Greg., II, 59-61, 365-370; and below, p. 469 f.

348. Lanciani, *The Destruction of Rome*, New York, 1899.

349. For Alaric in Rome: Greg., I, 117-172; Hodgkin, *The In-*

vaders of Italy, Oxford, 1892, book I, chs. 15-17; Lanciani, V.

350. Greg., I, 375-479; Hodgkin, book V, chs. 4-9, 17-21.
352. Cassiodorus, VIII, 13; VII, 15.
   Greg., I, 81-2.
353. Lanciani, *Ruins and Excavations*, London, 1897, 10-16.
355. Marjorian, in Hodgkin, book II, 424.
357. *Homily XVIII*, in Greg., II, 41.
359. Greg., IV, 237-254; Lanciani, *Destruction*, XIV.
361. Greg., V, 323-327.
362. I, 82-116.
365. Lanciani, XVI.
367. *De Gestis Anglorum*, III, 134; cf. Greg., IV, 249.
368 ff. Rome in the thirteenth century: Greg., V, 657-680; the Campagna: Tomassetti, *Campagna Romana*, I, 116.
371-373. Petrarch and Rome in the fourteenth century: Greg., VI, 319-323.

380. The Crusaders: Greg., IV, 287-292.
382. Legends: Comparetti, *Virgil in the Middle Ages*, London, 1895.
383. Urlichs, *Codex Urbis Topographicus*, 95, 113, 178.
   Cf. *I Reali di Francia*.
   Nichols, *The Marvels of Rome*, London, 1889.
385. The *Graphia:* in Nichols.
392. Cola di Rienzo: Greg., VI, 217-327.
393. Belisarius: Greg., I, 442.
396. Tosti, *Storia di Bonifazio VIII*, ii, 284; cf. Greg., V, 560.

CHAPTER X

402. On the state of Rome: Greg., VI, 671-732; VII, 1-88.
403. Poggio, *De Varietate Fortunæ*, in Greg., VII, 61.
405. McKilliam, *A Chronicle of the Popes*, London, 1912; Greg., VII, 530-655; VIII, 120-174.

412. VIII, 293-411.
418. VIII, 17.
421. Egidius of Viterbo, in Greg., VII, 528.

428-440. The aspect of the city: Ludwig von Pastor, *Die Stadt Rom zu Ende der Renaissance*, Freiburg im Breisgau, 1916; Greg., VIII, part 1.

CHAPTER XI

443. The sack of Rome: Gregorovius, VIII, 500-656.
446-453. The architectural growth of the city: Alfred von Reumont, *Geschichte der Stadt Rom*, Berlin, 1867-1870, III, 2, 728-735, 738-745.
The popes: McKilliam, 415-457.
453-458. Æsthetic, intellectual, and social ministry of Rome: von Reumont, III, 2, 687-826.
458. *Lettres familières;* cf. von Reumont, III, 2, 824.
459. The popes of the counter-Reformation: Ranke, *History of the Popes*, tr. Austin, London, 1840, I, 133-276, 511; II, 3-149; McKilliam.

462. The growth of the spiritual and temporal power: Beet, *The Early Roman Episcopate*, London, 1913, II-IV, VIII, IX; Greg., *passim;* Ranke, I, 3-33; Halphen, *L'administration de Rome au moyen âge*, Paris, 1907; Grisar, *Histoire de Rome et des Papes*, Paris, 1906.
466. Jerome, *Epist. XXXVI, 1, ad Damasum:* postquam epistulam tuae sanctitatis accepi.
469. The patrimonies: Greg., II, 57-62; cf. above, 345.
471. Greg., II, 53.
475. Halphen, part 2.

480. The character of the popes: Ranke, I, 241-386; McKilliam, Paul the Third to Gregory the Sixteenth; Ludwig

von Pastor, *Die Geschichte der Päpste*, Freiburg im Breisgau, 1901-1907.

483. On the papal administrations: Ranke I, 387-528.
486. Pasquino: Emilio del Cerro, *Roma che ride*, Turin.
490. De Brosses, II, 5.
492. Silvagni, *La corte e la società romana nei XVIII e XIX secoli*, 1881-1885.
497-498. Grisar, II, 79; Greg., II, 403.
498. Greg., V, 7.
502. Montaigne, *Journal de Voyage*, Paris, 1909, 259-261.

CHAPTER XII

Thayer, *The Dawn of Italian Independence*, Boston, 1899; *The Life and Times of Cavour*, Boston, 1911.

Trevelyan, *Garibaldi's Defence of the Roman Republic*, London, 1912; *Garibaldi and the Thousand; Garibaldi and the Making of Italy*, London, 1914.

Holland, *Makers of United Italy*, New York, 1908.

Orsi, *Modern Italy*, New York, 1900.

De Cesare, *Roma e lo stato del papa*, 1850-1870, Rome, 1904.

Del Cerro, *Roma che ride.* Gregorovius, *Roman Journal of*, tr. by Annie Hamilton, London, 1907.

CHAPTER XIII

Garlanda, *The New Italy*, New York, 1911.

Zimmern, *Italy of the Italians*, London, 1906.

Villari, *Italian Life in Town and Country*, New York, 1902.

Underwood, *United Italy*, London, 1912.

Page, *Italy and the World War*, New York, 1920.

INDEX

A BIB, 384
Aborigines, 25
Abraham, 279
Absalom, 385
absolutism, 237
absolutist reaction at Rome, 529
abuses of papal officials, 543
academies, 482
Academy, 427
Accius, 70
Achæans, 10
Acilius Glabrio, 284
acolytes, 290
Acqua Felice, 448; — Marcia, 546;
— Paola, 449, 535
Acropolis, 152
Actium, 240
Actresses, 260
Acts, The, 282
Adalberga, 382
Adam and Eve, 279
Adams, 549
Admiralty, 123
Adriano Castelli, palace, 428
Adriatic, 56, 57, 61
Aduatici, 138
ædiles, 141
Ælian, 220
Ælius Pætus, Publius, 73
Æmilians, 203
Æmilius Lepidus Porcina, Marcus,
86
Æmilius Paullus, 98, 99, 112, 136,
163, 181
Æneas, 24-25, 153
Æneas Sylvius, *Commentarii,* 405
Æneas Sylvius on abuse, 418
Æneid, 183
Æquian colonies, 61
Æquians, 54
Æsculapius, temple, 431
Æsernia, 61
Æsium, 61
Æsop, 210

Ætna, 4, 156
Ætolians, 78
Africa, 57, 101, 133, 137, 141, 242,
289, 290, 306, 510, 585
African, 205, 239
African conquest, 339; — soil, 98
Africano, 200
Africanus, 149
agape, 278, 328
agriculture, 45, 46, 74, 75, 80-84, 140,
470, 490
agriculture, primitive, 12
Agrippa, 25, 128, 130, 387, 576
Agrippina, 213, 220
Ahenobarbi, 413
Aix, 366
alabaster, 201, 365
Alan, 336, 342
Alaric, 248, 326, 338, 349, 353, 393,
446; — in Italy, 336; — in revolt,
335; — in Rome, 336
Alba, 25
Alba Fucens, 61
Alba Longa, 15, 25, 27, 28
Alban crater, 200; — foothills, 22;
— Hills, 70; — lake, 5; — Mount,
5, 6, 8, 15, 25, 88, 237, 576; —
mountains, 40
Albani, 450, 493
Albano, 369, 469, 539, 546
Alban people, 28, 35; — slopes, 70,
75, 151; — worship, 27
Albans, 148, 359
Alberic, 343, 473
Alberti, Leon Battista, 409
Albigenses, 476
Albinus, 228
Alboin, 342
Albula, 25
Alcaic, 153
Aldobrandini, 448, 485
Aldobrandini, Pietro, 483
Aldovrandi guide, 455
Alemanni, 241
Alexander, 56, 58, 165, 167, 239